Visioning
A Mi'kmaw Humanities:
Indigenizing the Academy

Marie Battiste, Editor

CAPE BRETON UNIVERSITY PRESS
SYDNEY, NOVA SCOTIA

The editor and contributors wish to thank the many contributions and funding provided to make this book possible, including the Social Sciences and Humanities Research Council of Canada through the Animating Mi'kmaw Humanities Project, Mi'kmaw Kina'matnewey and Unama'ki College of Cape Breton University.

Cover Image: Quill box by Caroline Gould, courtesy the Beaton Institute, Cape Breton University.
Cover design: Cathy MacLean Design, Chéticamp, NS.
Layout: Mike Hunter, West Bay and Sydney, NS.
First printed in Canada.

Library and Archives Canada Cataloguing in Publication

Visioning a Mi'kmaw humanities : indigenizing the academy / Marie Battiste, editor.

Includes bibliographical references and index.
Issued in print and electronic formats.
ISBN 978-1-77206-057-7 (softcover).
--ISBN 978-1-77206-058-4 (PDF). --ISBN 978-1-77206-059-1 (EPUB).-
-ISBN 978-1-77206-060-7
(Kindle)

1. Micmac Indians--Study and teaching (Higher)--Canada.
2. Humanities--Study and teaching (Higher)--Canada. I. Battiste, Marie, 1949-, editor

E99.M6V57 2017   971.5004'97343   C2017-900707-6
                                                 C2017-900708-4

Cape Breton University Press
PO Box 5300
Sydney, Nova Scotia B1P 6L2
Canada

Distribution and Sales:
Nimbus Publishing
3731 MacKintosh St
Halifax, Nova Scotia B3K 5A5
Canada

Visioning a Mi'kmaw Humanities

Table of Contents

Marie Battiste

Preface

Mi'kmaw Humanities: Dreamed and Storied

Coming into Cape Breton, Nova Scotia, over the Bras d'Or Lakes from Saskatoon, Saskatchewan, my research partner and colleague Lynne Bell asks me about feelings about coming home. Immediately my mind and heart rumble through the huge storehouse of my own personal and collective consciousness. Where does home start? Was it in the airport of Halifax or in the air over Cape Breton that I begin to get those nostalgic feelings about being home, a home whose reach was now far greater than the reserve of Potlotek that my parents called home. It was much more than Eskasoni where Alex Denny built us a house next to his, generously inviting us to live on his land, to suggest that I was part of his family who he would guide over time like his own family. I had just come home from Stanford, California, finishing my doctorate degree and travelling to Canada to think about where I would work. He must have known that to go and get me in California would give him about a week to talk me into staying in Cape Breton—to make the vision of bilingual bicultural education my action project for more than twenty years.

Still, there was much to consider about "home." Home. Was it the land that was rich with the stories of my father and mother who travelled from one place to another, pointing to one landmark after another telling me about how it came to be a memory and a story to be told and retold until it landed fully in my memory? Each of their stories had the same punch line or the same funny, or sad, ending. Both were great storytellers, although Mom could remember far more detail. Dad and Mom liked to tell stories of their homeland, some not so happy like when my dad drove off the road and into the ditch and my mother was in the hospital for many weeks after, or other sad memories that held a place in the history of the Mi'kmaq that should be remain in our memory. One of those was the place on King's Road where Mi'kmaq lived but were removed. The people of Sydney wanted the Mi'kmaw land on the shores of the harbour and created a backlash against them to get them removed in 1929 to a piece of land on the outskirts of Sydney where there was no access to the water and where only one road led in and, on entering, two signs read "NO EXIT." The local papers reported that the Mi'kmaq had an unsightly village, dirty and unsanitary, although a local doctor said it was not unlike the rest of the town.

Home has come to have many connotations for me and to consist of many stories from many places where I have lived. These stories were littered from Maine to Boston to Nova Scotia to California and back again and then back and forth to Saskatoon. Considering where to start to answer Lynne's question, I think about the few days ahead of us that will support these stories and try judiciously to think about a shorter story.

This time my return home came with a dream to unfold. Several months after writing a proposal with a team of friends and my husband, as principal investigator I received the promised letter from the Social Science and Humanities Research Council (SSHRC) that the proposal we had written was successful, and we got the full amount requested. That night, after receiving the notice, a prophetic dream arrived just before waking so that it was vivid and memorable to relay. I had long heard that these dreams just upon waking were dreams that held some very special meaning and needed to be carefully considered.

In my dream, I was travelling alone from my very posh home that seemed to be in the suburbs of Boston, where my husband Sa'ke'j was, to visit my mother and father in Potlotek. On the way, I stopped in to visit my long-time family friends Murdena and Albert Marshall. Murdena and Albert had a little girl at their house, one who was still quite small, in diapers but walking. She was a small-framed child, looking a bit underweight. Knowing Murdena's family well, I asked Murdena who she was and Murdena said she was from a family who was not able to take care of her and that she had agreed to take her in and raise her. She was a beautiful child who I was drawn to immediately. She was not able to talk though. Murdena and Albert were quite old and Murdena seemed particularly frail and older looking. I saw that Murdena had fallen asleep, so I took care of the little girl while she got the needed extra rest. I was playing with her and saying in Mi'kmaq, "Who's little girl are you?" She looked at me and asked, "What's your name?" I said "Marie." She said, "I am Marie's little girl." I smiled with contentment with this feeling, although I knew she was not mine. While Murdena slept and Albert was distracted, I began to think that I could adopt this little girl, I could take care of her, because Sa'ke'j and I were, after all, well off. Murdena and Albert were now old and poor and she did not even have pampers. She was on her last cloth diaper and I was problem-solving, "How can I get some pampers tonight?" And how could I get a car seat for her if I took her home? I would need a baby car seat and then to get her across the border. And I would need her papers. I then thought of Sa'ke'j and thought he may not be happy with my taking this on, but I thought she really needs us. I was cradling her in my arms, and she fell asleep. As she slept, she started to talk clearly about her day and playing, and I marvelled at her speaking so well in Mi'kmaq. When Murdena woke up, I said, "Listen to this, Murdena, she talks in her sleep." Murdena said, "I know, she does that."

When I woke up and lay in bed thinking of this child and the vivid dream, I had the warm feelings of going to visit my mother and father who had long passed. As I storied the dream to my husband, I lay thinking about its vividness and the little girl when I came to a realization: the child represented the project already birthed in Mi'kma'ki (Mi'kmaw territory that stretches from far and wide from Cape Breton through to Boston) and that she is a child of the Mi'kmaq that I was about to adopt and nourish to full growth. Murdena and Albert have already helped to raise the child and start her on her way; she was the child of the Mi'kmaq. Now they were older and needed our help. It is now ours to raise to full growth—the Mi'kmaw humanities. I had dreamed all the things I needed to get her going, the basic necessities to start the project (money, diapers, car seat) and the papers (the ethics proposal) to take her home over many borders (provinces and countries). I knew I couldn't do it alone and I needed Sa'ke'j and friends to help me with this project, to create the community to bring it growth. In the end, the proposal and the project, born from dreams, will be fed by the dreams of others and by those dreams we will be guided.

This current project in Mi'kmaw humanities started with relationships carved out of an earlier SSHRC grant in 2000 when Lynne Bell, an art historian, and Len Findlay, a professor in the English department, and I were working on our project of decolonizing of the university, a project that arose from our prior work. From the start of our working together, we were prone to take on the big issues, reading, analyzing, sharing knowledge gained in our various interdisciplinary niches, orating the persistent issues of justice, while unloading our own issues with the systems using all manner of critique.

Animating the Mi'kmaw humanities was not unlike other projects, deliberate in its connections to social and ecological justice, vitally important for the future of education, directed at the educational system, aimed at limiting the effects of all its hierarchical Eurocentrism and supportive of new knowledges and skills for both Aboriginal and non-Aboriginal students. We were joined often and supported by my partner Sa'ke'j Henderson, Chickasaw legal theorist and philosopher, and Isobel Findlay, a postcolonial scholar of Co-operatives, and others from many community Mi'kmaw partners at Cape Breton University, Dalhousie University, St. Thomas University, Mi'kmawey Kina'matnewey in Membertou and Set Annaway School in Newfoundland. Drs. Murdena and Albert Marshall were among those whose deep, long friendships and known passions in the Mi'kmaw language, the land, the culture were necessary and vital to our work. They had already birthed the Mi'kmaw integrative science project at Cape Breton University with Dr. Cheryl Bartlett. These were our co-collaborators and friends who could see the vision and were prepared to help mobilize the vision forward.

From our proposal in 2009 to the journey on the plane to Cape Breton in late 2010, there were many meetings, five ethics proposals for each of the institutions involved and one for the Mi'kmaw

Ethics Watch. The latter I have spent the last ten years reading and responding to proposals as a result of the Grand Council's interest and care in making sure that Mi'kmaw people and knowledge were not inappropriately used or secured. This was part of the protection of the Mi'kmaq nation that is under the guidance of the Grand Council.

The humanities was once described as a story of beginnings, of how a people story their own civilization. How does one story a Mi'kmaw humanities into Mi'kmaw consciousness? Into a non-Aboriginal consciousness? This story, rather many stories, then are my preliminary and evolving understanding of Mi'kmaw humanities with the hopes that it will add to what exists, and by my own story and that of others, bring the coherence that the Mi'kmaw humanities have had in our life. Using Mi'kmaw concepts of humanity embedded in Mi'kmaw language and teachings, I draw attention to the concepts of humanity that could be focal points for education and for curricula.

The questions asked are: What are the humanities and what do they include today? How is it that centuries of Western education and intensive global era relations have created more distance between people (and themselves), rather than bringing us together symbiotically and appreciating our differences? What were the motivations of the Western humanities and how does it differ and relate to the Mi'kmaw worldview of socialization, transmission of knowledge and teachings and their educational sovereignty? Why is it important to frame a unique Mi'kmaw humanities? What sources are already available in Canadian indigenous education literature for contemplation? Mi'kmaw culture is inimitable, how might this be reflected in a Mi'kmaw humanities framework? And what questions do we need to ask Mi'kmaw knowledge carriers to develop the Mi'kmaw humanities? In asking and addressing these questions, the next shift in the humanities should begin to respect and serve the cultural diversity of Earth and understand that each humanity is unique and equally integral to the health of the whole.

M.B.

Notes from the Editors

The spelling of Mi'kmaq, Mi'gmaq and Micmac represent variations of orthographic conventions; most historical documents before 1979 used Micmac in reference to the people. Smith-Francis has been the preferred orthography of the Grand Council of the Mi'kmaw Nation since 1979.

The word Mi'kmaq is plural and is also used when referring to the whole nation. For instance: "The Mi'kmaq of Eastern Canada…."

Mi'kmaw is the singular and adjectival form of Mi'kmaq. Examples: "I am a Mi'kmaw" or "A Mi'kmaw man told me a story" or, "As a Mi'kmaw speaker … etc." It is also used to refer to the language itself. Examples: "I speak Mi'kmaw." "Mi'kmaw is my first language." "All the Mi'kmaq spoke Mi'kmaw up to the 1950s…."

In a few cases, editors have respected the local orthography used by the author.

Mi'kma'ki, the territory of the Mi'kmaq, includes the island of Newfoundland, all of Nova Scotia and Prince Edward Island, much of New Brunswick and the Gaspé, and part of northeastern Maine.

Responsibility for the writing, research and permissions obtained for this publication rests with the authors.

Marie Battiste

Reframing the Humanities:
From Cognitive Assimilation to Cognitive Justice

Indigenous peoples have the right to maintain, control, protect and develop their cultural heritage, traditional knowledge and traditional cultural expressions, as well as the manifestations of their sciences, technologies and cultures, ... oral traditions, literatures, designs, sports and traditional games and visual and performing arts. They also have the right to maintain, control, protect and develop their intellectual property over such cultural heritage, traditional knowledge, and traditional cultural expressions.

In conjunction with indigenous peoples, States shall take effective measures to recognize and protect the exercise of these rights.

Article 31, United Nations Declaration on the Rights of Indigenous Peoples (2007)

To understand indigenous humanities is to first understand the exclusions of indigenous peoples from colonial systems of education or their enforced subordination to their Eurocentric imperatives and goals, and then to consider what it means to reframe humanities through the respectful re-encounter of the original peoples of Canada with Eurocentric humanities. To do so, one needs to go through a process of decolonization, an unpacking of the Eurocentric humanities and the reclaiming and restoration of the indigenous humanities. What is clear is that indigenous knowledges, perspectives, histories and presence have been so undermined, misunderstood and overly controlled in Eurocentric discourses and disciplines that little is known about what indigenous humanity really means, except by indigenous peoples themselves. When indigenous knowledge (IK) is omitted, ignored or misrepresented in the schools, and a Eurocentric foundation is advanced to the exclusion of other knowledges and languages, these conditions define for indigenous students an experience of cognitive imperialism and racism. Cognitive imperialism is about whitewashing the mind as a result of forced assimilation, a condition that has normalized Western humanities as the normative discourse for centring education with certain peoples and diminishing others as lacking civilization and real or full humanity. Euro-humanity affirms itself by inhumanely dehumanizing indigenous peoples.

Today many generations of indigenous peoples, in ways that affect everyone, have had to endure a Eurocentric education forced on them, not just in residential schools, but also in provincial public and federal schools and in postsecondary institutions. Those Eurocentric approaches to their education have cost indigenous peoples plenty: erosion and even loss of many of the indigenous languages in the world, loss of spiritual identities and traditions linked to their traditional and evolving ways of knowing, disconnections from elders, lands, livelihood and spiritual communicative connections to the land and much more. Formal education has also supported a hierarchy of privilege and entitlement that has erected barriers to a transformed education and perpetrated epistemic violence against indigenous peoples who continue to be silenced, marginalized and alienated from education and even further from the outcomes of success that the majority of Canadians expect and enjoy.

In an allegedly ever-smarter world with its ever-smarter technologies, little is known about indigenous knowledges and the diverse epistemologies, pedagogies and methodologies by which they may and ought to be comprehended in Canadian schools and universities. And there is no app to cure racist ignorance. For at least the last decade or more, provinces and territories through the Canadian Council of Ministers of Education have declared priorities to improve Aboriginal education, and university presidents have declared their intentions to indigenize and improve success outcomes for indigenous students. Despite these declarations (Universities Canada 2015; Association of Community Colleges of Canada 2014), the re-encountering and re-learning of indigenous knowledges, peoples, histories and perspectives for academic purposes is a vast undertaking that is meeting both hesitancy and fear, a form of coded resistance to the realignment of priorities for many faculties and their students. Eurocentrism and its traditions have created multiple layers of cognitive imperialism that have controlled disciplinary knowledges, values, beliefs and research practices for generations. What knowledge counts, what gets produced and disseminated in these institutions, what is prioritized, funded and given institutional space, what metrics are used to determine validity, usefulness and accessibility to resources are all controlled by and through Eurocentric academic norms and traditions. The long-term implication for indigenous peoples is that their knowledges, their scholarship and their relationships to land, place and resources will continue to get little attention, support or uptake unless tied to economic or scientific rationalizations arising from the use of IK and its exploitation for local and global gain for dominant economic and political interests.

Since the early 1980s the political and economic awareness of diversities that exist in Canadian society and the value of such diversities in problem-solving and achieving peaceful relations with one another have been a source of change in schools. Inclusion and diversity have marked the major movements for change in education policies and curriculum directions. Since the 1970s provincial education authorities have taken great strides to include multiculturalism, heritage and treaty rights, and human rights in research, policy reform and inclusive educational practices. But education has not yet transformed the social constructions of Eurocentrism. It has ushered in and sustained ordinary (dominant) practices. What Daniel Coleman (2006) calls "white civility" is alive and well, at least until indigenous peoples forget their place or assert their rights. Nor has there been the recognition of the legitimacy of diverse knowledges, languages and humanities among the diverse populations of Canada. Despite the provinces' directives to improve Aboriginal student successes in schools and despite the increased attention to the diverse conditions that create barriers to these successes, changes of curricula content and balancing distinctive knowledge systems and processes remain on-going challenges wrapped in confusion or racist skepticism. While confinement and control of knowledge exercised in exclusive disciplinary knowledge and methodology are thought to be neutral and fair in a just society, the disproportionate inequality and perpetuation of unequal outcomes have yet to be recognized as the outcomes of contemporary socialization, legal and social structures, and Eurocentric superiority covering as neutral and universal education. Canada in all its inequality today is the result of Eurocolonial effort, and crucial state instruments such as education have contributed greatly to producing and maintaining the unjust distribution of opportunity and reward.

Today, the critically important postcolonial quest for indigenous peoples is to bring their knowledge and practices fully into their children's lives. For public schools, it is to discern what is valuable about multiple humanities to include in core curricula. For both indigenous education and education that includes indigenous humanity, educators need to understand what is important to the people, what it is necessary to retain and how all groups can adapt and learn and be stronger because of their shared humanities and humanity. The key tools of that reclamation for indigenous peoples are in their languages, their ancestral relationships, their communal learning of the processes their ancestors used for holding to knowledge and deep relationships with their place, their ecologies and land. Reclaiming, recovering, restoring and renewing indigenous peoples' rights and their humanities clearly constitute a revisionist project of great magnitude. It is a project that indigenous leaders, scholars and educators have taken to their sites of work and study—whether in the political activism of blockades on the roads, in protests on the waters, in the courts, in dissertations and theses and in schools and classrooms. And teachers and students everywhere need to be aware of its significance and help advance its implementation.

This situation was brought home to a few researchers at the University of Saskatchewan as we sought to work on building an awareness of the cognitive imperial humanities' influence on our own education and to rethink and reframe another humanity that was part of my own heritage—Mi'kmaq. Though the Mi'kmaq once controlled the eastern door of Canada and some coastal areas in New England, they are currently geographically and politically dispersed over five Maritime provinces of Eastern New Brunswick, Eastern Quebec, Nova Scotia, Prince Edward Island and Newfoundland, making up forty-nine distinct reserves and twenty-six Mi'kmaw communities in Canada. The seven districts or tribes of the Mi'kmaw nation (*Mi'kmaw nationimou*) is situated within the boundaries of eastern Canada and the United States in the lands Mi'kmaq call Mi'kma'ki, the territory of the allied families. Despite colonial contact with the French, English and Scots for more than 400 years, the Mi'kmaq remain a distinct linguistic, cultural and political entity. In the 17th and 18th centuries, the district chiefs established alliances and treaties with the King of France and Great Britain and the United States of America.

Since 1820, most of the Mi'kmaq in Canada have lived on reserved land, in small parcels of land called bands, now First Nations, protected by law under the jurisdiction of the federal government under s. 91(24) of the *Constitution Act, 1867.* In this *Act,* Great Britain turned their protective responsibility for "Indians and lands reserved for Indians" to the federal government and denied provincial authority over them. In the constitutional reforms of *Canada Act, 1982* affirmed the existing Aboriginal and treaty rights of the Aboriginal peoples of Canada, including the Mi'kmaw Nation, as part of the supreme law of Canada. The constitutional reforms have generated a new imperative for curricula form for the federal and provincial education systems (Battiste 2009).

Although damaged by federal residential schools, Mi'kmaw is still spoken among several larger Mi'kmaw communities, as well as into the United States, where Micmac now are federally recognized as tribes.[1] In the United States, federal recognition of the Mi'kmaq has created an off-reserve community scattered throughout the Aroostook County of Maine, and a larger off-reserve community exist in the greater Boston area in Massachusetts.

We, academics in education, law, business, art and cultural studies came together to build a shared community around relationships, friendships, extended relations and decolonizing and postcolonial thinking. Together we prepared a proposal to the Social Science and Humanities Research Council to indicate our preparation and our commitment to make indigenous humanities a real and viable project for universities. The funding eventually made possible our dialogues with several Mi'kmaw communities, our research and formations of diverse animating activities that would ensure the livelihood of Mi'kmaw humanities, from the Tepi'ketuek Mi'kmaw Archives, the *Living Treaties* (Battiste 2016) book, to our conference presentations and hiring Mi'kmaw junior scholars to do research and literature reviews. We have done much to contribute to the on-going intellectual development of Mi'kmaw humanities in schools and universities.

What we aimed to achieve is the reframing of the Eurocentric humanities project that has been the status quo of conventional education.

In this time of fragile, vulnerable and tragic environments, humans are going to have to redefine and reframe what it means to be a human in every knowledge system. At a time when every living system is declining—and the rate of decline is accelerating, mostly because of the human activities and technologies—we have come to understand that the Earth's resources are finite, for humanity has become a constructed fantasy of global Eurocentrism fashioned within economic necessity or efficacy. The 19th and 20th centuries, with unprecedented scientific and technological expansion, brought to life artificial entities and reckless practices which have slowly but inexorably poisoned our ecosystems and destroyed life. The most important natural resource of any ecosystem—the capacity of life forms for self-regeneration—is already almost exhausted. Thus everyone has crossed a fatal boundary that reveals the dangerous lie about abundant nature and responsible humanity. Most peoples are globally aware of each other and of cultural diversity in an age of almost instantaneous circulation of information and the vast potential of diverse knowledge systems to enrich our lives, generate cooperation and solve shared problems. Most peoples are finally becoming aware of the multiple dangers that humans pose to an endangered living system that has placed before all people the spectre of a collective planetary doom.

In the past, many people have attempted to define, classify and measure this capacity of the human species for self-delusion. This was a complicated, hitherto unfinishable task. They have generated endless and different answers to these questions in stories, visual arts and written documents. The answers in international, trans-systemic, interdisciplinary, intercultural and interpersonal taxonomies and contexts remain elusive and often exclusive. Many of the typical answers in the past in Eurocentric (i.e., Western) knowledge systems have generated a damaging legacy of hierarchy, domination, intolerance, hatred and the annihilation of others. The Eurocentric answers have reserved the concept of human to some groups and created dehumanization, delegitimization, infrahumanization and moral exclusion of certain groups that have generated commonplace regimes of hatred and violence. In our current shared context of humanity, attempting to redefine or answer the question of the attribution and denial of humanity is a disturbing process.

These twin challenges are interrelated, and the awareness of the crisis is unique to our current consciousness of and within most knowledge systems. They generate the most amazing, challenging, astonishing, wonderful and hopeful challenge ever passed down to any generation of humanity. They generate a need for a more inclusive comprehension of humanity in all its diversity and its relations with place to create a sustainable future. Within this challenge is the opposition to a monopoly of culture and creativity in any knowledge system. It is a rejection of a past and present goal of European knowledge systems to produce a uniform world of being, behaving, consuming, thinking, learning and creating.

In Eurocentrism, the conflict over the basic terms of life, and especially the human, has fled the ancient arenas of philosophy, politics, arts and humanities to live under disguise and under constraint in the narrower and more arcane debates of the specialized professions. We must reveal and reconceptualize this conflict, and bring the best ideas back, transformed, to the larger, more inclusive version of humanity.

This book is addressed to both the global awareness of peoples and the ecological crisis that require new answers to the human and to the humanities. This reframing the human and the humanities to the Mi'kmaw consciousness and experience is an attempt to merge Mi'kmaw knowledge systems with Eurocentric knowledge systems to create a trans-systemic concept of the humanities. This trans-systemic concept of cultural and linguistic domains could generate across the knowledge system a cognitive space for learning, to think together and eventually to act together. In creating this trans-systemic synthesis, this book attempts to introduce a concept of Mi'kmaw humanities, a concept ignored under Eurocentrism. This book attempts to expand Eurocentric narratives of the humanities into a more inclusive and complex concept of human science. It seeks to animate the indigenous humanities to the very centre of secondary and postsecondary education as well as to reanimate the intellectual traditions of thought.

We recognize that each indigenous nation has its own distinctiveness and beauty and strength and each nation's humanity can be a part that can unfold the whole. In working on this book together, our research team has recognized our responsibilities to engage the regions and peoples in their particularities, and not redefine them as a pan-indigenous civilization where they lose their distinctiveness in time and place. There are deep complexities in each nation as well as similarities among indigenous peoples, especially when they share proximity to each other. We recognize that each has a right to exist on their own, to have their knowledges embraced in their languages and to be shared on their own terms as the peoples determine. Such are the rights as the United Nations Declaration of the Rights of Indigenous Peoples (2007) has revealed. So for us, due to our proximity to the Mi'kmaq in relationship, we have collaborated to engage Mi'kmaw humanities, and in so doing arrive at our own understandings of what we missed by our own incomplete education and what we have come to understand by our willingness to be open to relationships, to lessons learned and to new possibilities. We seek to clarify the resistances and the challenges of divesting from Eurocentrism, while urging an agenda of restoration within a multi-disciplinary context for human dignity and the collective dignity of Mi'kmaw peoples. We also aspire to bring new perspectives to our living in relation with each other and with our place, giving new sensibilities to how Mi'kmaq and other indigenous peoples have come to know and appreciate these relationships and the deep spiritual treasure they have in them.

Over the last two decades, with much resistance by the school systems, by indifference, silence, intolerance and hostility, fragments of an indigenous humanities have been developed across a variety of school systems and postsecondary disciplines and studies (English, fine arts, history, legal studies, women's and gender studies, cultural studies and co-operative studies). In their present disjointed and fragmented state, the indigenous humanities have limited value as an educational tool or source of identity formation for First Nations students. Teachers concerned with indigenous knowledge(s) and ways of knowing often find themselves working in isolation within the disciplinary silos of the Eurocentric humanities. Indigenous knowledge, if and when addressed at all, is read or counterposed against authoritative Eurocentric knowledge. This crosscutting interdependence of the indigenous humanities with education is a site of struggle between exclusive Eurocentric cultures and inclusive multicultural reconciliation.

Focused on therapeutic understandings, sensitivities and knowledge(s), these authors, both Mi'kmaq and non-Mi'kmaq, academics and non-academics, seek to displace assimilation strategies and find new ways of engaging First Nations Elders, communities, women and students' understandings of their heritages, humanities and identities. This transformative initiative seeks to provide First Nations youth with a politics and pedagogy of hope and agency. Perhaps it will begin to address the lack of hope among First Nations youth who leave school early or who find a lack of inspiration, engagement and identity formation within (and beyond) current education programs, grounded as they are in Eurocentric disciplines.

In developing a map and structuring the indigenous humanities as a holistic area of study, this book has many goals. It is an attempt to avoid getting lost in the vagueness of an everlasting academic conversation without direction. It seeks to demonstrate how people can build a better and therapeutic educational system together by analysis of existing curriculum materials in human science. New insights of human sciences in Eurocentrism are revealing the weakness, absence or fragmentation of Eurocentric humanities. They reveal that the proclaimed universality of Eurocentric humanities is an academic illusion that has generated devastating human suffering. These insights affirm and animate the indigenous humanities within secondary and postsecondary educational consciousness and curriculum. They support and enrich indigenous peoples. They share with non-indigenous peoples, educators and graduate students an understanding and commitment to an indigenous humanities as a process of decolonizing secondary and postsecondary education. In addition, they illuminate areas of study based on indigenous knowledge(s) and methods of knowing in trans-systemic humanities.

Our research methodology and design propose to bring the indigenous humanities into existence as an interconnected area of transcultural or transformative study that cuts across the cluster of professional disciplines of postsecondary education and teaching certificates presently known as the humanities. Within the indigenous humanities, previously separate areas of study such as the oral traditions and visual arts are interconnected within indigenous knowledge systems and ways of knowing. They comprise a distinct worldview and performance literacy. Narratives and stories, for instance, cannot be taken away from worldview, the structure of their languages or traditional visual culture (such as totem poles, ivory carvings, button blankets and medicine wheels). They have legal meaning as well as normative values. These parts cannot be disconnected as a written literacy.

Indigenous peoples have earned the recognition of their existing right of self-determination in the UN Declaration of the Rights of Indigenous Peoples. They may promote, develop, exercise and maintain their orders and laws and have the right to determine their political status and pursue freely their cultural destiny within supportive social and economic development. In so doing, it requires each of us to recognize those elements foreign to our knowing and to see experiences with new eyes or, as Mi'kmaw Elders Murdena and Albert Marshall have said, using "Two-Eyed Seeing" (Hatcher et al. 2009). In looking at our collective histories, we hope to account for the absences in current educational policy and its impact on Indigenous peoples, while taking ourselves to the doorways of understanding, discovering new possibilities, other strategies and watching as sources of power and strength emerge to reveal themselves in a new light. We seek a trans-systemic concept of linguistic, cultural and educational domains that could generate a cognitive space for learning to think and act together. From this place, we seek to revisit the past, to tell a new story, re-order the present and inspire a different future.

It is not enough to analyze the multiple ways in which imperialism's educational legacy continues to separate indigenous from non-Iidigenous peoples and designate them as primitive and civilized. It is not enough to study racism and anti-racism theory. These problems reside in the Eurocentric narratives that must be deconstructed and neutralized and eventually eliminated. This analysis must engage the omissions as systemic discrimination, and generate a positive agenda about what it means for an indigenous person to be an indigenous human or practice indigenous humanities. It is about generating a vision of society and education where knowledge systems complement, not exclude, each other—where knowledge systems and languages are reinforced and not diluted, where they can respectfully gather together without resembling each other, and where peoples can participate in the cultural life of society, education and their community. To address this task, it is now necessary to articulate and animate the indigenous humanities at the very centre of secondary and postsecondary education in Canada. In many ways, this is to say that the time has come to see innovative learning and education take the ascendancy over the political and commercial order in maintaining and sustaining relationships.

For a long time, Eurocentric scholars, both in natural or social sciences, have known and recognized that the process of knowledge is dependent on place. They have misunderstood the meaning of place-based knowledge systems and transformed the concept into rhetoric and stereotypes of First Nations. Place-based knowledge systems are part of the interrelationships of living entities within an ecology. In the continent called North America, indigenous humanities are also comprised of dynamic place-based knowledge systems and ceremonies of the indigenous peoples. They are organized around three insights: the insights of embodied spirits, the implicate order and transformation. These complementary (but resistant) insights inform the depth of indigenous world views. These insights suggest a starting point for reflecting about whatever is most significant in indigenous humanities. They persist through many variations. They replicate and are revealed in languages, ceremonies and stories. The implications of the insights that inform indigenous humanities become manifest little by little. Despite being ignored by the colonizers and their education systems, there is no reason to believe that their significance and their implications are even close to disintegrating. The indigenous humanities are an ecological vision of being a human. They are not a romantic view of ecology, but a deep understanding of the interrelationship in a particular ecology, some good and some bad.

This book seeks to address and facilitate educational and academic reform by displacing and expanding these existing representations of human science in curriculum and pedagogy. It argues that the mapping and structuring the indigenous humanities is of vital concern to the educational success of First Nations teachers and students. It seeks to broaden the spectrum of knowledge systems, and to generate a dialogue, not only with the past but also toward the present and future. It seeks to become an instrument of transformation, animating diversity and pluralism through trans-systemic comprehension of knowledge systems with the decisive purpose of furthering education in significant and visible ways.

We use the notion of sites of animation to connect a variety of audiences and educators with the work of such leading theorists of decolonization as the Maori educators Linda Tuhiwai Smith and Graham Hingangaroa Smith and postcolonial theorist Cathryn McConaghy. Postcolonialism is the term used in Eurocentrism to describe the study of cultures who have emerged from colonial rule and who are undergoing the processes of decolonization. This, as postcolonial theory makes clear, is far more complicated than merely gaining political independence. It requires decolonization of the Eurocentric mind. Colonized cultures will be saturated with the influence of the imperial power from language, through its education system to the economic and political systems imposed during colonization. Together, we have developed a number of sites of animation that allow differing communities to come together to share their thoughts about decolonizing practices and principles in education.

This book seeks to enrich the capacities of First Nations' knowledge keepers, scholars, educators, performers, artists, storytellers, historians and scholars to get past a critique of the Eurocentric canon by animating the indigenous humanities. If successfully implemented, the indigenous humanities will become part of every school and university curriculum and future teachers and researchers will be engaged in this work which moves beyond the current narrative of Native studies which is too often narrowly focused on the histories and tensions of Indian-White relations in Canada. The Eurocentric canons of humanities have not demonstrated relevance to First Nations students, and thus this book can provide a nourishing and revolutionary space in schools and universities that mobilizes the Indigenous humanities as a core way of knowing and creating positive identities.

Languages are an essential dimension of indigenous humanities and concrete tools of communication. Given this twofold nature of languages, they are not only components of humanities and dialogue, but also targets of trans-systemic or interdisciplinarity collaboration and intercultural dialogue. The indigenous humanities will have to provide space and support to safeguard and promote linguistic and cognitive diversity, especially endangered languages, as a vehicle of intangible cultural heritage.

Indigenous humanities as a concept of human nature deserve to be taken seriously. It has to be developed in ways and venues that illuminate First Nations civilizations, achievements, resiliency and capacities. It needs to be developed to resolve immediate negative experiences and disarray, and to help people to survive the everyday surprises and personal disappointments of life. The methods involved in an indigenous humanities will have to face many troubling particularities. They have to generate diagnostic and explanatory implications of contextuality, solidarity and identity to be therapeutic and based in healing.

To comprehend the dual crises and very serious threats facing humanity now and in the future, people need a mindset that appreciates diversity of knowledge systems and life as an element of betterment and growth, thus going beyond the older paradigms that perceive diversity as a threat or, worse yet, as a synonym for the "enemy." People need to grasp the importance of the knowledge systems; the love of our natural and cultural worlds, the knowledge of the capacity of the ecosystem and its sustainability, the interrelationship of all components of the ecosystem, the interdependence of all humanity and our shared responsibility to protect the global environment are just a few of the values shared by all humanity. Better education, the enhancement of collective wisdom by understanding knowledge systems, the work of tolerance, sympathy and indulgence for the manifestation of human diversity are the attributes that will pave the way for solutions to our shared crises.

Review of the author contributions

Stephen Augustine, Dean of Unama'ki College, Cape Breton University, offers his understanding of the teachings of his relatives in the story of Creation through the life of the first Mi'kmaw relative Kluscap, and how the Mi'kmaw world was created and how the first Mi'kmaw people came into being. Through the relationships with the animate universe in a location, Mi'kmaq have been given a way to understand and be present with their relations, world, ecology, environment and geography. These teachings begin our Mi'kmaw humanity.

Margaret Robinson is a researcher, scholar, professor and feminist whose people come from Epekwitk though she was raised in Eski'kewaq. Her essay draws from some original teachings of stories, legends, pictographs and the traditions of Mi'kmaq and their contemporary significance to Mi'kmaq today. She illustrates the importance of understanding how the early lives and teachings of Mi'kmaq and their relationships with animals, plants and ecology provide guidance for contemporary applications to her research, and to living with humanity—a mutual vulnerability that both ties us together and urges our responsible behavior to all our relations.

Len Findlay is a professor of literature and cultural studies and director of the Humanities Research Unit at the University of Saskatchewan whose early education and intellectual traditions were framed in the superiority and hierarchy of Eurocentric patriarchal traditions and ideologies. His arriving in Canada and working in and through First Nations contexts have provided the true grit of learning that has framed his new insights and allied him to Mi'kmaw humanities through the teachings of many indigenous scholars and their indigenous knowledges, including the Mi'kmaw Creation Story. He offers further insight into the contemporary significance to the Creation Story to all Canadians.

Marjorie Gould is a former teacher, Indian Affairs Superintendent of Education, education director, founding executive director of Mi'kmaw Kina'matnewey, and long time resident of Wagmatcook, her home community. She earned her BEd from St. Francis Xavier University, he master's degree from University of Maine at Orono, and received an honorary degree from St. FX. Marjorie joins Marie Battiste in a chapter that honours her mother Caroline Gould whose life gives some insight into the everyday journey of living to find one's gifts and share them with humanity.

James [Sa'ke'j] Youngblood Henderson is a member of the Chickasaw Nation and is a legal and philosophical historian and researcher and former director for the Native Law Centre at the University of Saskatchewan. His essay is a personal exploration and interpretation of the concept of Lnu'uk civilization and how many of its dialectal variations of the language create a distinct version of indigenous humanity. It examines how the knowledge keepers in the shared creation stories generate the covenants and teachings of how to be human is reflected in Mi'kmaw humanities and language.

Marie Battiste is editor of this collection, Mi'kmaq professor at the University of Saskatchewan and principal investigator of the funded Social Sciences and Humanities project "Animating Mi'kmaw Humanities." She offers a background to the research foundations on which this collection was initiated, the elders who guided its emergence, in particular Caroline and Marjorie Gould from Wagmatcook whose lives give some insight into the everyday journey of living to find one's gifts and share them with humanity. The essay shares some of the narratives of the research on which the core of this edited collection has been guided. In a second essay building on her doctoral research, she describes the symbolic literacies and communication forms used among the Mi'kmaq prior and after contact with European literacies, illustrating that Mi'kmaw ways of knowing and their forms of communication were vibrant and functional for their communication needs and continue through their contemporary lives.

Isobel Findlay is a Scots-born Canadian professor emerita of the University of Saskatchewan, a co-researcher in the Mi'kmaw humanity project who shares her deeply personal, sociocultural and intellectual journey in and through Eurocentric institutions. Through demystifying and displacing colonial residues, she illustrates an intellectual respect and learning from Mi'kmaw researchers, worldviews, values and measures to do some justice to relationships in a postcolonial Canada worthy of the name. She reconsiders the inherited narratives about superiority of Canada's intellectual traditions to recognize a much longer and largely unheralded story of traditions living in and as livelihoods that have sustained Mi'kmaq for generations.

Nancy Peters received her doctorate from the University of Saskatchewan and was one of the graduate researchers in the Mi'kmaw humanities project. Her essays are both the result of her research into how Mi'kmaq have been depicted, regarded, dismissed and stereotyped in Nova Scotia curricula over time, leading her to rethink her own educational experience in Nova Scotia as a settler and what she was taught to think and believe about Mi'kmaq. She begins to rethink the legacy of Mi'kmaw people and what it means to live in the shadow of Eurocentric superiority and perhaps what it requires to come out from that blind spot to become an informed and active ally of Mi'kmaq.

Jennifer Tinkham is an assistant professor at the University of Saskatchewan whose doctoral dissertation from St. Francis Xavier is a study of Mi'kmaq youth and their experiences with social studies curricula in Nova Scotia leading to her dissertation and essay title "That's not my history! Examining the role of personal counter-narratives in decolonizing Canadian history for Mi'kmaw students."

Lisa Lunney Borden is an assistant professor at St. Francis Xavier University where she did her doctoral research in Mi'kmaw concepts of math. In this essay she stories her early learning in Nova Scotia and becoming a teacher to learning a new cultural paradigm as she steps into her new role as teacher on a Mi'kmaw reserve in Wagmatcook. She shares how this experience and her inquiries into math thinking, called *mawikinutimatimk*, coming together to learn together, not only transformed her own perceptions of Mi'kmaw people's contributions but also helped her to transform her teaching and curriculum of math to better meet the needs of Mi'kmaw learners.

Jaime Battiste, Treaty Lead in Nova Scotia, resident of Eskasoni First Nation, and a member of Potlotek First Nation, writes about his experiences and concerns about how Mi'kmaw identity and citizenship are being shaped from Eurocentric discourses of blood, race and DNA. He analyzes their utility and contested foundations and considers how the teachings of Elders about Mi'kmaw humanity offer a different more robust analysis of family and collective community connections.

Ashley Julian is a Mi'kmaw educator whose master's degree research into Mi'kmaw language immersion programming takes her through her own journey of learning from her grandmother and elders in her community and to the Mi'kmaw immersion program in Eskasoni. Through these narratives and teachings she begins to frame how living with shame, marginalization and cognitive imperialism have generated language loss in Mi'kmaw communities with continuing challenges despite the resurgence of Mi'kmaw revitalization and reconciliation. Much more will need to be done she urges to correct these absences and it goes beyond Mi'kmaw healing and self-determination but to a humanity that accepts and encourages diversity of humanities.

Lynne Bell, a valued member of the Animating the Humanities research team, joins for the afterword, reflecting on our research and offering insights and lessons learned on the significance of the work.

Note

1. In Maine, the spelling is Micmac. See http://www.micmac-nsn.gov.

References

Association of Canadian Community Colleges (ACCC). 2014. An Indigenous Education Protocol for Colleges and Institutes, 1-11. https://www.collegesinstitutes.ca/wp-content/uploads/2014/05/ACCC_IndigenousEducationProtocol.pdf2014 (accessed August 24, 2016).

Battiste, Marie. 2009. Constitutional Reconciliation of Education for Aboriginal peoples / La réconciliation constitutionnelle des Autochtones et leurs droits éducationnels. *Directions* 5 (1): 81-84.

———, ed. 2016. *Living Treaties: Narrating Mi'kmaw Treaty Relations*. Sydney, NS: Cape Breton University Press.

Canada Act 1982, 1982, c. 11 (U.K.).

Coleman, Daniel. 2006. *White Civility: The Literary Project of English Canada*. Toronto: University of Toronto Press.

Hatcher, A., C. Bartlett, A. Marshall and M. Marshall. 2009. Two-eyed Seeing in the Classroom Environment: Concepts, Approaches, and Challenges. *Canadian Journal of Science, Mathematics and Technology, Education* 9 (3): 141-53. **doi:** 10.1080/14926150903118342.

Universities Canada. 2015. Principles on Indigenous Education. http://www.univcan.ca/media-room/media-releases/universities-canada-principles-on-indigenous-education/ (accessed August 24, 2016).

Stephen J. Augustine

The Mi'kmaw Creation Story

Mi'kmaw humanities are not comparable to Eurocentric concepts of humanities: the basic world view of indigenous peoples in North America is not grounded in the same historical experiences as the European cultures that came here to our territories. European humanities are founded in the philosophies of the early Greeks, like Socrates, Plato and Aristotle. Christian religious philosophies were founded on the teachings of Christ and the Bible. Mi'kmaw humanities have their origin in our Creation Stories, *ta'n wetapeksulti'kw*, each story specific to certain families and regions of Mi'kma'ki. There are many versions of the Mi'kmaw Creation Story—this is one of them.

My grandmother Agnes (Thomas) Augustine, who lived to be 100 years old (1898-1998) passed down to me and my siblings the oral history and traditions she had collected over her entire life. She was born on Lennox Island, Prince Edward Island, in a birch bark wikuom. She had many stories to share from her four grandparents and her great-grandparents—stories handed down from their ancestors—about the time before Europeans lived on our *wskitqamuk*. One of the stories kept hidden from the eyes and ears of the strangers is our Creation Story, *t'an wetapeksulti'kw*, "where we come from." It explains how the Mi'kmaw people, *L'nu'k*, came into existence here in Mi'kma'ki—*L'nue'katik*, northeastern North America, or eastern

Canada. Our Elders teach us the significance of the number seven. Seven is more than a "lucky" number, as it is often referenced in Eurocentric cultures; seven is very sacred to the Mi'kmaq.

There are seven levels of creation, the sacred directions explained in our Creation Story, that the Mi'kmaw people honour and offer smoke from our burning sweet grass, tobacco and pipe ceremonies— the smoke symbolically representing our words wafting to the spirits, our prayers. Our Elders say that there are seven council fires that represent the seven *mawio'mi* or the seven districts of the Mi'kmaw Grand Council, as it is known today. The Mi'kmaq represent one of the seven original Algonkian-speaking nations; the Elders tell us there were seven original families created in the Creation Story. Also, there were seven sacred medicines that were honoured during the telling of the Creation Story. They were called the *kji-npisun*, the Great Spirit medicine made up of seven ingredients of leaves, barks and roots of plants representing the medicinal nature of the Mother of Kluskap.

Before the *l'nu'k* were created, there were three spiritual entities that were here in *wskitqamu*, our world: Kisu'lkw, Niskam and Wskitqamu.

Kisu'lkw is a Mi'kmaw word which means "we have been created" and sometimes referred to as *ankweiu'lkw* "the one who takes care of us." After the introduction of Christianity to the Mi'kmaq, Kisu'lkw became known as God. Our notion of Creation is not as a singular "big bang" when everything began to be created nor is our story grounded in a Garden of Eden and the expulsion of Adam and Eve. Mi'kmaq generally understand that our world is a cyclical motion of events, we have been created, we are being created; in the future, if we wake up in the morning and see our world before us, then we are continuing to be created. Kisu'lkw is the Great Spirit or Giver of Life.

Niskam, is a Mi'kmaw word used to refer to the sun in a spiritual context, and because we honour and respect our grandfathers, *nijka-mij*, we call the sun our grandfather. The everyday Mi'kmaw word for sun means "it shines during the day," *na'ku'setewik* or simply *na'ku'set*. Because we descend from our grandfathers, *nij*, "to come down" *nija'si* or *nisa'si*, and correspondingly *nijink* "my children," our children and grandchildren descend from us. It is a sacred relationship. Our Elders tell us that the Grandfather Sun gave us our shadows, *mjijaqmijk*, and our shadows are the images of our ancestors following us around all day, protecting and guiding our spirits. In this way we are attached to our ancestors who have died and gone to the land of the shadows or spirits, we are attached to them by our feet and through our blood. When Mi'kmaw spirit leaders perform ceremonies they give thanks to Grandfather Sun, Niskam; they offer smoke to grandfather sun in the sky and within himself and to his shadow.

Wskitqamu is our Mother Earth. *Weskitk* or *wskitk* means "upon the surface" and *kaqma'latl* means "she/he is standing up" so *wskitqamu* means the surface of area upon which we stand and share with all the other living entities, or simply Mother Earth. Because our mother bore us in her body for nine months and sustained us with her milk for the early parts of our lives, we have great love for our mothers. The Mi'kmaq have great love and respect in a similar way for Wskitqamu our Mother Earth. For the reason that the birds, plants, animals and fish are part of Creation and part of Mother Earth, we give thanks to Her for allowing us to make our food, medicines, shelter, tools of survival and modes of travel—all from elements of Wskitqamu. Mi'kmaw spiritual leaders are grateful for what we receive from Mother Earth and perform sacred ceremonies, the sacred fire, tobacco offering, burning sweet grass, sweat lodge and sacred pipe, singing, dancing, drumming, fasting and feasting, giving gifts and sharing to give thanks; these are our way of negotiating our survival with Wskitqamu.

Kluskap is created from three bolts of lightning hitting the surface of Wskitqamu our Mother Earth. *Kisu'lkw* caused three bolts of lightning to hit upon the surface of Wskitqamu—and Kluskap was created. This lightning shook the earth and a shape of a person formed with the help of all that was part of the earth, plants, animals, birds, fish, air, fire, water and soil. The person's head was in the direction of the rising sun, the feet were in the direction of the setting sun and his arms were outstretched, one to the north and the other to the south—constituting the four cardinal directions. It was not until after the second bolt of lightning that hit Kluskap where he was laying after the passing of one winter, *newtipuk*—that he was given the extremities of his body, his fingers and toes. As well, he was given the seven sacred parts to his head, two ears to listen from the goodness of his heart, two eyes to look from the goodness of his heart, two nostrils to sense his place in the world and, finally his mouth to take the sacred breath, to drink the water that comes from Mother Earth and to eat the food from Wskitqamu. Our Elders tell us that Kluskap was still stuck on Mother Earth like the babies that mothers carry on their backs in the cradleboards. Babies start learning everything from their mothers who prepare animals, plants, fish and birds for food, clothing, medicines, shelter and tools of survival. Kluskap had to learn from his Mother Earth by listening, looking, smelling, eating, drinking and speaking from his heart. Kluskap had to observe the snow fall during the winter. He observed the changing colours of the leaves; he saw the changing colours of animal fur from brown to white of the rabbits and witnessed the colours of the world Wskitqamu transformed.

After the passing of another winter, a third bolt of lightning hit Kluskap where he was stuck and thereafter he gained his freedom. He gained the freedom to stand up, to walk, to move around his world. He was so excited to be able to move his hands, to hear his world and see it in different ways, and to smell it—to sense his place as well as to breath the air, drink the water and now be able to eat the food. He observed the land and its formations, the water, lakes, rivers, brooks, seas and shores and the forests. He saw the stars and the moon in the sky. He felt the wind and the rain and snow.

Kluskap, after he got up, gave thanks to Kisu'lkw for his life. He thanked Niskam, Grandfather Sun, for giving him his shadow which he could now see following him around. He gave thanks to Wskitqamu, Mother Earth, for giving up parts of herself for his creation. He turned around seven times and then followed the path of Niskam toward the west, the setting sun. Later, he decided to travel south until the earth became red and narrow and he could see water on both sides, in the east and in the west. Having spent some time in the south, he decided to travel up north to the land of white, the land of ice and snow. It was too cold for him so he decided to go back to the east where he owed his creation.

One day he came to the big circle of sparks and embers left over from the three bolts of lightning that caused his creation. He saw an impression of himself on the ground in the centre of the circle of sparks where he was peeled off of Wskitqamu. Kluskap had become a *wskijinu*, a surface-dwelling being. The last part of the word *wskijinu*, *inu* makes reference to indigenous people as "people of the earth," Mother Earth, and so we call ourselves Ilnu. The Montagnais and Attikamekw call themselves Innu. The Cree are called Iyu Atch.

Kluskap was the first Mi'kmaq who spoke, *keluliskip*, "he spoke to you." As he was standing in the centre of the circle, he saw Grandfather

Sun high up in the noonday sky, and while he was looking, he observed a large bird with a white head and a white tail circling around the sun. The bird slowly descended and landed in front of him. The bird, an eagle, spoke to him and said, "I am Kitpu. I have been sent by Kisu'lkw, Niskam and Wskitqamu to be a messenger to you. Because I fly the highest of all the birds and see the farthest of all the birds, I have been chosen as the messenger." Kitpu, the eagle told Kluskap he would be joined by his family on Wskitqamu in order for him to understand the world and his place there. The eagle flew up in the sky and an eagle feather fell down; Kluskap picked it up before it hit the ground. The feather made him feel strong and self-assured.

Nukami, a white-haired old woman appeared sitting on a rock when Kluskap, still holding on to the eagle feather, turned around. He approached her and asked her, "Who are you, where do you come from?" She said, "I am Nukami, your grandmother. I was brought into Wskitqamuk to guide and teach you how to survive. I owe my existence to this rock on the ground. Early this morning *kikpewisk*, dew, formed over this rock and with the help of Kisu'lkw and Niskam, Wskitqamu brought me into existence as an old woman already wise and knowledgeable. I will teach you everything you need to know about surviving on Mother Earth." Kluskap was so glad that his grandmother came into his world. He called upon a little animal, *apistane'wj*, marten, and asked him to give up his life so that Kluskap and Nukami could continue to live. They needed food to eat, medicine to stay healthy, clothes and shelter, tools of survival and a means to travel about. In order to negotiate their survival Kluskap offered *apistane'wj* a gift of *tmawey*, or tobacco, in return for giving up his life. Grandmother picked up *apistane'wj*, broke his neck and laid him down on the ground. In the meantime, Kluskap raised his hand with the eagle feather and apologized to Kisu'lkw for taking the life of his brother *apistane'wj*. He apologized to Niskam for taking the shadow of his brother and he apologized to Wskitqamu for taking a part of Her creation, *apistane'wj*, for the continuance of their, Kluskap and Nukami, existence. Kluskap said to them: "if you are all so great in making the world and putting us in it, why don't you give back *apistane'wj* his life so in that way we can have this relationship with him and the rest of the animals forever. We can negotiate our survival with the animals." And so, when Kluskap turned around *apistane'wj* woke up and Kluskap told him to return to the forest. In the meantime, his grandmother, Nukami was preparing an animal to make their clothing, their food, tools and so on.

Nukami told Kluskap to prepare a fire. She told him to gather seven sparks or embers left over from his creation and scattered in a circle around him. Kluskap picked up seven sparks and put them in the centre of the circle. Then Nukami told Kluskap to put seven pieces of dry wood and build a wikuom over the sparks. Kluskap did as he was told. Finally, Grandmother told Kluskap to invite *weju'sn*, his cousin the wind. The wind came in from the east and continued its way west and then north. In the meantime, a fire started to burn and this is how the *kjipuktew*, Great Spirit Fire, came to be in existence. Nukami cooked the meat of the animal on the *kji puktew* so they could celebrate her arrival to Wksitqamu. Nukami taught Kluskap everything he needed to know to survive.

One day while Kluskap was walking along the seashore in the east, *wjipenuk* or *wabanakik*, he was startled by a tall young man of great stature and sparkling white eyes rising up from the sweet grass, *weljema'kl*. Kluskap asked him, "Who are you? Where do you come from"? The young man replied, "I am Netawansum, your sister's son. You are my uncle. I owe my existence to the wind *wju'sn* that passed by over the ocean heading in the direction of the setting sun, *tkisnuk*, in the west. It caused the water to roil up and foam began to form on top of the water. The foam was blown on the shore picking up seaweed, driftwood, pebbles and sand, fish scales, bones, leaves and every part of Mother Earth, Wskitqamu, and with the help of Kisu'lkw and Niskam gave me a body of a young man, strong and able to help you and Nukami. I am a gift from our ancestors and I have a special gift of two eyes. Netawansum said he was a *kinap* and a *puoin*. If you respect my strength, my vision for the future, my youth, you will find your place in this world." Kluskap realized that young people have the gift of the eyes to look at the adults as role models so he had to make sure he left a legacy of survival for the future generations. Kluskap was glad that his nephew came into creation to join him in Wksitqamu so he called upon the fish of the waters. He gave them a gift of tobacco and then asked them if they could give their lives so he, Nukami and Netawansum could continue to live. The fish agreed to give up their lives and he asked his nephew to gather them and take them to Nukami so she could prepare a feast of fish to honour and celebrate the arrival of his nephew in their world. In the meantime, Kluskap raised the eagle feather and apologized to Kisu'lkw, Niskam and Wskitqamu for taking the fish for their survival. And they continued to look after the *kjipuktew* or the Great Spirit fire.

Kluskap was sitting by the fire one day and a woman sat beside him and asked, *"kewjin kwi's*? Are you cold my son?" He said, "Yes, who are you and where do you come from?" She said, "I am your mother, Nikanaknimkusi'skw. I owe my existence from a leaf on a tree which early this morning fell to the ground. Dew, *kekpewisk*, formed over the leaf and, with the help of Kisu'lkw, Niskam and Wskitqamu, gave me a body of a woman." She said, "I bring all the colours of the world, all the blues of the sky, the greens of the forest and the yellow skies of the setting sun." His mother said, "I also bring strength so that you will withstand the different elements of the world, the temperatures, the snow, wind and the rain. I bring understanding and love so my children will look after each other; they will rely on each other for their survival." Kluskap was happy that his mother arrived into the world. He asked his nephew to collect the food from the plants and the trees. Kluskap again raised the eagle feather to the sky and thanked Kisu'lkw, Niskam and Wskitqamu for bringing his nephew into the world. Nukami prepared a meal of fruits and vegetables in honour of Kluskap's mother's arrival to Wskitqamu.

Soon enough Kluskap realized that in order to exist in this world he had to rely on the wisdom and knowledge of his grandmother as to where to look for food. He had to rely on his nephew who was very strong and could bring an animal for their food and nourishment. Kluskap's mother brought him strength and understanding and all the colours. She was inspiring them to get along and rely on each other. She helped Kisu'lkw, Niskam and Wskitqamu to bring life into the world. So after some time, the eagle, Kitpu, came to visit Kluskap with a message. Kitpu told Kluscap that he would have to leave the world with his grandmother, and that his nephew and mother would have to look after the *kjipu'ktew*. They have to make sure the *kjipu'ktew* never goes out, no matter what happens.

Kitpu told Kluskap that one day seven sparks will fly out of the fire and when they land on the earth they will form seven women. Seven more sparks will fly out in a different direction and seven men will be formed when they land on the earth. Seven women and seven men will come together and form seven families. There will be seven original families sitting around the *kjipuktew*. Kluskap was told by

Kitpu that after the passing of seven winters the seven original families will disperse in seven different directions. One of those seven families will be the Mi'kmaw people and they will settle in the east, *wjipnuk*. In order not to forget the seven levels of creation, the Mi'kmaw will divide themselves into seven clans, each with their own spirit fire made from the sparks from the *kjipuktew*. The *mawio'mis* are: *Keskpe'k, Kikniktuk, Epekwitk aq Piktuk, Kespukwitk, Sipekne'katik, Eskikewa'kik* and *Unama'kik*. They will gather together every year into a *mawio'mi*, a gathering of their *saqmaq*.

Kluskap was told by the eagle that after the passing of seven winters, the Mi'kmaq will have to gather the sparks from their seven *mawio'mi* fires and return to the place of the Great Spirit fire (somewhere near present-day Montreal), a place surrounded by seven small mountains. They will have to give thanks to their place in creation. This giving of thanks involves ceremonies. It is a method of negotiating our survival on Mother Earth, Wksitqamu. The ceremony starts with the rekindling of the seven fires.

Kjipuktew Fire Ceremony

A spiritual leader is responsible for bringing all of the seven fires together. He is responsible for the fire ceremony. The fire ceremony is to honour the first four level of creation, Kisu'lkw and Niskam that caused a bolt of lightning to hit Wksitqamu that created Kluskap.

Nkani'kwom Sweat Lodge Ceremony

In order to honour the arrival of Nukami, twenty-eight stones will be placed in the *kji puktew,* and a dome-shaped circular structure, *nkani'kwom*, the "place of the spirit water" will be built out of seven saplings and covered with seven skins of animals with the opening facing the direction of the rising sun, *wjipnuk*. About fifteen paces away in the direction of the rising sun, the *kjipuktew* will be burning with the twenty-eight rocks inside it. There are four rounds of the sweat lodge. The first round involves bringing seven hot rocks from the fire into the sweat lodge and placing them in the centre of the circle. The first round is dedicated to the east and our leaders and also the first seven levels of creation: Kisu'lkw, Niskam, Wskitqamu,

Kluskap, Nukami, Netawansum and Nikanakunimkosi'skw. Once the door of the lodge is closed, the lodge-keeper will pour water on the rocks and steam begins to form. The lodge becomes very hot and the seven representatives of the seven original families who are sitting around the rocks will take their turns, one by one, and begin talking to the spirits of our ancestors and the birds, plants, fish and animals, apologizing and giving thanks, negotiating for our survival. The second round is dedicated to the south, to our grandmothers and to the seven original families in the Creation Story, the Mi'kmaq being one. Seven more rocks are brought in to the lodge and added to the seven that are already there. More water is poured over the rocks and the lodge gets hot once again. Everybody is hot and sweat pours out of their bodies onto Wskitkamu, an offering of ourselves to our Mother Earth. *Wela'liek aq msit nokmaq!* Thank you and all of our relations.

The door of the lodge opens. For the third round, seven more rocks are added to the fourteen that are already there. The door of the lodge is closed and the lodge-keeper pours more water on the rock creating heat and steam inside. This round is dedicated to the direction of the west, to the young people and to the seven clans of the seven original families. The seven *mawio'mi*s of the Mi'kmaw Grand Council are given honour. Each of the seven leaders talk to the spirits collectively, all together they sing to the spirits. The door opens and the steam rises outside. All my relations! Finally the fourth round begins with seven more rocks added to the twenty-one already inside the lodge making twenty-eight rocks for the final round. The sweat lodge door is closed. Water is poured on the rocks. The final round is dedicated to the north for the mothers because of the medicinal nature of their bodies and because Kluskap's mother came from a leaf of a tree, we bring seven sacred medicines inside the lodge to make our *kjimpisun*, our Great Spirit medicine. Each of the seven leaders say their words to the spirits of our medicines and ask the Giver of Life, Grandfather Sun and Mother Earth, to give strength to the medicine and each time water is poured on the rocks. The final round is very hot. The medicine is divided into seven equal parts so that each of the leaders has the seven parts of the *l'nuimpisun* so they can heal their people. They sing to the spirits of the medicines and then ask for the lodge door to be opened.

"All my Relations! *Msit nokma'q.*" So, all of the leaders are naked, they are red and shiny from the steam and heat, and because they are so happy, they are emotional, they crawl out of the sweat lodge like shiny new babies when they are born. The sweat lodge ceremony is honouring our grandmother Nukami. We go back into the womb of Mother Earth and we celebrate our recreation.

Weljama'jkewe'l Sweet Grass

In order to give honour and respect to the creation of the nephew who came from the ocean and was created on the sweet grass, we take this hair of Mother Earth and braid it and give it honour, dignity and respect. Then we light the sweet grass on the *kjipuktew*. We offer the smoke to the Giver of Life, Grandfather Sun, Mother Earth, Kluskap, Nukami, Netawansum and Nikanakunimkosi'skw—seven levels of creation. The smoke from the burning sweet grass represents all of our collective words or prayers. We offer the smoke or smudge to the seven sacred directions. We also take the smoke and direct it upon ourselves, to our head to cleanse our minds, our ears to clear the path to our heart, to our eyes so we can look with goodness from our heart, to our nose so we can sense our place on Mother Earth and everyone around us. We cleanse our mouth so we speak the truth and share the food, medicine and the water that comes from Mother Earth. We are a part of Mother Earth, we are part of Her creation so we belong to Her and all of Her abundances are not something that we can call our own. They do not belong to us so we have to share it with everybody.

Tmawey Tobacco Ceremony

We take the leaves of *tmawey* and prepare it to smoke in our pipes but first we offer the tobacco to the sacred fire and the smoke which rises represents our words to the spiritual entities of our ancestors, the animals, birds, plants and fish. We offer the smoke to the Giver of Life, Grandfather Sun, Mother Earth, Kluskap, to his Grandmother, his nephew and his mother—seven sacred levels. We also smudge ourselves with the smoke from the tobacco leaves.

Tmaqn Pipe Ceremony

To celebrate the coming together of our negotiations for survival, we take the stone that represents Nukami and shape it into a pipe bowl. We take a branch of a willow which represents Kluskap's mother, Nikanakunimkosi'skw, and we make the stem of the pipe. Then we take the leaf of the plant, the tobacco which also represents Nikanakunimkosi'skw and we put it in the bowl of the pipe. We fill it seven times, each time offering to the seven sacred directions and to the seven levels of creation.

When the pipe is filled with tobacco we light the sweet grass—which represents Kluskap's nephew—from the Great Spirit Fire and then light the pipe with the sweet grass. We blow the smoke to Kisu'lkw, then we take another mouthful of smoke and blow it to Niskam, we take another smoke and blow it in the direction of Mother Earth. We take another puff and blow it east to Kluskap. We take another puff and blow it to the south for Grandmother. We take another puff and blow it to the west, to the nephew, and finally we blow the smoke to the north for our mothers. After we have blown smoke to the seven sacred directions the pipe-carrier will offer the stem of the pipe to the seven sacred entities and invite the spiritual entities to join us in our ceremony. The pipe is then passed around the circle of leaders four times and then finally the pipe is separated or put apart, the bowl from the stem, by the spiritual leader and placed on Mother Earth. The ceremony is complete. This is not a full description of the ceremonies that are done, however this is an explanation on what they mean to some of our indigenous peoples in North America.

There are many principles, morals, ethics and values of how to live as a Mi'kmaw Ilnu that are hidden in the creation story, and when our Elders tell the story to our people, they emphasize the parts they want to use as their teachings. Our humanity is embedded in our oral history and traditions. Our humanity is also embedded in our language.

Msit no'kmaq, all my relations.

James Sa'ke'j Youngblood Henderson

L'nu Humanities

We are the stars that sing; we sing with our light.[1]

Across countless generations, comforted by the safety of the sounds of the language (*lnui'simk*)[2] and ceremonies, the Elders, knowledge keepers and storytellers have relied on and revealed the structure and teachings of the Lnu'uk civilization.[3] The Lnu'uk civilization establishes the foundation of at least seven other civilizations of L'nu (Augustine 1977, 1996, 2008) including the Mi'kmaw civilization (which I will use as an example).

In the dialogues on Mi'kmaq humanities, many Unama'ki Mi'kmaw Elders continue to prefer the ancient concept of L'nu to describe themselves to the concept of Mi'kmaq or the allied families. They all agreed that L'nu is the correct term. They say the root concept of L'nu is embedded in their concepts of living people (*skwinjinu*). They say their concept of humanity is *skwinjinu's* and humanities are *skwijinu'kinuek*, which is related to being from the earth and being people of the earth. They say where you are born is *skwijinuwa'skit*. They say these concepts also inform the idea of myself as a human (*l'nui*), the inclusive concept of humans (*wskwijinu'k*), as well as being a human (*mimajuinu*). They say their inclusive way of thinking like a human is *l'nui'suti* and looking like a *l'nu* is *l'nuamuksit or l'nuamuksit*.

When a Mi'kmaw-speaking person tells another to speak *l'nu*, they say *l'nui'suti* or speak the language of the humans. Their preference for L'nu reveals a foundational Lnu'uk civilization that has been and remains part of the endless process of knowing and balancing of the ecological and human diversities in the unfolding flux (represented by the prefix "*pema*").

The Elders reflect that while they have been using these words in daily life, they have not realized the depth of what they were saying. Because this ancient preference for L'nu is not deeply understood, it generates some confusion about Mi'kmaw identity and knowledge that I am attempting to unravel here. My original understanding derives from the Cheyenne (*Suhtai*) dialect of Lnu'uk (*Erenyiwa*). I had the good fortune to fall in love with a Mi'kmaw woman, my wife Marie Battiste, thus my entrance to the Mi'kmaw consciousness (*koqqwaja'ltimk*) is through the spirit and language of love (*kesaltim-kewey*) and relations. Many Mi'kmaq continue my intensive learning about the living linguistic structure of the Lnu'uk civilization, especially as enfolded among the Unama'ki Mi'kmaq. It has been helpful to be a legal advisor to the Sante' Mawio'mi in the constitutional battles of the Mi'kmaq and to find Elders to translate their thoughts and insights to me. This privileged position allows me to glimpse how the deep structure of Mi'kmaw knowledge, thought and law is related to the Lnu'uk civilization, how it adapted in the generations to generate new alliances and treaties, and informed the collective attempts to explain Mi'kmaw law and treaties to the courts.

Also, the yearly seasonal Mawio'mi discussions of humanity and human rights revealed the seven levels of Mi'kmaw language and thought. Mi'kmaw thought is more than daily conversational Mi'kmaq; it moves to an expanding understanding of place, nature and the universe. Grand Keptin Alex Denny of the Mawio'mi taught me the first of seven levels of Mi'kmaw versions of Lnu'uk; the top surface, the iceberg of what we know, is the environment, and because it exists, we are. These are the ancient teachings about learning from all the spirits and forces in the environment or ecology on how to live within its gifts and blessings. This is often comprehended as spirituality (*ktlamasitasuti*).

The second level is spoken from the heart (*nkamlamun*); learning is the gift of each person and the emotional intelligence of loving, caring and interconnected responsibility for relatives and others. It is learned from parents, community and relatives. The third level is how to be a human, how to be hospitable to relatives and others, how to greet people and how to be connected to all peoples. It is an understanding of how to create good relations with people and nature, and for learning how to get along in a respectful way with people and nature. It is learning about the ancient covenants of the Life Giver in the creation story. There are at least four other levels beneath these three, but these are beyond my knowledge. I have not mastered any of the levels.

The understanding of these levels was helpful in revealing indigenous humanity and translating the inherent rights of indigenous peoples in the UN Human Rights documents with the Sante' Mawio'mi team of Patrick Johnson, Marie Battiste and selected Mi'kmaw Elders. We strived for three decades to translate and generate inherent rights of indigenous humanity in the UN Declaration of the Rights of Indigenous Peoples (2007). All these experiences have taught me how and why we are all related and slowly and partially revealed the Lnu'uk civilization. Although my understanding is liminal, this chapter attempts to communicate the Elders' inseparable connection to the ancient concept of Lnu'uk civilization and to Mi'kmaw humanity.

Lnu'uk Civilization

The mystery of the Lnu'uk civilization is embedded in the languages, stories, songs and performances of the seven civilizations. The first teacher to the Lnu'uk civilization is the stars, including our sun. The stars taught the earth to live, and the spirits of the earth taught the animals, plants and then standing animals. The various languages of the standing animals generate and contain the knowledge of Lnu'uk civilization, and the various languages can unravel the teachings of the environment and humanity.

In the original teachings concerning "the people," the Lnu'uk, the rays of the sun, the sparks of the stars and the breathing earth shaped the people and related life-forms. This is captured in the Lnu'uk teaching that everything is alive and is my relation (*msit no'kmaq*). Their teachings provide lessons about loving, respectful, caring and interrelated ways to live in the dynamic, living and ever-changing environment of the great St. Lawrence basin of the Atlantic Ocean, its regions, rivers and forest. These teachings generate a unique concept of being human, living as humans in an ecosystem and of a particular form of humanity.

Eurocentric linguistic confusion and diffusion over the various languages, however, and changes over the generations may obscure close linguistic relationships and introduce problems in the recorded sounds in the Eurocentric traditions. I have found several linguistic variations among related Algonquian languages that illustrate this point.

L'nunape may be the original name for the Lnu'uk civilization. The Lnu'uk language may be the Proto-Algonquian language or Algic language family, which the Eurocentric linguists have been reconstructing. For example, the linguists who have been exploring Proto-Algonquian language argue that an ordinary man or human being is *elenyiwa*, where the *elen* is the concept of ordinary and *yiwa* is human, which is a y dialect related to *l'nu* (Proulx 1976: 71-72, n4; Hewson 1993).

The nations of the Wabanaki or Abenaki call themselves people or *alnoback*, which is translated in English as people, or human being in general or collectively. Similar to other L'nu people, they use the suffix *nape* to define their collective. L'nunape is the crux between L'nu and *nape* or *nabe*.[4] Many variations exist; for example Lenape and Anishnâbe. And it goes all the way to the Blackfoot where they say their Creator or trickster was a *napi*, revealing something very deeply embedded in the language.

Moreover, the sounds of Lnu'uk transform in the northern dialects to Innu or *iyu* and then to Inuit. They transform to the western plains as variations of the translated sounds for people. For example, Cree have many dialects: Iyiniwak, Iyiniwork, Ininiwork, Iyiniw, Iynu, Eenou, Eeyo or Nêhiyawak (people of the four directions). The Cheyenne use the term Erenyiwa and the Arapahoe use the term Inuna-Ina.

Lnu'uk is often translated in English by Eurocentric linguists as "human," the characteristics of or relating to human beings or people. Although it is often translated as man in various sound systems, the Lnu'uk language has no gender marker. For examples of the linguistic translations of man, the Algonquins use Inini', the Lenape use Lënu, the Munsee use Lu'nu, the Ojibwe use Inini or Anishnâbe (coming down to be human), the Illinois use Alenia, the Kickappoo use Inenia, the Sakuk use Neniwa, the Potawatomi use Nlne and the Blackfoot use Ni'naawa.

Over the generations of experiences and reflections, the Lnu'uk teachings, ceremonies, symbolic literacies, art, stories, songs and language gave vibrant expression to its interrelated knowledge systems. A linguistic consciousness of Lnu'uk civilization maintains the unity among the civilizations,[5] while each respected the others' diverse responses to common problems and experiences. Since the Lnu'uk language referred to everyone as "the people," most of the names for the Aboriginal confederation and their nations described the resources or attributes of their territories.

The L'nu civilizations extend along the north Atlantic coast and across North America across the Rocky Mountains to the Pacific Ocean, from Labrador south to North Carolina and Tennessee. They surround the linguistic islands of the Iroquoian and Lakota confederacies. The Mi'kmaw civilization was one of the seven civilizations of Lnu'uk. The other six that sprouted from that civilization (Dickason 1992: 63-67; Inglis 2002: 390-91) following the path of the sun and moon, are, to the northwest of the Mi'kmaw, the Inuit from the north, Innu (Montagnais, Naskapi, Attikamekw), to the southwest, the Wabanaki confederacy (Penobscot, Passamaquoddy, Maliseet, Abenaki), the Wampanoag confederacy, the Narragansett confederacy, and Lenapi confederacy (Delaware), and to the west the Anishinaabe confederacy (Anishinaabe, Anishinabek, Ojibwa, Chippewa), Iynu (Cree or Eeyouchi) and Nitsi-pol-yiksi confederacy (Blackfoot) among others. The various performative contexts and forms of these expressions reveal the enduring knowledge and styles of the Lnu'uk civilization with its unique order and humanity. The shared consciousness and knowledge did not separate orality from symbolism or literacy: the images are inseparable from the sounds of the languages.

The shared Lnu'uk linguistic traditions are contained in the various dialects of the land, oral traditions and stories, and the symbolic and visual arts and jurisprudence often inscribed upon the faces of the rock formations or birch bark. They are the linguistic framings of teachings and sensory experiences. This unity of sound and symbols transcended, evoked and complemented all written forms on rocks and birch barks. The written forms, however, never replaced the primacy of sounds, ideals and images.

Each of these modes of expression and humanity was generated to represent or shape the continuous movement and transformation of energy or spirit into different waves of knowing. Each sound and image unravelled a remembrance containing energy that had the potential to generate a new manifestation in cognitive modes of the changes in an environment.

The Lnu'uk teachings of those beneficial rhythms and actions that sustain life in the Earth lodge (*kinuw wsitqamuk*) are sung and told in the Mi'kmaw language, affirming the first teaching that the Earth lodge is, and thus we exist. Mi'kmaw language and its dialects are shared with other members of the Lnu'uk civilization (Inglis 2002). The conceptual structure underlying these languages is related but different. The Lnu'uk language structure and rhythm make translations into English and other European languages difficult but possible. The language systems construct meaning and package information in distinct ways. Neither the speaking nor writing of the languages resembles each other. Each language differs in the way "reality" (however that concept is translated) is segmented into sounds or words.

The Mi'kmaw version of the Lnu'uk languages, similar to other languages, is a culture of sound, often borrowed from the rhythms and sounds of the environment [*weji-sqalia'timk*] (Sable and Francis 2012: 17).[6] Mi'kmaq tend to wrap their insights into the energy of nature in sound, with each unit of sound unfolding a multilayered meaning of awareness and comprehension (Inglis 2002).[7] Sounds create motion, appearance or configuration through their measure, cadence, emphasis and rhythm. These created patterns translate into observed or experienced insights about embodied spirits into sounds. The Mi'kmaw language and knowledge systems reveal the secrets of comprehending the continually transforming motion of the Earth lodge.

Mi'kmaw language, knowledge and thought capture and manifest the endless transformation of energy in nature and life. Mi'kmaq learn from and through this dynamic place. They learn from being part of a complementary relationship within a net of spiritual energies that exist in the places where they come from (*weja'tijik*) and they live (*wl'k*, or as ending *-iktuk* or *-e'gadil*). They learn to experience the beauty and creativity of life and to release such inspiration back to where they came from without fear of loss.

With the fluidity and rhythm of the sound and learning system, every speaker can create new comprehensible vocabulary "on the fly," custom-tailored to meet the experience of the moment, to express the very finest nuances of meaning. This generates a language of sensations and feelings, which reflect a deep enchantment with land, place, nature and human relationships.

The Lnu'uk language arose as a method to explain or to change energies, to contain or express them and their transformations. This is the vital and significant context embedded in their knowledge system. It expresses a realm formed out of the energies, which the people comprehend and act out. Through unique word-endings, the language acknowledges the multi-levels of energy by reference to breathing or non-breathing. Breathing, thinking, blowing, praying, smoking, talking, singing and dancing all have transformative energies, a spectrum from creative to destructive energies.

Mi'kmaw knowledge, derived within the Lnu'uk language, combines an oral or performance style with ceremonies, teachings, stories and visual art that are passed down from generation to generation. These stories are either about treasured or experiential knowledge (*a'tukwaqn*) or about new experiences (*aknutmaqn*). Many versions of the treasured teaching about the long cycle of the creation of the Earth lodge exist. The framework of the teaching is constant, but the meanings of the teaching are covert and fluid. Knowledge keepers and storytellers often innovate in the song or tell the two types of stories in the knowledge system. Each singing or retelling of the story-cycle or stories is slightly different, and story-cycles weave both types in a retelling.

Most Mi'kmaq agree that the creation story version of Stephen Augustine (1977, 1996, 2008)—the hereditary Mi'kmaw territorial chief (*saqmaq*) for Sigenigteoag ([Siknikt] now called the New Brunswick district) and *keptin* of the Santé Mawio'mi—detailing the constructing, telling and teaching of the creation of the Earth lodge is the best and most accurate. His version is derived from older Lnu'uk stories. Augustine's teachings unravel the fragmented parts of the stories into the original conception.[8] The first part of the teachings established the covenants (*l'nuapskun*) and relations between the

Mi'kmaq and their ecology (or Mi'kmaw science); the second part of the covenants generated Mi'kmaw knowledge and the humanities. I will use the second part of the teachings to illustrate the structure and teaching of Mi'kmaw humanity.

Knowledge Keepers and Kaqmik

In the Augustine creation story and teachings, human form gradually sprouted from the earth under the spirit of the sun and moon and stood up as a breathing entity, thus becoming known as standing person (*kaqmik*). Kluskap, the first standing man sprouted from the Earth lodge, asked the Life Giver (*kisu'lkw*) how to live in the land of the rising day star or sun. In response, Kluskap is taught to give thanks to all the forms of life and to respect the seven directions: the sky above, the earth, and then the east, south, west, and north and,[9] equally important, Kluskap learned also to respect the abilities, energies and sensations available to the human form, which make up the seventh direction.[10] Since Kluskap taught the people their first lessons about language and learning, he is referred to as the "one who is speaking to you" or the "teacher creator."

In response to Kluskap's thanksgiving and prayers for learning, the Life Giver sent a bald eagle (*kitpu*) to carry a special message to Kluskap. The Life Giver's message told that Kluskap was going to be joined by other knowledge keepers in human form who were to help Kluskap understand the covenants of the Earth lodge. These covenants are to be shared with the spark people, when they are sprouted from the Earth lodge and activated as surface dwellers and standing people. These spiritual energies are conceptualized in the teaching in terms of a family to emphasize the importance of learning from family and guests about loving, relations and living in the Earth lodge.

The first knowledge keeper sent to Kluskap is called the force that teaches about nature and animal people (*kukumi*). This knowledge keeper says she is Kluskap's grandmother; the Sun has transformed spirit into the body of an older woman. Grandmother is the collective energy (*mntu*) of and within the ancient hard minerals of the deep Earth lodges—the allied rocks or stones (*kun'tew*) that are the bones of the dry earth. Nukami symbolizes the privileged role of an Elder woman among the people and teaches about the power of the moon in sharing and balancing relationship, the importance of the wisdom and guidance offered by Elders and the importance of language. Nukami taught Kluskap how to call upon the pine marten (*apistane'wj*), to speak to the guardian spirits to ask permission to consume other life forms to nourish human existence.

Marten is the keeper of an agreement (*kisa'matimk*) from the guardian spirits of the animal life forms who teaches about cycles of reincarnation, forgiveness, gift giving and the importance of ceremony. This agreement generates a treaty covenant with the land animals and their guardian spirits that ordered and guided the kinship relationship of shared obligations. These covenants constitute beginning teachings about the responsibilities of a person to be mindful of the energies of creation, the consent of the gifts needed and the required sharing of the gifts (*netukulimk*). Nukami covenants become enfolded in the Lnu'k language as well as in songs and rituals associated with the covenants of the Earth lodge and the role of alliances in acquiring knowledge and energy.

In terms of humanity, Nukami taught about the different spirits of learning, the importance of holistic knowledge and communal wisdom about the processes of life and of reflection in their personal journey. One could learn from studying the various forms of the earth—the so-called rocks, animals, plants—which had been given special gifts and kinship. They could learn from human life similar lessons about their emotions and values.

The next knowledge keeper to arrive was Netawansum, the force that teaches about the ancient, restless and eternal Water lodge (*sam'qwan*). This knowledge keeper told Kluskap that he is to be called nephew. Netawansum's human form was generated from the energy of the rolling foam of the ocean tides that swept upon the shores. This energy transforms to the energy of the sweetgrass, or holy grass (*wlima'qewe'lmsiku*), the first grass to cover Earth lodge, in the summer. Netawansum brought the covenants and comprehension of the water realms, the use and importance of spiritual energy and respect and the amazing ability of dreams and visions to see far away and to find their way over distant territories. This generates a treaty covenant with the water animals and guardian spirits that ordered and guided the kinship relationship and shared obligations. In terms of humanity, Netawansum taught the L'nu the amazing ability of the spirit of dreams, forerunners, telepathic experiences and visions (*mjijaqmij*) in comprehending knowledge of the various lodges of the earth and in finding their personal gifts.

The third and last knowledge keeper arrives. This knowledge keeper told Kluskap to call her mother (Nikanakanimquisiwsq) or Kiju'. Kiju' told Kluskap that the human form is generated by the interaction of the sun with delicate and sparking droplets of dew from the ocean's fog on the tip of a leaf on a tree (*kmu'j*). Kiju' revealed the knowledge of the covenants of the breathing plants of the forest ecology, which generated the atmosphere and establishes the *netukulimk* protocols of the kinship relations and obligations among the animals and humans. Kiju' revealed how to honour the strength and wisdom inherent in the knowledge of the forest earth and the changing colours of the forest in the cycles of life. Kiju' stressed that when the plants breathe, animals and humans inhale. The old mother trees were named "*kokom*" in honour of the mother's knowledge. They could learn from the language of the plants of the earth and the stars by way of learning to hear, listen and silently reflect, as well as speaking, chants, songs and dances.

In terms of humanity, Kiju' revealed to Kluskap the force of love (*kesaluek*) in nature and humans that would become the most sacred gift to the Mi'kmaw from the Life Giver and become the overarching framework of Mi'kmaw thought and society (*kesaltimkewey*). Kiju' teaches the knowledge of how to maintain strength and harmony in the diversities of the cycles of life, the laws of maintaining and sustaining peace with the Earth lodge and preventing any cycle of violence. And Kiju' introduced the concept of the future (*elmi'knlk*) to Kluskap and the ceremonies and protocols on how to know events before they happen (*ni'kaniqanimkwweuiku'skw*).

Teachings of the Spark people

The knowledge keepers became the first teachers of the Lnu'uk civilization. The stories, ceremonies, dreams, prayers and visions are called the teachings of the spark people who were generated from lightning bolts that created the Great Spirit fire (*kjipuktew*). In a cycle, seven sparks flew out of the fire to sprout the spark people in a process similar but not identical to the creation and sprouting of Kluskap as a standing person (*kaqmik*). These sparks are embodied in the people as the inherent spirits of living, especially the learning spirit. These sparks are often called the Creator's flame or soul-flames.[11] The spark (of fire) people created seven couples and they developed seven families.

The Life Giver sent the four sacred knowledge keepers to teach the spark people how to learn the covenants of the Earth lodge. The covenants are the first treaties with the guardian spirits and the animate forces of the Earth lodge. The stories say the knowledge keepers live with many generations of the spark people. They taught them how to learn and live cooperatively with the life forms and energies of the many lodges within the Earth lodge. The spark people learn from these lessons the potency and fragility of their humanity (*skwijinu'kinuek*) in the Earth lodge.

The teaching of the sparks of the Great Fire is inherent in every person to comprehend their own inherent and unique gifts. Every person is born sacred and given the gift of a body with the choice to care for it and use it with respect or not. They have the inherent capacity and the choice to learn to live in respectful relationships. Their personal strengths or talents are to be discovered and nurtured, to complete their unique gifts over a lifetime, and then shared for the benefit of all.

These covenantal teachings generate a holistic, ecological, structured family of the spark people in the Earth lodge. Through learning the covenants and performing their teachings by ceremony and daily activities, the families could generate peace and harmony with the ecosystem and each other. These teachings are integral to the concept of sustaining relations or honourable harvest (*netukulimk*).

Some of the stories reveal how Kluskap becomes known among the spark families and generations as a potent teacher (*ekina'muete'w*), a gifted person who acquires energy and uses it to expand their strength and perceptions (*kinapaq*) and a gifted person who uses energy to heal, a curer, a shape-changer or power spirit (*puoin*).[12] These roles involve learned gifts and skills that were shared with the families to assist them in learning and innovation in the Earth lodge. These gifts and skills enabled the generations to learn and manipulate the energies through intentions and ceremonies to create and sustain relationships and alliances with the changing Earth lodge.

As each newborn generation of the spark families awoke in a certain environment or place they, like Kluskap when he awoke, were unaware of everything in the Earth lodge. They had to learn how to live. Following the teachings of the knowledge keepers, their grandparents, parents and relatives taught them the art of listening, the gift of hearing nature and humans, and the art of loving nature and humans. They also learned from the consequences of the choices they made and situations they had experienced.

The generations carried the Lnu'uk language and teachings of the spark peoples and taught the youth their language and how to use their perceptions or awareness. They taught successive generations to comprehend the uniqueness, gifts and difference of all peoples; they belong to an ecology and to a family and relatives. They taught them that their learning spirit is bestowed upon them by processes of creation to generate their humanity. Their language, thus, contains much of the accumulated knowledge and wisdom of the families. It was considered a sacred language, related to the breath of life and shaped and informed by the sacred teachings and lessons of nature. It animates the sounds of persistent transformations, revitalization and enhancement of the teachings and experiences of the peoples.

The relationship with a dynamic Earth lodge, family, friends and their vision of humanity are embodied in their covenants (l'nuapskun) or teachings. These teachings stretch far back into the animated and silent past. Comprehending and teaching these covenants is a foundational accomplishment for each person, but much more learning was both desirable and possible.

The knowledge keepers did not give the families the maxims of life, detailed commands or answers; they give teachings, stories and dialogues about the various covenants of the Earth lodge. These teachings contained ideologies and urgings to continue to learn from their own journey, guided by love, intuition, vision and dreams, rather than to rely on outside directions or answers. They are taught to learn from family members and others, but not to have their spirits trapped by these stories and teachings. They have the ability to learn more from the energies than the existing teachings knew or thought.

Many more levels of knowledge could be learned through each generation, each person's life experiences. The knowledge keepers and families oriented the youth to watch and observe the sun, sky and water and lands in the ecosystem. They were told that all forces and life in the Earth lodge—even the air they breathe and the land and sea that nourished them—contain parts of the spirit. They were taught that other life forms and their spiritual energy contain more teachings and mysteries inherent in the changing Earth lodge. With each change, new learnings arose.

In a lifetime, each person has important communal roles to learn and serve. These interconnected roles enable knowledge and learning to flourish through their family, relatives, communities and among other peoples. In every generation, each person must find his or her implicate gifts in their various roles. When people find their gifts, they become human and the gifts are shared with the whole community and humanity. Each person achieves their gifts by sharing them with others and revealing the depth of the gift of empathy and care for those around us. Each person needs also to sustain the cumulative knowledge and wisdom of previous generations and to enrich the traditions by their personal experience of living successfully in a changing Earth lodge.

The knowledge keepers and families taught the youth that every realm of the Earth lodge reveals knowledge and learning; that everything they see, touch or are aware of in the Earth lodge and its spiritual energies must be respected and appreciated. They are taught that since all objects have similar, though not identical, energies; these energies create the standards for proper behaviour and generating the concepts of acting in a respectful way (*kepmite'ltimk*) and dignified way (*espa'teket*). Every life form should be given respect for its innate and inalienable dignity, since we are all connected in ways that are invisible to the eyes. Therefore, this respect requires a special consciousness that discourages carelessness of thought and behaviour about life forms and energies.

Youth are taught that the possession of a part can confer the energy and the responsibility of the Earth lodge. When people gather roots or leaves for medicines, for example, they respect the spirit of each plant by placing a small offering of tobacco at its base, knowing that without the proper rituals or protocols that seek the cooperation or sharing of the inherent energies of the plant, the mere form cannot activate its energies.

The Teaching of Spiritual Energies

These teachings of the intrinsic energies helped the spark family to comprehend that each person contains at least three spiritual energies (*mntu*).[13] These spiritual energies consist of a form of guardian sparks or spirits that help people find their humanity during their Earth walk, identified as embodied life spirits (or seat of life). A form of energy that after death transforms back into the environment identifies them as the embodied guardian spirit (or external soul). And an energy that travels after death to the lands of the souls, is identified with the ecological spirits (or free-soul). Some people have acquired, by skill and learning, a deeper knowledge of these and other energies.

The embodied life spirits (heart soul—*wijaqami*)[14] are the functional and emanating spirits within an object, conceptualized as being located in the processes associated with a human heart. This concept of the heart links the intuitive or emotional to the mind—intellectual or cognitive.[15] These forces are viewed as inseparably related and generated the concept of heart knowledge. The heart is the seat of the consciousness and "free will" (to use a Eurocentric analogy) and experiences love, pleasure and passions. These energies are responsible for the vital manifestations of every person's knowledge, learning spirit and humanity. They are responsible also for the cognitive space where relationships are sustained.

These spirits are capable of travelling outside the body for brief periods. During a vision, for example, these spirits could leave the body and travel about with the guardian spirits. If the spirits remain separate too long, the person will become senseless or unconscious and the related organ will cease to function. Some of these impaired conditions because of the loss of these embodied spirits are understood as a condition in which a spirit is unable to return to the body. A disordered mind or heart, for example, is said to have lost some of its life spirits or is disconnected from the heart and therefore no longer has the ability to comprehend.

Upon the death of a person, these spirits remain with the body for four to eight days, then transform into the realms of the Earth lodge or traverse toward the stars of the Milky Way and ultimately blend with the energies called the Land of the Spirits or souls. Although these disembodied spirits in the Land of the Spirits have the capacity to return to the Earth lodge on occasion, especially during dreams and ceremonies, they did not usually appear in vision quests nor are they able to bestow power on people.

The related guardian spirits (shadow or external souls—*mimajua-gen* or *mimajuagan*)[16] organize and protect the embodied life energy in the body of a person. They function within the entire body instead of the heart. Each part of the body has many unique embedded guardian spirits or energies: for example, pulse-spirits, heart-spirits, stomach-spirits, bone-spirits, head-spirits and breath- or language-spirits.

Some of the guardian spirits generate the "eyes" of the people's consciousness and language, the energy that allows them to awaken and experience the Earth lodge. These energies collectively comprising the learning spirit, give intelligence, allowing the people to learn and perceive and talk to other *mntu*, to contemplate and to remember and to establish relationships and alliances with other forms of energy and life. Sometimes, the learning spirit is "actually life." These spirits are personal and more indefinite than the embodied life spirits. Every once in a while, a human is allowed to view the external spirits in the same appearance as the body. The loss of *minajuaqan* is viewed as the process of death to the human form.

The guardian spirits communicate silently and easily with the collective consciousness of the embodied and guardian life spirits. They are said to help with informing or making one aware of other energy and things. For example, when you come upon another person, you must always acknowledge their existence before they pass you; this acknowledgement respects the person's guardian and embodied life spirits. It is essential that one's spirits acknowledge another's spirits. If you want to argue with another person, you must not do so until your guardian spirits have continued on their way. While your embodied life spirits can disagree, such disagreements will pass quickly if your guardian spirits are not involved or affected.

When a guardian spirit appears to a person in a vision, it can be or become that person's guardian or spirit helper. When such a spirit reveals itself, it enumerates in the vision the blessings to be gifted upon a person and the capacities the person might accomplish with its cooperation. The spiritual helper does not guard and protect against all contingencies, but rather aids the person in definite, prescribed situations.

Occasionally, the guardian spirits of a person may conflict, one spirit wishing to cooperate with an embodied life spirit, another body spirit or spirits, or with an ecological spirit. Such conflicting desires or doubts are viewed as creating discomfort in the consciousness and disease in the body. Sometimes such conflicts are seen as power spirits' work, but most often it is said to be the cause of bad conduct—the embodied life soul and guardian spirits have left the body and moved a distance away from them, so that the person consists only of body. Correct behaviour or ceremonies can loosen the ecological spirits to return an embodied life soul, but not always the guardian spirits.

The ecological spirits (free souls—*skite'kwj*) comprise many spirits that are active in the Earth lodge and outside of the heart and body of a person. They are related to the more distant spirits of the stars and the Land of the Spirits (*skite'kmu'jawti*, road of spirits or Milk Way) that created the Earth lodge.[17] They learned from the vitality of the stars, and the constellations of the Milky Way, the path their spirits take to return to the source of their Earth lodge. They operate in an indifferent but reciprocal relationship to the embodied life-spirits and guardian-spirits.

The people do not know all the ecological spirits of the water, earth, sky, rocks, plants and animals. Yet they are understood as belonging to the same animate spirits. The ecological spirits are infinitely greater than those embodied spirits of the Earth lodge and are a source of awe and requests for assistance. During the silent and isolated vision quests in the deep forest lodge, people can acquire relationship with these ecological spirits, learn from them, and they can become personal allies, often as animal spirit helpers (*waisisal*). Alliances with ecological spirits give people the ability to work mutually with and construct respectful relations with the embodied spirits of an ecological space.

Kesaltimkewey

As part of the covenant and integral to the structure of the knowledge keepers, the people are taught to respect the force of love in their community and nation. *Kesaltimkewey* teaches adherence to intimate ordering of loving and of proper bonds of relationships. The way of love is not entirely understood, however; it is conceptualized as a similar process to the energy exchanges of plants, which is called photosynthesis in English. The energy exchange of *kesaluek* or love operates between humans and all living forms in different but related ways. It teaches the primacy of heart knowledge (*wijaqami*) over mind knowledge. *Kesaltimkewey* generates the communion, loyalty, fidelity relations among nature and Mi'kmaq that creates cohesion, belonging, friendship, solidarity and empathy. It generates the inner strength of acceptance, nurturing, protection, caring and healing for the Mi'kmaq. It generates the concept of respect, gentleness, kindness, honesty, fairness, cleanliness, sharing and helping. It generates the idea of peace and harmony by familial relationships and seeking to have a good mind to generate beautiful relations (*kelu'lk*) and live a good life (*e'plewek*). It creates the implicate law that urges everyone to conduct themselves in a manner such that they generate positive or good relations in all relations and makes one feel good inside (*welkwija'luek*), even in times of conflict or sadness. It provides direction and guidance for achieving self-worth, dignity, integrity, cooperation, empathy and transformation. It creates the code of personal conduct among the Mi'kmaq to nourish:

(1) heart knowledge, a keen mind (*wtip*), and understanding to be able to speak with precision, accuracy and truthing

(2) a keen sense of alert and discerning sensory faculties to create the inner capacity of respect and kindness

(3) the inner senses of industriousness, work and cooperation to survive and prosper

(4) the inner energy to move or develop shared and personal initiative to generate liberties or freedoms.

Kesaltimkewey limits the awareness of fear, security and the quest for power. While the framework is not idyllic, it is a continuing dynamic collaboration of being and belonging, which does not preclude moments of intense disapproval and discontent. The Mi'kmaw concept of the spirit of love generates a love of family, community and peoples. It accepts them as they exist and refuses to betray them. It generates openness to people, affirming self-assurance of each person's gifts to the community. To the Mi'kmaq, to love your community without betraying it, love must reimagine, remake and help the family, community and people become what they should be and attain the highest values. The communion of love and belonging outlasts personal conflict, and conflict, deviations and surprises and drive Mi'kmaq into a deeper understanding of the blessing of love and shared involvement that makes them feel deeply responsible for one another's fate (*a'nus'tumakwek, or telite'tasik*).

As part of the covenants, the people are taught to respect their families and relatives, as they are their teachers to seek help and advice. They are taught to remain passionate for the quiet joys of peace and live pleasantly through the mutual support and cooperation of the families and relatives. Sustaining harmony and peace is the first teaching of the covenant of the knowledge keepers about the people. Each family will survive and flourish together and with other families because belonging in a web of respectful relationships with relatives is the path to a good life. Consensual agreements enable solidarity with nature and humans and add strength to the people.

In the Augustine creation story, after the passing of seven winters, the seven families that comprised the Lnu'uk, including the Mi'kmaq, were taught the necessity of gathering together to renew the covenants. This ceremony generated the gathering (*mawio'mi*). The seven families were told to return with their seven fires to rekindle the sparks of the original Great Fire. To renew the covenants and teachings of Life Giver and the knowledge keepers, seven hereditary leaders represented the seven original families. These renewal ceremonies generate the L'nu consciousnesses, knowledges and versions of the language. These gatherings were repeated for generations and each family generated different ceremonies as they dwelled with and comprehended the different forces of the Earth lodge.

The L'nu civilizations extend along the north Atlantic coast and across North America across the Rocky Mountains to the Pacific Ocean, from Labrador in the north, south to North Carolina and Tennessee. They surround the linguistic islands of the Iroquoian and Lakota confederacies. The Mi'kmaw civilization was one of the seven civilizations of Lnu'uk. These confederacies generated the Nikminen order, a voluntary transnational law among the spark people or Lnu'uk that equals the Law of Nations in Europe. This transnational order in North America was not based on the family structure; instead the order was based on consensual alliances, agreements and treaties (*anku'kamkewe'l*) (Marshall 2000)[18] among the civilizations, confederacies and nations of the confederacy under Lnu'uk protocols and ceremonies. This order created interlinking relationships of friends or allies who spoke similar languages (Henderson 1994: 246-69). Central to these vital and living relationships was the sanctity of spoken sounds and promises, which were understood to be manifestations of the holistic spiritual realm. These oral agreements imposed freedoms and obligations where none had existed before. Promises were binding and sacred. By treaties, the Haudenosaunee (Iroquois) empire was a member of the Nikminen order.

L'nu Humanity of the Mi'kmaq

From the Lnu'uk teachings, as represented by the Mi'kmaw and allied humanities, L'nu humanities arise from the ecology of the Earth lodge. It is part of the collective genius of their approach to humanities. The heritage of Lnu'uk knowledge among the Mi'kmaq is a distinct knowledge system of a place with its own concepts of epistemology, philosophy, methods and scientific and logical validity. The diverse elements of the heritage can be fully learned or understood only by learning the language and the teaching employed by these peoples themselves. The heritage represents the accumulated experience, wisdom and know-how unique to many nations, societies and/or communities of people, living in specific environments of North America. It embraces a philosophic and cognitive system within distinct language structures and categories, which transcends the boundaries of Eurocentric humanities and sciences. The heritage represents one of the terrestrial voices of the Earth Lodge. It represents the accumulated knowledge of a people long ignored in Eurocentrism.

Versions of L'nu humanities are grounded in the Lnu'uk knowledge system and worldview that is orientated to the energies of ecological places and situations rather than centred on humanity or its will, character or choices. The interconnected ideas of embodied spirits, implicate order of nature and transformation are the core insights of Lnu'uk knowledge. These interrelated notions generate an ecological sovereignty that rejects man-made or artificial rules for an order that was generations in process. This concept of humanity is based on trying to maintain harmony with the implicate order of an ecology, which was viewed as divine and sovereign, rather than attempts to overcome or humanize, anthropomorphize or zoologicalize the ecology. In this concept of humanness the relationship between situations, both unseen and seen, and human conduct has powerful influences as revealed by energy, locality, language and proper behaviour. It does not have a clear division or dualism between nature and humans, but has division about relations to nature and spirit and different human-ness or personhood (such as newborns). No clear division between spirit and structure exists in the L'nu view of the spectrum of ecology or humanity; the spectrum can change into many forms in different realms of the Earth lodge. This orientation is slowly emerging in Eurocentric thought in Canada.

L'nu humanity has a more holistic, naturalistic and internal orientation, rather than one based on the concept of artificial time and deductive thought. Time is the silent generator of the cycles of seasons and life. L'nu humanity, in English terms, is more verb-based processes based on sensations and emotions or action-orientated rather than noun-based or object-orientated.

The concept of empathic love is the foundation of the L'nu un-derstandings of nature, humanities and law. This empathic love is a feeling similar to attractions of the force called Eurocentric scientific gravity. Empathic love is like dark matter; its manifestation is like the lights of the stars. It reflects a loving way of life that expresses a sus-tainable humanity. Through the generations, the Mi'kmaw concepts of love and truly, truly caring for each other generated a safe feeling, a belonging, that has been described as a big blanket always wrapped around the family and relatives that held everyone together in every Mi'kmaw community.

The different versions of L'nu humanity are grounded in the end-less capacity to learn the awareness of energies and their transforma-tions and to communicate the knowledge. These learning spirits or energies are manifested in many different ways. They teach how to live together peacefully on the land with all its diversity and challenges. They teach how to make a living and a beautiful life. This learning spirit is the concept of L'nu rationality.

The L'nu humanities among the Mi'kmaq is a performance-based worldview. It is about actions not theories of behavior. The interweaved processes of performing a worldview are embodied in relationships, songs, ceremonies, symbols, story-telling, baskets and artworks. L'nu languages, stories, ceremonies and conduct are integrated with visual arts to renew or revitalize the ecological covenants and their teaching about being human in various situations. They are about the process of finding one's gifts and establishing good and interconnected relationships and feelings with all life forms. The learning spirit animates the transmission of knowledge in stories, ceremonies and visual arts.

L'nu humanity, which dictates the high value to be placed on all life forms and peoples, is an important source in Mi'kmaw justice, leadership, governance and law (Barsh 1986; Henderson 1995; Barsh and Marshall 1998). The wise people and leaders over the generations worked at developing a consensual union of the families into a vast nation that transcended the tribe or kinship authority and united with other nations into the Wabanaki Confederacy. Mi'kmaw leadership and governance was selfless, and listened, shared and deliberated widely with the family, community and other leaders in making decisions (*waym* or *tplutaqn*). They allowed the families and communities to lead themselves. They did not develop a lifestyle different from the community and lived among them and shared the gifts and sorrows of life with them. They united the people in amity and friendship from birth to death. The wise people devoted their thoughts to understand L'nu humanities to generate the fundamental law of justice, kindness and peace based on shared love of the spirits and forces with the environment and the families within their territory (Young 2016). They understood that because the environment existed, they lived; they sought to protect the ecologies and cause them to flourish. They advised both the peoples and families on how to live together in love and righteousness and to generate the law of trading between peoples to meet their needs.

The alliance of the families was neither complete nor final; it was a vibrant and changing relationship based on the gifts of the ecological flux. In structuring the personal conduct, ceremonies, teachings and laws, the wise peoples and the leaders sought to harmonize their laws and way of life with the energetic flow of the seasons. The kinship relations were mobile within its ecological territory and their shared territories with relatives; every family or district or tribe lived under conditions generated by the presence of the other in generous and gifted ecological imperatives. The nations and confederacy vigorously lived through the entwined, shared visions and resilient teachings of the wampum laws that established collaboration and renewal of their cognitive solidarity; however, the ceremonial structure insisted that each nation or tribe operated separately and freely through kinship to pursue their chosen way of life. The kinship organization of each nation required no institutions or elite that involved control over the families or people; the extended relatives and families in alliance with each other were an animate source of each nation as well as over the generations of the confederacy.

The consensual, entangled and balanced tensions often remade the organization of the Mi'kmaw nation and Wabanaki Confederacy to respond to diverse situations and fluxes. The Mi'kmaw nation became a teaching civilization rather than a dynasty or centralized authority, which exhibited great traditions of knowledge, creativity, flashes of problem solving and accomplishments. It became diplomatically linked with other confederations, nations and tribes as well as European nations. While conflict did arise with other confederacies, they were usually resolved as quickly as possible because of the necessity of peace and collaboration in a shared fate within an ecology. These conflicts were never transformed into dominance but rather exhibited the vitality of their skills to design normative standards of justice for lasting acquiescence, reconciliations, renewals and peace.

In determining justice (*habenquedoic*), the wampum law developed to maintain justice by thoughtfulness and ceremonies that strove to convert tensions and conflicts into balances or harmonies. Heart knowledge was valued more than normative behaviour in their knowledge system and laws. The wampum laws arose as manifestation of love and justice, rather than force. Heart knowledge of the wampum laws is linked to the values of inherent dignity of love, compassion, kindness, courteousness and respect for ecologies and humanities. Its teachings are a significant and vital part of healing strained or broken relationships that urges the art of intercession, harmony, conciliation and reconciliation. These teachings favour graciousness and restorative remedies and mutual comprehension of others, which contrast with mean-spiritedness, confrontation, vengeance and punishment. Mi'kmaw justice brings people together in all their imperfection.

In different situations, L'nu humanities continue to inform Mi'kmaq thought, action and life. It competes with other versions of humanity on a daily basis. It continues to pursue a respectful conciliation with the best of many other knowledge systems to generate a truthful, self-determining human that can generate friendship and peace among people by braiding knowledges, like the baskets and bead and quill work of their artistic traditions. It regenerates better stories using ancient teachings in contemporary situations to generate a better ecology, communities and humans, knowing that L'nu get the relationship with the world through learning, actions and visions.

Notes

1. Lnu'uk song, transcribed by Leland 1968: 379.

2. There are many different spelling systems of the sounds of Lnui'simk or the Algonquian language group based on dialects: Lnu'uk, L'nuk, L'nu'k, Lnuk and Lnu. The Unama'ki Elders noted that Lnu'k is related to the Mi'kmaw term for tongue or *kilnu*. The art of thinking like an *l'nu* is *l'nuwita'simk*. In this material, the Doug Smith-Bernie Francis system of the Mi'kmaw language (Mi'kmawi'simk) is used. This spelling system is the official phonemic orthography of the Santé Mawio'mi (Grand Council) of the Mi'kmaq. It is different from the English orthography of Mi'kmaw languages that will also be used at times.

3. Lnu'uk is singular, L'nu is plural. Lnu'k is currently used to describe a human person (male); Lnu'kske'sk: human person (female); Lnu'kswa (plural female persons). However, when discussing humans or people, *l'nu* is the adjectival and singular concept. It has many spellings: *lnu'k, lnu'g, lnu'g, el'nu, n'nu* or *ulnoo*. In Listuguj Mi'kmaq, the term *n'nu* is used as a general description of people. In Eurocentric knowledge system, the Lnu'uk civilization is categorized as the Algonquian language family or the Algic language family. This language family name, Algonquian, is said to be derived from the French understanding of the sounds and spelling that referenced the distinct rock formation from around the Great Lakes, where the ancient idiographic script or rock drawings were carved (Biggar 1922: 105). Champlain the explorer mistook the sound for the name of the indigenous nations of this place (Algonquins). It is often spelled Algonkin or—in anthropologist-linguist spelling—Algonkian. Later, Eurocentric linguists and anthropologists used the word as an appellation for a language group (Lnui'simk or L'nui'sin). Mi'kmaw Elders assert that the word is derived from the Mi'kmaw term *el legorn' kwin*, or *amalka'tite'wk* (friends, allies) or *allegon/ein* (the dancers) or *alkoorne* (people who stand in the canoe and spear fish in the water) or *alligewinenk* (people come together from distant places). Others say that Algonquin is a dialect of Ojibway, or that Algonquian is the entire language group. This is a typical chicken-or-egg issue in Mi'kmaw linguistics.

4. The "b" sounds in English are closer to the "p" sound in Mi'kmaw but not voiced.

5. Lnu'uk speakers could easily understand each other when speaking face to face, since specific pronunciations, gestures and situations gave meaning to the words, and dialects identified where the speaker came from. A fluent speaker could form compound words and phrases that would clearly indicate the speaker's intent, the relationship of the speaker to the audience, the time of the events being spoken of and the importance of this informa-

tion. There were, however, distinct differences between the Western Abenaki languages (spoken in New Hampshire, Vermont, parts of northern Massachusetts, southeastern Canada and upstate northeastern New York) and the Eastern Wabanaki languages of Malecite, Mi'kmaw, Passamaquoddy and Penobscots (spoken in Maine and the Maritimes). The Wabanaki Confederacy move through the pages of the colonial records as the Eastern Indians under the names of river or villages, rather than their names or totemic identities used in the confederacy.

6. *Wejisqalia'timk,* in its inclusive form, reveals that the language grew from the environment, which is expressed in the creation stories. The people are rooted in the "langscape" of Mi'kma'ki; when this relationship is generated in an exclusive form, *wejisqalia'tiek* translates into English as "we sprouted from the land," much like the forest ecology. *Wejiaq* is translated as "comes from it." In the Sipekne'katik Declaration (1720), the Sipekne'katiki *saqmaq* explained to the British governor Phillipps of Nova Scotia that they "believe that this land that God gave us, on which we could be counted even before the trees were born, does not appear to us to be disputed by anyone" (French version of the letter, Blanchet 1883: vol. 3, 46-47). See also the Mi'kmaw response to Governor of Ile Royale, Saint-Ovide, in 1730, who attempted to explain the French King's cession of Mi'kmaw land to the English King in the *Treaty of Peace and Friendship at Utretch*: "learn from us, that we are on this earth that you tread and on which you walk, before the tree which you see began growing, it is ours and nothing can ever force us to abandon it" Charlevoix Papers (1720).

7. The multiple layers of meaning in the Mi'kmaw language are characterized in Eurocentric linguistic disciplines as polysynthetic "verb stems" or "roots" and "inflectional prefixes and suffixes." The inflectional prefixes relate the context of the appearance to the motion or verb stem and the suffixes relate the process involved with the motion. In contrast, English tends to have one or two ideas per word-sound, despite the fact it has multiple morphemes drawn from the mixture of at least four different language families. In Mi'kmaw suffixes such as "*ikan*" and "*aquan*" can generate the illusion of nouns but they are old Mi'kmaw verbs or emotions.

8. A Wabanaki version of the creation story of "Klose-kur-beh, The Man from Nothing" in Joseph Nicolar (1893) is a more Catholic version of the creation story. Nicolar stated that in the Wabanaki language, *klose-ki* means simple or nothing; *klose-ki-nerquatt* means simple appearance; and *klose-kur-beh* means man from nothing. The Penobscot call the man from nothing Gluskabe, with emphasis placed on the suffix "abe," which is related to "*nabe*" in the Ln'luk.

9. These directions are associated with link to the earth; the colours associated with them are process words or, in English, intransitive verbs.

10. The different process of creation is contained in diverse energies available to humans: inclusive energies that created us (*kisu'lkw*); energies that are with us (*tekweyu'lkw*) and the energies that look after us (*ankweyu'lkw* or *jikeyulkw*). These energies reflect the changing seasons of the Atlantic woodlands and rivers ecosystem.

11. In the *nakawê* and *nêhiyaw* (Cree) language, the "y" dialect of Lnu'uk language, the Creator's flame is *manitow iskotêw*. The soul flame is called *ahcahk iskotêw*.

12. In Mi'kmaw thought, one is not supposed to use the concept of puoinaq. puoinaq has many spellings in Eurocentric literature: "*Bouhinne*," "*Booin*," "*Buion*," "*Pouin*," "*Aoutem*" and "*Aoutmoins* (Prophet)." These concepts do not translate with ease in English or French or other European languages; they have become known as "jugglers" of harmony and, more recently, as "shamans." The Catholic missionaries interpreted and labelled Kluskap as a "liar" for their own purposes, which many Mi'kmaq were taught and some believed.

13. These three generalized embodied spirits are known in English as "souls" or in Latin as *anima*.

14. To understand this translation from the Mi'kmaw language, "*wji*" is the sound that represents the personal, "*jag*" represents mirror image, and "*mij*" represents alive, animate energy.

15. This concept is essential in treaty talks with the nations of the Wabanaki Confederacy with the representatives of the King of Great Britain. They talked with a "good heart" (Mandell 2003: 108). For example, "I Panaouamskeyen [Penobscot Speaker, Loron], do inform ye—ye who are scattered all over the earth take notice—of what has passed between me and the English in negotiating the peace that I have just concluded with them. It is from the bottom of my heart that I inform you; and, as a proof that I tell you nothing but the truth, I wish to speak to you in my own tongue" (Calloway 1991: 115-18). Or as Auyoumowett (or Auyaummowett), the Arsignategok *sagamore* from St. Francis and spokesman for the nations to Governor Dummer of Massachusetts Bay, said: "I now declare to your Honour, as the Hearts of my Brethren are with you (making a Motion towards the Penobscots) so is my Heart also with you, As my Brothers Hearts who are here now are all with you, so is my Heart and the Hearts of all the Indian Tribes round about us. [...] Our Hearts and Hands are ready now [to sign the ratification of the proposed 1725 Articles of Peace of the Wabanaki Compact]" (Mandell 2003: 360).

16. This concept is related to *mjijaqmij* as a shadow or spirit of a shadow that one tries to possess or control but cannot. Often it comes as a dream or vision. *Njijaqamij* means a personal shadow, or something appearing as a mist. Often, Mi'kmaq say the spirit of the shadow arises from your body when you die. *Mimajuaqn* is the process of life, the energy of your life force that

can transform, generated from *mimajit*, meaning alive or moving. It is often used to refer to the human need for food so that the body can live. The terms *mimajuaqn* and *mjijaqmij* are not the same.

17. Mi'kmaq believe there are other worlds that exist besides the earth. The ancestors' or ghost lodge is where the people's spirits go when they die. They travel along a trail that can be seen in the night or the Milky Way. If someone has not been good in life, they are sent back to be born again and to learn more lessons in life. An ancient Mi'kmaw legend of *papkutparut* concerns an elderly man and woman whose young child dies. Inconsolable with grief, the father goes to the Land of the Dead to try and "win back" his son from the guardian of the souls by playing a game of dice (LeClercq 1910: 210). The stars can transform themselves into humans in the stories of the "Two Weasels and Mi'kmaw Women Marry Star Husbands." Also the story of Waso'q about reincarnation.

18. This term has not been fully translated by the Mi'kmaq Elders. The word *ankua'tumk* signifies the process of adding to an existing group or collective, thus the treaties are a method of adding members to the kin-group.

References

Augustine, Stephen. 1977. Mi'kmaq Knowledge in the Mi'kmaq Creation Story: Lasting Words and Deeds. April 8. http://www.muiniskw.org/pgCulture3a.htm (accessed August, 23, 2016).

———. 1996. English translation of the Creation story. *Looking Forward Looking Back Report of the Royal Commission on Aboriginal Peoples*, Ottawa: Minister of Supply and Services Canada.

———. 2008. Preface: Oral History and Oral Tradition. In *Aboriginal Oral Traditions: Theory, Practice, Ethics,* ed. René Hulan and Renate Eigenbrod, 2-4. Halifax: Fernwood Books and Gorsebrook Research Institute.

Barsh, Russel L. 1986. The Nature and Spirit of North American Political Systems." *American Indian Quarterly* 10:181-98.

Barsh, Russel L. and Joe B. Marshall. 1998. Mikmaq Constitutional Law. In *Encyclopaedia of Native American Legal Traditions,* ed. Bruce E. Johansen, 192-209. Westport, CT: Greenwood.

Biggar, H. P. ed. 1922. *The Works of Samuel de Champlain*. Toronto: Champlain Society.

Blanchet, Jean Gervais Protais, 1883. *Collection de Manuscrits, contenant lettres, mémoires, et autres documents Historiques relative à la Nouvelle-France*. Quebec: Coté.

Calloway, Colin G. 1991. *Dawnland Encounters: Indians and Europeans in Northern New England*. Hanover, NH: University Press of New England.

Charlevoix Papers. 1720. Discours fait aux Sauvages. Library Archives Canada, Manuscript Group 18, E-29.

Dickason, Olive P. with McNab, David T. 1992. *Canada's First Nations: A History of Founding Peoples from Earliest Times.* Toronto: McClelland and Stewart.

Henderson, James (Sa'ke'j) Youngblood. 1994. Empowering Treaty Federalism. *Saskatchewan Law Review* 58: 241-329.

———. 1995. First Nations Legal Inheritances: The Mi'kmaq Model. *Manitoba Law Journal*, 23: 1-31.

Hewson, John. 1993. *A Computer-Generated Dictionary of Proto-Algonquian.* Ottawa: Canadian Museum of Civilization. Canadian Ethnology Service: Mercury Series Paper 125.

Inglis, Stephanie. 2002. 400 Years of Linguistic Contact between the Mi'kmaq and the English and the Interchange of Two World Views. *Canadian Journal of Native Studies* 14: 389-402.

Le Clercq, Chrestien. 1910. *Nouvelle Relation de la Gaspésie,* translated by William F. Ganong, Toronto: Champlain Society.

Mandell, Daniel R., ed. 2003. New England Treaties, North and West, 1650-1776. In *Early American Indian Documents: Treaties and Laws, 1607-1789, vol. 20,* ed. Alden T Vaughan. Washington, DC: University Publication of America.

Marshall, Joe B. 2000. Overview of Mi'kmaw, Maliseet and Passamaquoddy Covenant Chain of Treaty. Presentation at the Assembly of First Nations Conference, "Looking Forward: Treaty Implementation." February 1, n.p.

Nicolar, Joseph. 1893. *Life and Tradition of the Red Man.* Bangor: C.H. Glass.

Proulx, Paul. 1976. A New Algonquian Correspondence. *International Journal of American Linguistics* 42:71-73.

Sable, Trudy and Bernie Francis. 2012. *The Language of this Land, Mi'kma'ki.* Sydney, NS: Cape Breton University Press.

Sipekne'katik Declaration, Indians of Les Mines to Governor Philipps of Nova Scotia, (2 October 1720) United Kingdom, Public Record Office, Colonial Office 217/3, No. 18 Enclosure 13, item 241(xiv).

United Nations *Declaration of the Rights of Indigenous Peoples.* 2007. General Assembly Resolution 61/295.

Young, Tuma. 2016. *L'nuwita'simk*: A Foundational Worldview for a L'nuwey Justice Ssytem. *Indigenous Law Journal* 13 (1): 75-102.

Margaret Robinson

Mi'kmaw Stories in Research

This essay describes the techniques I used researching for my article, "Veganism and Mi'kmaq Legends," which appeared in the *Canadian Journal of Native Studies* in 2013. I describe how I gathered my data, the tools I used, and how I wove Mi'kmaw and settler traditions together where it seemed appropriate to do so.

In preparing this essay I examined the art of Mi'kmaw basketry, and a number of parallels with research became immediately apparent. According to the late Ellen Googoo of We'koqma'q, Cape Breton (1907-1987), the work of making a traditional wood split basket is mostly preparation (Caplan 1973). One needs tools designed for the task, such as the curve-handled blade called a crooked knife, and if the tools aren't available commercially, then they are fashioned from what is at hand. A basket maker works with the wood rather than against it, patiently, keeping it moist so it will stay flexible. Indigenous research is likewise about preparation, about having the right tools for the job or inventing them as we go, about working with our material—in this case, our data—slowly and carefully, and about knowing how far the data can flex—that is, which interpretations are legitimate—before it breaks.

My people come from the Lennox Island First Nation, but I grew up in the woods on the eastern shore of Nova Scotia, in Eski'kewaq, or skin dressers territory. In 1990 I moved to Halifax for university and then to Toronto for graduate school. In 2009, with my PhD in theology from the University of Toronto fresh in my hand, I began to think more regularly about how our Mi'kmaw traditions could fit into my daily life in the concrete warren of Toronto. Since I was trained in textual hermeneutics, the interpretation of written texts, I looked for the earliest Mi'kmaw stories I could find. This brought me to a two volume collection entitled *Legends of The Micmacs*, by Silas T. Rand. Rand was a Baptist missionary, born in Kentville, Nova Scotia in 1810, who translated the Bible into Mi'kmaw and Malecite, compiled a Mi'kmaw dictionary, and collected two volumes of oral tradition. He was the first to record stories about Glooscap, our cultural hero and the archetype of virtuous human life.

The choice to examine our stories was not a random one. Blair Alicia Metallic, a Mi'kmaw woman from Listuguj in Quebec, argues that our stories "assure continuity of the culture by creating and keeping a collective memory in the form of narratives that can be told and retold, or read, expressed, and interpreted many times over" (Metallic 2015: 15). Marie Battiste writes that our stories, and our languages, "tell of all that is meaningful for understanding ourselves, individually and collectively, as human beings" (Battiste 2000: xxvii). I suspect that most Mi'kmaw families have at least one good storyteller in them. In my own family the stories that we tell also tell us something—who we are, what we value and how we should live together. They hold the past, present and future together and give continuity and meaning to what might otherwise be isolated moments in time. I read the stories Rand had collected, and any others I could find, working to find the values and perspectives of my ancestors, even if filtered through the words of a settler missionary. These stories became my data.

My interpretations drew on intellectual knowledge, such as that collected in books about our Mi'kmaw history, culture, philosophy and tradition. I also drew on experiential knowledge, such as the values reflected in our art, my experience of ceremony, and what I knew from my relationships, particularly with my father, James Robinson, and my grandmother, Margaret Robinson (nee Paul), who everyone called Margie. As a visitor to Margie's house, the first thing you noticed was that it was full of cats. She had a way with cats, and she took in any cat that came to her in need. Once, when she was visiting us, a hungry and frightened tomcat emerged from the forest. His fur was so matted we thought he had vestigial legs growing from his haunches. Margie fed him, and over the span of an hour, with gentle stroking and talking, calmed the frightened animal and then slowly cut away the matted fur until a thin ragged cat emerged, sporting the regular amount of legs. Our home became his home. My father is a scholar and an artist who supplemented our household income by making birch bark baskets, fashioning jewelry out of shells and bobcat teeth, and carving totem poles, including one that stood on Barrington Street in Halifax for many years. He taught me to love and respect the world around me and the many lives it contains.

Just as Mi'kmaw basket makers impress their own esthetic onto the baskets they make, researchers bring our own interests and needs to our research, and our findings bear our fingerprints. As my journey into Mi'kmaw stories began, I reflected on what the Mi'kmaw view of animals might mean for me, as a woman who had lived in an urban environment for the past twenty-three years, and who did so now as a vegan (i.e., one who does not use or consume animal products). I was concerned about how to reconcile my veganism with my Mi'kmaw culture. The traditional Mi'kmaw diet was 90 per cent animal-based, and objects made of animal bodies, such as drums, regalia and art are ubiquitous in indigenous spaces. My question, as I read our stories, was not only "What do the stories reveal about the values of our people?" but also "What do our stories reveal about me?" The view that what can be found depends on who is doing the looking is standard in social constructionist approaches to research, but it is also, I believe, in keeping with the Mi'kmaw view of the human being as located within a web of interdependent relationships. So what I found in my data may not be what another researcher might find, going in with different questions.

Returning to the metaphor of basket making, a large part of the work is preparation. For research this generally means reading, in the form of literature searches, interview data or relevant media. By far, the best tools for such work include patience and an open mind and heart. Part of my process is allowing my subconscious to sift through what I have read, making connections. Another part is listening to the voices I encounter and being attentive to how they relate to my research. My first answer came to me in a room at the Native Canadian Centre on Spadina Road, where Mi'kmaw elder Wanda Whitebird was talking about "all our relations"—the two-legged and the four-legged, the finned and the winged and the webbed. I began to reflect on what the phrase *msit no'kmaq*, or "all my relations" meant, for the Mi'kmaq in general, and for me.

As I read, I did so with all my relations in mind. The Mi'kmaw view of the world is rooted in our relationship with the other animals that share our territories. I had long understood that part of my identity as a Mi'kmaw woman had to do with my relationships to the land of my ancestors. Growing up, I ran barefoot in our territory, and my identity developed like an evergreen emerging from the thin, rocky soil. The degree to which the sea was in my blood became more apparent the longer I remained in Toronto. I began to wonder how my identity was likewise rooted in my relationships with the animals of our traditional territories—the call of the loon, rabbit prints in the snow or the slow waddle of a porcupine. Reflecting on "all my relations," I wondered what it meant to be related to other animals.

In our stories, humans and animals both experience our lives in the first-person, having adventures, overcoming fears, falling in love, raising families, vanquishing enemies and having a relationship with the Creator. Anthropologist Anne-Christine Hornborg writes, "I think it is better to talk about personhood as the common essence of both animals and humans. A human is a human, a beaver is a beaver, but they are both persons" (Hornborg 2013: 22). Since I was trained as a theologian, I looked to see what had been written about personhood in European philosophy. Immanuel Kant, a German philosopher, defined a person as someone "whose existence has in itself an absolute worth," a rational being who is "an end in itself" (Kant 2011: 10) rather than a means to an end. I read Kant's essay, noting the places where our views diverged. Although Kant concluded that "animals are not self-conscious" and are merely "a means to an end" (11), the teachings from my father, my grandmother and from my broader Mi'kmaw culture framed animals as self-aware rational beings whose existence is for themselves rather than for us. In Kantian terms, they are persons.

This perspective, of animals as persons, was also present in our stories. In the story of "The Beaver Magicians and The Big Fish," for example, a Mi'kmaw hunter follows snowshoe tracks to a wikuom by a lake, where he finds an elderly man and his family (Rand 2004). The elder offers the hunter hospitality, feeds him moose meat and gives him a store of meat to take home. However, when the hunter returns to his camp he discovers that the meat has become poplar bark. The hunter realizes that he has dined with a powerful *puoin* (a person of great spiritual power). Although actually a beaver Elder and his offspring in a lodge, the hunter had experienced the family as if they were other Mi'kmaq, living together in a wikuom. Legends such as this present human and animal life on a continuum. Other stories feature animals who speak, transform into humans, marry humans and raise children with them. Some feature humans who are changed into animals against their will. This shape-shifting is possible, it seems to me, because humans and other animals are related and experience ourselves as persons.

How, I wondered, does a culture that recognizes other animals as persons and even more, as relations, reconcile this worldview with a traditional diet that is primarily meat-based? Again, I went to our stories for my answer. One "Mi'kmaq Creation Story" begins with the birth of Kluskap from the red clay of the soil (Burke n.d.). As a member of the Lennox Island First Nation, I immediately thought of Prince Edward Island. The Creator then makes an old woman, Nukami, from a dewy rock, to be Kluskap's grandmother (Burke 2015). She provides him with wisdom, and in exchange Kluskap must provide her with food. Nukami explains that she cannot live on plants and berries alone (which was presumably what Kluskap ate before her arrival), so Kluskap calls upon his friend, *apistanewj*, the marten, and asks him to sacrifice himself so that Kluskap's grandmother may live. Apistanewj agrees, and to acknowledge this sacrifice Kluskap makes him his brother. In this story two things stood out most clearly for me. The first is that the motivation for Kluskap's request is survival. Kluskap had not eaten Apistanewj before, so he presumably did not require meat to live, but Nukami does, and her survival motivates Kluskap to ask for the sacrifice. Second, in this story, our kinship with animals seemed rooted in our relationship to them as a food source.

Next, I looked to our Mi'kmaw traditions to see if what I had found in my analysis of our stories resonated there as well. At this stage of research we draw on our knowledge of what is available, and where it might be. To return to the metaphor of basketry for a moment, the basket maker knows where to harvest, what type of tree produces the best splits, and which plants can be boiled to make dye. As an indigenous academic, I draw upon my traditional knowledge (who our Elders are, what they've done) and my academic knowledge (which universities or researchers produce reliable, ethical research with our communities). I brought this style of "two-eyed seeing" (Hatcher et al. 2009; Marshall 2011) to my search for interviews or quotes from our elders and traditional knowledge keepers, to see if what they had to say related to what I had found in our stories. In social science research this method of verifying data by using multiple sources is called triangulation. As a researcher, it's a good way to tell if you're on the right track, or if you've wandered off the path. One such source was Lacia Kinnear's qualitative study conducted at Bear River First Nation, Nova Scotia. Kinnear interviewed fifteen members of the Bear River community, asking how they understood the concepts "nature" and "animals," and what role their cultural values played in shaping animal use, how the human-animal relationship was significant to them, and how settler use of animals has impacted the community (Kinnear 2007). She had asked exactly what I wanted to know.

One woman in Kinnear's study suggested that a respectful relationship with other animals was essential to maintaining their willingness to sacrifice themselves. She reports, "If we learn to live in good spirit with the animals they can continue to reproduce and that they will always be offering themselves; there will always be enough" (Kinnear 2007: 71). A number of sources mentioned that respect is shown to animals in the careful treatment of their bones, which unless used to create necessities must be returned to the area where the animal lived and given a respectful burial. Peter Christmas, former director of Micmac Association of Cultural Studies, notes that if the proper respect were not shown to an animal's remains then the animal's spirit would convey this information to its living animal brethren and the animals would not permit themselves to be caught and killed (Christmas 1977). My search for data that confirmed or challenged my analysis of such stories confirmed the belief that animals willingly sacrifice themselves, and also suggested that such willingness was contingent upon human ceremony.

The Confederacy of Mainland Mi'kmaq takes the requirement further and portrays all interactions with the environment as having both a physical and spiritual component:

Because they [the Mi'kmaq] believe all things are part of nature and must be respected ... when they cut down a tree, or dig up plant roots for medicine, or kill an animal for food, there are certain rituals they must follow to pay the proper respect—to give thanks for things they disturb for their own use. Some animals, like moose, give their lives so the Mi'kmaq may have food. They show respect to the moose by treating the remains with respect. The bones of the moose should never be burned or given to household pets, they should be used to make something or buried (Confederacy of Mainland Mi'kmaq 2007: 50).

Armed with this, I re-read our stories for examples of respect protocols and was rewarded. In "The Invisible Boy," for example, a Mi'kmaw child thoughtlessly smashes the leg bone of a moose that his mother was saving for the boy's father, who is away hunting. When the boy's aunt sees the smashed bone, she realized that her brother is now lying in the woods with a broken leg, indicating that the hunter and the moose are connected on a physical and spiritual plane (Rand 2005). Similarly, the story "Two Weasels" tells of a pair of sisters who spend the night in a deserted wikuom. There they find the neck bone of an animal. The older sister cautions her sibling not to touch it, but the younger sister kicks the bone. Later, as they try to sleep, the neck bone speaks, complaining of the rude treatment and terrifying the girls, the younger of whom attempts to hide in her sister's hair (ibid.). Stories like these communicate the importance of respect through examples of what happens when that value is breached.

Another mark of respect is to take only as many animal lives as we need for subsistence. In the story "Ki'kwa'ju and Ki'wa'jusi's" ("Wolverine and His Brother," mistranslated by Rand as Badger), Wolverine invites a flock of birds into his wikuom, asks them to close their eyes, and then begins to kill them silently, one after another. His younger brother is distraught because Wolverine has already killed more birds than they can eat. The younger brother whispers for the smallest bird to open his eyes. Seeing the carnage, the young bird cries the alarm and the remaining birds escape (Rand 2004; Joe 1997).

The importance of killing only for food was demonstrated to me early on, when my younger brother received an air-powered pellet gun as a present, and promptly killed a squirrel with it. My father forced him to skin, gut, cook and eat the squirrel, something in which neither of them had any expertise. The smell of burned squirrel meat filled our shack, and I watched with curiosity and revulsion as they ate. My father used the squirrel pelt in his craftwork, and my brother never attempted to hunt again. Sport hunting is frowned upon in Mi'kmaw culture, with one participant in Kinnear's study said that it "goes against the spirit of the relationship between humans and the animals" (Kinnear 2007: 78). Stories such as that about Wolverine affirm the idea that while animals may give themselves to provide food and clothing, shelter and tools, they must not be exploited or over-hunted, and must be treated with respect, even (perhaps especially) after death.

Kinnear describes the relationship between the Mi'kmaq of Bear River and the animals around them as one of "reciprocal obligation" (71). The concept of reciprocity got me wondering, since the benefit for humans was clear (food), what was the benefit for animals? Our stories and Kinnear's research suggest that the answer is kinship, honour and respect. One way that respect is shown is by maximizing the use of an animal's body. As one young Mi'kmaq in Kinnear's study said, "You should only take what you need, but then use everything that you can from what you kill. What you can't use you should give away and share, so that nothing is wasted and everyone gets what they need" (Kinnear 2007: 82). Once an animal has been killed, we have an obligation to use as many parts as possible: meat, hoofs, hides, feathers, bones, teeth, claws, fur and antlers are often traded among community members to maximize their use.

Respect is additionally expressed when the Mi'kmaq give thanks for animal sacrifice in the form of prayers or offerings such as sacred medicines (e.g., sage, cedar, tobacco and sweet grass), food or even jewelry. These are given at the time the animal is killed and at other times deemed appropriate (Kinnear 2007). One Bear River woman reported making an offering when she collected porcupine quills from animals whose bodies were found by the side of the highway (ibid.). While my childhood included gathering quills from porcupines killed by vehicles on the nearby road—dyeing them, and using them to make birchbark baskets—my education did not include ritualized thanks to the spirit of the porcupine. It did, however, include a general sense of appreciation and respect, both for the animal whose quills we used and for the crows, who, prior to consuming the porcupine body, would pull out each quill and stack them on the edge of the road according to size—saving us from the dangerous and time-consuming work of de-quilling the porcupine ourselves.

Another element of reciprocity for animal sacrifice is our responsibility to provide the conditions necessary for animals to thrive. Kinnear notes that the present-day Mi'kmaw community at Bear River First Nation practices principles of "environmental stewardship," including "never taking more than is needed, taking care of nature for the generations yet to come, and not being wasteful" (68). In addition to offering prayers for animals taken in hunting, individual Mi'kmaw people may feel drawn to, in the words of one Mi'kmaw woman, "take that spirit on ... be the protector of that animal" (Kinnear 2007: 72).

Given our socially subordinated position in Canadian society, our ability to direct environmental policy is limited, but as indigenous people experience a resurgence in political activism and form alliances around environmental conservation efforts, this may be changing. The Mi'kmaq Warriors Society, for example, has been active in its opposition to the incursion of logging, mining, oil and gas industries into our territories, allying themselves with settler allies such as The Council of Canadians, a social group who "advocate for clean water, fair trade, green energy, public health care, and a vibrant democracy" (http://canadians.org/about).

In the last stage of my research I looked for Mi'kmaw concepts that related to what I had found in our stories and in our cultural teachings. How, I asked myself, have my people already described our insights into animals and food? I found the Mi'kmaw concept of *netukulimk,* which has been variously translated as "sustaining ourselves" (Marshall 2011), as "gathering ... provisions" (Davis et al. 2011) as "use of the natural bounty" (Native Council of Nova Scotia 1993: 8) and as "the skills and sense of responsibility required to become a protector [or some say hunter] of other species" (Hatcher et al. 2009: 146). Davis and colleagues suggest that *netukulit* is related to the prefix *nutqw-,* indicating insufficiency, and is closer to the idea of "avoiding not having enough" than to accumulating abundance (Davis et al. 2011). This resonated with the subsistence ethic I had seen in our stories, such as "Wolverine and His Little Brother."

Research, like basket making, is also creative and artistic. Somewhere around 1860, Mi'kmaw basket makers began to add decorative flourishes called periwinkle curls, snail curls or porcupine curls to their work (Abbe Museum n.d.; Sark 2001). Likewise, as researchers, we sometimes bring our own twist to how we analyze or interpret our data and the theories we create from it. My own creative touch came when I wondered: If animals are my relations—if, I too am bound by the sibling relationship that Glooscap established with Apistanewj, the marten—then how might the concepts that we apply to our own survival as Mi'kmaq, such as *netukulimk,* apply to those of the animals as well? Given the changes that have taken place in our traditional territories, it is the animals that are now at risk for not having enough—enough space to live, enough food to eat, enough uncontaminated water to drink. We might, I thought, extend the concept of *netukulimk* to our animal siblings, ensuring that they do not live in scarcity. In recent years the Mi'kmaq have taken a lead role in opposing the environmental destruction caused by industrial processes such as fracking, highway construction, clear cutting or strip mining, which threaten physical animal habitats, the enspirited landscape and the cultural history that the land carries. This seems to me to be a good expression of our relational responsibility. What, I wondered, could be mine? I returned to examine my vegan practices, bringing with me a new sense of what such ethical choices could mean to me as a Mi'kmaw woman.

Ecologist Fikret Berkes notes that indigenous people are often portrayed as if we must choose between living exactly as our ancestors did or assimilating completely into settler society. Berkes proposes a third option in which "culturally significant elements" of our traditions are retained, and combined with new ways "that maintain and enhance" our identity, and provide space for our culture to develop (Berkes 1999: 168). This concept, of discovering contemporary ways of expressing our traditional values, has also been expressed in the phrase "cultural continuity" (Hallett 2005). Metallic defines continuity as "the forward-motion study of culture and the consistent existence of Mi'gmaq values, knowledge, and stories and how they have continuously evolved" (Metallic 2015: 4).[1] Since ongoing colonialism has erased so much of our Mi'kmaw culture, I value our stories as a touchstone for our traditional values.

Our Mi'kmaw stories provide not only principles by which to live, but as a narrative they also offer a world in which we can experience the source and meaning of such principles through a personal relationship with the story's characters. I have never seen a marten, but I feel I understand the character of the marten that lives in our oral traditions, and that I have relational obligations to the marten (and to other animals) by virtue of my Mi'kmaw identity. The values in our stories re-inspired me to offer my own sacrifice (in this case, the eating of animal products) to ensure the safety and wellbeing of our animal kin whose habitats and very lives are imperiled by industry and human encroachment. Given my access to plentiful vegan food, it runs counter to my cultural values to ask my animal friends to sacrifice their lives for me.

Living in Toronto, in a territory that is not my own, my vegan practice was also a way to live my Mi'kmaw cultural values, even if the way I choose to do so is at odds with our historical practices. The

Mi'kmaw attitude toward animals has been described as "a mixture of kinship, awe, and the pragmatic" (Wallis and Wallis 1955: 106). It strikes me as particularly appropriate to express my kinship and awe in this way.

As researchers in the humanities and social sciences, our research examines human beings and our social groups. These disciplines are different when done from a Mi'kmaw perspective because the Mi'kmaw view of the human person is different. In the European humanities tradition I am a brain, thinking as an individual, disconnected from my environment and from the people living in it. From a Mi'kmaw perspective, I am a physical, emotional, mental and spiritual, being, connected to and dependent upon the lives around me. I brought this broad holistic perspective to my reading of our stories, but I believe that it has useful implications for all the research work we do.

I'd like to end with a story. I mentioned that my research was shaped by my relationships with my family members, and this story, although true, has also become one of the tales that tell me who I am and how I should be with others in the world. It was a sweaty summer day, and the big rainstorm the night before hadn't put a dent in the heat. My father came in the house excited.

"Hey kids," he said, "I need your help. A frog laid a bunch of eggs in this puddle out back, and it's drying up now, and they're all going to die if we don't get them into the pond."

So for the next two hours, in the hot sun, we moved these gelatinous little frog eggs and these squirmy little tadpoles from their quickly shrinking puddle into the pond. As we did so, I realized that to my dad, the fragility of these animals mattered in the same way that our own fragility mattered. All that summer the air was alive at night with frog song, and the mosquito population was remarkably low.

For me, this was a concrete experience that "all my relations" reminds us not to forget our mutual vulnerability, and to let the way that we treat one another reflect the kinship ties that bind us all. It's been twenty years since I last held a frog in my hand, but through our stories I can hold our Mi'kmaw values close to me and strive to live them out in my daily urban life.

Notes

I would like to thank the Ontario HIV Treatment Network and the Canadian Institutes of Health Research for their funding support.

1. The original adheres to the Metallic orthography in the spelling of Mi'gmaq (Mi'kmaq).

References

Abbe Museum. N.d. Cake Basket, probably Micmac, ca. 1870. Maine Memory Network, http://www.mainememory.net/artifact/14417 (accessed June 22, 2015).

Battiste, Marie. 2000. *Reclaiming Indigenous Voice and Vision*. Vancouver: UBC Press.

Berkes, Fikret. 1999. *Sacred Ecology, Traditional Ecological Knowledge and Resource Management*. Philadelphia, PA: Taylor and Francis.

Burke, Paul. N.d. Native American Legends: Micmac Creation Story." *First People*. http://www.firstpeople.us/FP-Html-Legends/MicmacCreationStory-Micmac.html (accessed June 22, 2015).

———. 2015. Native American Legends: Nukami and Fire, *First People*, http://www.firstpeople.us/FP-Html-Legends/Nukumi_And_Fire-Micmac. html accessed June 22, 2015.

Caplan, Ronald. 1973. Making a Micmac Basket. *Cape Breton's Magazine* 2: 3-5, http://capebretonsmagazine.com/modules/publisher/item. php?itemid=34

Christmas, Peter. 1977. Supplement on Mi'kmaq. *Mi'kmaq Association for Cultural Studies*, http://www.mikmaq-assoc.ca/Historical%20Arzticles/Supplement%20on%20Mi%27kmaq%201977.htm accessed June 22, 2015.

Clark, Penney. 2011. *New Possibilities for the Past: Shaping History Education in Canada*. Vancouver: UBC Press.

Confederacy of Mainland Mi'kmaq. 2007. *Kekina'muek (Learning): Learning About the Mi'kmaq of Nova Scotia*. Truro, NS: Eastern Woodland Print Communication.

Davis, Anthony, L. Jane McMillan and Kerry Prosper. 2011. Seeking Netukulimk: Mi'kmaq Knowledge, Culture and Empowerment. Mount St. Vincent University, http://www.msvu.ca/site/media/msvu/ NAISA%20edited%20version%202010_2.ppt accessed June 22, 2015.

Hallet, Darcy. 2005. Aboriginal Identity Development, Language Knowledge, And School Attrition: An Examination Of Cultural Continuity. PhD dissertation, University of British Columbia.

Hatcher, Annamarie, Cheryl Bartlett, Albert Marshall and Murdena Marshall. 2009. Two-eyed Seeing in the Classroom Environment: Concepts,

Approaches, and Challenges. *Canadian Journal of Science, Mathematics and Technology Education* 9 (3): 141-53.

Hornborg, Anne-Christine. 2013. *Mi'kmaq Landscapes: From Animism to Sacred Ecology.* Hampshire, U.K.: Ashgate.

Joe, Rita and Lesley Choyce. 1997. *The Mi'kmaq Anthology.* Lawrencetown, NS, Canada: Pottersfield Press.

Kant, Immanuel. 2011. Rational Beings Alone Have Moral Worth. In *Food Ethics,* ed. Paul Pojman and Louis P.Pojman, 10-12. Scarborough ON: Cengage Learning.

Kinnear, Lacia. 2007. Contemporary Mi'kmaq Relationships Between Humans and Animals: A Case Study of the Bear River First Nation Reserve in Nova Scotia. Master's thesis, Dalhousie University.

Marshall, Albert. 2011. Two-Eyed Seeing – Etuaptmumk: Mainstreaming Indigenous Knowledge for Sustainability, IntegrativeScience.ca, May 9-11, http://www.integrativescience.ca/uploads/articles/2011May-Marshall-Two-Eyed-Seeing-indigenous-knowledge-red-path-sustainability.pdf (accessed June 22, 2015).

Metallic, Blair Alicia. 2015. Forward Motion: Cultural Memory and Continuity in Mi'gmaq Literature. Master's thesis, Université de Sherbrooke.

Muin'iskw, Jean and Dan Crowfeather. 2013. Mi'kmaq Spirituality 101. Mi'kmaq Spirit, http://www.muiniskw.org/pgCulture2.htm (accessed June 22, 2015).

Native Council of Nova Scotia. 1993. *Mi'kmaq Fisheries: Netukulimk, Towards A Better Understanding.* Truro, NS: Native Council of Nova Scotia.

Rand, Silas T. 2004[1893]. *Legends of the Micmacs vol. II.,* West Orange, NJ, USA: Invisible Books.

Rand, Silas T. 2005[1893]. *Legends of the Micmacs vol. I.* West Orange, NJ, USA: Invisible Books.

Robinson Margaret. Veganism and Mi'kmaq Legends. *Canadian Journal of Native Studies* 33 (1): 189-96.

Sark, Tiffany. 2001. Mi'kmaq Baskets: Our Living Legends, The Government of Prince Edward Island, last updated January 14, 2001. http://www.gov.pe.ca/firsthand/index.php3?number=44605&lang=E (accessed June 22, 2015).

Wallis, Wilson D. and Ruth Sawtell Wallis. 1955. *The Micmac Indians of Eastern Canada.* Minneapolis, MN, USA: University of Minnesota Press.

Whitehead, Ruth H. 1989. *Six Micmac Stories.* Halifax, NS: The Nova Scotia Museum.

Whitehead, Ruth H. 1988. *Stories from the Six Worlds: Micmac Legends.* Halifax, NS: Nimbus.

Len Findlay

From Smug Settler to Ethical Ally: Humanizing the Humanist via Solidarity ... Interrupted

I am a long-time member of the Indigenous Humanities group at the University of Saskatchewan and a co-applicant on our SSHRC-sponsored study of the Mi'kmaw Humanities. In this essay I use my own experiences in Scotland, England and Canada to show how young people can be shaped by an education in the Eurocentric humanities and how that education stays with them into professional adulthood, from student learner to tenured professor, in ways that keep their understanding, instincts and actions profoundly but not necessarily permanently colonial. My studies in classical Greek and Latin, and in their modern derivatives—English, French and German—predisposed me to consider indigenous languages inferior, and to consider the speakers of those languages inferior too—unless and until they learned what I had learned. My study of other humanities subjects like philosophy, history and theology reinforced my tendency to dismiss or depreciate what I did not know and had little reason to inform myself about while I lived in Britain. I believed in knowledge monopolies and racist hierarchies, though I, and my teachers and peers, would have been outraged if accused of either. Arrogance and ignorance can guide the thinking of self-styled progressives and radicals at least as much as they fuel the delusions of brazen bigots. But at least the former, among whom I count myself, can be educated by their indigenous brothers and sisters into better ways of imagining, thinking and doing, if only they can show they deserve and will accept such an invaluable and urgent (re)education.

Poverty, Education and Prejudice

I grew up in a poor neighborhood in Aberdeen, Scotland, part of a big baby-boom by which people reaffirmed themselves after the insanity of yet another World War caused by the poisons still lurking in the heart of Europe and its extensive colonies around the globe. I was the second of four children in a fortunate family. We were fortunate because my mother was not a widow, like so many women were in our neighborhood. My father had steady work in a relatively well-paying trade as a ship's rigger in what was still a major fishing port before the factory ships emptied the oceans and the North Sea oilrigs arrived. We lived from weekly paycheque to paycheque, but we were lucky too in that, after a couple of years living in a former army barracks, my parents had been assigned a council house to rent in an estate close to schools, close to my dad's work and close to those cheapest of recreational facilities, public parks and the tidal seashore. I walked to elementary school every day and came home for lunch with my siblings, passing each way a fenced-off German bomb crater that at the time was little more than a backdrop for little boys' war games (including cowboys and Indians).

People did not seem to mind the ongoing rationing of all sorts of products (including children's candies). We were no longer at war. New parents could look to a public school system in which the whole of Scotland took pride for its effectiveness and relative inclusiveness, its commitment to "the democratic intellect" (Davie 1961; cf. Paterson 2015). If you had ability and good work habits and did not fall foul of the very stern teachers, then you could go far socially and geographically. That was the presumption. And it was backed up by the evidence of Scottish "success" in every outpost of the British Empire and in the post-imperial United States, including even "inventing" Canada (McGoogan 2010). The education system was broadly meritocratic, though not without the costs of prematurely streaming children aged eleven into academic and technical programs in different schools, and keeping financial challenges part of a "free" education in the form of school uniforms to be bought for the academically talented, and bus fares to be found for the journey across town to the elite school with a Latin motto where, unbeknownst to me, a recent pupil had been Bertha Wilson who would become the first woman justice on the Supreme Court of Canada. I would do well enough to remain at this school, Aberdeen Academy, as it was then known, for six years before going to university. This too was a financial challenge for my parents because they had to forego earnings from a male child who could have been out in the workforce at fifteen as were my two brothers and my sister. When you are just scraping by, every little bit helps. Sacrifices were made to give me a special opportunity, and I felt powerfully the responsibility not to disappoint. The school motto was *Ad altiora tendo:* I aim toward higher things. Those "things" were not specified. However, they were presumed by all to include material advantages as well as knowledge and the capacity to do good in the world. You were getting a chance to do better than the generation that preceded you, and you'd better not forget it!

The first member of my extended family to attend university, I did so as a working-class kid with many a chip on his shoulder. Growing up poor meant you spoke a certain way—and more often than not in Scots dialect rather than "proper" English—dressed a certain way and suffered doubts that seemed not to feature in the consciousness of peers from more privileged backgrounds. The solidarity and egalitarianism born of hard times in the "'hood" where everyone is poor helps you to face challenges, but you learn also to suspect your own success and not to flaunt it when you are among your own kind. In the great psychodrama that is adolescence, you threaten daily to drown in shame, doubt and guilt, to conceal what you already know of economic hardship and play down what you are now learning about better times and larger possibilities. In a class system like the United Kingdom's, where a colonial system was also developed and globally implemented, you learn to pass in two quite different worlds. Luckily, this was an experience that would eventually help me become an ethical ally to First Nations, Inuit and Metis people wrestling with a "split mind" of a far more taxing kind (Cajete 2000: 186-87) than I had to contend with. Empathy would eventually nourish new, anticolonial solidarities.

I was the Seafield Gold Medalist in my year at Aberdeen University, and this was especially thrilling for my father and my paternal grandparents. The Duchess of Seafield, an immensely wealthy aristocrat, lived at Cullen House in her vast estate in northern Scotland. When guests came to visit my family in the summer, my great grandfather would take them out fishing from the tiny Cullen harbor into the dangerous North Sea. Earlier members of the Findlay family had been recognized for their knowledge of the sea. So my family had a connection to the donor behind the academic medal. Now another was being recognized for academic achievement. I had also won a place at Jesus College, Oxford, to pursue postgraduate studies in English literature (as it was called). Moreover, I was engaged to be married to a girl I had met in my last year at Aberdeen Academy, Isobel Downie, and I was on full scholarship and not a direct drain on my family. Life was lookin' good, and I was pretty full of myself.

Oxford was full of intimidation as well as opportunity, all the old awkwardnesses and insecurities returned with a vengeance, and I found myself befriending and being befriended by Canadian students who felt like outsiders too. Wrong accent. Wrong background. Wrong connections. We shared experiences about our respective countries, and I became more actively interested in Canada as an escape from the British class-system and from aspects of its imperial past, especially as those were playing out in a South Africa still riven by apartheid, and in an America now animated by the Civil Rights movement. I heard faintly of the American Indian Movement, but their struggles seemed less important and dramatic than Black struggles. Meanwhile, despite my best efforts to remain "true" to my working-class origins, I was being gradually compelled to pass, in the eyes of Oxford University, an institution key over centuries to the perpetuation of the class system at home and the acquisition of empire overseas (Symonds 1991). I became an accidental, unconscious imperialist, as it were, in a process that paid tribute to my own considerable self-doubt and the enormous capacity of Western education to reproduce the same distribution of winners and losers, centrality and marginality, the informed and the ignorant, supporting some people and shamelessly, deliberately failing others. Part of me wanted to stay in Oxford forever, such is the allure of acceptance and authority. But another part of me, the one that experienced condescension and rejection in numerous academic encounters and job interviewees, wanted out. Time to go West, young man! Time to check out all those stories my Anglo-Canadian, white settler friends had shared with me. Not that I thought of my new friends in those terms. They were simply canonical or "real" Canadians, as understood from the heart of empire: they were colonials, to be sure, but certainly not colonizers. In thinking of Canada and Canadians this way, I could have been Stephen Harper denying Canada's colonial past to his fellow G8 leaders in Pittsburg in 2009 (Walia 2009), but at least I had more excuse than he had! I was not even a Canadian yet.

When I came to Canada in 1974, I was fresh from the Eurocentric marinade so well described by Marie Battiste. I was an excellent specimen of Eurocentric scholarly self-satisfaction and unconscious arrogance. I was bringing knowledge to a "young" country in need of my Old World skills. I would not have to adjust to my new job in a new city in a former British colony. My students, colleagues and (mostly white) neighbours would have to adjust to me. After all, Canada had little history and culture of its own, and what little it had was exported from Europe, by people just like me.

What is important and still puzzling in all of this is why, as someone who had known poverty and prejudice, I did not immediately show solidarity and common cause with those in Canada most clearly impoverished and victimized by prejudice, namely First Nations, Inuit and Metis people. One part of the answer was that, like so many immigrants before me, I was distracted by opportunity and dazzled by an apparent democratic difference. Canada seemed like a just society. (I had not yet read Harold Cardinal!) Canada seemed less hierarchical, more meritocratic, and more generous than a Britain soured and troubled by its loss of empire and its irreversibly diminishing place in the world. And Canada was evidently less violent and divided than the United States, or so it seemed to me. Moreover, the Canadian academy proved incredibly welcoming, and I thought at first it was that way for everybody.

The second part of the answer to the question of why solidarity with indigenous peoples came only slowly to me can be found in the subtlety and pervasiveness of Canadian racism in the 1970s and 1980s. So much was hidden, softened or repackaged as exotic décor and ceremonial federalism. I could read and navigate with some confidence cultural codes and practices derived from the country I had come from, but I had little capacity to unpack claims I regularly heard about "our Indians," a "conquered people," being treated better than their American counterparts, and incomparably better than black and coloured South Africans. And even if one wished to do so, how could one begin such a difficult conversation with such nice people without sounding like an uppity immigrant more self-righteous than informed? Moreover, there seemed little space in the academy as yet for such questions, because postcolonialism, if evident at all, was focused on the separatist movement in Québec, a conversation among white Canadians divided by language but joined by common assumptions about the deficient and disappearing Indian so instructively confirmed and confounded by "the Last Huron," Zacharie Vincent/ Teraliolin, whose life and work I would later devote myself to understanding and promoting (Findlay 2006, 2007). It took a while—and plenty of hard work—for my attitudes to change, but change they did, and profoundly, thanks to patient, generous teachers of all sorts, the most important of whom continue to be Marie Battiste and Sa'ke'j Henderson. First Nations students like Lori Blondeau and Tasha Hubbard, the one a gifted artist and curator, the other a filmmaker and now professor and colleague, also helped transform my thinking (and teaching and writing), reminding me again and again how much universities lose when they refuse or reject or undermine indigenous students. Through such generous counsel and guidance, I have been led from the presumptuous and exclusive humanities to an engagement with the fully human, and from European and Euro-Canadian models and knowledge systems to a deep respect and admiration for indigenous knowledge and knowledge keepers. In this extended and ongoing process, I have not forgotten what I learned growing up and as a young scholar and teacher. But I have altered my sense of its status and effects, the fact that Europe has no monopoly on knowledge, and that when Europe acts as though it does, great damage is done to other languages, other cultures, other traditions, other ecologies.

No one can decolonize himself or herself on their own. But dialogue and cooperation across Euro-Canadian, Mi'kmaw and Great Plains difference have enabled me to realize what the humanities can do for all humanity rather than simply for me and people like me. I now wish to share more of what I have learned (and unlearned) so that others can appreciate how the power of the Eurocentric humanities can be used to deconstruct them, and how that power can be enlisted in the interests of a more just, respectful and fully decolonized Canada where diversity is embraced for the gift it is and immigrant and settler arrogance increasingly hard to find and even harder to justify.

Academic Work as Ethical Alliance

As someone schooled in the Eurocentric humanities, I bring to our indigenous humanities group at the University of Saskatchewan a capacity for insider critique and outsider alliance (Battiste et al. 2007). The critique entails a "hermeneutics of suspicion" (Ricoeur 2010) directed at what you usually take for granted, and an anti-colonial critique that grounds high-flying, allegedly postcolonial theory in Indian country, on the land, in the knowledge ecologies developed and protected over centuries by the First Peoples of Turtle Island. What I have learned about social class, personally and professionally, is now put to work in the context of "race," the key obstacle to building solidarity between the impoverished immigrant and the unjustly treated indigene (Findlay 2009). Meanwhile, acting as an ally requires the patient and respectful building of relationships with, and helping to honour the work and example of, indigenous scholars at home, in your home and theirs, and across the world. Becoming an ally also requires the explicit and recurrent disavowal of authority over the Other and the willingness to help, when needed, under indigenous leadership, and most emphatically not as some paternalistic saviour or corporate thief from away. This is difficult but enormously rewarding work. I will now briefly illustrate the roles of critic and ally, and apprentice, in order to bring out their (and my) strengths and limitations as humanist and neo-humanist practices.

Critical Reading against the Euro-humanistic Grain

Early encounters between Mi'kmaw people and Europeans are recorded in the Christian humanist prose of soldiers, diplomats, explorers and priests. This archive of encounter, in its publication, circulation and interpretation offers the text-based Euro-humanities an important opportunity to expose the complicity of humanist knowledge and skills with imperialism and colonialism. One such work from this massive archive is Father Chrestien Le Clercq's *Nouvelle Relation de la Gaspésie, qui contient les Moeurs et la Religion des Sauvages Gaspésiens Porte-Croix, adorateurs du soleil, & d'autres peuples de l'Amerique Septentrionale, dite le Canada* (1691), a work reissued in 1692, 1758 and then in an English translation by William Francis Ganong for the Champlain Society in 1910 (see Palstits bibliographical essay in

Ganong). The Champlain Society had been established five years previously to emulate the Hakluyt Society in Britain and the Prince Society in the United States. Significantly, the Society's founding was triggered by a lecture to an elite audience on "History and Patriotism" by the head of the McGill University department of history, Professor Charles Colby, and was envisaged as an instrument of nation formation, the nation in question being the British Dominion of Canada.

As we will see shortly, this recourse to history to affirm national identity was basically a reprise of what happened in accounts of the consolidation of New France in the 17th century. But first, a word about and sampling from Le Clercq. Father Le Clercq (ca. 1630 to ca. 1695), was a Récollet missionary from the reform branch of the Franciscan order, many members of which served as chaplains for the French army. Le Clercq's social formation and education were both tested and confirmed by his years among the Mi'kmaq and Maliseet peoples of what is now known as the Gaspé or South Shore of the St. Lawrence. In his writings he constantly reveals how Euro-humanistic learning, values and assumptions enable and disable his ability to understand the knowledge systems and humanity of the Mi'kmaq. Early in his narrative, Le Clercq warns his readers against dismissing as savages people who "have not been bred in the maxims of civil polity" (chapter 1, 82). However, this openness to otherness and awareness of the prejudices of his countrymen cannot save him from the very lapses he warns others against. These lapses into incomprehension and paternalism are facilitated by his view of the Mi'kmaq as "not so ridiculous as the Indians of South America" yet susceptible to "master frauds" (chapter 3, 90) around child birth and their refusal to be impressed by either the dress or the buildings introduced by the French (chapter 4, 99). Le Clercq alternates accordingly between bouts of sober or sympathetic observation and reassertion of a rigid, racialized hierarchy:

> The Gaspesians do not know how to read nor how to write. They have nevertheless, enough understanding and memory to learn how to do both if only they were willing to give the necessary application. But aside from the fickleness and instability of their minds, which they are willing to apply only in so far as it pleases them, they all have the false and ridiculous belief that they would not live long if they were as learned as the French. From

this it comes that they are pleased to live and die in their natural ignorance. Some of the Indians, however, for whose instruction some trouble has been taken, have in a short time become philosophers and even pretty good theologians. But, after all, they have ever remained savages since they have not had the sense to profit by their considerable advantages, of which they have rendered themselves wholly unworthy by leaving their studies in order to dwell with their fellow-country-men in the woods where they have lived like very bad philosophers, preferring on the basis of a foolish reasoning, the savage to the French life. (LeClerq in Ganong, 1910[1697]: 125)

The humanist skills exemplified by Le Clercq expose the imagined deficiencies of the Mi'kmaq. They are constructed by the newcomer as actually educable and hence potentially human. Yet in the ongoing interplay of acceptance and refusal the missionary recurs to racial essentialism to clinch his case (or so he thinks) for European superiority and plenary, authentic humanity. "Fickleness [inconstance] and instability" apparently produce a settled, self-evidently ludicrous conviction among the Mi'kmaq that being the equals of the French in learning (*aussi sçavans que les François*) is for them a virtual death sentence—a conviction that Canadian history would seem to confirm as remarkably prescient, particularly in residential schools and endlessly unwelcoming universities. There are exceptions to the rule of Mi'kmaw obtuseness, Le Clercq concedes, in the person of those who display aptitude while being intensively instructed in the two preeminent disciplines in the Euro-humanities, philosophy and theology, with predictable missionary prejudice showing in his assigning to theology the greatest difficulty and utility of all. However, despite these cases of the exceptionally educable, the roots of Mi'kmaw inferiority seemingly remain. In time, these promising students show themselves utterly undeserving *(tout-à-fait indignes)* of the trouble taken to educate and improve them, and the advantages adhering thereto in the "new" world as well as the "old." They turn their backs on real knowledge in favour of traditional pursuits with their own people. Study for them is not the abandonment of indigenous for foreign knowledge, or of society for self-sequestered studiousness. Their wayward (extravagant) reasoning is, as Le Clercq's chapter heading indicates, a study in "ignorance." As philosophers whose judgment is drastically flawed, they are not the real thing but "very bad" ("*tres méchants*") parodies of scholarship (but for a compelling refutation of such claims (cf. Henderson and Battiste 2013). In sum, the only learning that counts is European learning. Theology as first among disciplines requires the convertibility of the Mi'kmaq, but only to compliant inferiority and ongoing dependency. They cannot be true human peers of the Europeans, not least because they go to school in the woods and in the company of their fellow savages, in land-based, protocol-infused knowledge ecologies rather than the stone sanctuaries dear to monastic orders and Renaissance humanists. Civic humanism does not go walk-about except for conquest and plunder, while clerical humanism does so only in the search for souls. Therefore, indigenous humanism and indigenous humanities cannot even be imagined by LeClercq. Instead, nature doubles in the passage cited above as the domain of the indigenous Other and the doom of indigenous "ignorance." Humanity as monopoly and zealously guarded franchise is manifestly out of its depth in Gaspesia, and necessarily lacking in self-awareness regarding its own origins:

> Our Gaspesians, however, can teach us nothing certain on this subject, perhaps because they have no knowledge of letters, which could give them knowledge as to their ancestors and their origin. They have, indeed if you will, some dim and fabulous notion of the creation of the world, and of the deluge. (84)

So much for the Mi'kmaw Creation Story I will discuss shortly! So much for blind allegiance to the Book of Genesis as sober, incontrovertible fact!

William Ganong, an expert on maps, mollusks, Acadian history and much else, takes on the editing, translating and contextualizing of the *Nouvelle Relation* with a revealing mix of academic seriousness and personal zeal. New Brunswick is Ganong's homeland; he knows its history, topography and biology well, and also the reasons for its Mi'kmaw and Maliseet place names, on which he wrote a series of essays for the Royal Society of Canada; and he is eager that others understand more fully the complex history of New France. Yet his substantial preface to his translation reveals curiously mixed feelings from the outset: "it narrates no very important events ... but it yields to no other in the value and interest of its matter from other points of view" (2-3). Ganong is writing more than two centuries after Le

Clercq, but little has changed in the mind behind the white settler gaze (except the levels of betrayal of the Mi'kmaq by white settler society: "The existence of the Cross among these Indians being granted, there are two possible explanations of its origin, aside of course from the Indian explanation, which is not to be seriously considered" (38). Mi'kmaw "religion" is a topic which Ganong thinks Le Clercq could have "treated as a master" (13-14), while the Mi'kmaw "explanation" of their spirituality—and much else—can provide only "materials of value to modern critical study"(17).

Ganong has degrees from Harvard and Munich as well as University of New Brunswick, and a long career as Professor of Botany at Smith College in Massachusetts. He also has a bad case of academic arrogance. He concedes mastery of "religion" to Le Clercq while insisting the latter was "no naturalist" (15). The master narrative of Euro-modernity driven first by religious faith is now driven by science. But, irrespective of the driver, the delusional apparatus of European superiority calls itself knowledge while most clearly performing its own ignorance. Over time, academic explanations may change, but the claim to mastery and modernity remains unchanged. At the same time, the meaning of the peace and friendship treaties is skewed ever more violently in the interests of colonial predation and dispossession. Is it any wonder that indigenous peoples are wary of settler education, the claims it makes for itself as well as the evil that *resided* in the schools where it forcibly confined and abused Mi'kmaw and so many other First Nations children? Bringing out the dark solidarity between greed and learning in the Euro-Canadian tradition is therefore work for all of us to undertake, but perhaps especially the erstwhile smug immigrant seeking to be an ethical ally.

Alliance as an Apprentice's Openness to the Mi'kmaw Creation Story

In contrast to Le Clercq and Ganong and so many others, I approach this story with a sense of the sacred, the sacred in the keeping of others, most notably Stephen Augustine (n.d.). I approach this story also with a humanist scholar's sense of the power of stories to bind people to a particular territory. In the words of the Gitxsan Elder whose words gave Ted Chamberlin's 2003 book its title: "If this is your land, where are your stories?" This question from a First Nations' source confirms for me the existence of the Mi'kmaw humanities, not least because the humanities disciplines derived from the understanding, interpretation and sharing of sacred texts, songs and speech from within universities that have for most of their history acted in the service of spiritual teachings rather than scientific, secular rationality. Notions of the canon derive from the distinction between canonical and apocryphal books of the Bible, even though they now govern and police what counts as knowledge across a wide range of inquiry and reflection.

So, in coming to this Creation Story, I remember the Book of Genesis in the Scottish Episcopalian tradition in which I was raised; I remember also how as a student I felt a pull to the priesthood even while I was learning about many other similar accounts in very different traditions, and how I concluded that these stories have the power of being held and preserved, and retold by particular communities as a way of binding them to each other within a particular language, while binding them also to a particular territory, real or imagined.

Creation stories, I have for some time thought, as an immigrant to a vast country only a few of whose creation stories I know—are stories that record and recurrently perform a deep and defining impulse to situate ourselves in relation to time and place and community, framing human existence in ways that assert or demonstrate or imagine connections to other peoples and other life forms in an arrangement and unfolding which relate to meaning and meaning-making, even if the meanings in question are too elusive or too rich for one person to capture or fathom (Battiste et al. 2007). I know the transcriber of this story to be a highly respected person from an important Mi'kmaw family. I will be reading the words of a scholar and knowledge keeper of a particular tradition whose people's Concordat with the Holy See I have read, and whose treasury of past, present and future meanings Sa'ke'j Henderson and Marie Battiste and their gifted children are helping me to approach respectfully, on Chapel Island and elsewhere. The first thing that impacts on me in the Creation Story is a Mi'kmaw word I do not understand. It is the first of a number of such words or names, each both resisting me and intriguing me. This is not my language; but what does it mean and how is it pronounced? The provision of pronunciation tells me up front that this is a living language with oral and other rules that I am ignorant of yet curious about. The explanation of this word immediately admits to an alias, establishing, I think, the principle that language is always exceeded by experience and the Creator. The fact that the Mi'kmaw version of the Creator is genderless reminds me instantly of the patriarchal traditions of Judaeo-Christianity. This reminder is gratifying but also unsettling. As a male feminist I am glad to get beyond patriarchy every chance I get; however, I think of this as progress—a recent development in modernity in the West—not as foundational moment in a culture so often figured as "backward" among the intellectual and spiritual authorities with whom I grew up. I also register that Creator has responsibility in two senses: for making this world; for caring for what happens to it.

We now move to two fundamental creations, the earth, both the planet and the territory on which the Mi'kmaw dwell, and the first being in human form, Kluskap.

The Earth is the mediated source of abundance and of relation to the Sun as guardian and provider of day and night. Kluskap is the product of a momentary interaction of energy and territory, the sky and the land. More particularly, it is the product of lightning and sand, whose meeting is always dramatic (and hence memorable). I find it notable that material form comes first, then life requires a second lightning bolt. Like an infant child, Kluskap is immobile to begin with, but this limitation allows for orientation and observation: the disposition of his body in relation to the seven directions and the opportunity to observe the world through which he will soon move. The ability to move comes from a request to the Creator after Kluskap knows what he is asking. Kluskap moves from the horizontal to the vertical, performing the basic human transition into *homo erectus*, his freedom conditioned by dependency on Creator and the connections of his corporeal extremities to directionality on the earth. This freedom is first marked by a ceremony of sorts, the giving thanks in a way that returns movement to circularity, to the symbolic implications of the number seven, and connects the spiritual interior to the spirits at work in and above the earth. His travels reflect the shape of Turtle Island and affirm his special relation to Mi'kmaw territory. His gaze is curious but respectful, while two key points are re-emphasized: Kluskap's dependency on Creator, and his role as steward, not "improver" or exploiter of the natural world. Then comes the promise or prophecy of meeting "someone soon."

Nukami is encountered in Mi'kmaw territory (the East). She is very old and his grandmother. She does not come from a human lineage but from a natural one: rock and dew and sunshine, in contrast to lightning and sand, but still the convergence and combination of energy and matter. I puzzle how, since she is very old and Kluskap is not, how he could have been the first to take on human form. But this apparent discrepancy seems to have been taken care of by a kind of *parthenogenesis* in which she is born old. Rather than questions about whether the Biblical Adam had a navel, a different kind of curiosity seems piqued by this account of parallel creations of grandson and grandmother outside sequential time but in a foundational relationship that cannot be undone and must be nourished through attentiveness and respect. It is as though the folds and fissures in the rock have been moistened by the dew into the wrinkled skin and durability of a wise old woman, stone not hurting skin but somehow becoming it, in accord with the transformative powers of the heavens: lightning and the sun.

We then see again Kluskap's impulse to give thanks for those he meets and for what he learns from these interactions. He makes a request of the marten. What follows is the demonstrating of respect in asking before acting and in the power of consensuality. Kluskap has a duty to consult. Nukami snaps the marten's neck with his permission, and Creator restores him to life in an allegory of responsible harvesting of animals for food and fur and shelter. The kinship system expands from grandson and grandmother to brothers and sisters, a web of relations that blurs or philosophically refuses the customary Aristotelian distinction between humans and animals. Harmony is desired and worked for. It can be best achieved by looking and listening (i.e. learning), before acting so as to live with rather than "disturb" creation.

Nukami knows how to prepare and cook food, and the fire she starts derives from the initial bolt that brought Kluskap into existence. Connectedness is thus emphasized, as is the notion that nothing need be wasted in a respectful economy. The convergence of matter and energy in fire is a powerful version of the sacred, and the sociability that develops around it, from survival to governance. Attentiveness is the key to respect, and we learn for interdependence rather than for selfishness and personal advantage.

Then comes Kluskap's nephew, the hunter who can bring down much larger animals than a marten, but only to share, not for the "thrill" of the kill or for something to sell. Here is the third generation and a symbol of the future, a young man who has to identify himself by "where he came from," a place-based inquiry that seems still alive and well today, perhaps especially among indigenous peoples and immigrants/exiles. Kluskap offers hospitality to his nephew by calling consensually on another Mi'kmaw resource, salmon, while offering a lesson about the connection between a diversified, seasonal diet, and the preserving of an important food source. Stewardship makes sense in all sorts of ways the Atlantic cod fishery could have learned from. This nephew, Netawansum, is born of sea and sweetgrass and the elemental aeration of water into foam through the agency of wind. This is biological kinship of a different sort than I normally think of. Mi'kmaw genealogy begins with energy and the elements, combining human ties with territorial ones and the principle of productive convergence of difference.

Kluskap is then claimed by his mother (Ni'kanaptekewi'skw (nee-gah-nap-de-gay-weeskw). Her birth echoes the grandmother's birth, but she comes from a leaf, not a rock, and brings colours to the world that remind us that the changing colours of leaves are one of the most pervasive expressions of time and place and the inescapability of process and change. I also think of how so many pigments come from earth and plants, and how the primary ones mix and combine to form secondary colours. Kluskap's mother's name is not translated but obviously has a bearing on the gifts she brings and her teaching that peace and harmony are other names for survival and a good life. Once again, Kluskap adjusts his impulse to hospitality in the harvesting from the plant word for the feast in which all the company will honour the appearance of his mother.

The final section of the creation story unfolds Kluskap's life with a mix of prophecy and rooted consistency. The future can only be anticipated if one looks to relationships and values, and to the conditions of one's own formation: biological, social and spiritual. The Mi'kmaw will not need Kluskap's presence unless they are "in danger." He offers them a warning and a reassurance. The numerology of seven shapes the narrative in a holistic yet dispersive way, including the growing of a people, its social organization, and the use of ceremony to keep the past alive and the present peaceful. The sweat lodge brings the grandfathers in in the form of other rocks, ritual purification admitting to the inevitability of personal contamination and the collective capacity for purging it. The innocence of infancy is for men recoverable in this way, re-establishing their internal harmony and respectful relations with all the women in their lives. The sweat, like the smoking of tobacco, is a tribute to the sacredness of fire and its transformative force when there is air and combustible material to feed it. The spiritual agency of fire needs special forms of human receptivity, attentiveness, respect and indeed belief. I come away from this experience with a strong sense of the power and limitations of written language, and with the power and limitations of the notion of the Humanities in which I was trained. My impressions recorded here surely attest to both my knowledge and my ignorance.

Language is not the whole of experience, and to pretend that texts contain everything is reductive and damaging. But language, carefully used and listened to, can help us record and develop our relationship to ourselves and others, all life forms and life systems. Every language is a "social treasury" (as Umberto Eco [1992] says), but it is a cognitive and ecological treasury too, one where value is recaptured from money and returned to relationships, not commodities to be traded.

Holistic knowledge can be mapped onto the current array of academic disciplines but cannot be confined to them. Its difference and independency may be threatening to some, but it offers a great opportunity to rethink and redirect the project of the human species from mastery to interdependence, from hubris to humility, from greed to generosity. It offers a great fire round which to gather for new dialogues, conversations and thoughtful silences. The Mi'kmaw knowledge system expressed in the creation story is for me not romantic or superstitious but highly disciplined and insightful. It is faithful to fundamentals yet endlessly adaptive. Land and language are at its heart, and it depends on the respectful relations made possible by an understanding and acceptance of the seven directions. Everyone can learn from this story. Its teachings, to which I am very new, are urgent, challenging and creative. It can animate the human, the humane and the humanities in us all.

The Eighth District, the New Knowledge Truckhouse and M'set Nogemaq[1]/All My Relations

The year 2016 has witnessed some remarkable developments at the federal level. The Trudeau government has made clear its unqualified support for the United Nations Declaration on the Rights of Indigenous Peoples (UNDRIP). This new national government has also begun to make good on its promise to accept and implement the Calls to Action issued by the Truth and Reconciliation Commission (TRC). This is all very inspiring for those intent on making Canada a truly just society, but it is complex and daunting too. Where do we start? How do we start? Who takes the lead? Even the new federal Minister of Justice, Jody Wilson-Raybould, with her wonderful activist genes, rich Kwakwaka'wakw heritage, and great intellectual and ethical gifts, is being watched for signs of backsliding even as she tries to clear some ground for real decolonization and an animated treaty federalism. The naysayers want to define Canada's "Indian problem" as either the fault of the First peoples themselves, or as an insurmountable challenge that can be solved only by the good old colonial standbys of elimination and/or assimilation. Either way, it should be business as usual after the posturing stops. The reconciliation that ought to prevail is that all Canadians should reconcile themselves to the inevitability, if not the desirability, of the neocolonial status quo. UNDRIP and the TRC notwithstanding, "the" economy and institutions it makes possible must continue to reproduce the conditions that favour the dominant. Otherwise, the country will be bankrupted in trying to better the lives of the incapable and the undeserving. Such remains the racist state of things.

There is a clear challenge for Canada's universities at this pivotal moment. These institutions that did so much to advance the objectives of colonialism are now being asked by the TRC to become part of the solution rather than furnishing additional alibis for colonial injustice, and new methods for refining and accelerating exploitation and the casual or concerted violations of the treaties signed by the Crown with indigenous peoples. The call to "indigenize" universities is not new (Findlay 2000), but it is now being taken up more widely and sincerely than ever before. And, in my experience, and consistent with treaty consciousness and traditional indigenous practice, it can be effectively done by forming alliances between indigenous and non-indigenous scholars working under indigenous leadership and with conceptual frameworks and protocols unique to particular First Nations, their particular histories and territories. The ongoing Mi'kmaw humanities initiative can feed invaluably into a national and international reconciliation effort while remaining a sweet-grass-roots movement, building on resources such as the new collection edited by Marie Battiste, *Living Treaties: Narrating Mi'kmaw Treaty Relations*. To this end, I conclude by invoking the seven districts of Mi'kma'ki which constitute a unique territory which has a long history of peace and friendship treaties with those coming from various parts of the eighth district (Pestie'ma'ltimk, the Boston, MA, area) which lies beyond Mi'kma'ki. This history must not only be widely known and its lessons respected, but the indigenous stewards of the treaties, their provisions and promises, and the territory that has witnessed the treaties' misrepresentation and betrayal. And there is a need too for truckhouses such as were mandated by the British Crown in 1725 to regulate trade between the British and the Mi'kmaw. But this time a new Proclamation should designate our schools and colleges and universities as truckhouses for a truly fair trade in knowledge systems and values overseen by the kind of "learning spirit" and the teaching of the baskets of which Marie Battiste has so compellingly written, spoken and acted. All our children deserve no less, and so does Mother Earth.

Notes

1. Elsipuktuk spelling, as rendered by Patrick Augustine in Battiste 2016: 62.

References

Augustine, Patrick J. Mi'kmaw Relations. In *Living Treaties: Narrating Mi'kmaw Treaty Relations*. Sydney, NS: Cape Breton University Press, ed. Marie Battiste, 52-65. Sydney, NS: Cape Breton University Press.

Augustine, Stephen J. *Mi'kmaw Creation Story*. www.muniskw. org?pgCulture3a.

Battiste, Marie. 2013. *Decolonizing Education: Nourishing the Learning Spirit*. Saskatoon: Purich Publishing.

Battiste, Marie, ed. 2016. *Living Treaties: Narrating Mi'kmaw Treaty Relations*. Sydney, NS: Cape Breton University Press.

Battiste, Marie, Lynne Bell, Isobel M. Findlay, Sa'ke'j Henderson, L. M. Findlay. 2007. Thinking Place: Animating the Indigenous Humanities in Education. *Australian Journal of Indigenous Education* 35:7-19.

Cajete, Gregory. 2000. Indigenous Knowledge: The Pueblo Metaphor of Indigenous Education. In *Reclaiming Indigenous Voice and Vision*, ed. Marie Battiste, 181-91. Vancouver: UBC Press.

Cardinal, Harold. 1969. *The Unjust Society: The Tragedy of Canada's Indians*. Edmonton: M. G. Hurtig.

Chamberlin, J. Edward. 2003. *If This Is Your Land, Where Are Your Stories? Finding Common Ground*. Toronto: Knopf Canada.

Davie, George Elder. 1961. *The Democratic Intellect: Scotland and Her Universities in the Nineteenth Century*. Edinburgh: Edinburgh University Press.

Eco, Umberto. 1992. *Interpretation and Overinterpretation*. Cambridge: Cambridge University Press.

Findlay, L. M. 2000. Always indigenize! The Radical Humanities in the Postcolonial Canadian University. *Ariel* 31:307-26.

———. 2006. Spectres of Canada: Image, Text, Aura, Nation. *University of Toronto Quarterly* 75: 656-72.

———. 2007. Towards Canada as Aesthetic State: François-Xavier Garneau's *Canadien* Poetics.*Studies in Canadian Literature* 32 (2): 18-42.

———. 2009. After Systemic Racism: The Canada We Can Be. *Differences: Journal of the Canadian Foundation for Race Relations* 5 (1): 18-20.

———. 2013. The Long March to Recognition: Sákéj Henderson, First Nations Jurisprudence, and *Sui Generis* Solidarity. In *Shifting the Ground of Canadian Literary Studies* ed. Smaro Kamboureli and Robert Zacharias, 235-47. Waterloo: Wilfred Laurier University Press.

Ganong, William Francis ed. and trans. 1910. *New Relations of Gaspesia, With the Customs and Religion of the Gaspesian Indians*. Toronto: Champlain Society.

Henderson, James (Sa'ke'j) Youngblood and Jaime Battiste. 2013. How Aboriginal Philosophy Informs Aboriginal Rights. In *Philosophy and Aboriginal Rights* ed. Sandra Tomsons and Lorraine Meyer, 66-101. Toronto: Oxford University Press.

Le Clercq, Fr. Chrestien. 1691. *Nouvelle Relation de la Gaspésie, qui contient les Moeurs et la Religion des Sauvages Gaspésiens Porte-Croix, adorateurs du soleil, & d'autres peoples de l'Amerique Septentrionale, dite le Canada*. Paris: Amable Auroy.

McGoogan, Ken. 2010. *How the Scots Invented Canada*. Toronto: HarperCollins.

Paterson, Lindsay. 2015. George Davie and the Democratic Intellect. In *Scottish Philosophy in the Nineteenth and Twentieth Centuries* ed. Gordon Graham. Edinburgh: Edinburgh University Press.

Ricoeur, Paul. 2010. *Freud and Philosophy; An Essay in Interpretation.* Trans. Denis Savage. New Haven: Yale University Press.

Symonds, Richard. 1991. *Oxford and Empire: the Last Lost Cause.* Oxford: Clarendon Press.

Walia, Harsha. 2009. Really Harper, Canada has no history of colonialism? *The Dominion: News From the Grassroots.* 28 September, www.dominionpaper.ca/articles2943 (accessed October 1, 2009).

Marjorie Gould with Marie Battiste

"Teach from the Baskets": Lessons Learned in Life

The highlight of many of my trips to Cape Breton has always been found in visiting with my friends and relatives, now Elders in the community, who continue to give their guidance, love and gifts of story, both in theirs renewed and mine refreshed. Stories bind us as a people to our past and our present because through our language and our relations we continue to build with and upon each other, sharing our teachings and memories in what has become our oral tradition. They are perceived as the tall tree roots that Eskasoni Mi'kmaw Elder Murdena Marshall aptly noted are holding hands below the ground. Stories provide the nourishment for our imaginations as we participate in our Mi'kmaw humanity. Each storyteller has a style and a flow, a language and dialect that localizes one to a place, and grounds the flora, fauna, animals and people together in coherence and comprehensibility.

So when Marjorie (Marge) Gould and I decided to share our thoughts and stories together about the life and teachings of her mother Caroline Gould, we decided that the narrative we had was both a flow and an intertwining of our stories and memories that would govern our writing as well. Our focus was dear to both of us—Elder Caroline Gould, Marge's mother, and my mother's best friend, a woman whose talents and experiences reached far into Mi'kmaw humanity through her many experiences over her 94 years and her passion for basket making. She started off her life, like all Mi'kmaw women, being part of a family-based economy that required everyone's hands and hearts and creativity to make a living in times of scarcity which were many.

As a backdrop to why this was an important topic, we take the reader to a special meeting time in December 2010 when my research colleague Lynne Bell, a professor in art and art history, and I were visiting in the Maritimes. We had come to town to conduct our first dialogue with Mi'kmaw Elders and leaders on Mi'kmaw humanity. On this first day, we needed to make our rounds visiting, using the traditional "tea diplomacy" that is common to Mi'kmaw people's relationships. Our visits with Mi'kmaw Elders around Cape Breton was paramount to introducing my friend and guest at my home.

At the time of our visit, I had known that Auntie Caroline was sick with cancer, and while she was open to talking about it, without need for fear or pity, she viewed it like most elder Mi'kmaq as a fact of life, or her fact of her life. She was a self-determining woman and would continue to live each day like the last—fully and amply with family and friends around her. She was woman with so much love and affection for company that I knew that it would not be a problem to visit. If she was not in a visiting mood, we would know how to quietly come in and go out. We had initially wanted her to be part of our Elders dialogue at Cape Breton University where we were convening, but I knew that might be just too much for a 94-year old woman to sit in circle for two days. But she continued to give encouragement and advice when we asked for it, and I knew that if she were able, she would give us her time and much more. She was an exemplary model of how to live through to her last day, which occurred eleven months after our visit with her.

Marge noted on her last day of her mother's passing, that all her family and friends in true Mi'kmaw fashion stood around her, and as she took her last breath seemingly without struggle, it was a surprise to her that no one cried. It was like she taught them how to live and then how to die with dignity, with having given her all to her family and friends and then moved on. After her passing, the family needed time to heal and to readjust to life without their mother. So it was not until the summer of 2013, two and half years later that Marge and I met again and arranged to spend a full week talking about her mother. This time, Marge came to visit me in Saskatoon. This was to be a time together, a time to write this chapter, focusing on her mother's last wishes to us as researchers—to centre the baskets in our humanities project. What we needed to consider was what was it about her mother's teachings and her life that would have motivated her to urge us to centre the basket in the Mi'kmaw humanities? So inviting Marge to town to have a long talk about this without distractions was what was needed.

As our visit commenced, we sat for a day over tea and food, and quiet time discussing our family updates, relating events that occurred in earlier times and in between; then when that was done, we started our talk and naturally achieved a routine of work that worked for both of us. We would start our day with a typical large breakfast, and morning rituals of cleaning and gathering ourselves for our day's work, some preparation of our in-between-meals and getting the teapot going. Our morning chores ended and we started our conversations. Then we settled down with our fresh cup of tea and a computer that recorded our conversation.

We carried on like great old friends getting caught up on all kinds of news. Marge, however, like a true administrator, first wanted me to give her an overview of the project I had been part of and she wanted a full overview of what we were doing and where we were. I recounted the project of Animating the Mi'kmaw Humanities and its funding from the Social Science and Humanities Research Council of Canada and the processes we had since achieved, including the launch of the Mi'kmaw humanities website that honoured her mother as a stimulus for it. I had this arranged from afar with the help of my son, Jaime, who was the local organizer for the website launch. He had made sure she and her sisters were invited and each were given engraved plaques that acknowledged their mother's contributions to the project. She had been our inspiration when we left Cape Breton with that in our mind and hearts but there had been so much left unsaid.

My main goal at this time was to sort out Marge's mother's interest and focus on baskets, and the witness of her teachings and her style and what these teachings had revealed. I have to admit that I anticipated special teachings, deep in the basket making and the materials, and underlying stories that went with them. Yet I was surprised that, as I sought this out, Marge started with the actual basket making process and how she herself had helped her mother to carve out a lucrative basket-making course that had lasted several years. The class structure went well with Marge's own teaching experience and the management of students, sometimes as many as thirty people taking the three-day course. Having the right set of materials, one for each of the students, was the critical facet, because after her mother talked about the basket making story of the past, and how Mi'kmaq have made these baskets, and how her own life followed on the path of her parents and others in the community, she would have to get down to the business of finding the right materials and starting the bottom of the basket.

"Imagine," Marge said,

having thirty students and if you didn't have all their materials sorted out, they would be shuffling through the materials, looking for strips, not knowing that there was a specific kind of wood strip that was needed to be used for each of the different processes. There was one kind of strip with a specific width and thickness that was used for the bottom, and thinner strips for putting those strips together, then another width and thickness for the layering of the sides and top. There were at least four or five different strips for different purposes and each student had a bundle of ten strips in total. This would be havoc trying to educate students to this refined knowledge.

Marge laughed at the prospect of the chaos she imagined and continued.

So we put together a bundle for each student so that they each had all the kinds of strips needed, the right number for each level. They would be at first instructed to feel the strips. They had to get the feel for the thick ones and thin ones and in between. They then would know which ones were the thickest because those ones would go on the bottom.

The refined knowledge of basket making came from a long-nurtured history of learning, and Caroline's were much like other Mi'kmaq at the time. Mi'kmaq have been making baskets for hundreds of years and maybe more. For Caroline Gould, daughter of a well renowned basket maker, Michael L. (Louis) Paul, whose nicknames were well known in the country—"Mikel Dada" and "Janie Peck," was "Janie Kiju'" especially among her many grandchildren and the community. There was much knowledge she would gain from her parents that all would have to acquire over time.

Caroline was one of the ten children of "Mikel Dada" and "Janie Kiju'." Having lots of children was both a given for Mi'kmaw families, partly because they loved their children and thought having a child was a true gift from Creator, but also that birth control was not something practiced in these communities. Mikel Dada and Janie Kiju' and all their ten children were renowned for each having many gifts of their own beyond basket making. With a large family, providing for them required Mikel D. develop refined indigenous knowledges as a fisherman, a farmer and a basket maker. He was a good businessman as well, Marge noted, and knew many languages. Mi'kmaw was his home language, but he could easily move out beyond his community by train to sell his baskets in the surrounding areas where there was a large French population; he often went as far as the Gaspé peninsula where French was the core language. He spoke French well enough to do his business and he spoke English as well.

"Janie Peck" had a unique story, Marge added, although the story has many versions. Marge told hers. "Mom's mother was something else. She was a full-blooded white woman!" The unique part of her history was one that was not uncommon among the Mi'kmaq of the day. Many non-Mi'kmaq had become members of our communities over time, from being given away as an infant to Mi'kmaw families; or another was a story of being dropped off at our communities or pushed into boats to float to the reserve. I too recalled this practice talked over in my own family. I had heard of Mi'kmaq finding babies at their doorstep or in boats that drifted to shore knowing that Mi'kmaq frequented the waters every day. These children were then raised in Mi'kmaw families, learning to live in Mi'kma'ki and learning to speak Mi'kmaw—accepted fully into the families.

The Catholic Church was very influential in all church-going families, framing attitudes toward unwed mothers and their babies. Many families gave up their "unwanted" babies to the families on reserve where the children were raised. That seed of thought about unwanted babies was initially rejected by Mi'kmaq who accepted all children, although as Christian values were taught in schools, a growing number of Mi'kmaq began to hold these biases and prejudices as well, although few gave their children away. The shunning attitude developed by the church and surrounding white communities toward children went with the term "pata'l," meaning children from unwed mothers. The great and legendary Alex Denny, the Kji Keptin, Grand Captain, of the Mi'kmaw nation, was himself a pata'l and he spent all his adult years trying to change the attitudes that the church crept in with their Sunday teachings. Alex, himself, was raised not by his mother but by an Elder in the community who taught him to be proud of who he was and in particular to be not ashamed of his status as pata'l. I recall how when I first went to his family home, and watched over the years, as I was their neighbor, that he gave extra special treatment to children who came to his house who were also pata'l. They had special sandwiches, special places at the table, often he sung them a special song, and he kept a special place in his heart for them. All of this was to dispel the community attitude toward these children, so that when they were referred to as *pata'l*, the young person would smile delightedly with that fact. The special status given to children, instead of being a stigma, became a feeling of pride and joy and especially worthy in his home.

Marge shared a story of Janie Peck she had heard from her mother, of how Janie Kiju found her way into the Mi'kmaw community. Though inconsequential for the purposes here, baby Janie was given to the Peck family in Wagmatcook, near We'koqma'q. Little is known about that life she led with her parents, although Janie Peck from Wagmatcook, now a fluent Mi'kmaw-speaking woman met her husband-to-be at the St. Ann's mission at Chapel Island (Potlotek) and married him and moved to Barra Head, having a typical Mi'kmaw life, raising her family of ten children with her husband Mikel Dada. Mi'kmaw families with blonde hair, fair skin, and blue eyes became a common sight in Mi'kmaw communities over the years. They had absorbed these children into their communities and all learned Mi'kmaq as their primary languages and the ways and habits of those they lived with. Janie Peck was among those who were fully absorbed into the Mi'kmaw community. Marge relayed how this practice was common as she named several others who also had white parentage but had been raised Mi'kmaq.

Mikel Dada and Janie Kiju' lived in Barra Head, a special place that had been named the capital of the Mi'kmaw Nation in 1750, and the location of an annual St. Ann's Mission. This land was sacred to the people, for it was also the burial ground where Mi'kmaq brought their people—in their canoes—who had passed in the winter and by early spring they were buried on Chapel Island on blessed ground with all their other ancestors. So Caroline's parents lived, as everyone else, off the land and off the knowledge they held in their place. These skills were plentiful and their knowledge of their territory was immense.

Caroline met her own husband Lo'li (Roddie) Gould during the mission at Chapel Island. The St. Ann's Mission was an occasion for spiritual prayer and meditation, gathering of all families who set up their wikuoms, tents or shacks beside one another. This had been an on-going activity since 1750. In those social interactions where everyone met once a year across many Mi'kmaw communities in Mi'kma'ki, there were many who found their future spouses. Finding a partner was normal activity, and getting married right away was a normal activity. It is important to note that when the English colonists banned priests and missionaries from Nova Scotia in 1758, there were no priests living in Mi'kmaw communities or among the French for more than a hundred years. Mi'kmaq often petitioned the governor of Nova Scotia from that time onward that they wanted a priest at least one once a year to officiate the marriages of their youth and baptize their children. This then led to their allowing a priest for only this occasion, and it was well accepted that the French would also come to officiate their nuptials as well.

With a priest present, baptisms and marriage ceremonies were often conducted even when young people had just met each other at Chapel Island. Families knew each other and would be acknowledging who one married, knowing that it would be another year before they would be allowed to get married. That fact alone held many stories of how young people would meet and get married over a few days. Caroline and Lo'li had known each other for some time as they came from the same community, but they were married at Chapel Island. Lo'li, or Rodrick, Googoo was a man with well-honed carpenter skills, having been responsible for building his own family home in We'koqma'q.

As time went on, Loli and Caroline were greatly pleased to have five daughters: Ethel, Marjorie, Margaret, Eunice and Annie, but no boys. In 1943, at the height of the Centralization Policy, the federal government decided unilaterally to move all Mi'kmaq to centralized reserves. This came without much if any consultation with Mi'kmaw leadership, but came as a policy of convenience for the local white communities to move onto Mi'kmaw lands. After much family deliberation, Lo'li and Caroline decided to move their family to Eskasoni.

Centralization Policy was the government's initiative to move all the Mi'kmaw families to two centralized reserves in Nova Scotia, one in Eskasoni and the other in Shubenacadie. Centralization to reserves occurred throughout Canada, although each community had their own unique experience with government officials and negotiations for servicing in the new area. All families were required by government dictates to move to these centralized locations although, like many such policies, it took more than a dictate to move the people—many other government policies were enacted to achieve this end. Marge recalled her mother's stories about the government closing the school and burning down the church to ensure families did not return. A few families refused to leave, even though they were left with no services by the government. In order to expand the lands in the central reserves, the government bought out some of the houses in neighbouring non-Native communities as was done for Eskasoni. Several large farmhouses were then made available. Caroline and Lo'li moved into one of these farmhouses, although they had to share the house with two other families until their own house was built. As a house contractor himself, Marge noted that this assured Lo'li a house more quickly and they did not stay too long in the cramped quarters.

Mi'kmaq were to be moved to the shores of Eskasoni, a tract of land that had 15 km of seashore and had several Mi'kmaw families already living there on large tracts of land, which were divided up to make room for other incoming Mi'kmaq. Eskasoni was a beautiful site on Bras d'Or Lake behind a mountain and large tracts of forest that needed to be cleared. The land was not well suited for farming, however, as the soil was very rocky. As a carpenter in Eskasoni, Lo'li had no end of work in the growing community. He first completed his own house then began to work on the homes of other families.

I recall my own mother, Annie Battiste, talking about how she and my dad moved from Barra Head to Eskasoni, having to move in with her cousin in a two-bedroom house with their children. My father worked in the mill cutting lumber for the houses, and my mother looked after the children and made baskets on the side to support them. Their combined incomes was not enough to cover the costs of living of a growing family and soon their borrowing from the government subsidy store got them so far behind that my dad decided to go to work in Maine to pay off the bill. My mother was adamant that she was not going to be left behind and so she packed up her needed goods and went by car with her husband taking her new born daughter Geraldine and her toddler son Thomas. My sister Eleanor was of school age by then, and her sisters-in-laws convinced her that they should take Eleanor to the Indian Residential School where she would be given food, clothing and lodging and would be cared for by the nuns while she also got her Christian education. Since neither had gone to the residential school, they were convinced this would be a good idea until they could get a place near a school and come get her. She would remain there for three years before joining the family in Houlton, Maine. My parents never returned to Eskasoni, but rather eventually made their way to Boston and then, twenty-three years later, they made their way back to their homeland of Barra Head, now renamed Potlotek.

Marge and I hopped around many topics as we sowed the stories of the basket-making economies of our families. Caroline's workshops also began with her stories shared with her students of how she came into this art and craft. As the ten hours of basket making workshop progressed over three days, Marge and one of Caroline's adopted sons, Bernie Francis, was called upon to help teach the Mi'kmaw language with her. Bernie was a well-known fluent Mi'kmaw speaker whose interest and passion in Mi'kmaw language earned him a role in working with a linguist by the name of Doug Smith and together they constructed a revised Mi'kmaw orthography which earned him an honorary doctorate. Mi'kmaw language was an important part of the workshop and all the tools, the materials, the wood types were important to know, how they were used and where they could be obtained. Bernie thus helped Caroline sort out all the names and spelling for each of the tools and teachings.

Baskets were made of many different kinds of wood. *Wiskoq* is black ash. *Aqamo'k* is white ash, which made strips called *kmu'ji'japi*. *Miti* is poplar, but the least desired wood as Marge recalled, because when it dried, it would snap like a matchstick. So finding the right wood was important, though not often easy. Marge relayed that during her mother's time, there was a lot of clear cutting of the trees in Cape Breton and getting the right wood became harder and harder to get as time went on. Paper mills and the wood mills were being set up around their area—wood was being sought and processed, some for paper and some for furniture or lumber for houses. It was a huge market and every man could find some work in the woods, cutting down trees and hauling them out of the woods for the lumber company, but the work was hard and low paying. Mi'kmaq were also well aware that part of their livelihood in the basket industry was being radically altered by the clear cutting of their forests. For many, it required that they look elsewhere for their wood, having to travel to mainland Nova Scotia, New Brunswick and Maine for the wood to make baskets.

Basket making was in mass production for a time, to serve farmers, and while there were women who became known for their dyeing of their basket strips and making what were called "fancy" baskets, basket making largely was a rough production of black ash baskets. These *wisqoq* baskets were rough wood that needed to be shaved well to get a smooth finish and this required a lot of work, largely done by the women. The sturdy *wisqoq* baskets that could withstand lots of handling were lucrative to farmers and it was often easy to sell off large lots of black ash baskets to farmers for the potato harvesting each year in Prince Edward Island, New Brunswick and Maine. These baskets were light, solid and hardy because Mi'kmaq made them with this in mind. Mi'kmaw baskets were treasured items for the farmers and every potato farmer had to have many hundreds of these for the harvesting of their potatoes. The cost for the lot was typically low, but for Mi'kmaw families with little money, and fewer skills in the white business world, including limited English, this business was vital to their survival on the land and a needed addition to the low government subsidies paid out as welfare.

Getting wood from the forest was a laborious task as well, finding the wood, knowing just which one was best, not too dry and not too knotty. This was an art that my own father and mother's brother uncle Mattie Lewis had achieved over time. My dad or Uncle Mattie could spot a tree a long distance away or know how to follow certain marshy area to find the right tree. Uncle Mattie often would make "v" notches on the tree and chew on the chip to determine if it had the right amount of moisture in it to peel or split well. They knew that only 54 inches of the maple was all that was good. This embodied knowledge came with practice and repetition and practice. So it was important to not just own this knowledge but to share it as well, which was part of every family undertaking when young boys were apprenticed in the woods to teach them how to choose trees and help with bringing the logs out as well. So having large families was an asset.

The Mi'kmaw family was first and foremost the central foundation for Mi'kmaw society. The extended family were teachers, the first schoolhouse, Marge recounted. As a mother, your children were not your own. Everyone had a responsibility to help raise the children and teach them all the knowledge one had, whether it was making bread or learning how to get wood from the forest. *"Mu keskelmu' kijun,"* Marge noted in Mi'kmaq. You were not stingy with your children. They were shared among the families, and in so doing, each learned from their aunties and their uncles the skills for living productively in the families and in their communities. Uncle Lo'li and Aunt Caroline could depend on their brothers and sisters to share their children, boys and girls in all kinds of activities from which learning was shared.

My own mother often related her living in Barra Head and having to be sent regularly by her mother to help her uncle Simon and his frequently pregnant wife Annie (Anji'j). There were lots of children in the house and Anji'j liked to chew tobacco and spit into the front of the potbelly stove. Often she missed and so the chew would splatter all over the front of the stove and across the floor, resulting in the floor being a dark black wood. These were rough wood floors, my mom Annie would tell me, and because she was named after this woman and the only girl in her family, she would be sent to help Aunt Anji'j clean house. My mother recalled having to get down on her hands and knees with a pail of soapy water and a scrubbing brush getting the wood floor clean again. This was hard work that she had to do often to help out this relative who fed her and sometimes sent her home with some bread or treats.

Family was important. Marge and her own four sisters were neighbours with her uncle and his wife who had five boys. Her parents often shared the needs for girls and they in turned shared their boys and all lived as one family, giving and getting what one needed to flourish. So food was an important element to give. No pot was too small for the people it fed and at every meal there were extra potatoes put in for the visitors. A saying Marge remembered was when her grandfather Mikel Dada would say to his wife in Mi'kmaw, "Don't forget the potato for Gabriel." Gabriel was a man who went house to house and, coincidentally, often at mealtimes. Marge relayed how her mother's cooking reflected that pattern while she was growing up and how having enough to feed any and all visitors who regularly come was a custom and tradition that she came to accept as norm. These always led to stories, laughter and good times because family and relationships were the core values of Mi'kmaq.

The community also helped in raising children. Teasing, laughing at people, and reminding them of transgressions through humour were ways to ensure proper behaviour. Everyone was a mentor and watched over each other. Nothing was hidden and everyone knew what was going on. Marge's male cousins would warn Marge and her sisters who to go out with and who to avoid, because they too talked among themselves about their behaviour. The brothers let their sisters know which boy was best to go out with and whom they should stay away from.

Caroline and Lo'li had a rich life filled with their five daughters and a supportive community always around them, and life skills drawn from their daily lives. But there were difficult times ahead. Caroline got tuberculosis and was sent to a sanatorium near Halifax. Her girls, including Marge, were sent to the Indian Residential School in Shubenacadie. Being there starting at the age of ten, she recalled little about the school experience but the girls were together while their mother was at the sanatorium. None of them had much English, and this experience afforded Marge, her sisters, and also her mother with more experience in English for the two years that they were apart, a skill they carried throughout their lives.

After the first year in the sanatorium, Caroline got some strength, but it was thought she was too weak to care for their daughters and they were kept in Shubenacadie Indian Residential School for yet another year. When they returned home, Marge finished elementary school in Eskasoni. There was no high school in the community, so she and her sisters went to a boarding school in Arichat staffed by nuns and finished at another boarding in Mabou to complete grade 11. This boarding school experience was much different from the Indian Residential Schools as these were for all students in Nova Scotia, in particular for those who had funds for a private school. They all were well treated overall by the nuns and she and her sisters had some memorable experiences. Their learning experience was enriched by meeting many new friends from all over Nova Scotia that enriched their learning of English that smoothed the way for her as she went on to St. Francis Xavier University. She would become the first Mi'kmaq to graduate from St. FX and later became among the first to receive her Master's degree from the University of Maine.

Caroline's husband's Lo'li had received a good grounding from his parents Joe and Annie Gould in many areas of his life in We'koqma'q. Eventually this homeland would call Lo'li back, although it would take several other moves to get there. When Lo'li married Caroline, he brought his bride (and her mother) back to We'koqma'q until Caroline felt at ease there, and then her mother returned to Barra Head. They set up a small canteen store, which Caroline managed, keeping the business running smoothly. Those business skills helped them when they moved to Eskasoni, where they built another store that she managed. Lo'li was again feeling the pull of his home community and when an opportunity arose for him to trade houses with a family in

We'koqma'q who wanted to live in Eskasoni, he and Caroline gave up their hand built house and moved to We'koqma'q yet again to continue to raise their family. There they set up yet another store that Caroline managed which eventually turned into a basket co-op. While Caroline could make baskets, having learned and practiced this skill as a youth and throughout her growing-up years, the basket making did not become an art form until many years later.

As she got older and the business was consuming too much energy, her family urged her to give up the store. The family reasoned to their mother that there were no longer any children at home, all the girls had found their lives elsewhere, some with families in other reserves and she should now take this time to rest and relax they reasoned. Marge herself had gone off to school to become a teacher and, later, to get her Master's degree. So Auntie Caroline gave up the store and instead of relishing the serene retired life promised her, she fell into a reflexive and sometimes bad mood. Her husband had his hobbies and was always busy. Marge was away too at school either as a teacher or principal or education director and her sisters were gone, except for their occasional visits with their families. There were community projects that Caroline busied herself with, especially with the church and she was especially helpful with organizing the bus trips of community members to St. Ann de Beaupre in Québec. She always did these, regardless if she worked or not.

One day she finally let it all out. Everyone had something to do but her. So Marge, with her counselling skills, asked her mother what she would like to do. Marge felt she needed a hobby. Well, she pondered, she liked making quilts. Marge was far more realistic however and shared with her that this hobby was nice, but few people needed quilts any more like in the past. Now with central heating, quilts were not needed as much. Considering this, she then decided that she would like to work on making baskets, something she liked to do. But this time it was not the huge lot of rough baskets of the past that she pumped out in great numbers, her skills were put to making the best basket she could, taking time and patience on each one, refining her skill so much so as to be named eventually the best basket maker among Mi'kmaq.

Marge recalls how her mother would make a basket and ask her family for honest comments on how she could make it better. Could the bottom sit more secure, could the top be fit better, were there some ways she could make the weaves look less common? So as the weeks went by, she experimented and refined her strip shavings, made different kinds of styles of fancy baskets, colored her strips and added many different kinds of embellishments on the basket, twisting the strips into what were traditionally called *jikiji'jk*. She got materials from various sources, but found the best were from a Mi'kmaw man in Québec.

Gabriel Joe, a welder, a great Mi'kmaw storyteller and a crafty person himself, discovered how to use his welding skills to make a machine that would pound the black ash without the labour of the axe used when done by hand. So he began selling the now easily pounded strips to those who needed them and he sent bundles on the bus to Caroline in We'koqma'q. These treasured materials then were the main source for Caroline to make her little works of art. There was demand for these baskets.

I remember Gabriel, whose nickname was Ko'ti, who visited families as he made his way in his welding work to many communities. He was famous for his storytelling and grand sense of humour. To this day, I recall him sitting at the table, telling stories about the missionaries and how they came to learn Mi'kmaw, but always imperfectly. The stories of how the missionaries misunderstood people and the advice they gave to Mi'kmaq in the confessional were the best and we would howl with laughter, tears rolling down our faces, imagining these scenarios and the people's reactions.

When a person died in the community or surrounding reserves, Caroline would often go to the funeral and put one of her baskets into the charity auction that we called *salite'*. These occur after the funeral mass when the community came together to share a meal with people who had travelled long distances to be with the local folk to share their grief and their stories. Each person would bring their household goods or whatever they wished to enter into the charity auction and all proceeds at the end of the auction would be added up and given to the closest family members of the deceased to pay for the costs of the funeral beyond the small amount that the federal government paid for the casket. Marge recounted how her mother, Caroline, would always bring a basket or make one special for the auction. Over time her baskets became the prize sellers at these auctions. Everyone wanted a "Caroline Gould" basket. Many baskets looked alike and other people put in their baskets as well, and if anyone knew who the basket maker was, it would raise the price of the piece in the auction—some going as high as $1,000 or more. I have several baskets from many older basket makers, including Caroline, by this means.

Marge told the story of a time at one of these auctions when a small well-built basket was being sold at the auction and it was going slow—$20, $25, $30, etc.—until Marge wrote a note to the auctioneer to tell people this basket was made by Della McGuire, a Mi'kmaq from Hantsport and a student of Caroline Gould. The auctioneer read the note to the assembled and immediately the basket shot up to the hundreds and kept on going, selling for more than $400. Her students thereafter could be easily identified, and Della's daughter Malglit (Margaret), Marge intimated, "became the artist who surpassed the teacher!" Marge's niece Ursula Johnson is another artist, a Mi'kmaw storyteller now performance artist, who had since a child often sat at her grandmother Caroline's table watching her make baskets and learning from her. She even made the basket the subject of her Master's thesis at the Nova Scotia College of Art and Design. Her unique performances told the story of basket making and shared the emotional impacts of colonization, neocolonization, capitalism and its effects on Mi'kmaq and their basket making.

So Caroline Gould was the paramount Elder basket maker. It wasn't politics exactly but rather it was a relationship that led to her receiving the honour to be selected to make a special basket gift for Queen Elizabeth II at the occasion of the 400-year celebration of the baptism of Grand Chief Membertou in Halifax. As the Mi'kmaw chiefs began to plan for this event with their ceremonies, they were asked to have a special meeting with the provincial members of the legislative assembly, a rare occasion. Caroline's nephew George Paul was the communications officer who, when the topic of gifts to give as protocol, suggested to the MLAs that they contract Caroline Gould to make the 75 baskets.

So when the prospect of having the Queen come to meet Mi'kmaw chiefs and Elders at the gathering in 2010—the 400-year anniversary of the Mi'kmaq entering into relations with Europeans through their political alliance sealed with their baptism—the gift to give the queen could be no other than a basket made by Caroline Gould. George, her nephew, called her to ask her to do this for the chiefs and she took it on with the greatest of delight.

Caroline began thinking about this basket, making drawings and sharing thoughts about the basket with her own artist in her family ... her daughter Malglit. What would be best to give and how could it be made more exquisite? She considered at first colouring strips but dismissed it as this needed to last a long time and colour strips did tend to fade. They considered that many would see it, and so it was to be a very special type, a different yet common to the style of Mi'kmaq but very special. The basket then was finally conceived and she began the process of finding the needed wood to make the strips. The strips could not be common either. They had to be made from white ash, which was hard to get. She talked to the Mi'kmaw people in Listigutj, Québec, about this and with their help she received the rarest and whitest ash strips. Then she worked on the parts, shaving them to perfection, and then began the process of crafting the basket in the manner of her parents and their parents and their parents before them. The basket evolved into a magnificent masterpiece with each detail more exquisite than any other. Marge relayed that the master let her daughter, the artist that surpassed the teacher, put some detailing on the edging of the basket that looked like lace. "Oh my God," Marge punctuated her thoughts. "The basket was beautiful!"

She received the contract and began to make these baskets called *kloqowe'ji'j*, or star baskets. They also became the object of her passion for the weeks that followed. She was on task each day, morning till night and as people came to visit her, they too became involved to the level of their skills. The community learned of her work and they pitched in, each providing some level of support to her work. I recall myself going to visit her at the time and the countdown was at fifty-seven baskets. She saw the light at the end of the tunnel, but there was still more to do. So while we told stories and visited and drank tea, she would make her basket. Eventually she achieved the order on time and, as her final tribute, she made one last basket, a much larger one for the Premier of Nova Scotia. The baskets were very well received and the chiefs and the MLAs sent their deep appreciation to Auntie Caroline for the exquisite baskets and all the work she had done.

So how was she going to look giving this basket to the queen? Well, the community got involved and the prize regalia experts in the community made Caroline a leather dress, beaded in the front, top and bottom in roses. She then had a photo taken in the dress with her basket. This picture, she proudly showed us when we visited her in late 2010. She was so proud and now she was ready to meet the Queen.

And meet the Queen Elizabeth and Prince of Wales she did, at the Halifax celebration where the Queen on a windy rainy day in Halifax took her walking tour through the Mi'kmaw village erected for that purpose in a Halifax park. The Queen was wearing a yellow jacket whose collar and cuffs had been sent to the Mi'kmaq to be beaded with Mi'kmaw curve designs by the women who made Auntie Caroline's dress. She also wore a raincoat poncho that showed off her cuffs, which delighted all who saw the photographs of her tour. It was a celebration like no other with a *mawio'mi*, a powwow, in a Halifax park and a concert with Buffy St. Marie and Shane Yellowbird. The crowds were huge and we were all so impressed!

So what teachings did the baskets serve? As Marge and I considered our many conversations, we realized that the basket is about the actualization of our deeply embodied knowledge as part of our daily lives, as story and art and history and language and values and teachings. Our relations are expressed in the performance of our being Mi'kmaq, in the ancient skills of our ancestors and in the new skills of our relatives and friends who keep and maintain traditions, customs and values. As process, the basket taught our children the preservation of our traditions and values, our economy and our survival, although not everyone will take it up today as skills of their own. To the extent that it is appreciated and serves a purpose today, it finds value and currency in our charity auctions, in our constant buying of baskets from the artists who are still around making them and sharing the skills with their children. It will serve as symbols of our past and present and hopefully our future.

An Anishenabe writer Heid Erdrich (2013) asked: "What helps us to know a place? Landmarks. And what helps us to know a people? The marks/signs they leave and we find" (14). In almost every home in Cape Breton and among the MLAs, the former Premier, and the Queen of England will be baskets made by Caroline Gould. They will tell her story and that of her family, past, present and future, and the work of the Mi'kmaq, their deep connection to their place and to their land. They will represent a deep long history in Atlantic Canada called Mi'kma'ki, it will show their exquisite artistry, and how it arises from the knowledge deeply embedded in their language and their knowledge of their land. It will demonstrate their love for their children, their relationships, their hard work and economies thwarted away by colonization, Indian Residential Schools, government paternalism, clear cutting, racism and poverty. For dignity, self respect, determination, focused activity, caring for the community, the church, the Elders and the traditions, Caroline Gould will be long remembered in the values and beliefs she was raised in and how lived a long life to teach so many others, both Mi'kmaq and non-Mi'kmaq. She was not stingy with her children, or her food, her baskets, her teachings, her language or her culture. She taught us that it was important to retain Mi'kmaw humanity.

Toward the latter years of her life, she did not want to go anymore to the local community school to do the show and tell with her baskets. She wanted serious basket enthusiasts who would learn from her and carry on the art. She was making sure that the basket craft and industry continued. Baskets had once created an economic system that worked for Mi'kmaq in the years before they entered into the Canadian economy—it continues to work for some. It is a distributive economy of building skills, males and females having different knowledges. It is important to share it with youth whose creative inner spirit might be sparked, or by young women who need to build some skills that they can do at home while they care for their own children.

While there are many who lament that the art of making baskets is fading with the loss of great artists like Caroline Gould, she did not live her nearly ninety-two years without a purpose. In fact, she had many purposes, which only she could evaluate how they turned out. What we know is that she centred the baskets and the baskets centred her. It was a reciprocal relationship that she grew into with a passion that fed her learning spirit and one that will continue to feed us as Mi'kmaq in more ways than a simple story can tell. Baskets still remain the one Mi'kmaw activity with deep roots in many peoples' lives which help us to understand our Mi'kmaw humanity as continuing to draw on our creative ingenuity and deep roots.

References

Erdrich, Heid E. 2013. Original Local: Indigenous Foods, Stories, and Recipes from the Upper Midwest. St. Paul, MN: Minnesota Historical Society Press.

Isobel M. Findlay

Weaving the Interdisciplinary Basket: Building Resilient and Knowledgeable Communities and Economies

When Mi'kmaw Elder, educator and basket maker Caroline Gould instructed our Animating the Mi'kmaq Humanities research team that teaching the Mi'kmaw humanities meant "teaching the baskets," it had each of us pondering what that might mean in our own disciplinary and institutional contexts. In my own case, it caused me to revisit my own personal and intellectual journey and reflect on what I have learned in working on cross-cultural, cross-disciplinary, trans-systemic projects over the last twenty years and in support of the Mi'kmaw humanities in particular over the last four and more years. This chapter is about what that learning means for reimagining the conceptual economies of our (inter)disciplines and our ability to enhance social, cultural, economic and ecological well-being in Canada and beyond.

In particular, I aim to rethink and reframe relations between the humanities and social sciences, between the sociocultural and the economic domains, how they have been conceived and with what consequences for whose activities and wellbeing. I reconsider inherited narratives about *homo economicus:* economic modernity, partial stories of the history of the economy, including the social economy, to recognize a much longer and largely unheralded story of traditions living in, and as, livelihoods that have sustained Mi'kmaq for generations—a story that we need more than ever in the current economic and ecological crisis.

Out of the Heart of Eurocentrism

When I came as a Scots-born and educated woman to Canada in the 1970s to begin my graduate career, I was deeply immersed in the Eurocentric humanities, having completed a degree in English language and literature at the University of Aberdeen, continuing a tradition embodied by David Hume and Adam Smith to beat the English at their own game. Yet I was already uneasy with the dominant narratives and value systems of the traditional humanities that marginalized and discounted the language and knowledges that I represented as a Scots woman. At no point in my earlier schooling, for example, had I been allowed, far less encouraged, to use the Scots language even in creative writing projects supposedly focused on my own experience. Scottish education policy drove home the inferiority of Scots as "not the language of 'educated' people anywhere, and ... not ... a suitable medium of education or culture" (Scottish Education 1946: 75) until a renaissance too late for my own education put Scots in the curriculum. Now Scots is seen as a rich resource giving access to "Scotland's vibrant literary and linguistic heritage and its indigenous languages and dialects" (Education Scotland 2016). And gender was a construct lived daily but beyond the educational ken. Nor did we study Scots language or literature except for the annual token representation of Robert Burns on the occasion of the birthday of the national poet (January 25, 1759). University offered some advance with opportunity to study Middle Scots language and literature (though hardly equivalent in class time to the study of Anglo-Saxon and Middle English) and to choose to write a special paper on Scots literature as part of the thirty hours of final exams at the end of my fourth year. And with the striking exceptions of Jane Austen and the Brontës, most of the literature I studied was overwhelming masculinist.

The uneasiness I felt led me—without ever being able to articulate why—to go on to write about authority and dissent, accounting and accountability, social justice and social cohesion. I probed connections between knowledge production and identity formation, to reflect on those who write and those who get written about or to consider censorship and constraint and resistance and struggle for legitimacy in writing a Master's thesis on English writer D. H. Lawrence whose writing had struck a chord with me when I read him as a teenager. I needed to understand why his work mattered to me when he was so widely characterized as misogynist, sexist, racist, pornographic and fascist. What was I experiencing and why did others not see or feel what I did? His railing against dehumanizing, industrializing modernity was famously misrepresented and censored (in the case of *Lady Chatterley's Lover*) until 1960 when prosecution of Penguin Books under the *Obscene Publication Act* resulted in a not guilty verdict. Lawrence's situated, self-aware style could hardly be more different from the "detached impersonality" favoured by high modernist T. S. Eliot who disdained Lawrence's "sexual morbidity," spiritual sickness, heresy and uneducated self-importance (Findlay 1995). Often accused of advocating "perpetual sex," Lawrence responded that he aimed for an "adjustment in consciousness" so that people learn to "speak out to one another," revalue the body and intimacy and avoid the will to power that denies people's Otherness (Findlay 1995). In the process of rereading Lawrence and the critical legacy, I came to understand something about the politics of language and the literary canon, the enabling fiction of studied neutrality that masks interests while omitting difference. I learned about the partiality of all texts (as well as their selective reading) and othering strategies to magnify, minimize or marginalize threats to the status quo—and their implications for the terms we live by: nation, class, gender and ethnicity.

I followed my Master's with an interdisciplinary PhD on Chartism, the working-class movement that arose in response to 19th-century industrialization and the twin evils of internal and external colonization (Findlay 1997). I needed to understand how a movement could have such an impact on democratic process that we now take for granted, while being disdained as a minor historical footnote unworthy of serious attention. The Chartists[1] aimed to remedy major obstacles to political rights, social, economic and democratic participation, in crafting the six points of the charter (only one of which, annual elections, was not achieved):

- All men to have the vote (universal manhood suffrage)
- Voting should take place by secret ballot
- Parliamentary elections every year, not once every five years
- Constituencies should be of equal size
- Members of Parliament should be paid
- The property qualification for a Member of Parliament should be abolished

My dissertation explores how, under industrializing conditions, relations among economy, society and culture were reconfigured to give priority to the economy, new social movements formed (Chartism, labour, women, co-operatives) and new business models emerged despite legal constraints on the communication of such social activities. It explores how these socioeconomic, political and cultural processes were understood and communicated by actors central to the processes and those professional experts (in the emergent social sciences) monitoring and measuring social change—and with what consequences for the institutions (including academic, economic and legal ones) we have inherited. Studying these developments highlighted communication's role in producing and reproducing identities and institutions, privilege or disadvantage, professional contests for authority and legitimacy, the disembedding of the economic from the socio-cultural domain with ongoing implications for communities, including scholarly ones.

That dissertation took me from humanities to social science theory and practice (and their deep embeddedness in Eurocentrism) and to rethinking what I thought I knew. In writing those graduate theses, I came to understand something about democratic freedoms and academic freedom—and whose values they represent. I came to understand something about academic overinvestment in objectivity and disinterest and the attendant tendency to discount, not promote and value, difference—the diversity of thinking on complex matters, the diversity of interests people represent and seek to advance, the diversity so crucial to a multicultural society and its democratic institutions. In an increasingly scientific and statistical culture, the surveillance of urban poor—and the construction of "problems" of poverty, women and the so-called Condition of England of growing inequality)—engendered professional classes whose social commentary appeared neutral and authoritative, while constituting people's sense of themselves and fostering a dependence discursively produced and economically enforced (Findlay 1997). And I remembered the warning of Fanon about "Disinterested expertise [repeating] colonialism's 'perverse logic' that 'distorts, disfigures, and destroys' the past of oppressed peoples" (qtd. in Lawrence 2002: 21). Disinterestedness and objectivity continue to be part of the university's self-branding—even self-delusion.

But these academic claims have histories that must be recovered and redeployed if we are to effectively resist the imperious self-interest of colonial powers and their legitimizing disciplines and institutions. My work on diversity and integrity, pluralism and engagement, continues to explore how communication is understood, valued or undervalued (especially by positivist disciplines in law and business), what knowledge counts and why, what performance indicators and evidentiary standards apply, and with what consequences for identities. The composition of "we" and "us" can never be presumed, but communities, including academic communities, can be nourished and empowered in discursive space beyond disciplinary dialects and (life)styles of disinterest, autonomy and independence.

Learning with and from Indigenous Scholars

It was only as I was completing my dissertation that I came to a critical stage in my learning. Working with and learning from indigenous scholars and educators, especially Marie Battiste and Sa'ke'j Henderson, I learned a language and developed a set of sociocultural and conceptual frameworks that allowed me to name what I had experienced growing up in Scotland and to recognize the even more violent effects of colonialism in Canada and elsewhere. I remain deeply grateful for the opportunities to learn from these two powerful teachers. If Gramsci (1971) is clear that hegemonic relationships are educational ones, Marie's (Battiste 2000; 2013) decolonizing education efforts to renew the learning spirit brought home the fundamental violence of colonial education. While working together for two years on a book on Aboriginal tenure in the constitution of Canada (Henderson et al. 2000), Sa'ke'j's patient teaching similarly drew me into the world of indigenous law and justice and helped me see how I could use that learning together with my cultural training to unpack the biases and predispositions of the law and the broader culture. The experience of the 1996 International Summer Institute on the Cultural Restoration of Oppressed Indigenous Peoples (Battiste 2000) added to my learning by introducing me to many more influential indigenous thinkers (Linda Tuhiwai Smith and Graham Hingangaroa Smith, Linda Hogan, Leroy Littlebear and Gregory Cajete, to name just a few). Cumulatively, that learning taught me to argue against the inevitability of cultural and other divides and to elaborate new modes of accounting and new communities of resistance and respect displacing colonial categories and re-mediating justice in writing and teaching about community economic development and law and culture.

Groups exercise enormous social power by controlling the discursive practices and perceptual lenses through which realities are understood (Bourdieu 1984). I became interested in the formal and informal shaping of public discourse in contemporary Canada and the consequences for public policy, economic participation and the administration of justice. The September 17, 1999, *R. v. Marshall* decision and the Supreme Court's unanimous November 17 "clarification" of its divided decision proved an important site for considering kinds of coercion, of whom and what, and in the interests of what kind of "clarification." *Marshall* demonstrates how permeable the boundaries between law and public discourse continue to be, and how, as a result, a select group of mainstream academic experts and media pundits can define and re-define issues so as to exercise undue influence on public policy, the administration of justice and community capacities to exercise their Aboriginal and treaty rights. A careful reading of *Marshall* and its public circulation and spinning reveals how "facts" are understood or remade, how accounts are framed, whose accounts are granted authority, where accountability is assigned, whose rights are protected or infringed and whose injuries or offenses are visible. Most importantly, the Marshall decision clarifies the priorities and privileges of legal argument (preconstructed as adversarial and hence as pitting Aboriginal against non-Aboriginal argument and authority) and the modest financial means of First Nations against the deep pockets of the neocolonial Canadian state. The decision also underscores the importance of "equitable access" to media and academic authority as much as to natural resources in nourishing a pluralistic Canadian future that will promise and deliver respect for diversity and postcolonial justice.

The challenge of intercultural understanding, of effective communication across difference, lies at the heart of current efforts in Canada to rethink the tests and evidentiary standards of colonial legal rationality. To that end, the Supreme Court acknowledges, in its 1996 *Van der Peet* decision, the failure of "liberal enlightenment" thinking to respect Aboriginal rights "recognized and affirmed" in the *Constitution Act, 1982*, and the Court's 1997 *Delgamuukw* decision urges an intercultural vantage respecting equally oral and written evidence. Still, in these and the *Marshall* decisions the Court fails to live up to the challenge of sharing what Mohawk lawyer, educator and activist Monture-Angus (1999) calls the "definitional power" (43) so as to avoid reinscribing old habits of merging, submerging, subordinating different legal, economic and cultural traditions. This failure, despite the *R. v. Badger* (1996) ruling that the honour of the Crown was at stake in treaty interpretation, and that *flexible* interpretation of ambiguity should therefore favour Aboriginal parties (*R. v. Sparrow* [1990] affirming *Nowegijick v. The Queen* [1983] at 36: "treaties and statutes relating to Indians should be liberally construed and doubtful expression resolved in favour of the Indians.")

When a divided Court reversed (Gonthier and McLachlin JJ, dissenting) the trial court and Nova Scotia Court of Appeal and recognized the Mi'kmaw treaty right to fish and trade and make a "moderate livelihood," and hence Donald Marshall Jr.'s right to catch and sell 463 pounds of eels for $787.10, the Court (like the dissent) did so by focusing rather narrowly on the English text of the treaty which departs from intentions and agreements registered by Mi'kmaw chiefs and Governor Lawrence of Nova Scotia (Barsh and Henderson 1999: 3).

Yet the decision occasioned virulent backlash among the media, the public and even the federal government. *Marshall* both affirmed and "broadened" (Barsh and Henderson 1999: 1) the 1985 *Simon v. The Queen* (which ruled that the 1752 treaty with the Mi'kmaw nation remained in force and placed the burden of proof for extinguishment of treaty hunting and fishing rights on the Crown) so that *Marshall* determines the Mi'kmaw right to fish for a "moderate livelihood" within their territory without external regulation, provided they do not endanger stock survival. If the widespread outrage at "**special** rights" or "**extended** rights **given** to Natives" "undermin[ing] the whole principle of property in Canada" (Warren; qtd. in Rotman 2000: 627) or signifying "the death knell for the east coast fishery" (628) seems disproportionate to the recognition of **existing** treaty rights assuring something like legislated poverty for Aboriginal peoples, it is a response undeniably revealing of the complexities and contradictions of Canadian multicultural realities and the communications circuits unevenly available to Canadians today.

Battiste's 2016 *Living Treaties: Narrating Mi'kmaw Treaty Relations* is an important and timely contribution in this regard, using the archives and teachings of the ancestors as "a form of counter-memory of the nationhood and treaty relationships that had been suppressed, ignored or edited out of Canadian law and history" (Henderson 2016: 106). Despite the worst efforts of the *Indian Act* and other colonial impositions, the treaties have remained alive in the hearts, minds and daily practices of Mi'kmaw people living their treaty relations and respect for *m'set nogemaq* (in the orthography traditional to Elsipuktuk), or "all my relations," an ethic of generosity and inclusive understanding of obligations to Creation and to relationships with communities and nations indigenous and non-indigenous (Augustine 2016: 62). Similarly, Metallic (2016) attests, in his Listuguj orthography, to "*ta'n tett tleyawultieg*—how we truly belong to this territory" (43) and related responsibilities to the sustaining land and waters, to share, to give thanks and to respect All my relations.

Yet, as much as I thought I had learned from what Battiste calls "cognitive imperialism" (2000: xvi) and the "process of systematic fragmentation" at the heart of imperialism's dominating universals (Smith 1999: 28), I still had much to learn on the road to "cognitive justice" (De Sousa Santos et al. 2007). When I was first asked to speak in public in my indigenous language (at a 2001 Aboriginal Education Symposium at the Banff Centre), the full horror of internalized colonialism and my own complicity hit me. I realized that I had never spoken Scots in public and that I had thoroughly internalized the value system that promoted the English language while marginalizing and reducing to the status of dialect the Scots language that was at the heart of my family and friendship relationships. That was another important step in a deeply personal, sociocultural and intellectual lifelong learning journey informing this chapter's double strategy. Demystifying and displacing colonial residues, while respecting and learning from Mi'kmaw researchers, world views, values and measures (Battiste and Henderson 2000), aims to do some justice to "*rewriting* and *rerighting*" (Smith 1999: 28) relationships in a postcolonial Canada worthy of the name.

"You cannot be the doctor if you are the disease" (Daes 2000: 4). Without the assistance and authority of the colonized other, as *Marshall* and other decisions show, decolonization stops paternalistically short of a more plenary, healing sociocultural and legal hermeneutics. The collaborative, crosscultural and cross-disciplinary practices of the indigenous humanities theorized and implemented by our team at the University of Saskatchewan developed as a necessary corrective to past paternalism and resurgent neocolonialism (Battiste et al. 2006: 2013; Findlay 2003). The extended, self-critical and revitalized humanities are dedicated to justice and public re-education, to rebuilding institutions and disciplines and to displacing Eurocentric singularities and nominal universals that denied and distorted the felt realities of difference and commonality that help define us all. These research projects have made significant contributions to intellectual life and capacity building. Harnessing civic and entrepreneurial knowledge and energy, they have generated publications, conferences, community-university partnerships, presentations and dialogues. And these intercultural and interdisciplinary projects challenge and shift the founding myth of a singular Western economic modernity that still informs so much of what counts for disciplinary research in the academy today.

Animating the Mi'kmaw Humanities

In this research project, we continue our work as ethical allies working together to unpack and kindle in a two-row project of re-educating ourselves and others and reimagining education as enriching differences and enablement for all. I focus on the ongoing unlearning and the new learning and teaching underway under the aegis of basket making as pedagogy, sustainability, relationship building and the fusion of physical and knowledge ecologies for the production of skills and meanings at the heart of resilient and knowledgeable communities and economies. What becomes clear is how selectively humane learning and expanding trade in the early modern world provided the academic and economic foundations for racializing and dispossessing practices which long preceded, and were by no means fully curtailed by, the Royal Proclamation of 1763. Revisiting the archive of encounter clarifies the extent to which dispossession and displacement of indigenous peoples, languages and knowledges depended on culture as a key enforcement tool. The story of economic modernity, of *homo economicus*, promoting the rational, self-interested human as guide and guarantor of wealth creation, civilization and progress was disseminated as both natural and reasonable (Findlay and Findlay 2013). That dominating, exclusive narrative both allowed settlers to legitimate their theft of land and obscured their own savagery and ignorance (Sullivan and Tuana 2007) and their dependence on indigenous knowledge and labour.

That social construction, what Mills (1997) called a "consensual hallucination," is based on "an epistemology of ignorance, a particular pattern of localized and global cognitive dysfunctions (which are psychologically and socially functional), producing the ironic outcome that whites will in general be able to understand the world they themselves have made" (18). That construction has proved especially hard to dislodge because it is so deeply embedded in institutional, disciplinary, discursive and other realities as to be invisible. In Canadian universities and colleges today, its priorities remain clear. Business is in the ascendant and the humanities and social sciences are under siege or in decline. This shift remains profoundly Euro-Canadian despite appeals to the postcolonial and the global, as an extractive economy demands compliance from its extractive academy. However, indigenous knowledge holds answers for and antidotes to the twin trajectories of destroying the land and imprisoning the land's most respectful and reliable stewards within discourses of deficiency and nominal consultation (despite the honour of the crown and the duty to consult). Holistic, fully contextual, and cooperative indigenous practices are helping us recover "the learning spirit" (Battiste 2013) in and as territory.

Taking inspiration from the words of Caroline Gould and from the many others who shared their wisdom with us in dialogues in communities in Eskasoni Mi'kmaw Nation, Cape Breton; St. Mary's First Nation, New Brunswick, and Listuguj Mi'gmaq First Nation in Québec, I aim to animate intercultural exchange and trans-systemic knowledges, weaving the interdisciplinary basket and engaging capacity for insider critique and ethical alliance. In the process of learning from dialogue participants, the basket moves from object of the anthropological or curatorial gaze and association with the past, to multiple ongoing meanings as cultural activism, social process, economic ingenuity, legal evidence, sustainable practice and place-based knowledge.

Dialogue, a generous discursive and cultural economy, aimed to counter the waste, violence and injustice of Eurocentric discursive and other monopolies that controlled memory and limited imaginative possibilities in educational, economic and legal settings. As painful and destructive as research and education has proven in the past (Smith 1999), Mi'kmaw humanities dialogue participants embraced the opportunity, as one put it, "to research ourselves back to life; open ears and hearts." They shared their stories of navigating a school system where they found no respect for language that "houses the teachings": "labels were confusing" and "a lot of words that were sacred to us were demonized." They were clear too that they were not responsible for a loss of language: "It was stolen." Entering high school proved "the most traumatic time" when one participant said she "noticed she was different" and even laughing could mean experiencing strapping. Children found refuge in "a corner of the school in Cultural Awareness Week where we could go to be safe." Recognizing that "kids only want to fit in," participants felt a special obligation "to keep the teachings going" and "to listen to the young people; they go to gangs because they do not feel like they belong." For many, school meant "forgetting who they were." Only at university did some learn the history of their self-sustaining societies, learning that "everything we were taught in early school years, we weren't." As a result, they "go into professions to help and heal"—to "help people let go of the anger." One woman learned to let go only "when she realized that they did it to everyone—even their own women who didn't get the vote until the 20th century." That new understanding taught her solidarity, a sense that she was "part of something bigger" and a movement that was needed more than ever today.

Despite the experience of violence and trauma, there was much resilience and a pride in language as "a treasure of knowledge of relationships and possible producer of new knowledge and social treasures." For others, culture was empowering, a means not to "change the past" but to "work on today." Yet another was "trying to find her voice" after "years of being quiet." Others were inspired by the knowledge that indigenous science has been feeding and healing the world" and the land continues to teach and shape language. That knowledge led to a commitment to a "curriculum [that] reflects you," and Mi'kmaw symbols (including baskets and canoes) celebrating identities and achievements throughout the schools, which in turn gives people "purpose." Nor did celebrating Mi'kmaq come at the expense of Canadian symbols as children proudly showed their skills in singing the national anthem in the Mi'kmaw language.

Not only were the baskets on show in the schools, but they were a recurrent theme in the dialogues that underlined the cultural and economic importance of wood and a sustaining knowledge ecology. As one participant argued, "Our language, our artwork, porcupine baskets, birches and ash baskets ... were suited to the area, to living among trees and water." And "sharing stories, food, roles, routines, and rituals is all about renewing relationships." Unlike Eurocentric thinkers, Mi'kmaw practice is about relationships, respect and reciprocity: "We don't externalize but live our worldview and work with the tree.... The tree has memory and personality.... After harvesting a tree, we left an offering of tobacco as a mark of gratitude." In fact, "exclusive ownership was beyond comprehension" for those for whom "sustaining balance and reciprocity is a dynamic relation between humanity and mother earth" which "meant ceremonies as a negotiation process." And ceremonies always meant "storytelling, genealogies, and relationships." What participants described was an ancient history of a social economy weaving social relations of production in a co-operative economy, a local economy sustained by rich resources managed respectfully. Nothing was wasted in the process; children learned basket making using smaller pieces and in the process heard the stories of Creation's plenty and their stewardship responsibilities. Far from economic modernity's founding story of its efficient use of scarce resources, the Mikmaw story is a celebration of plenty and obligation to share in building community with all my relations.

The case of *R. v. Sappier, R. v. Gray* [2006] (on appeal from the New Brunswick Court of Appeal) demonstrates ongoing colonial legacies in charges against Maliseet and Mi'kmaq for "the unlawful possession of or cutting of Crown timber" despite Aboriginal and treaty rights. In an appeal of the respondents' acquittal, Eurocentrism's continuing control over the past was clear in the appellant arguments. Based on colonial presumption about the uninventiveness of Aboriginal peoples, those arguments could not conceive of the centrality of the culture of wood in meeting the *Van der Peet* [1996] test for Aboriginal rights: "the purposes underlying s.35(1) activities must be an element of a practice, custom or tradition integral to the distinctive culture of the Aboriginal group claiming the right" and be "central to the Aboriginal societies ... prior to contact" (par. 44-46). Appellant arguments focused on wood as incidental as opposed to the overwhelming record of sophisticated, purposeful use of the knowledge of wood, what to use, when, how and where. Although the appeal was dismissed in recognition of the respondents' defence of their Aboriginal rights, the case is a reminder of why we all need to care and remain vigilant about ongoing colonial legacies even where justice should reign.

Conclusion

The Mi'kmaw story of economic ingenuity and sustainability challenges myths and mainstream interpretive monopolies. It helps us get beyond some of the most tenacious and pernicious conceptual boxes and thus to animate new thinking and action by learning from alternative models of fair trade and sustainable development long ignored or disparaged by the mainstream until it thought it "discovered" those terms. Reframing some old stories helps elaborate why indigenous success stories have been hidden in plain view, why the predisposition to get things wrong persists, and why policy makers continue to invest in misunderstanding that obscures what investments might best serve the public interest.

The cultural pressures to accept as real currency Eurocentric thinking diffused as the natural and neutral way of conceiving of the world depended on culture being both used and abused. Culture is both necessary to the project of modernity and colonial expansion and necessarily subordinated to the emerging sciences that legitimated their growing authority by delegitimating and subjugating other knowledges. Science disdained cultural, women's, experiential, indigenous knowledge, creating culture's Others—those beyond the domain of civilized culture. Culture was then as now saturated with social and economic hierarchies—and with boundary promotion and policing—literal fences of property regimes and conceptual fences. Those fences elide power relations as natural facts—boxing selves in in the process behind walls of ignorance that will not learn from different knowledge economies in part of the waste of modernizing processes (Bauman 2004) so emphatically defined by the colonial project.

Teaching the baskets importantly sustains learning communities and "the learning spirit" (Battiste 2013). It offers a model for rethinking what counts for knowledge and for remediating the Euro-Canadian curriculum and its unequal socioeconomic outcomes. It teaches how the triumphal narratives of economic modernity overlook talents and answers hidden in plain sight and overlooks the histories of how we have come to the current economic and financial crises and what knowledges and whose humanities have been sacrificed in the process. Teaching the baskets helps reimagine the conceptual economies of our disciplines, historicizing, re-socializing and indigenizing terms for research, writing and communicating in the interests of sustainable futures for all of us. It teaches us the opportunities and obligations of what we communicate and reminds us, as RCAP (1996) insists, "Communication is much more than a cultural glue.... We actually construct who we are" (621).

Note

1. Chartist, from The People's Charter, a reformist movement in Britain calling for universal suffrage (1837-1848),

Cases cited

Delgamuukw v. British Columbia [1997] 3 SCR 1010.

Nowegijick v. The Queen [1983] 1 SCR 29, 144 DLR (3d) 193

R. v. Badger [1996] 1 SCR 771, 133 DLR (4th) 324.

R. v. Marshall [1999] 3 SCR 456, 177 DLR (4th) 513. [*Marshall No. 1*]

R. v. Marshall [1999] 3 SCR 533, 179 DLR (4th) 193. [*Marshall No. 2*]

R. v. Sappier, R. v. Gray [2006] 2 S.C.R. 686, *2006* SCC 54

R. v. Sparrow [1990] 1 SCR 1075, 70 DLR (4th) 385.

R. v. Van der Peet [1996] 2 SCR 507, 4 CNLR 177

Simon v. The Queen [1985] 2 SCR 387.

References

Augustine, Patrick J. 2016. Mi'kmaw Relations. In *Living Treaties: Narrating Mi'kmaw Treaty Relations*, ed.Marie Battiste. 52-65. Sydney, NS: Cape Breton University Press.

Barsh, Russel L. and James Y. Henderson. 1999. Marshalling the Rule of Law in Canada: Of Eels and Honour. *Constitutional Forum* 11 (1): 1-18.

Battiste, Marie, ed. 2000. *Reclaiming Indigenous Voice and Vision*. Vancouver: UBC Press.

———. 2013. *Decolonizing Education: Nourishing the Learning Spirit*. Saskatoon: Purich.

————— ed. 2016. *Living Treaties: Narrating Mi'kmaw Treaty Relations.* Sydney, NS: Cape Breton University Press.

Battiste, Marie and James (Sa'ke'j) Youngblood Henderson. 2000. *Protecting Indigenous Knowledge and Heritage: A Global Challenge.* Saskatoon: Purich.

Battiste, Marie, Lynne Bell, Isobel M. Findlay, Len Findlay and James (Sa'ke'j) Youngblood Henderson. 2006. Thinking Place: Animating the Indigenous Humanities in Education. *Australian Journal of Indigenous Education* 34:7-19.

Battiste, Marie, James (Sa'ke'j) Youngblood Henderson, Isobel M. Findlay, and Len Findlay. 2013. "Conversations with Daniel Coleman: Different Knowings and the Indigenous Humanities." In Rethinking the Humanities [special issue] *English Studies in Canada* 38 (1) (March 2012): 141-159.

Bauman, Z. 2004. *Wasted Lives: Modernity and Its Outcasts.* Cambridge: Polity.

Bourdieu, Pierre. 1984. *Distinction: A Social Critique of the Judgement of Taste,* trans. Richard Nice. Cambridge, MA: Harvard University Press.

Canada. Royal Commission on Aboriginal Peoples (RCAP). 1996. *Gathering Strength.* Volume 3. Ottawa: Minister of Supply and Services Canada.

Daes, Erica-Irene. 2000. Prologue: The Experience of Colonization around the World. In *Reclaiming Indigenous Voice and Vision,* ed. Marie Battiste, 3-8. Vancouver: UBC Press.

De Sousa Santos, Boaventura, João Arriscado Nunes and Maria Paula Meneses. 2007. Introduction: Opening Up the Canon of Knowledge and Recognition of Difference. In *Another Knowledge is Possible: Beyond Northern Epistemologies,* ed. Boaventura De Sousa Santos, xiv-lxii New York: Verso.

Education Scotland. 2016. Knowledge of Language. http://www.education-scotland.gov.uk/knowledgeoflanguage/scots/scotsandliteracy/curriculum/index.asp

Findlay, Isobel M. 1995. Word-perfect but Deed-demented: Canon Formation, Deconstruction, and the Challenge of D. H. Lawrence. *Mosaic: A Journal for the Interdisciplinary Study of Literature* 28 (3): 57-81.

—————. 1997. Reading for Reform: History, Theology, and Interpretation and the Work of Charles Kingsley and Elizabeth Gaskell. PhD dissertation. McGill University.

—————. 2003. Working for Postcolonial Legal Studies: Working with the Indigenous Humanities, Special issue on Postcolonial Legal Studies, ed. W. Wesley Pue, *Law, Social Justice and Global Development (LGD)* (2003-1). http://www2.warwick.ac.uk/fac/soc/law/elj/lgd/2003_1/findlay.

Findlay, Isobel M. and Len Findlay. 2013. Co-operatives: After the Crisis and Beyond the Binaries. In *Genossenschaften im Fokus einer neuen Wirtschafts-politik [Cooperatives in the Focus of a New Economic Policy]* 2012 XVII International Conference on Cooperative Studies, Assoc. of Cooperative Research Institutes, University of Vienna, ed. Johann Brazda, Markus Dellinger, Dietmar Rößl (Hg.), 809-20. Vienna: LIT Verlag AG.

Gramsci, Antonio. 1971. The Intellectuals. *Selections from the Prison Notebooks*, ed. and trans. by Quentin Hoare and Geoffrey Nowell Smith. New York: International Publishers.

Henderson, James (Sa'ke'j) Youngblood. 2016. Alexander Denny and the Treaty Imperative. In *Living Treaties: Narrating Mi'kmaw Treaty Relations*, ed. by Marie Battiste, 95-114. Sydney, NS: Cape Breton University Press.

Henderson, James (Sa'ke'j) Youngblood, Marjorie L. Benson and Isobel M. Findlay. 2000. *Aboriginal Tenure in the Constitution of Canada*. Scarborough, ON: Carswell.

Lawrence, B. 2002. Rewriting Histories of the Land: Colonization and Indigenous Resistance in Eastern Canada. In Razack, S., ed. *Race, Space, and the Law: Unmapping a White Settler Society*, 21-46. Toronto: Between the Lines.

Metallic, Fred. 2016. Treaty and Mi'gmewey. In *Living Treaties: Narrating Mi'kmaw Treaty Relations*, ed. Marie Battiste, 41-51. Sydney, NS: Cape Breton University Press.

Mills, Charles. 1997. *The Racial Contract*. Ithaca, NY: Cornell University Press.

Monture-Angus, Patricia. 1999. *Journeying Forward: Dreaming First Nations' Independence*. Halifax, NS: Fernwood.

Rotman, Leonard I. 2000. My Hovercraft is Full of Eels: Smoking Out the Message of *R v. Marshall*. *Saskatchewan Law Review* 63 (2): 617-44.

Scottish Education Department. 1946. Primary Education: A Report of the Advisory Council on Education in Scotland. Edinburgh: HMSO.

Smith, Linda Tuhiwai. 1999. *Decolonizing Methodologies: Research and Indigenous Peoples*. London: Zed Books.

Sullivan, Shannon and Nancy Tuana, ed. 2007. *Race and Epistemologies of Ignorance*. Albany, NY: State University of New York Press.

Marie Battiste

Mi'kmaw Symbolic Literacy

Indigenous humanities are the building blocks and foundation of heart, mind and spirit of indigenous peoples. They have many distinct teachings enfolded into indigenous knowledge system and literacies developed from indigenous brilliances, inspirations and teachings. Many are gifts and blessings attributed to spiritual sources. Unpacking the humanities in these knowledge systems is an illuminating venture into comprehending the deep consciousness of ancient ancestors and their search for meaning in their lives.

My own journey in seeking out a part of Mi'kmaw humanity began with my discovery and interest in the accounts and histories of symbolic forms of communication of the Mi'kmaq—and their systematic use—as I pursued my doctoral studies at Stanford University. My dissertation (Battiste 1984) was a foundation on which I began my rediscovery of my own people and humanity from within their consciousness and their creativity and their resilience. The timeframe of the thesis examines Mi'kmaq of northeastern Canada long before European contact and examines the communicating forms and writing systems used. In my dissertation, I sought to demonstrate the various functions and uses of these writing systems which continue to exist in Mi'kmaq consciousness today, a testament to the consistency and resiliency of literacy processes in Mi'kmaw heritage. My dissertation also revealed how cognitive imperialism was, and is, imposed through forced education on Mi'kmaw students, which eroded and concealed the functioning and enhancing elements of their communication forms.

This chapter seeks to describe some of the several symbolic forms of Algonkian literacy among Mi'kmaq, used before and during European contact and contextualizes these forms of communication within their socio-political history. Mi'kmaq is still spoken among several larger Mi'kmaw communities, as well as into the United States, where Micmac now are federally recognized as tribes in the northern part of Maine.[1] In the United States, federal recognition of the Micmac has created an off-reserve community in the Aroostook County of Maine, while a larger off-reserve community exists in the greater Boston area in Massachusetts. Mi'kmaw adventurers and travellers are found throughout Canada and the United States.

In Canada, Mi'kmaq have retained their own self-determining national council, the Sante'wi Mawio'mi of the Mi'kmaw Nationimou, also known as the Grand Council, comprised of Keptins, or Captains, from each of the seven districts of Mawio'mi (their traditional home-land) under the leadership of a Grand Chief (Kji Saqmaw) and a Grand Captain (Kji Keptin). In the 17th and 18th centuries, most political alliances and treaties were conducted in accordance with custom and tradition with the Grand Council and the district, usually solemnized with exchange of wampum laws. Mi'kmaw wampum, or *elnapsku'k,* was also used at this time as an important communicative device, which had its specialized orators and knowledge keepers who brought out and read the wampum strings and belts at gathering ceremonies.

The Mi'kmaq are among those indigenous peoples who have had a unique history of symbolic writing that began well before letters and orthographies were introduced. To understand these forms and their usage, it is important to consider the spiritual, practical and public uses of early communicating and writing forms of pictographs, petro-glyphs, notched sticks and wampum in Algonkian and Mi'kmaw tradition and epistemology. At some indefinite time prior to European contact Mi'kmaq communicated and recorded ideas, information and beliefs through pictographic writing on rocks, birchbark and animal skins. Hieroglyphics are found in some petroglyphs and rock drawings, having been alluded to in the early exploration accounts of missionaries and traders in the early 1600s.

In the late 17th and 18th centuries, Catholic priests adapted and formalized these early aboriginal symbols and reported to have developed "hieroglyphic" characters for teaching religious knowledge and prayers (Le Clercq 1910 [1691]; Maillard 1863). This modified Mi'kmaw symbolic epistemology, which will be discussed later, remains a part of Mi'kmaw and English literacy in Mi'kmaw society today. Four phonetic Roman scripts of Mi'kmaw languages have also been introduced to serve the purposes of missionary conversion efforts and government-funded efforts to communicate with them. These hieroglyphic forms never developed into any other form of writing such as those called syllabaries that missionaries developed among several indigenous nations such as Inuit, Ojibwe and Cree in Canada. James Evans, a missionary credited with the creation of the syllabic systems among the Cree, introduced syllabic writing to hunter-gatherer nations in the latter half of the 19th century, using a relatively simple geometric shape, each representing a consonant and a vowel (Murdoch 1981). Evans reasoned that the syllabary was a far more efficient system that one could learn with the least amount of effort and which could be used across diverse dialects of the same language (Murdoch 1985). Some of these systems remain today, while many others have fallen into disuse because of missionaries who have found them difficult for themselves. Rather, Mi'kmaw hieroglyphics remains holistic, not sequential, in its reading form.

The Eurocentric Unknown and Construction of Cognitive Imperialism

While little has been written of the early indigenous writing systems used among first peoples in North America prior to European contact, it is evident by a review of diverse systems in print that indigenous peoples throughout the continent have used a wide array of forms of communicating or writing or remembering that bear resemblance in symbolic meaning, design and function. Early Euro-Christian travellers and missionaries transformed, ignored or consciously destroyed indigenous literacies or knowledge system of America. In addition, they created myths that supported their own Eurocentric superiority and ascendency as they paid homage to their own writing systems and to their biases for print and paged writing. Some of this is reflected in their ethnocentric belief that Indians were not capable of writing.

In 1580, Montaigne spoke of the Tupi-Guarani of Brazil as "so new and infantile, that he is yet to learn his A.B.C." (Montaigne 1580:

141). However, the Tupi-Guarani are well known for their book that recorded their Creation story and traditions written in the Mbya Guarani language and compiled by Paraguayan anthropologist León Cadogan called *Ayvu Rapyta* (Origin of Human Speech) (Cadogan 1959). When European missionaries encountered undeniable evidence of a literacy equivalent to their own, such as Tupi-Guarani, Toltec and Mayan symbolic literacies and paper books, they did their best to eradicate it as a threat to the teachings of the written Bible they brought with them. These attempts were attempts to conceal the fact that the word of God as depicted in the Bible was silent to the existence of the American continent and its peoples, a fact immensely distressing to those holding to the Biblical knowledge system of Europe in the 16th and 17th centuries (Zerubavel 1992). The very existence of *terra cognita* of a new world unknown to the scriptures generated demands for a new explanation and justification of the dominant Biblical knowledge system—unknown facts that previously had been considered universal and divine, made it appear fragile, vulnerable and wrong.

These doubts shrouded the Christian world view and perceived destiny. Petit de Julleville summarized the impact of this discovery on the European world:

> The discovery of America enlarged the habitable earth and offered to Europeans unlimited fortune in the future and world domination. At the same time the earth, dispossessed of the central place it was to hold in the universe, was no more than a point lost somewhere in unlimited space. These two conceptions, the world at once enlarged and diminished, opened the spirit of conquest and enterprise, and in the eyes of [the] philosopher, reduced to but a grain of dust in the open and bold conceptions of a philosophy freed [from] the chain of authority. (Scott 1934: 3)

The lack of coherent answers about the enigma of the new continent and its indigenous nations, however, shattered the cloistered medieval universe of Ptolemy and the Holy See and challenged the existing sacred and profane thought of the European mind. The Biblical knowledge system was constructed around the assumption that everything that happens in nature, happens out of special conditions of necessity. The unexplained indigenous lands, resources and nations of the "New World" challenged the assumed necessity principle behind its knowledge system. The unknowns in the knowledge system of Europe had large, long and lasting consequences for the Church and its knowledge system. It generated an undirected response. Pope Alexander VI's papal bull *Inter Caetera* (1493) expressed its hope that the "barbarous nations be overthrown and brought to the faith itself."

The finding of indigenous peoples in the world began the knowledge transformation called the European enlightenment. The fissure in the Biblical knowledge system and absence of coherent justifications for the fissure fuelled the myth that indigenous people in the Americas were illiterate savages who "only" possessed an oral tradition. The illiterate savage myth was fundamental to European colonial and imperial interests. It both dramatized the Christian world vision and justified the confiscation of indigenous wealth. That the myth ignored centuries of Aboriginal communication forms and denied human dignity and rights to the natives was unimportant, since it was Canada's mythogenesis and colonial fortunes.

The living and all-inclusive tradition of Algonkian symbolic literacy was barely noticed in the European writing. Early travellers' reports emphasized the "bestial" nature of natives and only grudgingly admitted them into the ranks of humanity. A few examples of recorded Aboriginal literacy in North American nevertheless survive. In 1497, for example, John Cabot was intrigued by "fallen trees bearing marks" (Maine Historical Society 1897: 347). In 1602, the English captain John Bartholomew Gosnold encountered Mi'kmaq off the coast of Maine in a "Baske shallop" with sails and oars (Archer 1843: 73). The Basque-speaking Mi'kmaq gestured signs of peace and made a long speech that was partially understood by the sailors, as "they pronounced our Language with great facility." Gosnold wrote, "...with a piece of chalk [the Mi'kmaq] described the coast thereabouts and could name Placentia of the Newfoundland." They also told him where he could and could not go. In 1652, Father Gabriel Druilletes reported Algonkian Indians using coal for ink, bark for paper and writing with new and peculiar characters. He wrote: "They use certain marks, according to their ideas as a local memory to recollect the points, articles, and maxims, which they heard" (Le Clercq 1910{1691]: 22).

In 1653 Father Bressani reported Indians of New France using "littlesticks instead of books, which they sometimes mark with certain signs.... By the aid of these they can repeat the names of a hundred or more presents, the decisions adopted in councils and a thousand other particulars" (Le Clercq 1910[1691]: 23).

The illiterate-savage myth continued to dominate Europeans' assessment of Indian character, however. Father Pierre Biard's assessment of the Mi'kmaw mind in 1616, illustrates the inherent contradictions of the myth:

> [The Indians] have rather a happy disposition, and a fair capacity for judging and valuing material and common things, deducing their reasons with great nicety, and always seasoning them with some pretty comparison. They have a very good memory for material things, such as having seen you before, or the peculiarities of a place where they may have been, of what took place in their presence twenty or thirty years before, etc.; but to learn anything by heart—there's the rock: there is no way of getting a consecutive arrangement of words into their pates. [Y]ou will see these poor barbarians, notwithstanding their great lack of government, power, letters, art and riches, yet holding their head so high they greatly underrate us, regarding themselves as our superior. (Thwaites 1897: 73-74).

Father Biard ignored the fact that sequential alphabets of European aristocratic society were alien to the Mi'kmaw mind. Rather, the Mi'kmaw mind moved in a holistic and implicit world of symbolic literacy and collective dialogue. The ability to express every nuance of oral or syllabic expression was meaningless to the Mi'kmaq, their cognitive focus being on great ideals, which guided their thought, conduct and speech as was found in their wampum belts.

From the beginning of dialogue with the Euro-Christians, the difference in worldview was apparent to the Algonkian. The conflict between European pretenses and condemnation of native society and their conduct was carefully noted among the Algonkian. They always found it difficult to accept naively the romantic image of the righteous immigrant who laboured selflessly for mankind to spread Christianity and culture to non-literate natives.

The Mi'kmaq were deeply puzzled by the Europeans' inconsistencies. Clearly a gap existed in European thought between ideas and events, which was rare in the holistic Mi'kmaw consciousness and their verb-orientated language. Upon critical reflection, Mi'kmaq concluded that their own society was affluent and literate, comparable to European society. Mi'kmaw life was not "nasty, brutish and short," as so eloquently coined by Thomas Hobbes (1651), but a comfortable ecological stability producing a greater supply and diversity of foods than Europe. Mi'kmaw education was a vital and dynamic part of ecological life, not an imagined preparation for economic utility in an aristocratic society. Everything Mi'kmaw youths learned generated their knowledge of the world and guided them in how to fit harmoniously into it, and consequently expectations blended harmoniously with their visions and gifts in the scheme of the Good.

Mi'kmaq realized they had little need for the alien thought of aristocratic Europe. The puzzling failure between Euro-Christian thought and their conduct caused Mi'kmaq to consider Christian thoughts differently; they noticed the hypocrisy of actions of the Christians that revealed Christian teachings it sought to prevent. Since their literature addressed similar paradoxes of human life, the best of the spiritual teachings of the "Black Robes," the Jesuit missionaries, became synthesized into broader, but analogous, indigenous concepts of spirituality.

This mythic fact reinforced a prejudice that indigenous peoples were primitive and ignorant, forcing them into colonial European languages and sometimes their literacy without the benefits that it offered the colonists. It preserved, even assured, the moral ascendancy and economic objectives of Eurocentrism through cognitive imperialism (Battiste 1984). Cognitive imperialism is the Eurocentric framework for asserting its authority to define its own cognitive traits and preferences as normal and desirable and all other ways of thinking, learning and understanding the world as deficits and ignorance. It's the cognitive equivalent of racism. It assumes that the Eurocentric knowledge system way of thinking, of learning, of being is destined to overwhelm and replace all others. This approach reveals the nature and limits of Eurocentric knowledge systems with regard to the particular challenges of the "new"—the challenge that indigenous humanity presents to Eurocentrism.

Many generations of indigenous peoples, indeed everyone, have had to endure cognitive imperialism in a forced Eurocentric education imposed on them. They were enforced in Indian residential schools, day schools, provincial public and federal schools and in postsecondary institutions that continue to ignore distinctive indigenous knowledge systems and languages. Those Eurocentric approaches of cognitive imperialism in their compulsory education have cost indigenous peoples profoundly: the erosion and even loss of many of the indigenous knowledge systems and languages, loss of spiritual identities and traditions linked to their traditional and evolving ways of knowing, disconnections from their heritage, knowledge systems and spiritual communicative connections to the land and much more. Formal education has also supported a hierarchy of privilege and entitlement that has acted as a barrier to transforming education and enacting an epistemic violence on indigenous peoples who continue to be silenced, marginalized and alienated from education, and even further from the outcomes of success that the majority of Canadians enjoy. Modern studies characterize these education processes as linguistic or cultural genocide (Skutnabb-Kangas 2000; TRC 2015: 1).

Today, the cognitive imperialism embedded in English literacy in compulsory education systems is among the leading killer languages of indigenous languages, having amassed a greater structural power and material resources than its number of speakers justify, to the cost of other languages (Skutnabb-Kangas 2000). Only three of the seventy Aboriginal languages in Canada have been predicted to survive this century, along with only 100 of the world's languages. Such destruction of indigenous languages and literacies impinge equally on indigenous knowledges, with their consequence to sustainable resource development and biodiversity, resources that are threatened as well.

Context of Indigenous Literacy

Indigenous literacy of America was largely symbolic, reflecting a unified vision of knowledge and thought from Patagonia to Baffin Island. From the Tupi-Guarani's *Ayvu Rapyta* (Cadogan 1959), to the Yucatac-Mayan paper screenfolds (Roys 1933), the Nahua-Toltec screenfolds (Wauchope 1964-1975), to the Algonkian Walam Olum or Red Score (Brinton 1969[1884]), Midewiwin or Grand Medicine scrolls (Tanner 1830) and Mi'kmaw hieroglyphics, these mutually-intelligible ideological systems comprised an indigenous encyclopedia capable of providing the true history of early America (Levi-Strauss 1964-1971). They maintained a basic cognitive unity and balance, allowing indigenous peoples to explore universal ideals that lay beyond the grasp of their empirical world. Some symbols were practical representations of objects and time in the empirical world surrounding the people. Most symbols were never precisely defined or fully explained, however, since their purpose was to stimulate a dialogue rather than resolve the paradoxes of life concretely. They represented ideals which were infinite, dialectical (or relational) and indivisible such that their significance could not be adequately understood by any one person or generation.

This indigenous epistemology was derived both from the immediate world of personal and indigenous experiences, perceptions, thoughts and memory including experiences shared with others; and from the spiritual world discovered in dreams, visions and signs interpreted with the guidance of medicine men or elders. Holistic ideographs are interactive, invoking the memory, creativity and logic of the people. Their most significant meanings quickly passed from family to family and to succeeding generations through dialogue and appropriate rituals and legends. Through analogies or style, they modelled the harmony among humans and the environment. Knowledge was derived from the immediate world through personal and indigenous experience and, secondly, from one's interaction with the spiritual world. The indigenous texts thus catalogued essential knowledge of the two worlds in holistic meaningful ideas or visions, and through the oral tradition and appropriate rituals, the collective indigenous knowledge was transmitted to succeeding generations.

Wampum

The most common Algonkian ideographic texts recorded were in wampum, which appear to have served both public and private functions among several tribes. The word wampum is Algonkian in origin. It is purported to be derived from the dialect of the New England tribes, from the word *wamponpeag*, which means, "white string of shell beads" (Snyderman 1954)—*wa ba'bi*, meaning "white string" and *ka'ka'bos*, meaning "old dark string" of the Penobscots, *sogabi*, meaning "dark string" of the Abenaki and Wawenock, and *wo ba'p* among the Malecite and Passamaquoddy (Speck 1940).

In Mi'kmaw, the concept of "wampum" was expressed by three terms. The mainland Mi'kmaq referred to it as *wabe'k* in the singular and *wabe'gol* in the plural, meaning "white seed." The Mi'kmaq of

Unama'ki (Cape Breton Island), however, referred to them as "stones of man" or *elna'pskuk* (Speck 1917: 5). The word *uktogooloowokuna* was also cited in Rand's dictionary of Mi'kmaq as describing a type of wampum neckpiece that was worn by ancient heroes (Rand 1894: 62). In all the Wabanaki tribes, wampum was figuratively called *kelusewa'ngan,* or *klusuaqnn,* meaning "speech" (Speck 1915: 507).

Configuring wampum was accomplished by a method in which colored beads taken from shells of the quahog were woven into a desired pattern. In a Mi'kmaw legend (Rand 1971[1894]: 103) the process of stringing them together was called in Mi'kmaq *napawejik.* Wampum specimens have indicated that some conventional symbols were evident among the Algonkian tribes who used wampum extensively. Evident in wampum belts among the different Algonkian tribes were shared conceptions of peace, friendship, war, death and alliance, exemplified by the symbols of a pipe, clasped hands, a hatchet, purple beads around the emblem of a person, and a chain being held by two persons.

Two distinct periods of wampum use have been found among woodland tribes and their allies. In each period, a different type of wampum is used. The dividing line between the two periods roughly coincides with the establishment of European-indigenous relations. During the pre-colonial period, the "grave or discoidal" shaped wampum, measuring "one-tenth of an inch in diameter and one thirtieth of an inch in thickness to two inches in diameter nearly one-half inch in thickness" (Snyderman 1954: 469) was used. Snyderman proposes that because of its shape and weight, grave wampum was strung and exhibited in the form of necklaces and not displayed in the more common belts of the second period. This hypothesis is confirmed in part by the old Mi'kmaw word for wampum, *uktogooloowokuna,* which literally means "belonging to the neck" and referred to in Rand's dictionary as a "collar or yoke" (Clark 1902: 162).

Wampum was the medium of public records, maintained by a wampum keeper, their indigenous historian. These strings and belts of tubular shells were periodically displayed at ceremonial gatherings to recall past events and announce new alliances and treaties. International treaties, indigenous agreements and boundaries could be represented in conventional symbols woven into the strings or belts, the arrangement and colors conveying intent or attitude. Because of the utility and widespread value of the shells, however, the woodland nations and the European immigrants also used wampum shells as international, trans-tribal and commercial currency. Colonial officials fixed exchange rates for the wampum against sterling and later the dollar.

Pictographs and Petroglyphs

Since pictographic writing is visually similar to prehistoric art forms, it is often analyzed from this perspective (Begouen 1929). This analysis serves to reduce the drawings to mere symbolic representation. Thus, pictographic art has not been viewed as comprising a set of devices for the interactive communicative function of writing. Among Mi'kmaw petroglyphs, no clear distinction can be made between graphic forms of writing and those of art. Robertson (1973) frequently attributes some petroglyphic drawings to Mi'kmaw artistic expression when the function and usage of the designs are ambiguous.

Petroglyphic communication has been found throughout North America, especially near coastal areas where rock surfaces have been polished by sea or streams. The principal area of petroglyphic activity extends from Hudson Bay to South Carolina and from Nova Scotia to the Rocky Mountains. The large number of petroglyphs attests to their universal usage among North American tribes as Hoffman (1895) noted that the petroglyphs used among the various Algonkian tribes had similarities in design and may also have had similarities in intent.

Many examples of petroglyphic writings have been found in Mi'kma'ki. At the time of his research, Mallery (1893) identified bark records and petroglyphs designed by Mi'kmaq and Abenaki Indians of Northeast America. Robertson (1973) offers the most complete accounting of Mi'kmaw petroglyphs. While no method has proven successful in dating petroglyphs (Molyneaux 1980), some evidence of their antiquity exists; the drawings illustrate a period from ancient times up through European contact. Robertson described their general nature as follows:

> Most of the drawings are a solitary figure with no apparent relation to other drawings on the rocks. A few are picture stories of hunting and fishing; some depict ritual dances, the dancers in ceremonial dress. A few figures are of Micmac folk beliefs

about the world around them; others related to their chief and their medicine man, their wigwams and houses, their decorated peaked caps, and artistic designs. Drawings of hands and feet identified by symbols delighted the old Micmac, as did etchings of animals, and birds, and snakes, and the sailing vessels of the white man. (Robertson 1973: 1)

The interpretation of pictographs and petroglyphs has challenged subsequent writers to an understanding of how Indians portray ideas. Glidden (1843), in his classification of hieroglyphics of ancient Egypt, offers two methods of portraying ideas. The first is by metaphor; the second, by enigma. Among the Mi'kmaw petroglyphs illustrative of metaphor is the star design with five or eight points, called *kakwet*, which means "starfish." Similarly, a fan-shaped design is said to represent the northern lights, called *wae-g-a-disk, wekatesk* (MacLaren 1974: 169). An example of enigma in indigenous society is the eagle, which represents a deep spiritual connection to the Great Spirit and thus the mystical connection between the spirit of the bird and spirit world of the deity.

Ideographs representing abstract ideas, pictorially expressed, are more frequent in the pictography of Mi'kmaw tribes than is the mere portraiture of objects. Hoffman (1895) offers an example of ideographic representation in the Dakota tradition. In this ideograph, a person is sitting with his left hand drawn to accept a pipe; the pipe itself does not appear. The pipe, together with the ritual surrounding it, is universally understood among all nations as a symbol of peace and friendship. The example illustrates the incorporation of gestures into pictographic writing. In the Mi'kmaw hieroglyphics the similar idea is *kisutmi'tij* or "they came to a consensus" is represented by a dual peace pipe:

By the term "symbol" is meant "the representation of ideas by aid of certain analogies which the mind sees between the symbol and the idea attached to it" (Hoffman 1895: 555). The ability to illustrate ideas and abstractions symbolically is found in all Aboriginal writing

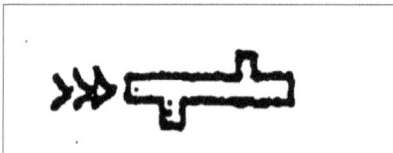

Fig. 7.1 – Taken from Schmidt and Balcom 1993. The dual peace pipes represent mutual promises and agreement (Schmidt and Balcom 1993: 120).

systems. The tomahawk symbol represented war, while the pipe represented peace. In another instance, the symbol of friendship among tribes was represented by hands clasped or by two hands with open palms approaching each other.

Besides the recording of events and stories, North American Indians have used pictographic symbols to record timing of events. Famous among these pictographs are the Dakota winter counts. Similarly, Mi'kmaq portrayed the seasons of the year pictorially, differentiating the seasons by the natural changes they observed. Spring had come when buds on the trees appeared, when wild geese appeared, when the fawns of moose had grown to a certain size in their mother's bellies, and when the seals gave birth. Summer had come when the salmon were running up the river and when the wild geese shed their feathers. Autumn was observed by the waterfowls' return from the north to the south. Winter was marked by the harsh cold and abundant snows, and the bears retiring until spring (Le Clercq 1910 [1691]: 137).

Europeans admired Mi'kmaw knowledge of their homeland in which they could identify every crevice, stream and hill with great accuracy. They were particularly adept in making maps, which portrayed their knowledge. Making maps and charting courses of travel with birch-bark scrolls marked one of the main functions of pictographic writing. Le Clercq observed:

> They have much ingenuity in drawing upon bark a kind of map which marks exactly all the rivers and streams of a country and which they wish to make representation. They mark all the places thereon exactly and so well that they make use of them successfully and an Indian who possesses one makes long voyages without going astray. (Le Clercq 1910[1691]: 136)

Rand (1850: 25) also noted Mi'kmaw skills in map-making. He observed that Mi'kmaq were in the "habit of making crude drawings of places for the direction of others. An Indian would often make these drawings on bark and leave them at places where he turned off the path." Speck (1922: 96-98) further pointed out that these birch bark maps not only charted travel routes but also described family and common hunting territories.

The function of pictographs has only been superficially studied. Schoolcraft (1853) and Mallery (1893) offered some insight into indigenous societies' uses of pictographs. They concluded that pictographs represented two forms of knowledge—one form was accessible to the whole tribe and indicated everyday existence, such as information about hunting and travelling, while the other form was known only to the *pa'tlia's*, or priests, and used to initiate spiritual lessons or religious rites or to manifest the power of certain deities. With the aid of signs and figures on birch bark, the *pa'tlia's* "recorded the oral tradition and, in considerable detail, material relating to the origin of their religion and its dissemination among the Ojibwe" (Vennun 1978: 774). Sacred songs were written and preserved in more than 1,000 texts of the Ojibwe Midewiwin society, with at least half of the texts written in text plus pictograph. While indigenous societies and their spiritual predilections have been rarely described with much accuracy, some research on specific tribes has nevertheless supported the thesis that pictographic texts were representative of two modes of experiencing the world: one through the spirits, the other through everyday existence. Reading of the various signs and symbols was known to those who practised the rituals. Repetition and association served as the primary means of learning to read the native texts. But, especially the rituals associated with the figurative sign or symbol manifested a relationship with the spirits from which knowledge was derived. Robertson (1973) also found this to be the case among Mi'kmaq. She noted:

> Animals, birds and fish were respected by the Micmac. They believed that the spirits of these creatures survived and if their bones were burned, the spirit of the bones would carry the news to others of their kind and they would no longer allow the Indians to capture them.... The number of animal drawings on the rocks of Kejimkoojik suggests that the Micmacs believed that drawing the likeness of an animal one wished to capture would ensure success in the hunt. (Robertson 1973)

The petroglyphs interacted with and depended upon the oral traditions in Mi'kmaw society. A mark on a rock in itself did not merely represent the image but was part of a lesson or a story. Without the oral text, most glyphs could not be deciphered as meaningful records. Robertson found written accounts of Mi'kmaw legends to help explain the various rock glyphs found in Nova Scotia. Legendary figures were often the focus of petroglyphic drawings in which the action

*Fig. 7.2 – http://www.historymu-
seum.ca/cmc/exhibitions/aborig/
storytel/images/petroa.gif*

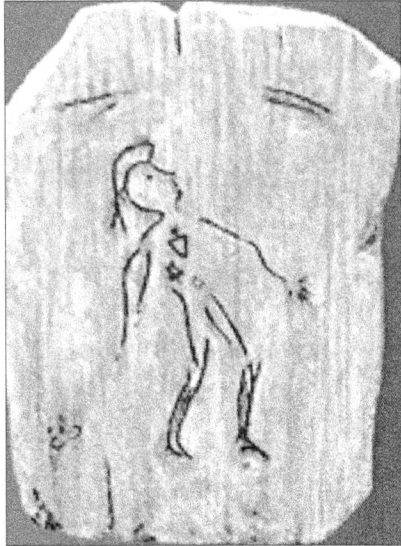

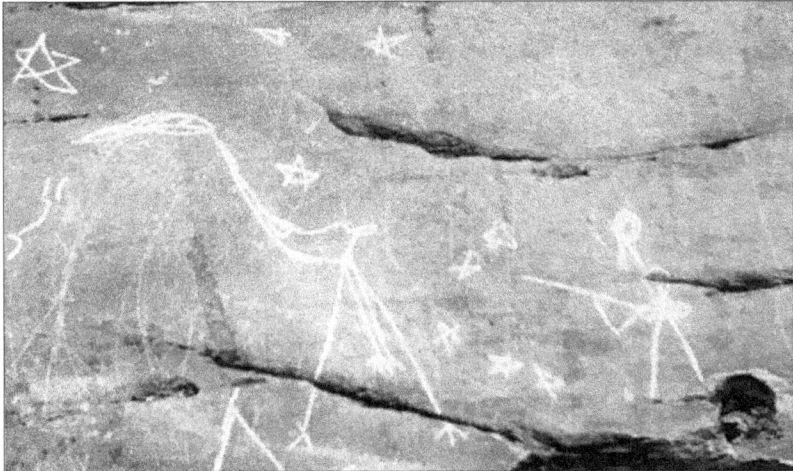

*Fig. 7.3 – Mi'kmaw petroglyph shows story representation of "Star Husband,
Star Wife and Crane": Two Mi'kmaw women wish to marry stars, and upon
awakening find two star men beside them who they take as their husbands.
Soon the women discover they are in the sky. They are told they could return
to earth but must obey certain instructions if they are to reach earth safely.
Unfortunately, they disobey and find themselves stuck in the branches of a tall
pine tree. The badger helps them out of the tree, and the crane helps them to
cross the river. Taken from Robertson 1973. http://www.muiniskw.org/images/
pgHistory3b_Kulloo.jpg*

and story was implied by various marks around and on the character. The following illustrations and texts (Robertson 1973) of Mi'kmaw petroglyphs offer examples of petroglyphs whose functions appear to be related to legendary heroes:

Algonkian pictographs, petroglyphs and notched sticks served more diversified uses. Like the Mesoamerican screenfolds, most described spiritual ideas and concrete experiences (Robertson 1973). The designs explained cosmogony and were used to communicate with the spirit and human worlds and to recall individual visions and experiences among the spirits. The pictographs incised on birch bark scrolls of the Algonkian Midewiwin or Grand Medicine society is one example of the Algonkian written literacy (Eliade 1964: 314ff). It is a text for an initiate into the spiritual society. The pictographs describe the rituals and stages to acquire wisdom and knowledge for its members.

Through this symbolic literacy, Algonkian nations achieved a written communication, which served a variety of social, political, cultural and spiritual needs. It maintained a deep and lasting communal bond affecting all aspects of indigenous life. Symbolic epistemology reconciled the natural facts of being born into a certain family, a certain language, a spiritual world and proper conduct in a material world. This common cognitive experience created a collective cognitive experience for indigenous societies and tolerance for other societies. It was, and remains, the core of indigeneity and tribalism (Unger 1976). A tightly bound community of sentiments and ideas united by symbolic literacy and collective dialogue identified "what ought to be" with "what is," dispelling moral doubt. All aspects of Mi'kmaw life (i.e. Mi'kmaw law, Mi'kmaw religion and Mi'kmaw art), expressed the view that the ideal and actuality were fundamentally inseparable. An endless series of interlocking face-to-face conversations sustained consistency between past and present, rather than criticism (the articulation of inconsistency) as the people sought to discover the universal lessons behind the ideals of a changing world. This unity of consciousness bonded the people into a strong worldview and of an ideal of the Good in which others participated as an intense moral communion in our knowledge system and language that was perceived as spiritual teachings and sensibilities. Reason was merely the awareness of a highly concrete ideal implicit in the reality of nature in a state of flux. It knew no distinction between "is" and "ought" or between theory and practice. Individual consciousness tended to reflect the collective culture and its understanding, which was the most important source of order in indigenous society. This unity was able to make the most of the better aspects of human nature while suppressing most effectively man's evil side.

Mi'kmaw Literacy and its Synthesis of Catholic Teachings

Rejecting any alliance with Europe's secular princes, Grand Chief Membertou and 140 Mi'kmaq reached a spiritual and political accord with the Catholic Church in the moon of good fishing, 1610. A symbolic indigenous ceremony witnessed the agreement, which included both the ceremonial exchange of sacred wampum and the Catholic ritual of initiation (the baptism) of the Grand Chief and his immediate family by Father Jesse Flesche. As the traditions of the Grand Council required, the Grand Chief sent his sons out to all the district leaders to tell them about his baptism and asked them to embrace his district union with the spiritual leader of Europe. Within a century, all Mi'kmaw families had entered the accord.

This political alliance provided for the establishment of churches within Mi'kmaw national territory, protection of Church property and priests, and the spiritual instruction of the Mi'kmaq. Consistent with traditional respect accorded grandmothers in the Mi'kmaw knowledge system and at the request of the Grand Council, the Holy Grandmother, St. Ann became the patron saint of the Mi'kmaq in 1630. From that time to 1762, Catholic priests lived and worked among Mi'kmaq, learning their indigenous epistemology and language. Catholic ideas of a universal God, the ideal of the Good, and asking God to reveal greater understanding of the faith through prayer were consistent with Mi'kmaw epistemology, and were viewed as supplemental to their knowledge system. Little progress was reportedly made in Catholic teaching, however, until a major breakthrough in 1677, when Father Chrestien Le Clercq transliterated Biblical ideals into Mi'kmaw symbolic "formulary," as he called it.

> Our Lord inspired me with the idea of [characters] the second year of my mission, when being much embarrassed as to the method by which I should teach the Micmac Indians to pray to

God, I noticed some children were making marks with charcoal upon birchbark, and were counting these with the fingers very accurately at each word of prayers which they pronounced. This made me believe that by giving them some formulary, which would aid their memory by definite characters, I should advance much more quickly than by teaching them through the method of making them repeat a number of times that which I said to them. (Le Clercq 1910[1691]: 131)

Le Clercq was very surprised with Mi'kmaw facility in tenaciously grasping "any association of word, fact, or simple idea with a written arbitrary symbol" (24). He wrote that Mi'kmaq have much readiness in understanding this kind of writing, and that they learn in a single day what they would never have been able to grasp in an entire week without the aid of these leaflets (126).

Once Catholic rituals had been transcribed as symbolic literature, using analogies with existing symbols, they diffused rapidly throughout the nation within traditional social contexts. Father taught son, mother taught daughter, and children taught each other. Prayers were recording in proper Catholic ritualistic order as charcoal designs on birch bark books, which each family preserved in birch bark boxes decorated with wampum and porcupine quill designs (Speck 1914, 1922, 1927).

Although Le Clercq reported successfully using these characters for the remaining ten years of his mission, little evidence of the original forms remains of them. In a search for the origin of the Le Clercq's characters, Ganong (1910) concluded that Le Clercq used all the indigenous designs he found, most having the typical double scroll patterns characteristic of nations of the Wabanaki Confederacy, of which the Mi'kmaq were the younger brother, and then developed a few characters of his own for new concepts found in prayers.

In 1735, Father Pierre Antoine Maillard began a twenty-seven-year mission among Mi'kmaq (Maillard 1758), during which he expanded the hieroglyphic ideographs and literacy and contributed to the transition from ideographic literacy to roman script. In the second year of his mission, Maillard reported having discovered an innovative method of using hieroglyphics to teach Mi'kmaq how to pray. Subsequent scholars investigating the origin of Maillard's hieroglyphics have concluded that Maillard was the beneficiary of Le

Clerq's work, although the new prayers, chants and instructions which he composed with the assistances of the Mi'kmaq probably required new understandings of Mi'kmaw symbols and new characters (Le Clercq 1910[1691]; Shea 1861; Hewson 1977).

Unlike Le Clercq, who frequently characterized Mi'kmaq as savages and barbarians incapable of advancing to letter literacy, Maillard perceived them as curious and intelligent people capable of learning anything they wanted. When Maillard became fluent in both the spoken and symbolic Mi'kmaq, he was frequently challenged by Mi'kmaw inquiring minds. He astutely realized that if Mi'kmaq became literate in the Roman script, their doubts about the new religion based on their experiences with Europeans would be strengthened by discovering further ideological inconsistencies in European books (Maillard 1863). Maillard also feared that if Mi'kmaq knew how to read and write letters, they could read and understand the interests of the English and be better able to correspond with each other, perhaps against French Catholic interests (ibid.).

Despite the fact that Maillard had developed a roman phonetic script, which he used for his own linguistic studies, he chose to withhold any knowledge of it from Mi'kmaq. Maillard continued to teach the Mi'kmaq only through hieroglyphics, thus deliberately closing European Roman alphabet literacy to them. In his absence, Maillard carefully appointed catechists among indigenous elders, whose duty it was "to see to the religious instruction of children, preside at public prayers on Sundays, administer baptism, receive matrimonial promises, and officiate at funerals" (Johnston 1960: 72).

The similarity in spiritual function between Catholic priests and medicine people ensured the success of Maillard's plan. Medicine people had specialized knowledge of reading and writing sacred symbols on birch bark, which for centuries catalogued the proper rituals and chants for various spiritual occasions and societies. The priest and his reliance on the Bible were analogous. Like the training of priest, the apprenticing of young men to the medicine society was a long and rigorous training involving the learning of symbols, chants and rituals, and learning the nature of the spirit world. As spiritual intermediaries, medicine people helped their people achieve personal communion with the spirits. Prayer and revelation were analogous to the traditional vision quest.

The spiritual foundation of the Mi'kmaw creation story, its knowledge systems and literacy also paralleled Catholic doctrines. Both systems addressed universal concepts. Catholic teachings of a universal God and his lesson to man affirmed aboriginal ideals, thus Mi'kmaw spiritual culture was broadened, not altered by Catholic theology. The Catholic teaching that man was destined to eternal damnation unless he practiced a Christian life involving faith, ritual and sacrifice was analogous to indigenous beliefs in the necessity of living up to the great ideals of Mi'kmaw life through self-control. Catholic doctrines of love of God and each other, its prayers for the dead to help them enter the spiritual world and sacred symbols were all analogous to indigenous beliefs and symbols. Mi'kmaw society embraced the two spiritual worlds as one, adding to rituals but not changing the ideological foundation. Hence, when the British eventually removed the French priests and evicted the French from their homes, Mi'kmaq held to the Christian faith for more than a hundred years without priests and churches, and eventually would enable Catholic priests to return to proselytize in the Canada (Henderson 1997).

Conclusion

The renowned psychologist Carl Jung stressed that the acquisition of modern human consciousness is a very recent and fragile experiment, which has not achieved any reasonable degree of continuity and remains vulnerable to the fragmentation of the soul and mind (Jung 1964). He also maintained that the ability to fragment consciousness and concentrate on a single thing, cannot exclude the rest of consciousness, any more than an automobile that disappears around the corner has not vanished into thin air. Rather, he noted other realms of consciousness arise to influence our mental clarity (Jung 1964). He also stressed that symbols and archetypes were wider "unconscious" aspects of the human consciousness and essential to meaning.

Modern sequential literacies were derived from symbols. The early picture-writing (pictograms), symbols and ideograms first represented general and abstract ideas. At some point in European history, the Phoenician traders created an alphabet of symbols, which represented individual sounds of speech, rather than ideas. Out of this notion grew the European alphabets and scripts.

The Mi'kmaw knowledge and literacy system and consciousness remain embedded in the ideographs and the oral traditions. The modern sequential literacies imposed on Mi'kmaq have supplemented their world view and knowledge systems, but the ideographic literacy continues to affect Mi'kmaw consciousness as does European-based linear scripts on the consciousness of modern humanity. Modern literacy research has shown that the dichotomization of language into the oral and written forms is recent (Goody and Watt 1963). In the dichotomized scheme, the terms "preliterate" and "illiterate" were used to characterize oral cultures, and the peoples were depicted as living off the fringes of society, unable to survive or thrive (Corbett 1981). Modern research has invalidated the dichotomized forms, finding that the two modes are superimposed and intertwined with each other (Tannen 1982). Tannen has argued that the difference between the oral and written culture represents a difference in approach to knowledge and thought. In oral cultures, knowledge is embodied in a collective repository of received wisdom, acquired through shared experiences and interpersonal relationships; in written cultures, knowledge is seen as a depersonalized and analytic compilation of facts and insights of decontextualized thoughts (Goody 1981).

The differing conceptions of the knowledge system also imply different modes of transmission (Goody 1977) and different modes of human consciousness (Ornstein 1972). These recent understandings reject the older illiterate and literate dichotomization of language skills. Nevertheless, the Canadian schools continue the process of cognitive imperialism under the illiterate savage myth and the banking concept of education. Despite good intentions and textbook reforms, the seemingly innocuous textbooks continue the mythical portrait of Mi'kmaq and their society, when they mention it at all. Conventional Canadian history remains a fictional history, a by-product of 19th century European society, in which the Mi'kmaq and other indigenous nations are mere bystanders. Stripped of their resource wealth in Eastern Canada, Mi'kmaq carry the burden of history and modern economics while myths continue to erode perceptions of their culture, language and indigenous identity. Their knowledge and values receive barely a quaint nod. This psychological and cultural regime remains substantially implemented in provincial, federal and many band-controlled schools.

The resiliency of early Algonkian literacy processes in Mi'kmaw consciousness has demonstrated that any system can function as long as the people value it and have use for it. The indigenous forms of literacy served a function for Algonkian society: universal symbols represented concepts and ideas, not sounds of language, and its legitimacy for contemporary indigenous society has not been replaced. Instead, missionary and governmental education has attempted to assimilate Mi'kmaq to the functions of cultural transmission of and adaptation to Euro-Canadian society.

A contemporary assessment of Mi'kmaw education suggests both curricula reform in provincial schools and the need for the continued development of traditional and contemporary functions of literacy and knowledge, as well as its systems. In Canada, this curricula reform is a constitutional imperative for the federal and provincial educational systems; it is required to implement the inherent, Aboriginal and treaty rights of Aboriginal peoples (*Constitution Act, 1982*: s. 35; Battiste 2009). It is a project that indigenous leaders, scholars and educators have taken to their sites of work and study, whether in the political activism of blockades on the roads, in protests in the waters, in the courts, in dissertations and theses, and in schools and classrooms. And teachers and students everywhere need to be aware of its significance.

Under the constitutional rights of the Mi'kmaq, Mi'kmaw Kina'matnewey is successful leading the way to curricula reform in the educational systems of the Mi'kmaw reserves and Nova Scotia, and other education organizations are attempting similar reform in the Atlantic Provinces. Indigenous languages and their symbolic systems are an essential constitutional dimension of indigenous humanities in the curricula reform. These language rights generate cognitive justice, reconciliation, cultural restoration and amelioration of the past harms and disadvantages of indigenous peoples. In addition, these language rights provide the therapeutic remedies space and support to safeguard and promote linguistic diversity of indigenous peoples, especially endangered languages, as a vehicle of intangible cultural heritage, inherent and constitutional rights in the twenty-first century.

Notes

1. In Maine, the spelling is Micmac. See http://www.micmac-nsn.gov.

References

Alexander VI. 1493. *Inter Caetera* ("Among other works") website accessed 1 September 2016 http://www.papalencyclicals.net/Alex06/alex06inter.htm

Archer, Gabriel. 1843. The Relations of Captain Gosnold's Voyage to the North Part of Virginia, 1602. In *Collections of the Massachusetts Historical Society*, vol. 3. Boston, MA: Massachusetts Historical Society.

Battiste, Marie. 1984. *An Historical Investigation of the Cultural and Cognitive Consequences of Micmac Literacy*. PhD dissertation, Stanford University.

―――. 2009. Constitutional Reconciliation of Education for Aboriginal peoples / La réconciliation constitutionnelle des Autochtones et leurs droits éducationnels. *Directions* 5 (1): 81-84.

Begouen, Count Henri. 1929. The Magic Origin of Prehistoric Act, *Antiquity* 3 (9): 5-19.

Brinton, D. G. 1969[1984]. *The Lenape and their Legends with the Complete Text and symbols of the Walam Olum*. New York: AMS Press Inc.

Cadogan, León.1959. Ayvu Rapyta, Textos miticos de los Mbya-Guarani del Guaira. Boletim no. 227. *Antropologia* no. 5. University of São Paulo.

Canada Act 1982, 1982, c. 11 (U.K.).

Clark, Jerimiah S., ed. 1902. *Micmac Dictionary*. Charlottetown, PEI: Patriot Publishing.

Constitution Act, 1982. Enacted as Schedule B to the *Canada Act 1982*.

Corbett, Edward. 1981. The Status of Writing in Our Society. In *Writing: The Nature, Development and Teaching of Written Communication*. Hillsdale, New Jersey: Lawrence Erlbaum.

Eliade, Mircea. 1964. *Shamanism. Archaic Techniques of Ecstasy*. Trans. Willard R. Trask. Princeton, NJ: Princeton University Press.

Ganong, William, trans., ed. 1910. *New Relations of Gaspesia*. Toronto: The Champlain Society.

Glidden, George. 1843. *Ancient Egypt*. New York: J. Winchester.

Goody, Jack. 1977. *The Domestication of the Savage Mind*. Cambridge: Cambridge University Press.

―――. 1981. Alternative Paths of Knowledge in Oral and Literate Cultures. In *Spoken and Written Language*, ed. Deborah Tannen. Norwood, NJ: Ablex.

Goody, Jack and Ian Watt. 1963. The Consequence of Literacy. *Comparative Studies in History and Society V* (3): 304-45.

Henderson, James (Sa'ke'j) Youngblood. 1997. *The Mi'kmaq Concordat.* Halifax, NS: Fernwood.

Hewson, John. 1977. Micmac Hieroglyphics in Newfoundland. In *Language in Newfoundland and Labrador,* ed. H. J. Paddock, Preliminary version. St. Johns, NL: Memorial University.

Hoffman, Walter James. 1895. *The Beginning of Writing.* New York: D. Appleton and Company.

Johnston, A.A. 1960. *A History of the Catholic Church in Eastern Nova Scotia II.* Antigonish, N.S.: Francis Xavier University Press.

Jung, Carl J. 1964. *Man and His Symbols.* London: Aldus Books.

Le Clercq, Father Christian. 1910[1691]. *New Relation of Gaspesia.* William Ganong, trans. and ed. Toronto: The Champlain Society.

Levi-Strauss, Claude.1964-1971 *Mythologiques.* (4 vols.) Paris.

MacLaren, George 1974. The Arts of the Micmac of Nova Scotia, *Nova Scotia Historical Quarterly* 4 (2): 167-77.

Maillard, Antoine Pierre. 1758. *An Account of the Customs and Manners of the Micmakis and Maricheets Savage Nations, Now Dependent on the Government of Cape Breton.* London: S. Hooper and A. Morley.

———. 1759. *Ideograms with Translation in Micmac Written in Roman Alphabet.* Eucologe. Archives do l'Archdiocese de Quebec.

———. 1863. Lettre de M. l'Abbe Maillard sur les Missions de l'Acadie et Particulierement sur les Missions Micmaques. *Soirees Canadiennes III*:291-426.

Maine Historical Society. 1897. *Collections and Proceedings. Second Series, VIII.* Portland, Maine: Maine Historical Society.

Mallery, Garrick. 1893. Picture Writing of the American Indians. *Tenth Annual Report of the Bureau of Ethnology. 1888-1889.* Washington, DC: Government Printing Office.

Molyneaux, Brian. 1980. Rock Art Research in Nova Scotia. In *Proceedings of the 1980 Conference on the Future of Archaelogy in the Maritime Provinces.* Occasional Papers in Anthropology no. 8 Halifax, NS: Department of Anthropology, Saint Mary's University.

Montaigne. 1603[1580]. *Essayes,* Trans. John Florio. London.

Murdoch, John. 1981. *Syllabics: A Successful Educational Innovation.* Master's thesis. Winnipeg, MB: University of Manitoba.

————. 1985. A Syllabary or an Alphabet: A Choice between Phonemic Differentiation or Economy. In Barbara Burnaby, ed., *Promoting Native Writing Systems in Canada*, 127-36. Toronto: Ontario Institute for Studies in Education.

Ornstein, R. E. 1972. *The Psychology of Consciousness*. New York: Penguin Books, Inc.

Rand, Rev. Silas Tertius. 1850. *Micmac Tribe of Indians*. Halifax, N.S.: James Bowes & Son.

————. 1894. *Legends of Micmacs*. New York: Longmans, Green, and Co., Reprints 1971 and 1898, Johnson Reprint Corp.

Robertson, Marion. 1973. *Rock Drawings of the Micmac Indians*. Halifax, NS: Nova Scotia Museum.

Roys, Ralph L. 1967[1933]. *The Book of Chilam Balam of Chumayel*. Norman, OK: University of Oklahoma Press.

Scott, J. B. 1934. *The Classics of International Law*. Oxford: Clarendon.

Shea, J. G.1861. Micmac or Récollect Hieroglyphics. *Historical Magazine V* (10): 289-92.

Schmidt, David L. and B. A. Balcom. 1993. The Règlements of 1739, A Note on Micmac Law and Literacy. *Acadiensis* 23 (1): 110-27.

Schoolcraft, Henry Rowe. 1853. *Historical and statistical information, respecting the history, condition and prospects of the Indian tribes of the United States / collected and prepared under the direction of the Bureau of Indian Affairs, per act of Congress of March 3d, 1847, by Henry R. Schoolcraft ; illustrated by S. Eastman*. Philadelphia: Lippincott .

Skutnabb-Kangas, Tove. 2000. *Linguistic Genocide in Education or Worldwide Diversity and Human Rights?* Mahwah, NJ: Lawrence Erlbaum Associates.

Snyderman, George S. 1954. The Functions of Wampum, *Proceedings of the American Philosophical Society* 98:469-494.

Speck, Frank. 1914. The Double Curve Motive in Northeastern Algonkian Art. Memoir 42. Ottawa: Government Printing Office.

————. 1915. The Eastern Wabanaki Confederacy. *American Anthropologist XVII* (3):492-508.

————. 1916. Wampum in Indian Tradition and Currency. Proceedings of the *Numismatic and Antiquarian Society of Philadelphia XXXVI*:121-130.

————.1917. The Social Structure of the Northern Algonkian. *American Sociological Society XII*, 82-100.

————.1919. The Functions of Wampum Among the Eastern Algonkian. *American Anthropologist IV* (1).

———.1922. *Beothuk and Micmac*. New York: Museum of American Indians, Heye Foundation.

———.1927. Symbolism in Penobscot Art. American Anthropological Papers. *American Museum of National History XXIX* (2).

———.1940. *Penobscot Man*. Philadelphia: University of Pennsylvania Press.

Tannen, Deborah. 1982. The Myth of Orality and Literacy. In *Linguistics and Literacy*. Ed., William Frawley, 37-50. New York: Plenus Press.

Tanner, John. 1830. *Narrative of the Captivity and Adventures of John Tanner*. New York, NY: G and C and H Carvill.

Thwaites, Rueben Gold. ed.1897. *The Jesuit Relations and Allied Documents, vol. III*. Cleveland.

Truth and Reconciliation Commission of Canada (TRC). 2015. *Honouring the Truth, Reconciling for the Future. Summary of the Final Report of the Truth and Reconciliation Commission of Canada*. Winnipeg: Truth and Reconciliation Commission of Canada.

Unger, Roberto Mangabeira. 1976. *Law in Modern Society*. New York: Free Press.

Vennum, Thomas. 1978. Ojibwa Origin-Migration Songs of the Mitewiwin, *Journal of American Folklore* 91 (361): 753-91.

Wauchope, Robert. 1964-75. *Handbook of Middle American Indians*. Austin: University of Texas Press.

Zerubavel, Eviatar. 1992. *Terra Cognita: The Mental Discovery of America*. New Brunswick, NJ: Rutgers University Press.

Nancy Peters

Learning Shame:
Colonial Narratives as a Tool for Decolonization

Stories can control our lives, for there is a part of me that has never been able to move past these stories, a part of me that will be chained to these stories as long as I live (King 2003: 9).

My name is Nancy and I'm a white, non-Aboriginal, fifty-something "come-from-away" who lives on never-ceded Mi'kmaw territory in Nova Scotia. From 2010 to 2012, I was privileged to be a research assistant with the "Animating the Mi'kmaw Humanities in Atlantic Canada" project. My role was to look at how the Mi'kmaq had been portrayed in the Nova Scotia school curriculum and textbooks. This task was similar to an assignment that Trent University professor David Newhouse (2005) has given to students enrolled in an introductory indigenous studies course. Newhouse asked students to examine their home communities and prepare a "homelands report" (47) about the Aboriginal peoples who have lived there. Inevitably, he observed, students "come back after a short while telling us that they can't find any information" (47). Just like Newhouse's students, at first, I found very little.

Turning to archives and second-hand bookstores, I eventually began to uncover long-out-of-print books containing stories about the Mi'kmaq written by European settlers. At about the halfway point in the research project, however, I wrote in my journal:

I'm finding this research more difficult than I ever imagined. [...] I don't know which is worse, the complete silences about the

Mi'kmaq or the fearful, hate-filled words that appear in other textbooks. I can't imagine what it must be like for someone who is Mi'kmaq, seeing these images and reading such poisonous stories about your ancestors, your family, and your community. I feel so sad. But even more than that, I feel so very, very ashamed....

Encountering overt racism in the works and words of respected white European colonizers shook me up in ways that academic articles about colonialism had not.

One of the strongest emotions I experienced was a profound sense of shame. As I started to recognize how settlers very much like me have thought about and treated the Mi'kmaq for centuries, I began to wonder how, or if, I was any different than them. I began to examine what I believed about Canada's past and started to question my own position in relation to Aboriginal peoples, including my own good intentions. Shame is a feeling commonly perceived as being disempowering or paralyzing, but when it comes to decolonization, a therapeutic dose of shame may be exactly the "medicine" that non-Aboriginal Canada needs right now.

The Peacemaker Myth

> So you have to be careful with the stories you tell. And you have to watch out for the stories that you are told (King 2003: 10).

In their interim report, the Truth and Reconciliation Commission of Canada (2012) observed that "Canadians have been denied a full and proper education as to the nature of Aboriginal societies, and the history of the relationship between Aboriginal and non-Aboriginal peoples" (26). Looking back on the years I spent in school, I can now see just how little mention there was of Aboriginal peoples. As one participant in a nationwide study by the Coalition for the Advancement of Aboriginal Studies (2002) commented more than a decade ago:

> I was barely taught ANYTHING regarding Aboriginal Peoples in school ... I am absolutely clueless with regard to these issues. I am uneducated on these matters and as such feel ill equipped to even have an opinion much less come to an understanding. (129)

From elementary to post-secondary classrooms, school curricula have consistently failed to provide an accurate, appropriate and balanced account either of colonial history or of Aboriginal peoples' rights, issues and concerns (Clark 2007; Godlewska, Moore and Bednasek 2010; Kanu 2011; Tupper 2011). All too often, though, settler Canadians deny that we have any responsibility for addressing the social, cultural, political and economic problems Aboriginal peoples face today.

The long-standing myth of Canada as a nation of "peacemakers" (Barker 2009; Day 2000; Regan 2010) is a major barrier when it comes to changing settlers' beliefs, attitudes and behaviours. I grew up believing that Canada has always been a country where diversity was tolerated, if not openly celebrated, a country renowned for its sense of fair play (Alfred 2005; Bolton 2009; Haig-Brown and Nock 2006; Mackey 2002). This story has been told again and again, not only in school textbooks, but also in museums and other public institutions that provide a storehouse for our collective memory. In 2011, for instance, the Art Gallery of Nova Scotia mounted an exhibit titled *Burying the Hatchet, and the Sword*. Prints and drawings created by white settlers in the decades immediately after the signing of the 1752 peace and friendship treaty depicted details of Mi'kmaw dress, encampments and livelihood activities. Even if the images in this exhibit were true to life, the larger story this exhibit told was not. What the exhibit failed to acknowledge was the violence used to wrest control of Mi'kma'ki from its traditional caretakers.

Shortly after assuming his post as the first British administrator of Nova Scotia, for example, General Edward Cornwallis issued a bounty of £10, which was later raised to £50, for the scalps of every Mi'kmaw man, woman and child or prisoner taken alive (Paul 2006: 112-22). British administrators subsequently imposed such harsh policies that the Mi'kmaq barely survived what was, in fact, attempted genocide (Coates 2000; Paul 2006; Neu and Therrien 2003; Parnaby 2008). With the exception of a single sentence in the *Burying the Hatchet* exhibit brochure, which admitted the "rapacious demand of new settlers for more land" (O'Neill 2011: 2), peaceful portrayals left viewers with the impression that European settlement brought no harm to the Mi'kmaq, their communities or traditional ways of life. By removing all evidence of aggression on the part of white European colonizers, however, the exhibit made "white entitlement seem natural and normal" (Schick 2012: 2) rather than the inevitable outcome of military force and oppressive political, economic and social policies and practices.

A few academics believe that national events like the Prime Minister's 2008 apology to Aboriginal peoples for Indian residential schools have been effective in raising awareness in settler Canada and instilling a much needed sense of collective guilt (Taylor, Caouette, Usborne et al. 2010: 193-96). Other Aboriginal and non-Aboriginal scholars have argued that, as a group, settlers still seem strikingly unapologetic, reluctant to even consider the possibility that we have unfulfilled legal, let alone moral, obligations toward Aboriginal peoples (Lund 2006; Nagy 2013; Schick 2012; Solomon et al. 2005; Stanton 2011; Warry 2009).

In the comments section of an article by Nie (2011) reporting that an Aboriginal woman had been granted a human rights hearing in order to investigate charges of discrimination towards Aboriginal peoples by a local nightclub, one reader identified only as "Fledgling" raved:

> I am so SICK of this ... I personally did nothing to anyone ... GET OVER IT !!!. Time to be one country not a bunch of people who cry and sniffle over stuff that happened how many years ago....
> (Nie 2011)

Another barrier that stands in the way of reconciliation, then, is the all-too-common assumption on the part of people of privilege that "I'm not responsible for what my ancestors did" (Cannon 2011; Caouette and Taylor 2007; Schick and McNich 2009; Schick 2012; Tupper 2011). The difficulty here is that, from a Eurocentric perspective, Fledgling's arguments make sense.

People from white, European cultural backgrounds are typically taught that there is no need to feel guilty unless we are *personally* responsible for harm done to others (Katz 2003; Young 2008). If, however, we have few, or no, interactions with those who have been wronged, and if there is no formal contract which lays out our obligations toward others, guilt is neither expected nor appropriate, and there is no need to make reparations. What can we do, then, to begin to "unsettle the settler within?" (Regan 2010). More often than not, settlers shy away from any examination of our role as "colonizer-perpetrators" (28). Even non-confrontational attempts at questioning the "naturalness" of Aboriginal inequality and "rightness" of white Euro-Canadian privilege may be interpreted as a deeply personal form of attack (Schick 2000, 2012; St. Denis and Hampton 2002; Tupper 2011).

Who Do You Think You Are?

Some psychologists believe that the starting point for any significant psychological and social change begins with the reclamation of aspects of ourselves, our lives and communities which have long been forgotten, suppressed or rejected (Kaufman 1989). Stories provide learners with a "safe space" where uncomfortable truths can be examined more openly and self-reflexively (Cloke and Goldsmith 2000; Episkenew 2009; Marks 2011; Nelson 2001). Humans seem to respond reflexively to stories, the "most effective form and the oldest form of teaching" (Gold 2002: 15). Narrative educators Carolyn Clark and Marsha Rossiter (2008), however, pointed out that we need different types of stories and stories told by different people in order to effect change. First, we need to listen to the stories others tell about themselves and their lives (Clark and Rossiter: 2008).

For some time now, Aboriginal scholars and settler allies have been urging settlers to pay close attention to Aboriginal peoples' accounts of our shared colonial past (Graveline 1998; Battiste 2000; King 2003, 2012; Chamberlin 2004; Dion 2009; Episkenew 2009; Regan 2010); for example, stories told by participants in Truth and Reconciliation Commission of Canada hearings. Stories that reveal the "harmful effects of one's action on a victim" (Barrett 1995: 54) are believed to be helpful in catalyzing restorative attitudes and behaviours on the part of people who are, or have been, the aggressor. Educators including Susan Dion (2009) have also used first person Aboriginal narratives about historical events, about family and community life and ways of living with the land, not only as a way of countering settler prejudices, but also as a forum for presenting Aboriginal peoples in a positive, empowering light.

Clark and Rossiter (2008) also argued we need to become more critically aware of stories "in which we are positioned" (6), stories like the peacemaker myth. While settlers are beginning to learn more about Aboriginal peoples, their cultures and their concerns, we still spend relatively little time learning about how we came here and secured our position on Aboriginal territories (Kuokkanen 2003; Lawrence and Dua 2005; Schick and St. Denis 2005; St. Denis 2007; Tupper 2011). As anti-racism educator Carol Schick has emphasized, Canadian settlers today need to be able to provide a more truthful answer to the question, "Who do you think you are?" (2009: 125). In the "Animating the Mi'kmaw Humanties" project, I had opportunities to read reports, letters, histories and school books written by respected white settlers who were, or later became, people with considerable privilege and power over the telling of Nova Scotia's history. Far from being peacemakers, the settlers' stories clearly revealed different ways white settlers were complicit in a whole host of "policies of devastation" (Episkenew 2009: 20-68) that resulted in the subjugation of the Mi'kmaq.

As Joanne Episkenew (2009), professor of English, explained, first the colonizers seized land and power. Then, they set out to ensure Aboriginal peoples were regarded as inhumane and less than human:

> Four hundred years ago nearly all this land was one unbroken forest, without roads or cities, or cultivated fields. Save the wild animals, which roamed through its forests, its only inhabitants were a race of savages scattered thinly over the country. How these people came here, whence they came, or how long ago nobody can tell. They had no history or written language. They lived in rough dwellings formed of poles ... for the most part they lived by hunting and fishing. They were a roving people, remaining but a short time in one place. [...] The different tribes were often engaged in war with one another. [...] Before a battle they held a grand feast followed by wild war dances during which they filled the air with hideous shouts and yells. Prisoners taken in war they tortured to death and then feasted on their bodies. (Calkin 1898: 2-3)

The author of this passage, J. B. Calkin, was nearly the sole author of history and geography texts used in Nova Scotia schools for some fifty years (Robinson 1979; Welsh 2005). Calkin taught at the provincial teacher's training college in Truro for forty-two years before becoming Head of Pedagogy and Psychology in 1869 and Principal of the College in 1898. These kinds of "external stories" (Cloke and

Goldsmith 2000: 7) that depicted the Aboriginal "other" as the aggressor and as a social and cultural inferior persisted well into the 1960s.

Son of the Hawk: A Canadian Yankee Boy in '76 (Raddall 1951), for instance, was included on the compulsory "Extra Reading" list for Grade 10 English from the mid 1950s through to the mid 1960s. In one passage, the teenage boy narrator recounts his experiences on a moose hunt accompanied by Mi'kmaw guides:

> We butchered him at once. Soon we were blood to the elbows, with dark clots spattered all over. [...] the Indians made a fire and roasted the dark liver on a stick and ate it like gluttons. I could eat none, for all my hunger, I wanted to retch. (9)

Later, the young narrator complained of sleeplessness as "the savages whooped and danced ... brandishing guns and hatchets, far into the night" (148). Author of *Son of the Hawk*, Thomas Raddall, was a popular historian and novelist whose influence extended well beyond the schoolroom. Raddall received no fewer than three Governor General's Awards for his fiction (Cockburn 1978; Seaman 1991). He also sat on Nova Scotia's Historic Sites Advisory Council, a group responsible for installing plaques and memorials commemorating important people, places and events in Nova Scotia (McKay 1993). Perhaps not surprisingly, from 1948 to 1964 the Historic Sites Advisory Council acknowledged "Native History" (McKay 1993: 439, 449) only once, referring to the site of a large Mi'kmaw encampment when white European explorers first arrived.

Settler stories that were even more troubling, though, were the "internal stories" (Cloke and Goldsmith 2000: 7) settlers told in an attempt at "excusing ourselves, justifying our actions or inactions" (ibid.). For instance, in a letter dated January 1, 1939, the Indian Agent of King's Country, Nova Scotia, wrote to his supervisor in Ottawa:

> Dear Sir: The Indians here in Cambridge Reserve were determined to have their children who is attending the Shubenacadie Indian School – home during the xmas vacation. I refused to grant their request and advised them that this was against the rules of the Dept. These people went so far as [to] have a man go to the school for their children. They did not get the children.... These people think they can have their own way and would like to do so and when they find out they cannot they get mad. I had

your rules and regulations regarding this matter. (Knockwood 2001: 116-17)

The Indian Agent seemed proud of unquestioningly following orders and expressed neither compassion for children entrusted to his care, nor empathy for family members who tried so desperately to take their children home.

Encountering these kinds of demeaning and openly racist viewpoints in textbooks which had been authorized for use in Nova Scotia schools was far more "unsettling" than reading about racism in academic journals. These settler tales left me with a hard pit of anger in my stomach and a deep sense of shame that I had known so little about the words and actions of Nova Scotia's "founding fathers." I began to recognize how the white settlers who came before me had secured my own privilege. I also began to wonder if I might be just as blind to the realities that Aboriginal Peoples around me are facing as well as equally oblivious to my own agency and responsibility.

Shame as a Catalyst for Decolonization

> Just don't say in the years to come that you would have lived *your* life differently if only you had heard this story. You've heard it now (King 2003: 167).

Guilt, shame and empathy have been described as being moral emotions (Price et al. 2003) that allow us to get in touch with *who we are*, rather just what we have or have not done. Shame is especially unsettling because it signals that we have failed to live up to our most important personal values and principles (Harder 1995: 373; Price et al. 2003). Consequently, shame prompts us to turn inward and critically examine what we believe about ourselves and our assumptions about others (Barker 2003; Barrett 1995; Price et al. 2003; Price et al. 1995;). Shame, therefore, is often believed to be the basis for the development of empathy and a moral conscience (Hartling et al. 2000: 2).

> In an international study that explored the willingness of people from dominant groups to participate in reconciliation, researchers found that individuals who admitted to feeling a sense of shame about their collective group identities were more open

to dialogue about social justice issues and were more likely to be active in initiatives aimed at healing (Allpress et al. 2010). In Canada, Regan (2010) has similarly concluded that, "the process of being uncomfortable is essential for non-Indigenous people to move from being enemy to adversary to ally" (27).

The Importance of Primary Sources

In the aftermath of conflicts where genocide was a factor, historian Sztompka (2000) concluded that aggressors need to undergo a process of "cultural disorientation" (ibid.) before peace can be restored. What usually catalyzes this disorientation is some significant, new "discovery, unraveling of facts, or emergence of evidence, throwing radically new light on events or persons and demanding basic reinterpretation of earlier judgments" (455). In the "Animating" project, stories told by white settlers such as Calkin, Raddall and others unsettled my own thinking and caused me to reconsider what I thought I knew about myself and about the province in which I live. As Mi'kmaw historian Daniel Paul (2006) has pointed out, "the proof of the horrors committed by the British in what is today Atlantic Canada has been readily available for examination by scholars and others for centuries. But it was never brought out of the closet for scrutiny" (370).

Narratives are "cultural artifacts" that provide a window into their time and place and into the character of the people who created them (Rossiter and Clark 2007: 62). White settler stories in learning materials approved for use in Nova Scotia schools revealed beliefs, assumptions and perspectives that have largely faded from public memory or have fallen out of favour because they are no longer "politically correct." Current research on history and social studies teaching increasingly asserts that *primary* documents, documents produced at a particular period in time including autobiographies, newspaper articles, audio recordings, photos or posters, even old textbooks, hold the key to helping learners reframe their false, faulty or distorted beliefs about the past and their assumptions about non-dominant or marginalized groups (Anderson et al. 2006; Foster and Padgett 1999; Newhouse 2005; Nokes 2013; Warren et al. 2004). Historian and teacher Jeffery Nokes (2013), for instance, commented that the collision of viewpoints enables learners to become skeptical about single truths and become more curious about what lies beneath taken-for-granted interpretations (133-44).

The Importance of Taking Action

North Americans have also been described as highly "shame phobic" (Price et al. 2002: 11) and shame is typically reserved for only very serious misdeeds (Barrett 1995; Barker 2003; Lu 2008). Feelings of shame can also cause people to turn away from, rather than toward, others—in part to sidestep the hard work demanded by change. For several months while I was working on this project, I felt "stuck," almost paralyzed, and was unable to read or write any further. Following a conversation with Dr. Jeff Orr, Dean of the Faculty of Education at St. Francis Xavier University, my sense of shame began to shift. Orr commented that even racist texts like the ones I had been reading can be useful in opening up dialogue about inequality, power and privilege (J. Orr, personal communication, February 15, 2011). His remarks interrupted the cycle of self-blame and pushed me to look at what these narratives could teach me, not only about the past, but also about what I might do differently right now as a settler living on Mi'kmaw land. I began to explore ways to use the power and privilege I have to shift conversations about Aboriginal peoples and Aboriginal-settler relationships in my community. As one anti-racism educator has observed, whites possess an abundance of agency and if "we make the rules," we are also in a position to change what the "rules" are (Leonardo 2009).

Colonizers or Allies?

The truth about stories is that that's all we are (King 2003: 2).

More than a century of psychological indoctrination has encouraged settlers to "keep their distance" from the Mi'kmaq and has interrupted settlers' awareness of the legal and moral responsibilities as foreigners living on Mi'kmaw lands. Alongside stories told by Aboriginal Peoples, the external stories settlers have told about First Peoples and the internal stories we have told ourselves excusing our actions or inaction offer a space where people of privilege may risk "revealing ourselves as vulnerable 'not-knowers'" (Regan 2010: 28).

Confronted with the racism and hardships that Mi'kmaq have endured over the past 400 years, I now more fully appreciate the resilience and dynamism of the Mi'kmaw nation. Observing the shifts and turns of beliefs and attitudes over the centuries, I also recognize that history is fluid and that dramatic shifts are possible if people like me take up the challenge to do things differently by working as allies with Aboriginal peoples.

On March 21, 2013, *Idle No More* co-founder Nina Wilson posted this call to action:

> I know it has been a long hard four months ... but we need you ... we need the messengers ... the ones who love this land, water, and the air and want it safe, clean, and pure ... the farmers, the unions, the educators, the poets, the writers, the singers, the artists, environmentalists, the settlers, and all allies ... we need you. (qtd. in Houle 2013)

Whether or not this happens will depend, at least in part, on the stories we choose to listen to and the stories we choose to tell now and in the generations yet to come (Chamberlin 2003; Lutz 2007).

References

Alfred, Gerald Taiaiake. 2005. *Wasáse: Indigenous Pathways of Action and Freedom*. Toronto: University of Toronto Press.

Allpress, Jesse A., Fiona Barlow, Rupert Brown and Winnifred R. Louis. 2010. Atoning for Colonial Injustices: Group-based Shame and Guilt Motivate Support for Reparation. *International Journal of Conflict and Violence* 4 (1): 75-88.

Anderson, Charles, Kate Day, Ranald Michie and David Rollason. 2006. Engaging with Historical Source Work: Practices, Pedagogy, Dialogue. *Arts and Humanities in Higher Education* 5:243.

Barker, Adam J. 2009. The Contemporary Reality of Canadian Imperialism: Settler Colonialism and the Hybrid Colonial State. *The American Indian Quarterly* 33 (3): 325-51.

Barker, Phil. 2003. Guilt and Shame. In *Beyond Intractability*, ed. G. Burgess and H. Burgess, Conflict Information Consortium, University of Colorado. http://www.beyondintractability.org/bi-essay/guilt-shame (accessed August 6, 2015).

Barrett, Karen C. 1995. A Functionalist Approach to Shame and Guilt. In *Self-conscious Emotions: The Psychology of Shame, Guilt, Embarrassment, and Pride*, eds. June Price Tangney and Kurt W. Fischer, 25-63. New York: Guilford Press.

Battiste, Marie A. ed. 2000. *Reclaiming Indigenous Voice and Vision*. Vancouver: University of British Columbia Press.

Bolton, Stephanie. 2009. Museums Taken to Task: Representing First Peoples at the McCord Museum of Canadian History. In *First Nations, First Thoughts: The Importance of Indigenous Thought in Canada, ed.* A. M. Timpson, 145-69). Vancouver: UBC Press.

Calkin, John B. 1898. *A History of the Dominion of Canada*. Halifax, NS: A. and W. MacKinlay.

Cannon, Martin J. 2011. Changing the Subject in Teacher Education: Indigenous, Diasporic and Settler Colonial Relations. *"Equity Matters" FEDCAN Blog* November 12. http://www.ideas-idees.ca/blog/changing-subject-teacher-education-indigenous-diasporic-and-settler-colonial-relationsx (accessed January 14, 2012).

Caouette, Julie and Donald M.Taylor. 2007. "Don't blame me for what my ancestors did": Understanding the Impact of Collective White Guilt. In *The Great White North?* ed. P. R. Carr and D.E. Lund, 77-92. Boston, MA: Sense Publishers.

Chamberlin, J. Edward. 2003. *If This is Your Land, Where are your Stories? Finding Common Ground.* Toronto, Canada: Vintage Canada.

Clark, M. Carolyn and Marsha Rossiter. 2008. Narrative Learning in Adulthood. *New Directions for Adult and Continuing Education* 119: 61-70.

Clark, Penney. 2007. Representations of Aboriginal People in English Canadian History Textbooks: Towards Reconciliation. In *Teaching the Violent Past: History Education and Reconciliation* ed. E. A. Cole, 81-120. Lanham, MD: Rowman and Littlefield.

Cloke, Kenneth and Joan Goldsmith. 2000. *Resolving Personal and Organizational Conflict: Stories of Transformation and Forgiveness.* San Francisco, CA: Jossey-Bass.

Coalition for the Advancement of Aboriginal Studies. (2002, November). *Learning About Walking in Beauty: Placing Aboriginal Perspectives in Canadian Classrooms.* Toronto, Canada: Canadian Race Relations Foundation. http://www.crrf-fcrr.ca/en/component/flexicontent/334-crrf-research-reports/23526-learning-about-walking-in-beauty-placing-aboriginal-perspectives-in-canadian-classrooms (accessed June 14, 2010).

Coates, Ken. 2000. *The Marshall Decision and Native Rights.* Montreal: McGill-Queen's University Press.

Cockburn, Robert. 1978. Nova Scotia is My Dwelen Pias: The Life and Work of Thomas Raddall. *Acadiensis* 7 (2): 135-41.

Day, Richard. 2000. *Two Canadian Solutions to the Problem of Diversity. Multiculturalism and the History of Canadian Diversity.* Toronto, Canada: University of Toronto Press, 72-100.

Dion, Susan. 2009. *Braiding Histories: Learning from Aboriginal Peoples' Experiences and Perspectives.* Vancouver: University of British Columbia Press.

Episkenew, Jo-Ann. 2009. *Taking Back our Spirits: Indigenous Literature, Public Policy, and Healing.* Winnipeg, Canada: University of Manitoba Press.

Foster, Stuart J. and Charles S. Padgett. 1999. Authentic Historical Inquiry in the Social Studies Classroom. *The Clearing House* 72 (6): 357-63.

Godlewska, Anne, Jackie Moore and C. Drew Bednasek. 2010. Cultivating Ignorance of Aboriginal Realities. *The Canadian Geographer* 54 (4): 417-40.

Gold, Joseph. 2002. *The Story Species: Our Life–Literature Connection.* Markham, Canada: Fitzhenry and Whiteside.

Graveline, Fyre Jean. 1998. *Circle Works: Transforming Eurocentric Consciousness.* Halifax, NS: Fernwood.

Haig-Brown, Celia and David A. Nock. eds. 2006. *With Good Intentions: Euro-Canadian Aboriginal Relations in Colonial Canada.* Vancouver: UBC Press.

Harder, David W. 1995. Shame and Guilt Assessment, and Relationships of Shame – and Guilt-Proneness to Psychopathology. In June Price Tangney and Kurt W. Fischer, ed *Self-Conscious Emotions: The Psychology of Shame, Guilt, Embarrassment, and Pride*, 368-92). New York: Guilford.

Hartling, Linda M., Wendy Rosen, Maureen Walker and Judith V. Jordan. 2000. *Shame and Humiliation: From Isolation to Relational Transformation* no. 88. Wellesley, MA: Stone Center, Wellesley College.

Houle, Shannon. 2013. Idle No More needs all of you, March 21. http://idlenomore.ca/articles/latest-news/global-news/item/170-idle-no-more-needs-all-of-you (accessed August 15, 2014).

Kanu, Yatta. 2011. *Integrating Aboriginal Perspectives into the School Curriculum: Purposes, Possibilities, and Challenges.* Toronto, Canada: University of Toronto Press.

Katz, Judith H. 2003. *White Awareness: Handbook for Anti-racism Training.* Oklahoma City, OK: University of Oklahoma Press.

Kaufman, Gershen. 1989. *The Psychology of Shame: Theory and Treatment of Shame-based Syndromes.* New York: Springer.

King, Thomas. 2003. *The Truth About Stories: A Native Narrative.* Toronto, Canada: House of Anansi Press.

King, Thomas. 2012. *The Inconvenient Indian: A Curious Account of Native People in North America.* Toronto: Doubleday Canada.

Knockwood, Isabelle. 2001. *Out of the Depths: The Experiences of Mi'kmaw Children at the Indian Residential School at Shubenacadie, Nova Scotia,* 3rd ed. Black Point, NS: Roseway.

Kuokkanen, Rauna. 2003. Toward a New Relation of Hospitality in the Academy. *American Indian Quarterly* 27 (1/2): 267-95.

Lawrence, Bonita and Enakshi Dua. 2005. Decolonizing Anti-racism. *Social Justice* 32 (4): 120-43.

Leonardo, Zeus. 2009. Reading Whiteness: Anti-racist Pedagogy Against White Racial Knowledge. In *Handbook of Social Justice in Education,* eds. B. Ayers, T. Quinn and D. Stovall, 231-48. New York, NY: Routledge.

Lu, Catherine. 2008. Shame, Guilt and Reconciliation After War. *European Journal of Social Theory* 11 (3): 367-83.

Lund, Darren E. 2006. Rocking the Racism Boat: School-based Activists Speak Out on Denial and Avoidance. *Race Ethnicity and Education,* 9 (2): 203-21.

Lutz, John Sutton. 2007. *Myth and Memory: Stories of Indigenous-European Contact.* Vancouver, Canada: University of British Columbia Press.

Mackey, Eva. 2002. *The House of Difference: Cultural Politics and National Identity in Canada.* Toronto: University of Toronto Press.

Marks, Stephan. 2011. Hidden Stories, Toxic Stories, Healing Stories: The Power of Narrative in Peace and Reconciliation. *Narrative Works: Issues, Investigations and Interventions* 1 (1): 95-106.

McKay, Ian. 1993. History and the Tourist Gaze: The Politics of Commemoration in Nova Scotia, 1935-1964. *Acadiensis* 22 (2): 102-38.

Nagy, Rosemary L. 2013. The Scope and Bounds of Transitional Justice and the Canadian Truth and Reconciliation Commission. *The International Journal of Transitional Justice* 7: 52-73. doi:10.1093/ijtj/ijs034.

Nelson, Hilde Lindemann. 2001. *Damaged Identities: Narrative Repair.* Ithaca, NY: Cornell University Press.

Neu, Dean and Richard Therrien. 2003. *Accounting for Genocide: Canada's Bureaucratic Assault on Aboriginal People.* Halifax, NS: Fernwood.

Newhouse, David. 2005. Telling Our Story. In *Walking a Tightrope: Aboriginal People and Their Representations,* ed. U. Lischke and D. T. McNab, 45-52. Waterloo, ON: Wilfrid Laurier University Press.

Nie. 2011. Re: Aboriginal Woman Granted Human Rights Hearing. *Castanet Forum,* May 25. http://forums.castanet.net/viewtopic.php?f=23&t=32340&start=15 (accessed August 6, 2015).

Nokes, Jeffery. 2013. *Building Students' Historical Literacies: Learning to Read and Reason with Historical Texts and Evidence.* New York, NY: Routledge.

O'Neill, Mora Dianne. 2011. *Burying the Hatchet and the Sword: Mi'kmaq in Nova Scotia Following the Peace and Friendship Treaty of 1761.* Early Canadian prints and drawing, January 22-July 17 2011. Halifax, NS: Art Gallery of Nova Scotia. https://www.artgalleryofnovascotia.ca/exhibitions/burying-hatchet-and-sword (accessed September 24, 2011).

Parnaby, Andrew. 2008. The Cultural Economy of Survival: The Mi'kmaq of Cape Breton in the Mid-19th Century. *Labour/Le Travail,* 61, 69-98.

Paul, Daniel N. 2006. *We Were Not the Savages: Collision between European and Native American Civilizations,* 3rd ed. Halifax, NS: Fernwood.

Price Tangney, June and Kurt W. Fischer. eds. 1995. *Self-conscious Emotions: The Psychology of Shame, Guilt, Embarrassment, and Pride.* New York, NY: Guilford Press.

Price Tangney, June and Dearing, R. L. 2003. *Shame and Guilt.* New York, NY: Guilford Press.

Regan, Paulette. 2010. *Unsettling the Settler Within: Indian Residential Schools, Truth Telling and Reconciliation in Canada.* Vancouver: University of British Columbia Press.

Raddall, Thomas H. 1951. *Son of the Hawk: A Canadian Yankee Boy in '76.* Toronto, Canada: John C. Winston.

Robinson, Paul. 1979. *Where Our Survival Lies: Students and Textbooks in Atlantic Canada.* Halifax, NS: Atlantic Institute of Education.

Rossiter, Marsha and M. Carolyn Clark. 2007. *Narrative and the practice of adult education.* Krieger Publishing.

Schick, Carol. 2000. By Virtue of Being White: Resistance in Anti-racist Pedagogy. *Race, Ethnicity and Education* 3 (1): 83-101.

———. 2009. Well-intentioned Pedagogies that Forestall Change. In"*I Thought Pocahontas was a Movie": Perspectives on Race/Culture Binaries in Education and Service Professions,* eds. C. Schick and J. McNinch, 111-28. Regina, SK: Canadian Plains Research Centre, University of Regina.

———. 2012. White Resentment in Settler Society. *Race Ethnicity and Education* November: 1-15.

Schick, Carol and James McNinch, ed. 2009. *"I Thought Pocahontas was a Movie": Perspectives on Race/Culture Binaries in Education and Service Professions.* Regina, Canada: Canadian Plains Research Centre, University of Regina.

Schick, Carol and Verna St. Denis. 2005. Troubling National Discourses in Anti-racist Curricular Planning. *Canadian Journal of Education* 28 (3): 295-317.

Seaman, Andrew. 1991. Thomas H. Raddall. In vol. 7 of *Profiles in Canadian Literature*, ed. J. M. Heath, 79-86. Toronto, Canada: Dundurn Press.

Solomon, Patrick, John P. Portelli, Beverley-Jean and Arlene Campbell. 2005. The Discourse of Denial: How White Teacher Candidates Construct Race, Racism and "White Privilege." *Race Ethnicity and Education* 8 (2): 147-69.

Stanton, Kim. 2011. Canada's Truth and Reconciliation Commission: Settling the Past? *The International Indigenous Policy Journal* 2 (3), article 2, http://ir.lib.uwo.ca/iipj /vol2/iss3/2

St. Denis, Verna. 2007. Aboriginal Education and Anti-racist Education: Building Alliances Across Cultural and Racial Identity. *Canadian Journal of Education* 30 (4): 1068-92.

St. Denis, Verna and Eber Hampton. 2002. *Literature Review on Racism and the Effects on Aboriginal Education. Prepared for the Minister's National Working Group on Education.* Ottawa, Canada: Indian and Northern Affairs Canada, http://www.ainc-inac.gc.ca/pr/pub/krw/rac_e.html.

Sztompka, Piotr. 2000. Cultural Trauma: The Other Face of Social Change. *European Journal of Social Theory* 3 (4): 449–66.

Taylor, Donald M., Julie Caouette, Esther Usborne and Michael King. 2010. Indigenous Peoples Are Disadvantaged, But They Were Here First. In *Words of Conflict, Words of War*, ed. Fathali Moghaddam and Rom Harr, 189-200. Santa Barbara, CA: Praeger.

Truth and Reconciliation Commission of Canada. 2012. *Truth and Reconciliation Commission of Canada: Interim Report.* Winnipeg, MB: Author.

Tupper, Jennifer A. 2011. Disrupting Ignorance and Settler Identities: The Challenges of Preparing Beginning Teachers for Treaty Education. *In Education* 17 (3). http://ineducation.ca/article/ disrupting-ignorance-and-settler-identities-challenges-preparing-beginning-teachers-treaty-e (accessed March 6, 2013).

Warren, Warren J., David M. Memory and Kevin Bolinger. 2004. Improving Critical Thinking Skills in the United States Survey Course: An Activity for Teaching the Vietnam War. *The History Teacher* 37 (2): 193-209.

Warry, Wayne. 2009. *Ending Denial: Understanding Aboriginal Issues.* Toronto: University of Toronto Press.

Welsh, Jeffrey A. 2005. Nova Scotia, Nation, and Empire: The Politics of Civic Education and Provincial Textbooks, 1864-1918. MA thesis Dalhousie University.

Young, Iris M. 2008. Structural Injustice and the Politics of Difference. In G. Craig, T. Burchardt, and D. Gordon eds. *Social Justice and Public Policy: Seeking Fairness in Diverse Societies,* 77-104. Bristol, U.K.: Policy Press, University of Bristol.

Nancy Peters

Tales Told in School: Images of the Mi'kmaq in Nova Scotia School Curriculum

In 2010, the Mi'kmaw Humanities project was born from a proposal prepared for and funded by the Social Science Humanities Research Council of Canada, with principal investigator Marie Battiste and co-applicants Lynne Bell, Isobel and Len Findlay, J. Youngblood Henderson and Albert and Murdena Marshall. The object of the research was to "shift educational and public discourses about the Mi'kmaq (in the humanities) from deficiency to accomplishment, from misunderstanding to respect, from exasperation to pride, and from division to cooperation" (project proposal). One of the first tasks was to explore what the prevailing literature has said about Mi'kmaw people, in order to understand what Nova Scotia settler society has been learning about them in Nova Scotia's public schools, with a focus on stories, images and discourses found in curricula and other authorized learning resources. Textbooks are still at the heart of the teaching/learning process in schools.

In the first part of this chapter I explore how the Mi'kmaq have been portrayed in Nova Scotia schools in authorized learning textbooks and learning resources. I sketch some important events which shaped life in Nova Scotia schools, provide a few examples of "tales" told in schools at that time and examine what these tales reveal about settlers' beliefs about and attitudes toward the Mi'kmaq at the time. Next, I look at contemporary Nova Scotia curricula in more detail, including how and where the Mi'kmaq are spoken about in learning resources, instructional methods, student learning outcomes and key policy documents. Last, I explore some of the barriers that may have prevented more complete, rapid integration of accurate information about the Mi'kmaq into Nova Scotia schools. Among the barriers is one exercised by the provincial government who has centralized control over educational thought, process and practice for more than two hundred years. Another barrier is that stories about the Mi'kmaq have—to date—more commonly been written by white settlers who use an evolving colonial Eurocentric lens. A more recent problem is that what information there is about the Mi'kmaq in Nova Scotia curricula is often invisible, buried in an ever-growing list of curriculum outcomes and authorized resources. As has been true in the past, the onus is on individuals, on classroom teachers, to fill in the silences in curriculum and replace worn out "tales" about "Indians" with more accurate, empowering and contemporary portraits of the Mi'kmaq.

This study has certain limitations. First, I do not take up what the experience of federal education for the Mi'kmaq in Indian Day Schools or Indian Residential Schools was like. Nor do I address the implications of programs intended to support Mi'kmaw learners in public schools. Teacher awareness, teacher training, local cultural discourses and the culture of individual schools are important factors that shape how Aboriginal peoples are represented in schools, but these issues are not discussed in any detail here. Instead, I examined official documents—the printed word—including curriculum guides, textbooks and other learning resources authorized for use in Nova Scotia schools.

Another challenge in relation to assessing representations of Aboriginal peoples is that "conclusions based on a single source can be misleading. Indeed, a true perspective can only be ascertained by comparing several reports in several locations over an extended period of time" (O'Neill 1987: 22). In this study, I attempted to find several textbooks used in a particular subject area during a specific time period. It was relatively easy to find contemporary curriculum guides and textbooks currently authorized for use in schools. What was more challenging was locating textbooks, curriculum guides and teacher resources from long ago—resources since delisted and withdrawn from circulation and evidently destroyed. The discourses shared here, therefore, are based on a comparatively small sample.[1] Particularly when it came to some of the earliest published works, I was not always able to confirm conclusively that all the items were authorized for use in schools. In light of factors such as the author's position or the relative scarcity of learning resources during a specific time period, in some cases I have assumed that a work would likely have found its way into the hands of textbook authors, teacher educators, teachers or even students in Nova Scotia schools.

Lastly, this chapter reflects what I learned about past and present Nova Scotia curricula, the images and factors that struck me, a white "come-from-away" settler, as interesting and important. I have three education degrees and have taught various grade levels and subjects in public schools in western Canada, but knew almost nothing about Nova Scotia school curricula when I started this research. As I searched for materials during my research, I was learning—sometimes for the very first time—about what European settlement in Mi'kma'ki was like, about the impacts of colonization, and how colonialism shaped what is (or is not) talked about in schools. I consequently share these findings as a record of what was, for me, a deeply moving and informative learning journey. Nova Scotia teachers and historians may find errors or omissions in my observations and conclusions. I encourage others who are interested to review curricula for themselves and draw their own conclusions.

Uncovering Tales Told in Nova Scotia Schools

In order to better understand the implications of what was said about the Mi'kmaq over time, I carried out a discourse analysis (after Fairclough 2000; McGregor 2003; van Dijk 2001). In discourse analysis, researchers examine not only what was actually said or the kinds of images or symbols that were used, but they also pay attention to how specific words or symbols are positioned in relation to other elements in a text, the silences or omissions and types of genres or subject areas in which a topic appears, including whether or not a text is labelled as being "fact" or "fiction." Discourse analysis also considers who has authored a text and the authority a text has depending upon an author's class, status, age, ethnic identity, gender, culture, profession, training or experience. Last, discourse analysis takes into consideration the broader social, cultural, political and economic contexts that shape how a text may have been used interpreted.

In this analysis of curriculum in Nova Scotia, I focused on three aspects: (a) *Genre:* When and where have the Mi'kmaq been represented in curricula? In what subject areas? In what types of resources (e.g., student texts, curriculum guides, teacher resources)? (b) *Image and interpretation*: How have the Mi'kmaq been portrayed in curricula? What messages, beliefs and assumptions do these representations convey? (c) *Intent*: In what ways do these representations support or challenge dominant educational understandings about colonialism, nationalism, multiculturalism or inclusion, equity and empowerment? To get a broader sense of what this discourse has looked like over time, I sought out such primary documents as curriculum guides, textbooks authorized for use in schools under the authority of the Minister of Education and "program of studies" documents[2] which lay out the framework for instruction in particular subjects, such as English language arts, social studies and science, etc.[3] Until the late 1970s, the program of studies also contained lists of prescribed and elective textbooks, student workbooks, teachers' manuals and supplementary teaching resources.[4]

Discourse analysis of representations of Aboriginal peoples in print and other forms of media is not new; many examples can be found in the literature. Francis (1992), Slapin and Seale (1992) and Clark (2007), for instance, have categorized the types of stereotyped images of Aboriginal peoples found in texts and other media such as "Indians of Childhood," depictions of indigenous peoples as one-dimensional figures from fiction or fantasy. In *Walking a Tightrope*, editors Lischke and McNab (2005) also looked at about how imagery, choice of language and media type all come together to paint distorted pictures of Aboriginal peoples. Other scholars such as Haig-Brown and Nock (2006), have outlined some of the beliefs and attitudinal perspectives which lie behind settlers' assumptions about Aboriginal peoples including "biological racism" the belief that people from non-white races are inherently inferior and physically and cognitively deficient. There has also been research on the ways in which Aboriginal peoples have been depicted in school textbooks (Clark 2007; O'Neill 1987) and the curriculum as a whole (cf. Ofner 1983; Shiu 2008). With the exception of a *Textbook Analysis: Nova Scotia* carried out by the Nova Scotia Human Rights Commission (1974), however, there appears to have been few—if any—similar studies which examine the discourse about the Mi'kmaq in Nova Scotia schools, what images are contained in curriculum, where these images came from, who produced them, what they mean and how these images and attitudes have evolved over time.

Discourses about the Mi'kmaq: A Nova Scotia Homeland Report

Discourses—what we say and write about a topic, event, experience, or people—are believed to be shaped by time and place and by the identities of the people who produce them. Discourses, then, are indications of what is going on in the society, providing a "mirror" on the nature of social, cultural, economic and political relationships (McGregor 2003; van Dijk 2001). In Nova Scotia, I found that different periods in history seemed to be characterized by different types of discourses: 1500s-1712, living with "the Other"; 1713-1863, ambivalence about "the Other"; 1864-1924, light, soap and water; 1925-1969, united we stand!; 1970-1990s, Nova Scotia's Multicultural Mosaic; and today, 2000-2012, hidden in plain sight. These divisions roughly correspond with those identified by other Canadian historians (cf. Jaenen and Morgan 1998; Miller 1991). For each of the first five time periods, I sum up some important historical events along with some examples of images of the Mi'kmaq, examining the beliefs and values these images suggest. In the second part of this chapter, I look at contemporary Nova Scotia curriculum in more detail, exploring how the Mi'kmaq are addressed not only in learning resources authorized for use in schools, but also in other aspects of the curriculum such as learning outcomes, instructional practices and policy approaches.

1500s-1712: Living With One Another

In the country we now call Canada, the Mi'kmaq have the longest experience of contact and interaction with European peoples. Historians typically have reported that first contact took place in the 1400s with the arrival of the Portuguese (Paul 2006; Reid 1995), followed by the French in the early 1500s (Paul 2006; Reid 1995). For some 200 years, "relations between the French and the Eastern Algonkians were extremely amicable" (Bailey 1969: 15). The Mi'kmaq were not only important political allies, they were also a source of invaluable information about how to survive in a new and unfamiliar land. In addition, Reid (1995) has concluded that French willingness to respect Mi'kmaw protocols and frequent intermarriage with the Mi'kmaq indicate that there was a sense of "mutuality" and "reciprocity" which "extended the boundaries of community" (74). Shared approaches to livelihood may be one reason why the French formed close relationships with the Mi'kmaq. One historian notes that "there was such a close connection between the early Acadians and the Micmacs that beleaguered British officials often complained that they could not tell the two apart" (Upton 1979: xv), even as to their lack of "initiative" or "industry" (xv).

Texts written by missionaries, expedition leaders, explorers and settlers describing the author's first-hand experiences with and observations of the Mi'kmaq have become important primary sources for contemporary historians, anthropologists and, more recently, curriculum writers. Published in 1691, one frequently cited work from this time is *Nouvelle Relation de la Gaspésie*, by Catholic missionary Chrestien Le Clercq who landed on the Gaspé Peninsula in 1676 and travelled the region for almost a decade (Upton 1979). Another text, *Concerning the Ways of the Indians* by Nicholas Denys, one of the "leading families of Acadia," was published in 1672. Denys "lived in European style" but his family members "spent much of their lives traveling with their Indian relatives" (Upton 1979: 26). Both these French writers provided detailed descriptions of the material, spiritual and cultural features of Mi'kmaw life, including house construction, hunting practices, style of dress, celebrations, burial customs and gender relations.

In these early works, it is surprising to note the extent to which French informants appeared able to recognize their own cultural relativity and were somewhat willing to consider Mi'kmaw points of view. Le Clercq, for instance, recorded a lengthy rebuke from his Mi'kmaw host who roundly criticized the Frenchman's assumption of superiority pointing out that Mi'kmaw lifestyles were perfectly adapted to the land and that the Mi'kmaq were content (as cited in McGee 1974: 45-49). In response, Le Clercq conceded that the Mi'kmaq did seem to "live in great harmony" with "continual joy in their wigwams" (McGee 1974: 50).

In Nova Scotia, the French Catholic missionaries were the "standard-bearers of pioneer educational effort" (Thibeau 1922: 13). Capuchin friars established the first schools in Nova Scotia in the mid-

1600s (13-25) in which Mi'kmaw and French children sat side-by-side, receiving the same instruction. Focused more on religious principles than the mechanics of literacy, classroom instruction emphasized values such as moral courage and recognition of interdependence (13-14). The prevailing ideology, however, might best be described as a "discourse of paternalism" (Henry and Tator 2006) through which missionaries like Le Clercq believed themselves to have a duty of care to "rescue" the Mi'kmaq from a fallen state of sin by converting them to Catholicism, and persisted in seeing their own beliefs and practices as morally and materially superior to those of the Mi'kmaq.

1713-1863 Ambivalence about the Other

With the Treaty of Utrecht in 1713, the British assumed control over Nova Scotia. This marked a significant shift in European-Mi'kmaq relations. Although a covenant chain of Peace and Friendship treaties was signed between the British and the Wabana'ki Confederacy in 1725, 1726, 1749, 1752, 1760-1761, peace for the Mi'kmaq was more "a consequence of their being outnumbered and militarily overwhelmed by a colonial population" (Reid 1995: 77) than a willing surrender of sovereignty. The arrival of the first British Governor of Nova Scotia, General Edward Cornwallis and the deportation of French Acadians in 1755 opened the way for successive waves of settlers from the Scottish Highlands and for American Loyalists, all of whom who took up lands "vacated" by the Acadians and/or wrested from the Mi'kmaq. Relocated to places where they found themselves in competition with newly arrived settlers or where the land was incapable of supporting them, by the early 1800s, many Mi'kmaw communities across the Maritimes were on the brink of starvation. The situation was so severe that in 1841, Louis-Benjamin Paul petitioned Queen Victoria for support (Paul 2006). Although newly appointed Commissioner for Indian Affairs Joseph Howe was given some latitude by the provincial government to address the crisis, Howe's plans for permanent settlements failed as a result of widespread epidemics, crop failures and the increasing hostility of white settlers (Upton 1979).

As early as 1730, British officials recognized that public education was the key to attracting white settlers from the British Isles as well as an important tool for inculcating a homogenous "British" identity in colonists who came from different geographic regions as well as different class backgrounds. At the same time, white loyalists from the United States and new colonists arriving from the British Isles attempted to deal with their own feelings of loss and dislocation by recreating British-style settlements and communities, including schools (Reid 1995). Early pioneer schools were typically "conducted in the home of the parents or in some vacant unpretentious building in the community ... supported by 'subscribers' and not a public expense" (MacDonald 1964: 57). In especially rural or remote areas, families often made do with the less than skillful instruction provided by itinerant teachers (Robinson 1967; Thibeau 1922). Families who could afford to do so sent their children to private academies. Beginning in the early 1800s and continuing throughout the century, the Church of England, Presbyterian and Anglican churches established postsecondary institutions such as the University of King's College at Windsor in 1788 and the Pictou Academy in 1816. Private schools also sprang up in Halifax and in larger towns such as Truro.

By 1811, the provincial government had passed legislation providing grants for the establishment of public schools in ten counties and laying out structures for educational administration, the appointment of trustees and hiring of teachers and the outlines for a common course of study (Robinson 1967.) Curriculum during this time emphasized subjects such as "English Grammar, the Latin and Greek Languages, Orthography, the use of the Globes, and the practical branches of the Mathematicks [sic], or such other useful learning as may be judged necessary" (Bingay 1919: 38). Prior to the establishment of a provincial "Normal School" or teacher training college in 1855, however, what these itinerant teachers actually taught was uneven at best. For example, in an annual report, one of the two provincial school inspectors observed that "in place of English grammar and geography, sewing and knitting are often accepted as legitimate occupations" (qtd. in MacDonald 1964: 12).

One of the earliest examples of literature for children in Canadian schools (Halifax Library Association 1967) is *Little Grace, or Scenes in Nova Scotia* (Grove 1846.) The author, Miss Grove, was a teacher in a private school in Halifax. *Little Grace* was written at a time when the Mi'kmaq had just begun to recover from the enforced starvation of a decade earlier and some Mi'kmaq had begun to settle semi-permanently in or near white communities (Paul 2006). In *Little Grace*, the young female narrator described her encounters with Mi'kmaw people living in their camps on the edge of Halifax. Like earlier authors such as Denys (1979[1671]) and Le Clercq (qtd. in Upton 1979), Grove provided some rich detail about the Mi'kmaq and their way of life, including emerging livelihood activities such as basket making and trading in local markets. A line drawing of a birch bark wikuom inside the front cover establishes the context for *Little Grace*. What was particularly interesting about this work was the author's frank recognition of the Mi'kmaq as the original inhabitants of Nova Scotia, a people "who were always here ... even before the French or any white people" (Grove 1846: 39). The Mi'kmaq were also acknowledged to be a distinct group, one of many groups of First Peoples who can be found worldwide. As Grace's father explained, there are "the Eesquimaux and Greenlanders; then there are the Patagonians and the Araucanians; the Knistenaux, the Objibbeways, the Assineboins" (34).

Alongside these admissions, however, a recurring debate among Grace, her parents and other adults in the novel focused on whether or not the Mi'kmaq should be regarded as "savage" (53.) Grace asserted that the Mi'kmaq were "so well-behaved ... they never talk loudly nor quarrel in the streets" (54) and even argued that living in a wikuom in the woods should not a measure of worth and character. In contrast, Little Grace's father countered that civilized people "build houses and towns, have shops and manufacturers" (53). This shift toward "binary polarization" (Henry et al. 2000), a sharp distinction between a superior white European and an inferior Aboriginal "other" was indicative of the growing divide between white settlers and the Mi'kmaq even when it came to the land where "wild country inhabited only by savage Indians" (Grove 1846: 17) was contrasted with the safety of farmers' fields, the physical industry and moral goodness of British settlers. In *Little Grace*, cultural deficiency or "social Darwinism" (Haig-Brown and Nock 2006) was cited as the reason why the Mi'kmaq had not been able to achieve a standard of living equal to that of white settlers. This assumption implicitly "blamed the victim" (Henry et al. 2000) and drew attention away from any examination of the impacts of decades of European aggression and oppression.

1864-1924: Light, Soap and Water

Confederation of the colonies in 1867 was accompanied by numerous social, cultural and political changes at a time when "economic growth and diversification combined with expanding civil liberties and political autonomy to inspire a sense of achievement and local patriotism" (Clarke 1991: 85). With the introduction of the 1864 *Education Act*, all children in Nova Scotia were entitled to attend school in the district in which they lived. School boards were established, school inspectors appointed and a standard academic curriculum was laid out by the provincial council on public instruction (MacDonald 1964; Nova Scotia Archives 1789-1989). In Nova Scotia, "the still new and expanding provincial educational systems were charged with explaining to young Canadian British subjects the new Dominion, its place in the world, and their place in the Dominion" (Welsh 2005: 2).

To instill a sense of belonging to the British Empire, school teachers in the province were tasked not only with the job of developing functional literacy and vocational skills, but also with the formation of "good citizens" who were willing and able to fulfil their "moral and patriotic duties" (Annual Report of the Superintendent of Education 1894: xiv-xv.) In 1898, annual Empire Day celebrations for schools were legislated with the express purpose of highlighting

> the causes of why it became great, and how it may continue to be great, if the history of the rise, growth and alliance of its different peoples ... and of the development of that spirit of Empire unity which is a new thing in history. (*Manual of the Public Instruction Acts* 1911: 167-68)

While teachers were instructed that "exercises should not be directed to develop boastfulness in the greatness of the Empire" (167-68), geography and history lessons emphasized the continuity of Western civilization, European heritage and achievements. Books recommended for school libraries included titles such as *Round the Empire* (Parkin 1892) and *Deeds that Won the Empire* (Fitchett 1897: 324-26).

In addition to loyalty to the British king, public school teachers were also obliged to provide instruction in "moral duties." These were described as service to the school—a "disposition to sacrifice some of his time, his convenience or his efforts, for that part of his country with which he comes first into contact ... the public school" (*Annual Report of the Superintendent of Education* 1895: xiv-xv). Students were expected to participate in activities such as Empire Day and Arbor Day activities, as well as to take up maintenance or beautification projects. Moral instruction also addressed the need for "good manners," "self-effacement," "putting others at their ease" and a "cautious attitude towards gossip" (*Manual of the Public Instruction Acts* 1911: 200-201). Physical hygiene meant not only "scrupulous cleanliness," but also "temperance" or abstention from alcohol,[5] physical exercise and the development of talents such as singing (ibid.). One historian described this period as "the age of light, soap, and water" (Valverde 1991), where middle and upper class British values fuelled "moral reforms" such as the elimination of alcoholism, prostitution and poverty.

Although the *Manual of the Educational Statutes* (1892) contained indications that some provisions were already being made for the "education of deaf or deaf, mute persons" (39) as well as "the blind" (41-43), public school superintendents' reports made only fleeting references to students' ethnicity or race. One of the few references to the Mi'kmaq was found in an 1895 superintendent's report which described the establishment of a day school at Schubenacadie as "a great boon to these Indian people" (*Annual Report of the Superintendent of Education* 1896: 74). In works used by students and teachers in schools, however, two types of tales predominant in this period are stories of "Savage Warriors" (Clark 2007) and tales about "Vanishing Canadians" (Francis 1992).

Savage Warriors and Vanishing Canadians

Another influential figure who emerged during this period was J. B. Calkin, who became an instructor and principal of the Provincial Normal School—the teachers training college. Calkin began his teaching career in 1857 and was the primary author of history and geography textbooks for more than fifty years (Welsh 2005). Calkin is known for two achievements: first, for promoting a "brand of mild, but stubborn Nova Scotian patriotism" that resisted nationalist, assimilative messages from Central Canada (214) and, second, for moral education (Berard 1984: 59-60). Although the *Education Act* of 1864 mandated that Nova Scotia schools were to be secular institutions, Calkin believed that lessons taught in school should be "freighted with rich and high-toned moral sentiment" (59). In one text reviewed for this study, Calkin (1898), for instance, cast an affirming eye on Chief Membertou's relationship with Champlain (34-35). More commonly, though, Calkin made derogatory generalizations about "Indians," who he described as "very hostile to the new colony and kept it in constant alarm ... ever lurking in the woods on the borders of the settlements ready to kill and scalp, or to carry off those who came within their reach" (125-26). This myth depicting Indians as "savages" "on the war-path" (McKinley 1929: 7) continues to appear in social studies textbooks like *Canadian Heroines of Pioneer Days*[6] well into the 1930s, when stories of "Heroism, Hardship and Loyalty" depicted the challenges of pioneer life so that students "fully understand how much had to be endured by the Early Pioneers of our Country" (McKinley 1929).

In histories published around the turn of the 20th century, however, another new tale about Aboriginal peoples was also emerging—a tale about Aboriginal peoples as "vanishing Canadians" (Francis 1992) soon to become, if not already, extinct. One example is *Markland or Nova Scotia: Its History, Natural Resources and Native Beauties* (McLeod 1903), a reference book that was suggested for school libraries until at least 1922 (*Journal of Education* April 1922: 88) and later recommended as a teacher resource for local studies courses throughout the 1970s (Nova Scotia Department of Education 1977: 28). In *Markland*, McLeod (1903) provided extensive descriptions of wildlife and livelihood practices (e.g., agriculture, mining) along with accounts about the settlement of various Nova Scotia counties. *Markland* is more than 600 pages long, yet a token ten pages is devoted to the Mi'kmaq, omitting them completely from county histories and chapters on subjects like "hunting and fishing." Perhaps this silence should be not surprising as McLeod commented that the Mi'kmaq had "passed away forever" (174) even if some Mi'kmaw names still "linger on each mount, and stream and bay" (174). The title *Markland*, McLeod's own suggestion, draws attention to the "discovery" of Nova Scotia by the Norse voyageur Leif Erickson (4). This subtle form of "terra nullius" implies that the province was uninhabited and free for the taking at the time white Europeans arrived.

The picture that emerges from the time of Confederation to the close of the 1920s, then, suggests a hardening of attitudes and, eventually, a rejection of the Aboriginal "Other." Authors such as Calkin (1898) seemed intent on fostering a sense of "moral panic" (Henry et al. 2000: 328), creating the impression that Aboriginal peoples were a direct and immediate threat to the safety of white readers. At the same time, the history of the province was being re-storied by erasing the Mi'kmaq entirely from the record of the past or by diminishing their role and importance. Increasingly, when there was any mention of "Indians" at all, both they and their territories go unnamed. One historian who has examined Mi'kmaq-settler relationships during this period noted that "despite the many voices that called for the entry of the Mi'kmaq into civilization,[7] the drive toward a purity of (white, British) identity negated the possibility" (Reid 1995: 64).

1925-1969: United We Stand!

From 1929 to 1969, Canada began to define itself as a nation at both a policy and at a program level. Tested by two world wars, the government renewed efforts around the centralization of services, and there was a push toward political unity at the national level as well as an emphasis on social and cultural homogeneity based on an assumed British-Canadian identity (Shore 2002: 93-117). By the end of the First World War, Canadians increasingly began to relocate from rural areas, congregating in emerging industrial centres (Valverde 1991). Not surprisingly, school curriculum from this time shows a marked shift in emphasis from the Classics and social studies toward math and sciences and training in technical skills for trades like mining (MacDonald 1964: 96). After the end of the Second World War, many small rural schools were consolidated and regional high schools were set up in order to "satisfy the economic thirst of the countryside by offering activities of a practical nature along with the fundamental academic courses" (164). There were, though, still ample reminders that Canada was a country with deep British/European roots. Grades 10, 11, and 12 English, for example, focused on Shakespeare and contemporary British authors. Instruction in both Greek, though discontinued in the mid-1960s, and Latin, discontinued in the late 1990s, signalled a faith in the value of classical western cultural knowledge and values.

Until 1949, the Education Office of Nova Scotia was under the control of the Council of Public Instruction. In 1949, however, that council was abolished and a Minister of Education was appointed, followed by the establishment of the Nova Scotia Department of Education in 1953. One outcome was increased provincial government control over curriculum and textbooks where a comparatively small number of texts were authorized for used in all schools. In some cases, these remained unchanged for decades. For example, the same reading series was used in grades 1-6 from at least 1956-1957 to 1969-1970 (Nova Scotia Department of Education 1956, 1962, 1969). Textbook publishers from the 1950s onward appear to have been primarily Canadian companies or divisions of foreign companies based in Canada (for instance, Addison Wesley, McClelland and Stewart, Copp Clark, J. M. Dent, W. J. Gage, Ginn and Company, or Holt, Rinehart and Winston). At the same time, there was increasing emphasis on the Canadian history and heritage. In 1956-57, for example, *The Story of Canada* (Brown, 1949) replaced *The Story of Britain and Canada* (Paterson 1933) as the prescribed text for grade 7 social studies. In this same year, grade 6 geography students studied *Canada and Her Neighbours* while grade 9 history and civics students were assigned *Building the Canadian Nation* (Brown, 1942). Few provisions were made for learners from different cultural backgrounds[8] Although the federal government's Indian affairs policy permitted integration of Aboriginal learners into public schools in Canada as early as the 1950s, some two decades later, only half of all registered Aboriginal learners appear to have been enrolled in public schools (Thomas 1972: 136). Curriculum documents, such as the subject-based Program of Studies fail to mention the needs and interests of Mi'kmaw learners. What references either dismissed the existence of the Mi'kmaq through claims of "*terra nullius*" or employed tokenism or cultural racism as a way of diminishing their humanity.

Terra Nullius: An Empty Land

One significant tool for controlling the discourse about Aboriginal peoples from 1930-1969 was the notion of "terra nullius," implying that the land was "empty" when European settlers arrived. This poem in *Canada – A Nation: And How It Came to Be* (Lower and Chafe 1958), was a frequently reprinted text which was authorized for grade 10-12 social studies and for history 11-12 until 1969-1970.

> I am a part of this, part of Canada
>
> Mine are the unlimited forests
>
> Mine the thousands of lakes,
>
> Mine the riches of mountains and mines,
>
> Mine the span of earth holding in firm grasp two oceans,
>
> This is Canada and it belongs to me – A Canadian.
>
> from *Song of a Canadian* by Eva Lis Wuorio in *Canada: A Nation: And How it Came to Be* (Lower and Chafe 1958 n.p.)

The monolithic "we," of course refers to whites of European descent. Students are reminded students that "our European civilization traces back some two or three thousand years" (Lower and Chafe 1958: 21). This notion of European right of possession is reinforced elsewhere in the text, including the chapter 1 description of Cartier and other European explorers' "discovery" of Canada" (22-31). In *Nova Scotia: A Brief History,* used for grade 6 History from 1956-57 to 1970-71, Blakely (1955) presented a similarly distorted account, stating that the "story of Nova Scotia begins with the story of Acadia ... the French name for what we now call the Maritime provinces" (ix). Both texts, *Canada - A Nation* (Lower and Chafe 1958) and *Nova Scotia: A Brief History* (Blakeley 1955) shaped the thinking of learners in the province for at least two decades. The Nova Scotia Human Rights Commission (1974) noted that one of the most potent weapons of discrimination is to simply avoid mention of "Other" groups, thereby rendering them invisible. Looking back on this period, one school inspector observed:

> We were brought up to accept by revelation that Antigonish was created at the date of its incorporation in the year 1889, and it appeared almost mandatory that each succeeding local generation should religiously commit to memory the families of the beneficent incorporators. (MacDonald 1964: 39)

Nova Scotia: A Brief History was subsequently singled out by the Nova Scotia Human Rights Commission (1974: 33-34) for its biased, racist portrayal of minority groups, including the Mi'kmaq.

Token "Indians"

When "Indians" did make an appearance in texts during this period, it is most often as token background figures. Prepared between the First and Second World Wars, *Nelson's School Geography: Maritime Edition* (Gunn n.d.: 65), for instance, asserted that "the story of Canada as a white man's country extends over less than four centuries" (65). Gunn also began with the "discovery of America" by Columbus and made only passing mention that the continent was already "occupied by a race of men whom [Columbus] called Indians" (42). Later, in the section on Nova Scotia, the Mi'kmaq are acknowledged as "the original inhabitants of the province" (65), but Gunn omitted them entirely from later descriptions of resources, industry and manufacturing in the province—events in which the Mi'kmaq did not seem to figure at all.

The literal way in which Aboriginal peoples were pushed to the sidelines can also be seen in a graph of "The different races from which Canadians have sprung" in *Canada - A Nation* (Lower and Chafe 1958: 490). A large, bold silhouette showed that some 47.9 per cent of the population of British origin with only a scarcely visible line represented people of "Indian-Eskimo" origins, 1.2 per cent. Another form of tokenism, more positive perhaps but tokenism nonetheless, are stories about a select handful of "good Indians" who came to the aid of white settlers. In *Nova Scotia: A Brief History,* Blakeley (1955), for example, devoted several pages to the interactions between the French colonists at Port Royal and the Mi'kmaq, recognizing the Mi'kmaq for sharing their provisions generously. *Canada in North America to 1800* (Brown et al. 1960) contains similar affirmations of Aboriginal peoples by early explorers and Loyalists:

> We discovered a fleet of ten Indian canoes slowing moving towards us, which caused considerable alarm with the women. Before they came within gunshot, one who could speak English came to let us know, "We all one brother!" They were of the Micmac tribe and became quite friendly, and furnished us plentifully with moose meat. (309)

The authors included a brief reference to Chief Membertou, yet denigrated his relationship with the French by suggesting that Membertou's feelings of sadness when the French departed was largely due to loss of ready access to European trade goods (87).

Cultural Racism

One of the more subtle forms of racism lies in the failure of textbook authors to explain how present day situations or concerns have been shaped by the events of the past (Nova Scotia Human Rights Commission 1974). Nova Scotia's or "Acadia's Age of Gold" (Machar 1932: 123), pre-European contact, was described as a time of peace and happiness. In a poem entitled "The passing of Gluskap" (123-28), however, the author recounts that Kluskap deserted the world when "an alien spirit" (124) broke the "peaceful compact" (124) between man and nature. As no clues are provided about the origins of this "strife" (124), the impression is that it is the Mi'kmaq who unleashed "havoc" (126) in paradise.

A similar glossing over of the harmful impacts of British colonial rule was found in *Nova Scotia: A Brief History* (Blakely 1955), authorized for grade 6 history from 1956-57 to 1970-71 and the only provincial history text in use in schools at this time. Blakely implied that the Mi'kmaq broke the 18th-century peace and friendship treaties without reason but failed to provide any comparable details about violations on the part of the British such as scalping proclamations issued by Governor Cornwallis in 1749 and 1750 and Governor Lawrence in 1756 (Paul 2006). Lower and Chafe (1958: 47) also repeatedly emphasized the warring tendencies of Aboriginal peoples, including "Iroquois enmity and savagery" overcoming the valiant Jesuits.

In addition, highly selective "facts" about the Mi'kmaq (usually negative) further reinforced a belief in European superiority. In *Canada – A Nation* (Lower and Chafe 1958), for example, the only indication that Aboriginal peoples were present at all was a single photo of a book of hymns written in Cree syllabics. This juxtaposition suggests that Aboriginal peoples had peacefully accepted the influx of settlers and European cultural values. Entries in the index reinforce the notion of Aboriginal inferiority by directing readers to entries on "Indians: effects of liquor on" and "placed on reserves" (501). In *Canada in North America to 1800* (Brown et al. 1960), and other textbooks from this time period, European practices and customs were held up as a standard for societal development:

> Imagine how overcrowded Montreal or Toronto or Vancouver would be if the people who live there had to begin to hunt and fish for all the food they need! Even if they tried to grow all their own food, they would have to spread out great distances from one another in order to have enough land to farm (36).... There are over fifty times as many people living in North America today as when the first white man arrived. That is because a country can support many more farmers and factory workers than it can people who live by hunting and fishing. (49)

In only one instance did the Mi'kmaq appear to be positioned as equal to white Europeans, and this comparison was not a favourable one. *Canada in North America to 1800* (Brown et al. 1960) contains assertions that the Mi'kmaq, along with Europeans, were responsible for the genocide of the Beothuk people in Newfoundland. Although they (Brown et al.) were some of the rare voices to acknowledge the negative effects of colonization on Aboriginal peoples, they too absolved white settlers of any blame by pointing to the "tragic effects of the misuse of alcohol" (49) in Aboriginal communities. In a time when cultural and political unity was the underlying theme of Nova Scotia school curriculum, discourses which continued to "blame the victim" (Henry et al. 2000) absolved settlers of any responsibility for taking action around the social, cultural, economic and political challenges the Mi'kmaw communities faced.

1970-1999: Nova Scotia's Multicultural Mosaic

The 1970s saw marked shifts in the organization, delivery and philosophy of education in Nova Scotia. In contrast to nationalist rhetoric of the 1950s and 1960s, there was growing awareness of the cultural diversity among groups in Nova Scotia. New policies highlighted the multicultural nature of Nova Scotia and teaching resources began to address the histories and experiences of non-white groups. These changes were fuelled by three factors: school amalgamation[9] the elimination of provincial examinations[10] and the federal government's 1971 policy on multiculturalism, which put forward a "pluralistic notion of equality" (Multicultural Association of Nova Scotia 1978: 1). Excerpts from interviews with teachers and administrators in the 1970s suggest qualified support for the idea that Nova Scotia schools should "educate fully ... *all students* [emphasis added] in the cultures and history of our minorities" (Nova Scotia Human Rights Commission 1974: 21). By 1980, a new aim for public education had emerged:

> Develop knowledge and understanding of history and geography ... so that the students may be aware of the cultural diversity of their country ... and have a basis upon which to assess current values. (Nova Scotia Department of Education 1979: 3)

One key learning outcome was to enable students to build "knowledge, understanding and appreciation of themselves, their fellow human beings, their environment, and the relationship among the three" (3).

An analysis of Nova Scotia school textbooks carried out by the Nova Scotia Human Rights Commission (1974: 68-71) assigned half of all textbooks examined "the lowest possible ratings" because of stereotyping, the use of misleading language or because the authors failed to acknowledge the perspectives, issues or concerns of minorities. The Commission also found that there were more frequent references to "blacks" than "Indians"—who were most likely to be mentioned in Grades 5/6 social studies or history. Only one text, *Nova Scotia: A Brief History* (Blakeley 1955) contained any substantive information about the Mi'kmaq, and the Commission strongly condemned it for its racist stance (1974: 33-34). Furthermore, the Commission recommended that a total of twenty-three textbooks "be removed altogether and replaced with more recent and better-planned texts in the interest of Nova Scotia unity" (67). More than a decade later, a study of the *Multicultural Assumptions of Selected School Boards in Nova Scotia* (Sullivan 1989) revealed that school boards had made some attempts to increase the amount of content about the "other" in their programs, but teaching practices and delivery systems appeared virtually unchanged. In the same year, a report by the Dalhousie University Task Force on Access for Black and Native People (1989) pointed to interlocking relationships among race, ethnicity and educational achievement at the primary and secondary level as the principle factors responsible for under-representation of Black African Nova Scotians and Mi'kmaw people in postsecondary education. In 1995-96, however, the *Education Act* was significantly revised and school boards were directed to:

> (a) provide and implement programs and policies promoting Mi'kmaq education; and (b) include in learning materials information respecting the history, language, heritage, culture, traditions and the contributions to society of the Mi'kmaq (*Education Act, Chapter 1 of the Acts of 1995-96*: n.p. section 138).

These revisions were reinforced by curriculum foundation documents which stated that classroom materials and techniques should "reflect students' abilities, needs, interests, and learning styles" so that "all students will be successful regardless of gender, racial and ethnocultural background, social class, lifestyle or ability" (Atlantic Provinces Education Foundation 1996: 42).

Indians of Childhood

During the 1970s, folk tales, myths and legends written by non-Aboriginal authors became popular vehicles for exploring cultural diversity. These included stories about Kluskap, framed as Canadian "fairy tales" (Macmillan 1974[1922]). One example was *Canadian Wonder Tales* (1974) by Cyrus Macmillan. As a young man, Macmillan had spent a few months in Mi'kmaw communities while working as a field assistant with the Geological Survey of Canada under the direction of Edward Sapir. Macmillan's "Indian" stories came to be widely distributed in Canada as well as in the United States and Britain. Dedicated his "fairy tales" to the "pleasure and delight of children" (x), Macmillan thanked his mother who "first taught me to see the fairy world and to hear the horns of elf-land blowing" (vii.) Macmillan thanked "the *nameless Indians* [emphasis added] ... from whose lips he heard these stories" (xi) and claims that his tales "are not the product of the writer's imagination" (xi), but his interpretations seem to have little in common with traditional Mi'kmaw stories. Unlike Silas Rand, Macmillan did not incorporate any Mi'kmaw names or words. The actions and motivations of the characters appear simplified, and even the cadence and flow of the language is markedly different from Rand's translations. In addition, Macmillan freely added details that had nothing to do with Mi'kmaw tradition; for example, "Glooscap waved his magic wand as was his custom" (145).

Rather than an entry point to understanding a different way of life, Macmillan positioned (white) readers as being superior to the Mi'kmaq, noting that although "their descendants live in certain of these parts still ... the real greatness has long since gone. They have grown smaller in size, and they are no longer powerful as in the old days" (34). He described the Mi'kmaq as "dwelling in settlements of their own apart from the white folk. You may still see them in their *strange* [emphasis added] tents or wigwams" (34). Macmillan's renditions, however, are dubious at best. Macmillan could not speak any Mi'kmaw and was released from his position as a research assistant with the Geological Survey of Canada when it was discovered that a significant part of his "field research" appeared to have been plagiarized, copied from the writings of Silas T. Rand and pioneer journalist Charles Leland (Parkhill 1997: 23-24). A publisher's note in *Wonder Tales* (1974) is similarly cautious:

It is not known ... from which particular areas of Canada Professor Macmillan gathered his stories, although some of the legends are peculiar to certain tribes or groups of Indians. A few stories are clearly European imports, remembered and retold by French-Canadian settlers; while others are basically Indian but show signs of assimilation, with an admixture of European fairy tale *motifs*, witch, wand, ogre and giant. Again, it is not clear how much of this assimilation is attributable to Professor Macmillan ... or whether it is because the storytellers were whites rather than Indians. (Publisher's Note, copyright page, *Canadian Wonder Tales*, Macmillan 1974)

The book jacket of *Wonder Tales* (1974) suggested that Macmillan's popularity was aided by his high profile career as a professor and dean at McGill University as well as his stature as a Canadian Member of Parliament and government minister in the 1930s and 1940. Fortunately for learners during the 1970s and 1980s, tales about fantasy Indians were being replaced with more accurate, empowering information about the region's First Peoples.

Diverse Canadians

Beginning in the 1970s, the Nova Scotia Museum of Natural History began to develop a range of learning resources and programs which highlighted the importance of Nova Scotia's cultural mosaic. The Museum, for instance, encouraged teachers to bring their classes to the Museum for self-guided tours and museum classes, where learners could access selected museum artifacts, equipment or visual aids ("Classes," *Learning Resources Catalogue*, Nova Scotia Museum 1983-1984: 2). The earliest mention of a guided museum class with a Mi'kmaw focus was a 1970 session on "The History of Indians in Nova Scotia" for grade 6 students (Nova Scotia Department of Education and Culture, 1970: 4). In 1980, the Museum organized an exhibition of "Micmac artifacts" which appears to have attracted wide spread attention from the general public (Nova Scotia Department of Education and Culture 1980: 12). By 1983, a guided class for grades 4-7 entitled "About the Micmacs" examined "aspects of a people's relationship with the environment through their quill work, basketry and decorative styles and techniques" had become a regular offering (Nova Scotia Museum 1983-1984: 2).

The museum also worked in cooperation with the CBC, the Nova Scotia Department of Education Media Services, St. Mary's University Department of Anthropology, and the Micmac Association of Cultural Studies to develop a five-part video series, *Mi'kmaq*, for educational television (Nova Scotia Department of Education and Culture 1981: 1-3). Launched in 1981[11], the goal of the series was to stimulate "curiosity and speculation" about the Mi'kmaq and to "expose English-speaking students to the experience of another culture totally independent of their own" (2). Episodes highlighted winter and summer livelihood activities such as the construction of an eel weir and significant cultural practices including marriage ceremonies.

Early museum resources such as monographs on *Rock Drawings of the Micmac Indians* (Robertson 1973) or *Early Man in Nova Scotia* (Hayward 1973) may have left readers with the impression that the Mi'kmaq had vanished with the passing of time. Resources produced in the 1980s were aimed at showing that the Mi'kmaq are still here and that they "have a long heritage, and are proud" (Whitehead and McGee 1983: 59). *The Mi'kmaq: How Their Ancestors Lived Five Hundred Years Ago* (Whitehead and McGee 1983), for instance, depicted the Mi'kmaq as capable human beings with a fully rounded society—one of the first publications by white authors to do so. Whitehead and McGee used language that affirmed Mi'kmaw cultural practices, noting that "the Mi'kmaq were *very skillful* [emphasis added] in setting bones and in treating wounds." The authors went even further to normalize animist belief systems, observing that "most Mi'kmaq behaviour involved what we think of as religious or spiritual attitudes ... everyday activities were all forms of religious devotion and respect for life" (54). An endorsement by Bernie Francis, the Mi'kmaw advisor to the project, expressed the hope that these materials would enable Mi'kmaw students to "gain a more positive image about themselves as a people prior to (European) contact"(Whitehead and McGee 1983).

This same, more positive tone could also be found in some authorized learning resources intended for use in all schools such as *Community Canada* (Cruxton and Walker 1993), listed for grade 7 social studies from 1996 to 2005. The authors asked students to:

> Imagine that you could spend a year with Membertou and the Micmac. [...] The Micmac could teach you how to use the *plentiful* sea and land resources of their environment. [...] They could

share their inventions – ways to travel on water and in snow. [...] Summer was a time of plenty. The Micmac *feasted* on fish and shellfish. (108-109, emphases added)

The Mi'kmaw way of life was being recognized as not only functional, but also equally satisfying as that of Europeans: Large families were a source of joy and pride to the Micmac. Children were welcomed into the family. The whole community was invited to a birth feast (113).

As the decades unfolded, however, there was more emphasis on the impacts of history and slightly less description of material artifacts and cultural practices.

In a few texts, authors were beginning to question inequitable power relations between Aboriginal and non-Aboriginal people. Massey's (1992) *Our Country, Canada,* for example, pointed out that: "Originally, the Native people of Canada welcomed the French and English explorers and first settlers to *their* [emphasis added] land. Think about how *we* have treated them in return" (302). In *Community Canada*, Cruxton and Walker (1993) were even more direct, outlining the genocidal impacts of European contact—destruction of the environment, disease, war, dislocation and starvation—and how the Mi'kmaq adapted in order to survive (113-14).

There were also a handful of new resources that illustrated the continuity of Mi'kmaw tradition and occupation over time, providing a glimpse into the lives of contemporary Mi'kmaq and their communities. Prepared by linguist Robert Leavitt at the University of New Brunswick, *Micmac of the East Coast* (1985) for example, was authorized for grade 6-7 social studies until at least 1998 (Nova Scotia Department of Education and Culture 1997: 72). Topics included traditional livelihoods as well as the impact of European contact, treaties and information about present-day Mi'kmaw communities. Maps, charts, photographs and a glossary of Mi'kmaw terms supplement the text. *Maliseet and Micmac: First Nations of the Maritimes* (Leavitt 1995), authorized for Mi'kmaw studies 10, focused on language and culture, religion and spirituality in greater detail.

Another notable text authorized for use in Nova Scotia schools, beginning in 1997, was *Atlantic Canada in the Global Community* (Crewe et al. 1998). The authors acknowledged that there are significant gaps in white European understandings of Aboriginal peoples and substantive differences among the cultures and histories of

Aboriginal peoples in the Maritimes. Sections on the treaties have been juxtaposed with information and discussions about stereotyping, prejudice and racism. The accompanying teacher's guide to this text also contains additional details such as the effects of contact and European settlement as well as sample questions teachers might use to help students uncover silences and contradictions in discourses about Aboriginal peoples. A case study entitled "Educating Against Racism," for example, includes a short biography of Rita Joe, photos of her receiving the Order of Canada in 1990, and a copy of her poem "I lost my talk" (90). The goal of this curriculum document is to enable students to "see the connections between power and racism" (158). Teaching suggestions include having students dramatize Rita Joe's poem and "imagining what it would be like to lose their language" (157). Students are also encouraged to draw from external resources such as "Friendship Centres and Native Organizations" and to apply what they have learned to planning and organizing anti-racism events in their school and community.

"First Voice" 12: The Mi'kmaq Speak for Themselves

Beginning in 1970, collaboration among the Department of Education, its audio visual services branch, libraries and the Nova Scotia Museum dramatically increased the number and types of learning resources that teachers and students could access. The audio visual services branch, for example, reported holdings of 45,000 films and 7,000 filmstrips available on loan to schools (Nova Scotia Department of Education and Culture 1972-73: 20). Audio visual resources also provided a platform which enabled the Mi'kmaq to tell their own stories. Produced by education media services, a 1979 video called *Wikuom and Ktantekewinu Aknutk* or "The Hunter Speaks" (Wright 1996: 7) features a Mi'kmaw trapper from Newfoundland talking about making his living from the land. This depiction is interesting because it illustrates contemporary Mi'kmaw lifestyles and the continuity of Mi'kmaw tradition. As mentioned in the previous section, not long afterwards, Educational Television began to broadcast the *Mi'kmaq* series, which was written and produced in Nova Scotia in collaboration with Mi'kmaw organizations and input from Mi'kmaw advisors (Whitley 1981: 1-3).

A few years later, the Department of Education inventoried a range of resources featuring different racial and ethnic groups (e.g., African Studies, Chinese, Mi'kmaq) with a focus on topics such as human rights and anti-racism. While the Multicultural Education Resource List (Wright 1996) listed nine print resources for "Aboriginal Studies," only two were about the Mi'kmaq. In contrast, the list of available audio-visual materials ran to almost twelve pages.[13] While the majority of these resources were by or about Aboriginal peoples outside the Maritime region, about thirty productions featured the Mi'kmaq, including *River of Fire* (Francis and Von Rosen 1991) in which Michael Francis told the story of the sacred fire, and *Justice Denied* (Harris 1986) detailing the wrongful conviction of Donald Marshall, Jr. Almost all of the Mi'kmaw-focused audio visual resources had been produced within the decade, and a number addressed contemporary Mi'kmaw activities, people and concerns. Topics ranged from livelihood strategies such as blueberry harvesting, fishing and basket making to treaty rights, including, for instance, the impact of quarrying on Kelly's Mountain, rights to fish and land claims. Directed by Catherine Martin, the first Mi'kmaw documentary filmmaker, *Kwa'nu'te: Micmac and Maliseet artists* (Nason et al. 1991) celebrated the power of creation in the lives of fifteen Mi'kmaw and Maliseet artists like Shirley Bear, who combined painting with family life and political activism. The visuals and dialogue position these individuals as artists rather than craftspeople, drawing from tradition (e.g., basketry) but using "non-traditional" media to communicate important social, cultural and political messages.[14]

One of the first books promoted for use in all schools, which contained interviews with actual Mi'kmaw people, was a compilation entitled *People of Nova Scotia* (Multicultural Association of Nova Scotia 1978). In one chapter, for example, Mrs. Lucy Paul offered a first-person account of her life history. In another section about the "Micmac Indians Today," Noel Knockwood asserted that treaty relationships have been "honoured by the Indians [but] not respected by their new European neighbours" (78), going on to describe how the Mi'kmaq have worked to secure their rights through formation of the Union of Nova Scotia Indians and the Micmac Institute of Cultural Studies. One drawback to this publication, however, was that the Mi'kmaq were still implicitly positioned as only one of many "ethnic minorities" in the province.

Since the 1950s, provincial history, geography, politics and economy had been a focal point for grade 6 social studies. In the 1970s,
"local studies" was also identified as a social studies topic for grades 1
through to 7 (Nova Scotia Department of Education 1977). Materials
such as an *Atlantic Docupack*, a collection of primary research materials
such as government reports, pages from newspapers, maps and letters,
was created to support this new emphasis (Nova Scotia Department of
Education 1975a: 28). In 1988, however, the Department of Education
went to launch a Maritime studies course at the junior high level,
which drew attention to ethnic diversity, histories and experiences
of non-British groups (Nova Scotia Department of Education and
Culture 1988a: 17). A new text was created especially for this course,
The Maritimes: Tradition, Challenge and Change (Peabody et al. 1987),
which covered the post-Second World War period, from 1945 onward.
This new Docupack adopted a multidisciplinary approach to the study
of geography, economy, social life, politics and culture and contained
different types of media and information including photos (e.g., different types of Maliseet baskets, 209); paintings and poems (e.g., a
poem by Rita Joe, 222) and first-person stories (e.g., a story by Charlie
Sark, 223) were vehicles for presenting information about Mi'kmaw
experiences and history. Aboriginal cultural practices were depicted
as dynamic and evolving rather than static, unchanging "traditions":

> "When I'm creating a story or a poem myself," Rita Joe says, "and
> I'm thinking about the next line, I sometimes wonder whether it
> would be better in English or in Mi'kmaq. Sometimes I use one,
> sometimes the others. Sometimes you just can't say what belongs
> there in English." (Peabody et al. 1987: 221)

Other narratives in *The Maritimes* provided an entry point for examining relationships among social, cultural, economic and political
forces (209). For instance, a case study by Battiste (qtd. in Peabody et
al. 1987) illustrated the dimensions of "structural unemployment" in
Mi'kmaw communities, and invited readers to compare and contrast
the Mi'kmaw experience with that of their own communities (319-
26). What made *The Maritimes* unique was that the Mi'kmaq were not
relegated to a separate "Indian" category; instead, Mi'kmaw-focused
content was integrated throughout. Unfortunately, *The Maritimes*
was only in use for a short time. Pilots began in 1987 (Nova Scotia
Department of Education and Culture 1988b: 17), but by the 1995-

1996 academic school year, the text appears to have been de-listed (Nova Scotia Department of Education 1994).

Other contemporary stories about the Mi'kmaq also began to appear in English language arts materials in the mid 1990s. *Voices of the First Nations* (Ahenakew et al. 1995), authorized for Grades 10, 11 and 12, for instance, contained a story called "Quill earrings" by Maureen Googoo (1992, 1995). Her story is a striking example of Mi'kmaw First Voice narrated by a young woman who has come home from university for a visit. Readers are introduced to her family, including her mother, who is a teacher, and her father, who works in a shipyard. The family lived in a comfortable, newly renovated house located in a modern Mi'kmaw community. Characters used slang when they spoke and teased one another with affection. Although they also encountered problems and did not—at first—always make the right decisions, they found ways to resolve the problems that arose. The conflict in Googoo's story focused on the need to find ways to honour Aboriginal identities and heritage, not as a static artifact from an ancient past, but as a way of life that enables the Mi'kmaq to be more fully human and stay connected with family. Rather than suffering victims or an "exotic other" (Clark 2007), the Mi'kmaq were portrayed as capable agents, people with rich lives and their own individual and collective gifts. The *Senior Issues Collection* in which this story appeared was de-listed in 2003.

An even more important milestone in the literacy landscape, however, was the publication of *The Mi'kmaq Anthology* (Choyce and Joe 1997). This collection of poetry, essays, traditional stories and autobiographical narratives by Mi'kmaw people featured the voices of Mi'kmaw leaders like Lindsay Marshall and Noel Knockwood, educators like Elsie Charles Basque and Murdena Marshall, and other Mi'kmaw poets, artists and writers. *The Mi'kmaq Anthology* was cross-listed for use in grades 10-11 social studies, Canadian history, Mi'kmaw studies and, by 2011, for English language arts 10 as well.

Cracks in the Mosaic

A 1971 Canadian multiculturalism policy (Leman 1999) offered protection for the expression of diverse cultural preferences and lifestyles. By the 1980s, some of its principles had been embraced by the Government of Nova Scotia and the Nova Scotia Department of

Education as a framework for curriculum in Nova Scotia schools. New learning resources such as the ones mentioned above were authorized, and some references to cultural diversity was incorporated into curriculum, particularly in grade 6 social studies, which focused on Nova Scotia and Atlantic Canada. Students were expected, for example, to be able to "identify the first known inhabitants of Atlantic Canada (Micmacs, Malecites, Beothuks) and tell how they came here" (96). In another theme, learners might also explore the ways in which "effective use of environment enabled native peoples to lead a highly developed lifestyle" (Nova Scotia Department of Education 1981a: 54).

Aboriginal peoples, though, still did not receive equal space, time and consideration. The curriculum remained largely Eurocentric. In grade 6 social studies, for instance, at least twice as many objectives highlighted the exploits and achievements of "key explorers." The curriculum also contained hidden assumptions about colonialism. Objectives like "examine the lifestyle of native people after the arrival of the Europeans and identify different ways they helped each other" (96), for example, implied that European settlement brought great benefits, not harms, to the Mi'kmaq.

Near the end of the 1980s, in a study of the Multicultural Assumptions of Selected School Boards in Nova Scotia, Sullivan (1989) concluded that although school boards had made increased the amount of content about other "diverse" ethnic or racial minority groups, goals, outcomes and teaching practices appeared virtually unchanged. More disturbing, however, was reluctance on the part of principals and administrators to admit that inequality and inequity were deeply rooted problems in schools. In part, this lack of awareness might be attributable to the emphasis multiculturalism placed on harmony among diverse peoples, on the importance of "balance." The 1971 federal policy on multiculturalism, for instance, asserted "no one group should have or maintain cultural superiority" (Multicultural Association of Nova Scotia 1978: 1). Even when it came to curricular reform, the goal was to "ensure that the Nova Scotia school curriculum reflects a balanced view of Nova Scotia's multicultural diversity and human rights"[15] (Nova Scotia Department of Education and Culture 1988b: 1). In reality, though, diverse ethnic groups in Nova Scotia were not equal. Multiculturalism ignored Mi'kmaw treaty rights and legal status as owners of the territory. In the 1970s and 1980s and even in the 1990s, the Mi'kmaq tended to be depicted as figures from an ancient past, rather than as a living people. As historian Thomas King (2012) has pointed out, colourful displays of "traditional" Aboriginal culture by "Dead Indians" at multicultural festivals pose little threat to the status quo and, in the majority of learning resources, there was little, if any, mention of hard-to-hear truths about colonial violence and the intergenerational impacts of colonization on Mi'kmaw families and communities.

Summary of Discourses

Studies of identity, inclusion and exclusion in Canada have revealed how highly selective "representations of cultural difference ... in national histories, national art, tourism, and government discourses and programmes" (Mackey 2002: 7) have shaped settler-Canadians' beliefs about and attitudes toward Aboriginal peoples. In public schools in Nova Scotia, imaginary images of Aboriginal peoples have been used to evoke fear of the Mi'kmaq and resentment in white settlers. Fuelled by colonial ambitions, distorted notions of the Mi'kmaq were present in school from the time of Confederation. Early binary representations of the Mi'kmaq as "savages" and settlers as "civilized" pushed the Mi'kmaq to the peripheries of settler consciousness. By the turn of the century, however, the Mi'kmaq were almost invisible in Nova Scotia curriculum. When Aboriginal peoples appeared at all, they were portrayed either as fantasy figures or as a relic from the ancient past, culturally inferior wards of the state. These distorted depictions of Aboriginal peoples began to change with the introduction of federal government policies on multiculturalism which sparked new thinking about the goals and practice of education. By the end of the 1970s, the Mi'kmaq were recognized as a living people, but were categorized as only one of many ethnic minority groups in the province. More recently, scholars have been speaking out about faulty images of Aboriginal peoples for decades (Clark 2007; Dion 2009; Francis 1992; Lischke and McNab 2005; Nova Scotia Human Rights Commission 1974; Ofner 1983; Slapin and Seale 1992; Welsh 2005) and the most blatantly racist depictions of Aboriginal peoples have been removed from school texts. At the same time, however, disempowering messages about the Mi'kmaq are still embedded in contemporary provincial educational discourse where the Mi'kmaq seem to be hidden in plain sight.

Contemporary Nova Scotia Curriculum: Hidden in Plain Sight

So, what progress has been made toward more accurate, empowering representation of the Mi'kmaq? To what extent is curriculum in Nova Scotia schools today different from what has been offered in the past? University of Manitoba teacher educator Yatta Kanu (2011) has argued that when it comes to inclusion, it important to look closely at a range of elements that make up the curriculum including: (a) the philosophical underpinnings of curriculum, the fundamental beliefs and values that shape our approach to schooling; (b) the kinds of learning outcomes we identity as important; (c) the content found in curriculum and learning resources; and (d) instructional methods, strategies and approaches used to catalyze learning.

In this section, I describe what and where I was able to see the Mi'kmaq in contemporary Nova Scotia curriculum. Although some new stories about the Mi'kmaq are certainly now being told in schools at many grade levels and in the majority of subject areas, the Mi'kmaq still appear to be "hidden in plain sight" (Newhouse 2005). Representations of and information about learning outcomes and instructional approaches seemed limited, confined to narrow curricular spaces and a small number of learning resources.

Philosophical Foundations

Aware of the limitations of politically neutral, colour-blind pedagogy, the Nova Scotia Department of Education began to take up issues around race relations and human rights in the early 1990s with the goal of helping "students develop life-long respect for others, and enhance their multiracial and multicultural understanding" (Nova Scotia Department of Education *Mission, Goals and Action Plans* 1992: 1). In 1993, the office of race relations and cross cultural understanding was established in order to "help educators prepare students to live in multiracial/multicultural society and to develop an understanding of their own background and culture and those of others" (Nova Scotia Department of Education and Culture 1993: 20). Responsibilities of the office of race relations included policy creation, development of curriculum resources and teacher professional development (10).

Not long after, "equity and diversity" statements began to appear in curriculum guides. The *Foundation for the Atlantic Canada English*

Language Arts Curriculum, for example, drew attention to the multi-cultural make-up of the region: "The society of Atlantic Canada, like all of Canada, is linguistically, racially, culturally and socially diverse. Our society includes differences in gender, ability, values, lifestyles and languages" (Atlantic Provinces Education Foundation 1996: 42).

Teachers were also expected to employ instructional and assessment practices "free of racial, ethnic, cultural, gender and socio-economic bias" (42). This stance was soon integrated into other subject areas such as the *Foundation for the Atlantic Canada Social Studies Curriculum* (Atlantic Provinces Education Foundation 1999), which highlighted the need to recognize inequality at different levels and to: "Promote a commitment to equity by valuing, appreciating, and accepting the diverse and multicultural nature of our society, as well as by fostering awareness and *critical analysis of individual and systemic discrimination*" (31, emphasis added).

In 2002, the Department of Education introduced a comprehensive Racial Equity Policy (Nova Scotia Department of Education 2002b), which brought together key points from earlier policy documents, addressing key principles around human resources management, curriculum, assessment, instructional practices, counselling, learner development, learning environment and community relations. This was later supplemented by a Racial Equity / Cultural Proficiency Framework (Nova Scotia Department of Education 2011) aimed at enabling administrators and teachers to learn "how to interact effectively with people in their environments who differ from them" (1). Proposed strategies included "department-wide plans for professional development for curriculum developers, directors, consultants, and evaluation staff" (4).

Although commitment to inclusion of learners from diverse cultural backgrounds is evident in these kinds of policy documents, one drawback is that no distinctions were made among diverse groups of learners. Acadians, African Nova Scotians and the Mi'kmaq, for example, bring vastly different experiences with them into the classroom and have very different interests and historical positions. In equity and diversity statements, however, it appears that the Mi'kmaq are subsumed as part of a "monolithic other" (Henry and Tator 2006), one of many unnamed "linguistically, racially, culturally and socially diverse" groups in the province (Atlantic Provinces Education Foundation 2001: 53). Moreover, equity and diversity principles appeared on a separate page and there were no examples illustrating how these principles could be put into practice. It was therefore left to teachers to determine how to best infuse these goals across the curriculum. In the remainder of this section, I examine how the Mi'kmaq have been addressed in learning outcomes, curriculum content and learning resources, and in instructional approaches.

Student Learning Outcomes

Beginning in the 1990s, the Department of Education began to lay out "essential graduation learnings," "what students are expected to know and be able to do by the time they graduate from high school" (Atlantic Provinces Education Foundation n.d.: 4). These learnings "cross traditional subject boundaries" (Nova Scotia Department of Education 2003: A-4) and are grouped around six themes: aesthetic expression, citizenship, communication, personal development, problem solving and technological competence. Only one theme, citizenship, draws attention to equity and diversity principles. For example, one of the essential graduation learnings for Citizenship states that students are expected to "develop knowledge, skills and attitudes that will enable them to have a sense of belonging and to understand, actively participate in, and contribute positively to local, regional, national, and global communities" with an emphasis on "participation in the democratic process" (A-6). Other learning outcomes associated with this goal indicate students will: "examine human rights issues and recognize forms of discrimination and demonstrate understanding of their own and others' cultural heritage, cultural identity and their contribution to multiculturalism in society" (6). Teachers are also instructed that students need to be able to "read the literature of many cultures and investigate how forms of language construct and are constructed by particular social, historical, political and economic contexts" (7).

The overall goal of essential graduation learnings, however, appears to be preparation for the labour market. Even themes like "personal development" emphasize the necessity of "preparedness for the transition to work and further learning" (A-4). Nowhere in the essential graduation learnings foundational documents (Atlantic Provinces Education Foundation, n.d.) or in curriculum guides referencing essential learnings did I find any mention of the Mi'kmaq. Rather, the phrase "difference and diversity" seemed to be used as a shorthand way of referring to learners from different racial and ethnic backgrounds, of different genders and sexual orientations and capabilities. One outcome for the Citizenship curriculum at the primary level, for instance, states that learners are expected to hear, explore and respect other viewpoints (Nova Scotia Department of Education and Culture 1999: 5). An accompanying statement explains that this extends across differences in gender, but fails to mention the need for more effective communication between settler people and the Mi'kmaq.

Subject-specific curriculum guides seemed similarly silent when it came to identifying goals and outcomes focused on the region's first peoples. Student learning outcomes identified for subjects such as social studies, history, geography and sociology contained some occasional references to Aboriginal peoples but only infrequently named the Mi'kmaq as a specific people. The Atlantic Canada Social Studies Curriculum: Social Studies 8 (Nova Scotia Department of Education 2006), for instance, contained four pages outcomes but mentioned the Mi'kmaq only once.[16] In subjects like English language arts curricula, art, dance and music, the Mi'kmaq were not addressed in any of the learning outcomes, with only very infrequent references to Aboriginal peoples. In science, math and education for sustainable development, it appears that neither Aboriginal peoples nor the Mi'kmaq are featured at all. Mi'kmaq studies 10 was listed as "a social studies alternative" and is not mandatory for students in Nova Scotia schools, and Mi'kmaw language is provided in only a handful of public schools.

Specific curriculum outcomes focused on Aboriginal peoples tended to be cognitive (e.g., "analyze," "explain") or, to a lesser extent, psychomotor or behavioural (e.g., "read critically," "present a report"). For instance, as outlined in the *Foundation for the Atlantic Canada English Language Arts Curriculum* (Atlantic Provinces Education Foundation 1996) that students will "*identify* some forms of oral language that are unfair to particular individuals and cultures and *use* vocabulary that shows respect for all people" (7, emphasis added). Another outcome aimed at fostering "critical literacy" stated that students must learn how to "detect prejudice, stereotyping and bias" and "read resistantly" (Atlantic Provinces Education Foundation 1996: 28-9; Atlantic Provinces Education Foundation 1997b: 157-59). Yet there seemed to be few, if any, outcomes that emphasized a need for affective learning (e.g., value, internalize, adopt a new outlook or behaviour) in relation to the Mi'kmaq. Outcomes that directed students to move beyond instrumental knowing and passive tolerance to more actively integrate, or adopt elements of Aboriginal world views or ways of knowing appeared to be absent entirely.

Curriculum Content and Learning Resources

Perhaps not surprisingly, the most attention seemed to be given to Aboriginal peoples and the Mi'kmaq in the social studies curricula for grades 7, 8, 10 and 11. Social studies texts such as Fitton's (2006) *Canadian Identity*, authorized for grade 8 were frank in describing how European settlement fuelled the forced displacement and relocation of Aboriginal peoples (44). *Canadian Identity* also drew up Aboriginal culture and history in order to explore key themes. Traditional and contemporary Aboriginal media, for instance, were used to illustrate the interaction of culture, identity and change (5). Aboriginal treaty rights were presented as being on par with other 20th-century struggles for social justice such as the women's movement, and Aboriginal self-government, provided one focal point for discussions around changing Canadian political relationships in the 21st century (263-67). Other textbooks such as LeBel and Orr's (2003) *Canada's History, Voices and Visions* authorized for grade 11 social studies/history provided more detailed insights to Mi'kmaw territory, traditional Mi'kmaw governance systems and the peace and friendship treaties (143-49). In addition, I found a small handful of new supplementary resources that took a critical stance on settler-Mi'kmaq relationships. Wicken's (2002) *Mi'kmaq Treaties on Trial: History, Land and Donald Marshall Junior, The Mi'kmaw Concordat* (Henderson 1997) and *Aboriginal and Treaty Rights in the Maritimes: The Marshall Decision and Beyond* (Isaac 2001) for instance, were listed for grade 10 social studies/Mi'kmaq studies and history 10-12. *We Were Not the Savages* (Paul 2006) was recommended in the margins of the grade 7 social studies curriculum guide along with new video productions such as *The Cross and the Eagle Feather* (Johnstone et al. 2003) produced by Prince Edward Island team which included Mi'kmaw filmmakers Brian Pollard and Joe John Sark.

Compared with the number of resources featuring groups such as African Nova Scotians, there were far fewer learning resources with content about the Mi'kmaq. Repeated searches of the Nova Scotia School Book Bureau database turned up fewer than fifty-five authorized learning resources with Mi'kmaw content across all grade levels and subjects. In some instances, resources were recent editions of items already in use for decades.[17] In subjects such as English language arts and science, there appeared to be almost no Mi'kmaw focused resources at all.

In addition, there seemed to a startling absence of resources in which the Mi'kmaq have told their own stories themselves. Unique, regional, resources from the 1980s and 1990s such as *The Micmacs of the East Coast* (Leavitt 1993[1985]), authorized for Grade 6 social studies in Atlantic Canada, until at least 1998 appeared to have been removed altogether. Prepared by University of New Brunswick linguist Robert Leavitt, *Micmacs of the East Coast* incorporates excerpts from historical documents, traditional oral stories and first hand narratives told by contemporary Mi'kmaw people. Topics include traditional livelihoods, as well as the impact of European contact, treaties and information about present day Mi'kmaw communities. Maps, charts, photographs and a glossary of Mi'kmaw terms supplement the text. Questions were designed to prompt not only critical analysis, but also empathetic engagement with Mi'kmaw people. For example, following a story that recounted what it felt like to be forced to leave your home and move to an entirely new community, the author asks readers to:

> Compare Moving Day in the 1940s with the young woman's account of Moving Day five years earlier. Why did each of these two young women move? Why did each one look forward to? Did they each have something to regret?

Videos like *Achieving Balance* (Nova Scotia Department of Education and Culture 2005) were flagged as being of interest to Mi'kmaw learners and there appeared to be an overall lack of information about contemporary Mi'kmaw people, communities, cultures and concerns. Although the three part *Wabanaki People of the Dawn* (Soosaar et al. 2005) video series begins with pre-history and ends with an examination of the contribution of Mi'kmaw youth today, the extent to which these few authorized resources can counter-balance the larger, Eurocentric "hidden curriculum" seems doubtful.

Social studies curriculum guides indicated that students need to "appreciate that there are varying perspectives on a historical issue" (Nova Scotia Department of Education 2006: 7); Aboriginal peoples and the Mi'kmaq appeared to appear to be compartmentalized, separated by artificial boundaries. In Canadian history 11 (Nova Scotia Department of Education 2002a), for instance, students compare different governance models but the curriculum guide noted that that "this outcome does not call for a complete study of each society, but rather only that which affected governance" (74). Mi'kmaw territory extends across the Maritime region, and the Mi'kmaq are members of the Wabanaki Confederacy, with ties to peoples east and west, north and south, but Mi'kmaw stories from outside the borders of Nova Scotia did not seem to be mentioned. Discussions about Aboriginal peoples often seemed to be confined to units on "culture"[18] or taken up as one of many "challenges and opportunities"[19] facing the Canadian state. These juxtapositions could leave learners with the impression that Aboriginal peoples are somehow outside "civil" society, little more than "problems" or "protestors" (Clark 2007). In addition, social studies and history curricula privileged post-contact "event history" (Braudel qtd. in Reid 1995: 18), a slim 400-year slice of time, rather than "structural history," broader patterns of events and interactions, which have unfolded over epochs. As Orr (2004: 168) has argued, understanding Aboriginal perspectives requires a more holistic approach where students move "back and forth between historical and contemporary issues and concepts."

Instructional Strategies and Approaches

Equity and diversity statements in foundation documents for social studies, English language arts, and arts education identifying some important "principles of learning that teachers and administrators should use as the basis of the experiences they plan for their students" (Nova Scotia Department of Education 2003: B-3). These principles include recognizing the background and experiences learners bring to the classroom, accommodating different learning styles and ways of knowing, and ensuring that all learners see themselves as capable and successful (B-3-B-4). The Foundation for Atlantic Canada Arts Education Curriculum (Atlantic Provinces Education Foundation 2001), for instance, outlines how students must be given opportunities to "use their own voices to understand, shape, and share their worlds" (42) as well as "challenge prejudice and discrimination which result in unequal opportunities for some members of society" (42).

In more contemporary social studies curriculum guides, there has been an evident shift away from rote learning and transfer of information toward an emphasis on dialogue and more critical thinking. Like the example below, suggested instructional activities for social studies 7, 8 and 11 prompt students to compare and contrast the experiences and perspectives of Aboriginal peoples with those of people from other groups.

Empowerment / Disempowerment of Groups in British North America			
Group	Empowerment		My evidence is….
	Strong	Weak	
Acadians			
Aboriginal peoples			
Irish settlers			
Black Loyalists			
United Empire Loyalists			
As a ____, I do / do not enjoy the privileges I should have *(Go on to explain why you would feel that way).*			
Source: Atlantic Canada Social Studies Curriculum: Social Studies, grade 7, Nova Scotia Department of Education 2005: 66).			

These kinds of activities reflect Orr's (2004) call for the use of more cooperative and collaborative approaches to learning about Canada's first peoples (172-73). One drawback, however, is that the onus is on teachers to ensure that students have access to adequate, accurate information about the Mi'kmaq and the impacts of colonialism. Uninformed teachers might also mistakenly assume that the experiences of Aboriginal peoples across Canada were all the same, rather than unique to each region, First Nation and group.

This emphasis on critical literacy is particularly evident at the high school level where learning experiences should, for instance, enable students to "reflect on the different social assumptions that different people bring to text construction and interpretation" (Atlantic Provinces Education Foundation 1997b: 158). One learning activity that meets these goals is an author study in which students examine "historical background and information texts, and cultural contexts in which the works were created or set" (122). These goals and activities are consistent with approaches to critical discourse analysis attempted in this study. Yet. what is missing in the both the English language arts foundation document and in the Grades 10-12 curriculum guide, though, is any indication of what controversial texts look like, who and why they might offend, or how teachers should address these issues when they arise.

Congruent with policy level changes recognizing and mandating respect for diverse people and the perspectives in curriculum documents in the 1990s begin to provide teachers with some guidance around addressing bias, stereotyping or racism embedded in learning resources. The *Foundation for the Atlantic Canada English Language Arts Curriculum 1997-1998*, for instance, devotes a page to "controversial texts" that "address issues and themes or contain content that may be sensitive or controversial in some Atlantic communities" (Atlantic Provinces Education Foundation 1996: 55). Although no specific examples are provided, the underlying debate appears to be about values, particularly those of "other cultures and times ... that may now seem deplorable were nonetheless facts of life in different times and places" (55). In deciding whether or not to use such "controversial texts," teachers are advised to consider the extent to which "society has evolved in understanding and tolerance over the years," whether these attitudes are those of an individual or if they are shared by a larger group, and the maturation level of students. The overriding consideration, though, is "respect for the students and concern for their feelings" (55).

At the primary level, curriculum guides provide examples of how teachers may deal with texts that raise controversial issues. One of the specific learning outcomes for *Atlantic Canada English Language Arts Curriculum Guide: Grades Primary-3* (Atlantic Provinces Education Foundation 1997a) outlines how "students will be expected to interact [with texts] with sensitivity and respect, considering the situation, audience and purpose" (59). In a folk tale/fairy tale unit, a Grade 3 teacher is illustrated as using a video of *Peter Pan* to focus students' attention on the use of "unfair or disrespectful language" and stereotypes. After listening to the song, "We're Off to Fight the Injuns," the class discusses the importance of using appropriate names, including "Aboriginal" or specific names such as Mi'kmaq or Maliseet. The teacher also highlights the importance of making generalizations about Aboriginal peoples as warriors and savages.

Suggested approaches for dealing with controversial texts like the examples above, however, gloss over the complex interdependences that Aboriginal peoples have with the land, let alone contemporary realities. In the discussion about the Inuit in Labrador, for instance, teachers might engage their classes in a deeper discussion about subsistence and sustainability, about the ways in which Aboriginal peoples limited their consumption and used every part of what they killed. Teachers might also talk about Aboriginal peoples' relationship with animals and the spiritual beliefs and practices that are carried out before, during and after a hunt. Teachers might also have contrasted traditional hunting practices and use of animals with contemporary practices, where we still rely upon animals for food, but the killing occurs in factories in less humane ways. Core values such as "respect for the students and concern for their feelings" (Atlantic Provinces Education Foundation 1996: 55)—in some instances—prompt teachers to shut down, rather than open up, more critical examination of ideas that seem strange or that make learners (or themselves) feel uncomfortable.

Summary of Contemporary Curriculum Discourses

New initiatives such as the Racial Equity/Cultural Proficiency Framework (Nova Scotia Department of Education 2011) help to sustain hope that long-standing inequalities and inequities will soon be addressed. In 2012, there was a distinct lack of representation of the Mi'kmaq across the curriculum, including policy frameworks, learning outcomes, curriculum content and learning resources and instructional approaches. As in previous decades, the Mi'kmaq were most likely to be visible in social studies (including Mi'kmaq studies, history and sociology), occasionally in English language arts and only in rare instance in music or art. The majority of mentions of the Mi'kmaq are at junior and senior high school levels, with far fewer at the primary level. Learning outcomes seem to have been aimed more at knowledge about the Mi'kmaq rather than at affective or behavioural changes. Particularly in social studies, there is evidence of an attempt to provide students with additional and more accurate information about the early pre-history and first peoples of the region, about colonialism and its impacts and about the treaties that European settlers signed with Aboriginal peoples, but curriculum which portrayed the Mi'kmaq as a vital, contemporary people was difficult to find. Even though curriculum framework documents contain rhetoric on the importance of diversity and equity, it is not completely clear who these documents are speaking about or what responsibility classroom teachers have in relation to the Mi'kmaq. Despite an explosion in the number of authorized learning resources in all subject areas, there are still comparatively few resources about the Mi'kmaq, most written by non-Mi'kmaw authors. Materials from Mi'kmaw organizations are difficult to locate in resource databases or have not yet been authorized for use. Although some new audio-visual resources with Mi'kmaw content have been introduced, non-print learning resources are positioned in a way that implies they are of less value and less importance than textbooks.

Curriculum Gatekeepers

Given that policies aimed at supporting inclusion of Mi'kmaw perspectives have been in place for more than two decades, why has the pace of change been so slow? I suggest that there are several "curriculum gatekeepers" which still have considerable power when it comes to determining how and where the Mi'kmaq are seen and heard in provincial schools today:

(a) The invisible authority of white authors;
(b) Centralized control over learning resources; and
(c) Problems with approaches to a more inclusive, socially just education.

The Invisible Authority of Non-Aboriginal Authors

Through to the 1980s, the relative scarcity of resources with Mi'kmaw content was a significant barrier in terms of accurate and empowering curriculum discourse. In the mid 1980s, for example, a bibliography of holdings at the Nova Scotia Provincial Legislative Library (Elliott 1986) listed numerous biographies about prominent European figures from Nova Scotia's past, stretching over six pages, as well as works about local and provincial history (twenty-one pages) documenting the experiences of British, Scottish and Acadian colonists. In contrast, there were a mere fifteen titles with reference to "Micmac Indians," which were almost exclusively focused on ancient pre-history or the period of first contact (87-88).

A more important gatekeeper, however, and one less readily identifiable, is that all of these authors were white, European settlers. As indigenous scholars have observed, it is the stories that settlers have told that have for too long determined what and how we think about indigenous peoples (Episkenew 2009; Lischke and McNab 2005; Smith 1999). In Nova Scotia, much of the information about the Mi'kmaq disseminated in schools can be traced to a handful of white historians, storytellers and academics. Some of the key figures whose works have been authorized for use in Nova Scotia schools and who continue to cited as authorities on colonial history, Mi'kmaw culture, politics are summarized in the chart below.[20]

Although these authors' works have often been cited as primary sources, the information they contain is often questionable. Far from fading away though, these works can still be found in academic libraries. Many have also been digitized and are available in electronic archives or online through Google books. In addition, both during these authors' lifetimes and after their deaths, other contemporary authors borrowed from what these individuals wrote, further distorting our understanding of Mi'kmaq world views and colonial history.[21]

The Historians	The Storytellers	The Academics
Thomas Chandler Haliburton (1820s-1850s): Judge; Member of the Nova Scotia Legislative Assembly; Member of Parliament	Silas Rand (1894): Baptist Missionary	Abraham Gesner (1849): Explorer; Indian Commissioner for Nova Scotia
	Charles Godfrey Leland, (1884, 1902): Journalist	J. B. Calkin (1859, 1891, 1898, 1911, 1916): Teacher and teacher educator; Principal, Nova Scotia Normal School
Beamish Murdoch (1866): Lawyer; Member of the Nova Scotia Legislative Assembly; Secretary Central Board of Education	Cyrus MacMillan (1918, 1922, 1974): Dean of the Faculty of Arts and Science, McGill University; Member of Parliament	
Thomas Raddall (1940s-1970s) Author (Governor General Award's for Literature); Historian	Kay Hill (1963, 1965, 1970): Journalist; Author; Broadcaster	Wilson Wallis (1911-1912); Wilson Wallis and Ruth Sawtell Wallis (1955)

Centralized Control over Learning Resources

Tight, centralized provincial government control over learning resources is one significant gatekeeper that seems to restrict inclusion of more accurate and empowering information about the Mi'kmaq. As early as the 1700s, school administrators had begun to express concerns about the procurement, selection and distribution of textbooks (Robinson 1979). Part of the impetus for the formation of Nova Scotia's public school system was the drive to provide teachers and students with access to learning resources, and to ensure that all schools used the same resources. Even before Confederation, textbooks were recognized as effective mechanisms for political control (Welsh 2005). A report to the British Parliament by Lord Durham in 1839, for instance, recommended that Canadian, not American, books be used in colonial schools in order to forge loyalty to the British crown. By 1869, the government of Nova Scotia assumed responsibility for authorizing texts that were to be used in particular subjects and grade levels as well as for the training and certification of teachers. As one study of textbooks in Atlantic Canada concluded, the assumption was that regional survival hinged on the promotion of a homogeneous (white) social, cultural and political identity, a process which could best be carried in schools (Robinson 1967). Today, curriculum resources used in school must still be approved by the provincial Minister of Education and teachers are still expected to be guided by resource lists prepared by the Department of Education and distributed by the Nova Scotia School Book Bureau.

Until the 1980s, a relatively small number of texts were used in all schools. For instance, the Nova Scotia School Series, which was printed and distributed by A. and W. MacKinlay in Halifax, were virtually the only learning resources schools used from the late 1880s through to the early part of the 20th century (*Annual Report of the Superintendent of Education* 1934: 114). Even as schools gained access to a wider range of learning resources, textbooks authorized for use in schools often remained unchanged for decades. George W. Brown's (1942) *Building the Canadian Nation*, for example, was used until at least the mid 1950s. Other texts by this author, such as *Canada in North America to 1800* (Brown et al. 1960), remained in circulation at least until 1970.

Although there has been a rapid, exponential increase in the total number of resources authorized for use in Nova Scotia classrooms from the 1980s onward, Mi'kmaw-focused resources are still conspicuously absent. Learning materials produced by Mi'kmaw organizations such as the Confederacy of Mainland Mic-Macs did not seem to appear in lists of authorized learning resources. Nor were there any links to these resources on the Nova Scotia Department of Education's "curriculum related websites" page. Although there are a few more authorized textbooks which positively acknowledge the Mi'kmaq and paint a more accurate picture of colonization in Mi'kma'ki, the ever increasing number of authorized textbooks and other learning resources means that items with Mi'kmaw content are proportionately fewer than ever before.

Instructional strategies in Nova Scotia schools still rely heavily on print resources as learning and teaching tools. One study of textbooks in Atlantic Canada even concluded that textbooks are "where our survival lies" because they provide a repository for our collective memory (Robinson 1979). In Nova Scotia education, long lists of authorized learning resources and numerous references to texts in curriculum guides suggest that the printed word is still at the heart of teaching and learning. Across all grade levels and subject areas, textbooks (most from national publishing houses) still make up the majority of authorized learning resources. This emphasis on print as a "container" for knowledge and reading as a way of knowing, however, raises questions about how Mi'kmaw knowledge, which is rooted in an oral tradition and embedded in relationships with people and the land, has been incorporated into curricula. A few curriculum guides suggested that teachers may want to "invite an Elder to speak to the class."

In 2012, a media library managed by the learning resources technology services division of the Nova Scotia Department of Education contained approximately fifty different audio-visual resources featuring the Mi'kmaq.[22] These included the *Mi'kmaq* video series produced in the 1980s, which is now available on DVD, as well as newer productions such as *The Spirit of Annie Mae* (Martin et al. 2002), the *Meeting of Nations* (Francis et al. 2006) and the *Wabanaki People of the Dawn* series (Soosaar and Fulmer, 2005). Most of these new audiovisual materials were been authored by or produced by Mi'kmaw people— including Mi'kmaw filmmaker Catherine Martin or Mi'kmaw organizations. Yet, almost all new media resources seemed flagged for use in grades 9-12 and could only be found by conducting a separate search of the media library, a structure which implied that these audio-visual resources were less important, informative, valuable or accurate than textbooks.

Teachers in Nova Scotia schools today clearly have access to a wider range of learning resources than ever before. The list of authorized materials for grade 7-9 social studies, for example, was more than fourteen pages long. Despite this, a significant proportion of Mi'kmaw focused resources suggested in curriculum guides such as *We Were not the Savages* (Paul 2006) listed for grade 7 social studies appeared to be missing from book bureau lists, the learning resources technology media library and the department's curriculum-related websites for teachers page. In 2012, information about authorized learning resources could be obtained from two databases: a database managed by the Nova Scotia book bureau (https://edapps.ednet.ns.ca/nssbb/default.asp and from a learning resources technology services database (http://lrt.ednet.ns.ca/) linked with the department of education website. On the surface, both of these databases appeared to be comprehensive, yet identifying resources with Mi'kmaw content was neither quick nor easy, suggesting new information-finding tools may be a barrier, rather than a help, to teachers who want to bring Mi'kmaw voices into their classrooms because of the complexity of subject indexing. Although subject-specific lists of learning materials contained headings such as "Multiculturalism and Antiracism" and "African Nova Scotians," there was no similar heading for the Mi'kmaq. Additionally, the online search functionality of the Nova Scotia book bureau and learning resources database was poor, even when the exact title and the type of material was known. Databases could only be searched separately and multiple search terms and spellings were required (e.g., "Mi'kmaw," "Mi'kmaq," "Mic-Mac," "Aboriginal," "Indians"). Nor was it possible to download a list of resources for either Mi'kmaw studies 10 or Mi'kmaw language 7, two subjects where the majority of Mi'kmaw learning resources were found. Materials were seldom cross listed for different subjects and/or grade levels, and it was not easy to locate other authorized items containing information about the Mi'kmaq. For instance, *The Peopling of Atlantic Canada* (Reynolds and MacKinnon 2000) was a multimedia package developed especially for the new Atlantic Canada social studies core curriculum and is one of the few resources that addresses the pre-history of the region. From database and other descriptions, however, there was no indication that this kit contained relevant Aboriginal content.

Problems with Approaches

Anti-oppression educator Kevin Kumashiro (2000) has identified four approaches to more equitable, socially just learning and teaching about the Other. The first approach, "education for the other" is what usually comes to mind when "Aboriginal education" is mentioned. Education for the other emphasizes the need for teachers and administrators to adopt new approaches, or provide specific strategies, services and supports that address the needs and interests of particular groups of learners so they can succeed within the mainstream school system; for example, as the Learning for Life Strategy II: Three Mi'kmaq Support Worker Pilot Projects (2005-2008). Education for the Other is also what takes places in band-operated schools under the control of Mi'kmaw Kina'matnewey (MK) school system (www.kinu.ca) with impressive results: almost 88 per cent of enrolled Mi'kmaw learners complete grade 12. With an emphasis on the seven sacred teachings, Mi'kmaw language and First Nations content and approaches, MK schools provide an environment in which Mi'kmaw learners thrive.

Although the language used in contemporary policy documents is becoming more critical, to date "education about the Other" appears to have been the most used approach where "content, concepts, themes and perspectives (have been) added to the curriculum without changing its structure" (Banks 1997: 233.) More commonly referred to as multicultural education (Banks 1997; Guo and Jamal 2007), education about the other attempts to integrate mention of cultural differences and the contributions of diverse cultural groups into curriculum content, learning resources and, less often, student learning outcomes. The assumption has been that increased exposure to information about diverse groups will result in "personal action and social transformation" (Kumashiro 2000: 38.) One benefit to such additive approaches is that it has indeed been possible to incorporate some information about, or references to, the Mi'kmaq into curriculum documents and materials, likely with no or only minimal resistance on the part of non-Aboriginal teachers, administrators or parents.

The way in which curriculum has been structured with an artificial separation into disciplines, however, means that what is taught about the Mi'kmaq is far from complete or well-rounded. For instance, one outcome around governance in Canadian history 11 explicates how "This outcome does not call for a complete study of each society, but rather only that which affected governance" (Nova Scotia Department of Education 2002a: 74). Courses such as Mi'kmaw language and Mi'kmaq studies allow for more holistic explorations of history and culture, but relatively few non-Aboriginal students have completed either subject, in part because these two courses have not been made available to all Nova Scotia public school students. Nor does there appear to be much space in Nova Scotia curriculum for an examination of Mi'kmaw world views and ways of knowing, concepts of space, time and relationship that are distinctly different from those of white, English-speaking settlers. This kind of "multicultural" content is urgently needed so that learners become more aware of what and how the Mi'kmaq think and feel, as well as become more aware of the gaps in our own knowledge and outlooks and the unimagined possibilities that lie outside Eurocentric frameworks. In the absence of specific goals, outcomes and content featuring the Mi'kmaq in learning resources, however, what learners are exposed to in the classroom is dependent upon the knowledge, discretion and good will of individual teachers.

Although policy language suggests that the Nova Scotia Department of Education is making moves toward other approaches to inclusion and diversity reflective of an "education critical of privileging" (Kumshiro 2000), this shift appears to be slow in making its way into the curriculum as a whole. One reason is that policies that mention issues around race and power have typically been broad rather than specific where groups like the Mi'kmaq who have been subject to violence may not even be named. In addition, as Kumashiro concluded, "the goal that students will first learn and then act 'critically' is difficult to achieve when there is much that the teacher cannot and does not know and control" (38). Although teachers have certainly been directed to incorporate instructional and assessment practices that are "free of racial, ethnic, cultural, gender and socioeconomic bias" (Atlantic Provinces Education Foundation 1996: 42), the extent to which white teachers in largely white public schools have been able to set their own privileged identities aside in order to create more inclusive classroom spaces seems doubtful. While foundation documents suggest that teachers need to be active in pursuing their own personal and professional growth in the area of anti-racism, curriculum guides fail to offer concrete suggestions about how educators can become aware of their biases or the prejudices learners bring with them from their communities. One of the guiding principles for instruction in Nova Scotia schools outlines how students are to "construct knowledge and make it meaningful in terms of their prior knowledge and experience" (Nova Scotia Department of Education 2003: B-3). What do teachers do, though, if neither they or nor their students experience racism or violence? If these topics lie outside their conscious experience? How can teachers best introduce the hard facts about colonialism and white privilege so that learners feel connected with, rather than separate from the Mi'kmaq?

Conclusions: The Way Forward

For more than three centuries, the "leaders and people of Nova Scotia have consistently shown a deep-rooted and constant faith in the powers of education to affect their destiny" (Parker 1967: Foreword, n.p.). The past decade has seen growing acceptance of the importance of anti-racist approaches to education, education critical of white, Eurocentric privilege. Kumashiro (2000), however, concludes that simply putting an end to "the repetition of harmful knowledge" is not enough. Instead, he argues, we urgently need to "construct disruptive, different knowledges" (42) as the foundation for an "Education that Changes Students and Society." This is a truly postcolonial perspective that addresses the partiality of school knowledge and actively incorporates the world views and voices of the Other into core subject areas and into the very fabric of life in schools—exactly what the Animating the Mi'kmaw Humanities project aims to do. What might be done, then, to redress faulty images of the Mi'kmaq in Nova Scotia curricula? How can we help all learners to hear what the Mi'kmaq have to say about their lives, their culture and concerns?

One key strategy for radically "altering citational practices" (Kumashiro 2000: 42) would be to bring Mi'kmaw voices into schools and to create space and time in all subject areas where Mi'kmaw stories can be told. This kind of approach would: (a) demonstrate respect for the Mi'kmaq, past and present; (b) show how Mi'kmaw humanity has evolved through time, adaptations and creativity; (c) uphold the importance of Mi'kmaw world views, values and perspectives; and (d) highlight the past and present relationships between the Crown and the Mi'kmaq, laying a foundation for new models of governance as well as new forms of relationships between settler Nova Scotians and the Mi'kmaq.

Learning resources produced by Mi'kmaw people and organizations are now widely and readily available. The Confederacy of Mainland Mi'kmaq, for instance, has produced a number of resource guides as well learning modules like Kekina'muek (learning) – Learning about the Mi'kmaq in Nova Scotia (Confederacy of Mainland Mi'kmaq 2007) with topics ranging from pre-history to education and the treaties. There are also several on-line Mi'kmaw oral history projects such as Kisiku'k Wklusuwaqnmuow "What the Elders Have to Say" (http://kisikuk.ca/) and new multilingual renditions of Mi'kmaw legends such as *Muin and the Seven Bird Hunters* (Marshall et al. 2010). In works like *L'sitkuk: The Story of the Bear River Mi'kmaw Community* (Ricker 1997), Mi'kmaw First Nations in Nova Scotia demonstrate the ways in which Mi'kmaw families and communities have maintained their ties as a nation and their connections with the land for generations.

Leading scholars, such as Mi'kmaq Stephen Augustine and Wolastoqey Andrea Bear Nicholas, have looked deeply into the implications of Wabanaki oral traditions in terms of reading, research, the writing of history and the production of media (Hulan and Eigenbrod 2008). In the curriculum, there are already some first person narratives like *The Mi'kmaq Anthology, Volume 2* (Meuse et al. 2011), which help readers recognize the all-pervasive impacts of colonialism and come to appreciate the value of Mi'kmaw culture. Biographies, autobiographies and memoirs such as *My Mi'kmaq Mother* (Pellissier-Lush 2009), and plays like Barlow's (2011) *Inspiration Point* speak with an authority and directness that allow readers to see through Mi'kmaw eyes. Rather than a single, static story about an extinct people from the distant past, contemporary Mi'kmaw film makers Catherine Martin and, more recently, Jeff Barnaby reveal the richness and diversity of Mi'kmaw experience across generations, locations and interests. Organizational websites, blogs and other electronic media are other valuable sources of information about Mi'kmaw creativity, innovation and achievement. Numerous Mi'kmaw communities, organizations, projects and approaches have been recognized for their outstanding contributions to fields ranging from the arts to education, environmental sustainability, business and politics. These kinds of success stories, stories about excellence and best practices extending beyond provincial borders, across the Maritime region and into the United States are sorely needed as sources of information and inspiration.

Not all Mi'kmaw stories, though, are told with words. Elder Caroline Gould's baskets, for instance, also speak volumes, as does the work of other Mi'kmaw artists like Alan Syliboy, Shirley Bear, Charles Doucette and Jerry Evans. Nor have the pedagogical applications of Mi'kmaw dance and other forms of performance art been fully examined. Ursula Johnson's *Elmiet* (Flinn 2010), for instance, invites participants to experience the physical, cultural and spiritual impacts colonization had on the Mi'kmaq.

Even if more Mi'kmaw voices are brought into schools, however, learners—especially learners who are settlers—still need to be willing and able to listen to what is being said, and to consider what omissions exist regarding Mi'kmaw people, history, treaties and contemporary governance in a neocolonial context. Rather than adding Mi'kmaw voices to a chorus of other perspectives, one approach might be to use Mi'kmaw examples as the focal points for instruction, where learners spend substantive time with Mi'kmaw perspectives, experiences and concepts, each excellent in its own right. One example of thematic teaching resources that have been cross-referenced with essential learnings and curriculum-specific outcomes is *Music: Cape Breton's Diversity in Unity – Mi'kmaq* (Beaton Institute n.d.). This unit focuses on diverse Mi'kmaw musical traditions and includes a teaching guide for elementary and secondary music and Mi'kmaq studies. Another similar module was *Work Through Time* (Community Access Program Society of Cape Breton County n.d.) an interactive oral history program developed by the Community Access Program (CAP) Society of Cape Breton County.[23] Drawing from firs-person narratives and primary sources including contemporary audiovisual media and archival resources, the purpose of the program was to "provide students with the opportunity to learn about the rich history of work, and its relation to culture, family and the environment, in Eastern Canada." Recognized Mi'kmaw Elders and educators including Murdena Marshall have helped to shape two units with a Mi'kmaw focus: a grade 5 unit, "Eel fishing in Eskasoni" (Community Access Program Society of Cape Breton County n.d.), and a grade 6 unit, "Mi'kmaq Work Poetry" (Community Access Program Society of Cape Breton County n.d.), which explored writing by Mi'kmaw authors Rita Joe, Lindsay Marshall and Shirley Christmas. These programs and units of study, however, do not explicitly uncover the deep differences between Mi'kmaw and Eurocentric world views or ontological understandings of space, time and relationships.

In contrast, new print publications like *The Language of this Land, Mi'kma'ki* (Sable and Francis 2012) reveal the meanings of traditional Mi'kmaw legends, place names and family stories. Even Mi'kmaw dance, the authors noted, provide clear evidence that Mi'kma'ki is not just a physical place, but a psychological space in which the land, and its people are one. Experiential, land-based programs with a focus on Mi'kmaw knowledge such as "Stone Bear Tracks and Trails" (stonebear.ca) provide another entry point to Mi'kmaw perspectives on the human and natural world. Cape Breton University's integrative science program (Cape Breton University n.d.), which promotes the concept of "two-eyed seeing," offers frameworks and concrete tools which can be used to help people learn to read the natural world as the Mi'kmaq have done for generations. Principles of holism, dualism, co-learning, multiple intelligences and reflexivity are not only congruent with the emphasis on critical literacy in essential graduation learnings and specific curriculum outcomes, they also provide concrete, practical tools for developing critical literacy skills. Although groups like Health Canada have been adopted integrative science and the concept of two-eyed seeing, there appears to have been no recognition by the Nova Scotia Department of Education to date.

Another important form of critical literacy is social literacy, knowledge and skills, which enable us to form and maintain more effective, egalitarian cross-cultural relationships. Positive examples of Mi'kmaq-settler relationships, and how they have unfolded, seem to be almost entirely absent from Nova Scotia curriculum today. Although *Micmac by Choice: Elsie Sark, an Island Legend* (McKenna 1990) was suggested as a curriculum resource in the early 1990s, it does not appear in current lists of authorized learning resources. In the advent of national-wide social movements like Idle No More, it has become clear that there are at least some settler Canadians who stand in solidarity with Aboriginal peoples but who these white allies are and how they became allies are among the many stories that have yet to be included in Nova Scotia curriculum.

In other provinces, like Manitoba for example, genocide education has been introduced in order to help (http://www.edu.gov.mb.ca/k12/cur/multic/genocideprevention.html) teachers and learners connect the threads among mass atrocities worldwide and to come to terms with our individual and collective responsibilities for human rights in the face of human aggression. Tools such as "life stories" (http://lifestoriesmontreal.ca/en/life-stories-in-education.html) have been developed to help learners engage with painful historical events and come to terms with the parts of ourselves as humans that we may not wish to acknowledge. Genocide education is a powerful new tool for implicating and engaging settler Canadians, defuse our resistance and prompt us to take action. Typically, however, genocide education has focused on events like the Jewish or Armenian holocaust, overlooking the genocidal violence of colonialism.

Introducing these kinds of disruptive knowledge, though, calls into question the purpose and structure of curriculum. As Kanu (2011) described, curriculum in Nova Scotia has been framed as a course to be completed, where learners are expected to acquire clearly defined knowledge objects along the way (204-205). Rather than a race to run, equity for and inclusion of the Mi'kmaq might be better served by framing curriculum as a "spiritual journey and transcendence" (206-13), a deep "conversation" with ourselves and others where the goal is the building of community with all other human, with other-than-humans beings, and with the earth itself. Perhaps the place where we might begin is by listening to what the Mi'kmaq have to say: "The story happens eternally, life goes from generation to generation. There is no end. The earth and our ancestors remain the same, but [the Mi'kmaq] are here now as today's people" (Marshall et al. 2010: 26.)

Msit no'komaq; all my relations.

Notes

1. A more comprehensive, comparative review could be carried out using reports, documents and textbooks housed in the *Little White Schoolhouse Museum* (www.littlewhiteschool.ca) in Truro, Nova Scotia. The museum houses an archive of educational resources from the mid 1800s to the mid 1970s.

2. The title of these bulletins has changed over time. In the late 1800s, they were called Manual of the Educational Statutes and Regulations of the Council of Public Instruction of Nova Scotia. By the 1950s, the title was Program of Studies in the Schools of Nova Scotia. In 1977-1978, the title was changed again to Public School Programs: Aims and Policies; Program and Course Descriptions; Procedures, Services and Publications. This is the title that was in use until 2012. In this chapter, I refer to all of these documents using the term "program of studies" because I feel this describes the bulletin's purpose. Beginning in the 1950s, bulletins appear to have been issued annually, with a few exceptions such as the 1980-1981/1981-1982 bulletin, which covered two instructional years.

3. I also consulted annual reports prepared before 1900 by the provincial Superintendent of Education for additional insights into what was happening in schools.

4. By 1977-1978, information about authorized texts was removed from the bulletin and published separately as Lists of Authorized Instructional Materials. These were available in print format until the late 1990s, when they were discontinued. Information about current authorized teaching resources is now available through an online database managed by the Nova Scotia School Book Bureau.

5. Instruction in moral and patriotic duties appears to have continued through until at least the end of the Second World War. Instruction on temperance, abstaining from alcohol, was mandated until at least the 1950s and possibly into the 1960s.

6. *Canadian Heroines of Pioneer Days* (McKinley 1929) was produced by a major Canadian school textbook publisher, but I was not able to confirm if it was authorized for use in Nova Scotia schools. By 1929, however, the province had begun the shift from provincially produced resources toward the use of materials from publishers in central Canada.

7. Among these voices was that of Joseph Howe, who became the first Commissioner of Indian Affairs for Nova Scotia in 1842 and later served as Premier of the province from 1860-1863. As Commissioner of Indian Affairs, Howe's first report to the legislature condemned government inaction and proposed a number of measures that might have put the Mi'kmaq on an almost equal footing with white settlers. The government of the day, however, refused to implement the majority of Howe's proposed reforms (Paul 2006: 204-16).

8. Programs of instruction in French for Acadian learners had been introduced around the turn of the century, but were discontinued by the 1920s due to "indifference" on the part of parents who elected to send their children to English schools (MacDonald 1964: 88-89).

9. Amalgamation of small, local school boards in the late 1960s was driven by a need to increase the tax base for schools as well as an expressed desire to provide a "comprehensive education" that would "serve the variety of needs, interests and capabilities of all types of students in the public school system" ("Amalgamation of School Boards" 1970: 18). This included improving student access to specialized courses and the development of a wider range of supplementary teaching resources.

10. Arguments for the elimination of provincial examinations included greater "flexibility, freedom and stimulus for local school authorities" ("Amalgamation of School Boards" 1970: 19), as well as more "variety and adjustment in courses and programs."

11. The series *Mi'kmaq* was regularly broadcast on School Television throughout the 1980s. By 1996, the series had been dubbed to video and was available to schools on loan (Wright 1996). In 2011, the series was formatted to DVD and could be borrowed from the Department of Education Learning Resources and Technology Services division.

12. "First Voice" is a term used by Graveline (1998: 116-27) to refer to narratives produced by Aboriginal peoples themselves. First Voice includes stories about creation, legends and traditional teachings; "non-fiction" accounts of the lives of individuals and communities; Aboriginal testimony; scholarly research and critique. First Voice is often, but not exclusively, a counter-story to white, European interpretations and perspectives.

13. Other notable examples distributed by the Department of Education's media services division were *Ktapeckiaq Kaqui-Tluek*, "The Song Says it All," a 1988 video featuring Rita Joe who talks about her work as a contemporary Mi'kmaw poet. The video includes a public performance she gave at a school at Whitney Pier, Cape Breton (*Education Nova Scotia* 1989: 3).

14. One of the featured artists in *Kwa'nu'te: Micmac and Maliseet artists* (Nason, Martin and McTaggart 1991) for instance was Alan Syliboy, who discussed how he came to use t-shirts as a canvas for raising awareness in non-Aboriginal society and expressing his own pride in his Mi'kmaw heritage.

15. For instance, human rights teaching/learning resources for elementary grades were field-tested in several counties in the late 1980s (*Education Nova Scotia* 1988: 1).

16. In the Atlantic Canada Social Studies Curriculum: Social Studies 8, Outcome 8.5.2 states that students will "Analyse the political challenges and opportunities that may affect Canada's future: Examine issues related to Aboriginal autonomy and self-government" (Nova Scotia Department of Education 2006: 25)

17. *Six Micmac Stories* (Whitehead 1989), for instance, was authorized from 1991 to 2002. It was replaced in 2007 by *Stories From the Six Worlds: Micmac Legends* (Whitehead 2006).

18. For example, in Canadian history 11 (Nova Scotia Department of Education 2002a), Aboriginal concerns are integrated into a unit on "culture and diversity (5).

19. "Challenges and opportunities" was the title of one unit in the Atlantic Canada Social Studies Curriculum: Social Studies 8 (Department of Education 2006: 25).

20. For example, Abraham Gesner's (1849) *The Industrial Resources of Nova Scotia* (http://www.biographi.ca/009004-119.01-e.php?BioId=38570) is recommended by the New Brunswick Museum's *Koluskap: Stories from Wolastoquiyik* project (see http://website.nbm-mnb.ca/koluskap/English/Bibliography/index.php)

21. Parkhill (1997) argues that a number of Kluskap stories used as the basis for Mi'kmaw and Maliseet cultural revitalization initiatives (Bear Nicholas 2008) were not "traditional" at all, but were invented by journalist Charles Godfrey Leland.

22. Several groundbreaking films from the 1990s which portrayed contemporary Mi'kmaw people, culture and concerns such as *Kwa'nu'te: Micmac and Maliseet Artists* (Martin 1991), however, were no longer listed for use in particular subject areas or had been removed.

23. As of 2016, *Work Through Time* modules could no longer be found at this address and appeared to have been taken down.

References

Ahenakew, F., B. Gardipy and B. Lafond. 1995. *Voices of the First Nations.* Toronto, NS: McGraw-Hill Ryerson.

Annual report of the Superintendent of Education on the Public Schools of Nova Scotia for the Year Ended 31ˢᵗ July, 1894. 1895. Halifax, NS: Commissioner of Public Works and Mines, Queen's Printer.

Annual report of the Superintendent of Education on the Public Schools of Nova Scotia for the Year Ended 31ˢᵗ July, 1895. 1896. Halifax, NS: Commissioner of Public Works and Mines, Queen's Printer.

Annual report of the Superintendent of Education for Nova Scotia for the Year Ended July 31, 1933. 1934. Halifax, NS: Minister of Public Works and Mines, King's Printer.

Atlantic Provinces Education Foundation. N.d.. *The Atlantic Canada Framework for Essential Graduation Learnings in School.* http://www.ednet.ns.ca/files/reports/essential_grad_learnings.pdf

Atlantic Provinces Education Foundation. 1996. *Foundation for the Atlantic Canada English Language Arts Curriculum*. Halifax, NS: Nova Scotia Department of Education and Culture, English Program Services.

Atlantic Provinces Education Foundation. 1997a. *Atlantic Canada English Language Arts Curriculum: Grades Primary-3*. Halifax, NS: Nova Scotia Department of Education and Culture, English Program Services.

Atlantic Provinces Education Foundation. 1997b. *Atlantic Canada English Language Arts Curriculum: Grades 10-12*. Halifax, NS: Nova Scotia Department of Education and Culture, English Program Services.

Atlantic Provinces Education Foundation. 1999. *Foundation for the Atlantic Canada Social Studies Curriculum*. Halifax, NS: Nova Scotia Department of Education and Culture, English Program Services.

Atlantic Provinces Education Foundation. 2001. *Foundation for the Atlantic Canada Arts Education Curriculum*. Halifax, NS: Nova Scotia Department of Education, English Program Services.

The Atlantic Readers: Fourth Reader. 1932. Toronto, ON: Thomas Nelson.

Bailey, A. G. 1969. *The Conflict of European and Eastern Algonkian Cultures 1504-1700: A study in Canadian Civilization*. Toronto, ON: University of Toronto Press.

Banks, J. A. 1997. Approaches to Multicultural Curriculum Reform. In *Multicultural Education: Issues and Perspectives* 3rd ed., ed. J. A. Banks and C. A. McGee, 229-50). Toronto, ON: Allyn and Bacon.

Barlow, J. G. 2011. *Inspiration Point* [Play script]. Toronto, ON: Playwrights Canada Press.

Beaton Institute. N.d. *Cape Breton's Diversity in Unity: Music*. Mi'kmaq. http://www.beatoninstitutemusic.ca/mikmaq/index.html (accessed October 15, 2016).

Berard, R. N. 1984. Moral Education in Nova Scotia, 1880-1920. *Acadiensis* 14 (1): 49-63.

Bingay, J. 1919. *Public Education in Nova Scotia: A History and Commentary*. Kingston, ON: Jackson Press.

Blakeley, P. R. 1955. *Nova Scotia: A Brief History*. Toronto, ON: Dent.

Brown, G. W. 1942. *Building the Canadian nation*. Toronto, ON: Dent.

Brown, George W. 1949. *The Story of Canada*. Toronto: Copp Clark.

Brown, G. W., E. Harman and M. Jeanneret. 1960. *Canada in North America to 1800*. Toronto, ON: Copp Clark.

Calkin, J. B. 1898. *A History of the Dominion of Canada*. Halifax, NS: A. and W. MacKinlay.

Cape Breton University. N.d. Institute for Integrative Science and Health. *Integrative Science*. http://www.integrativescience.ca/ (accessed August 15, 2016).

Choyce, L. and R. Joe. 1997. *The Mi'kmaq Anthology*. Halifax, NS: Nimbus.

Clarke, P. D. 1991. Beamish Murdoch: Nova Scotia's National Historian. *Acadiensis* 21 (1): 85-109.

Clark, P. 2007. Representations of Aboriginal People in English Canadian History Textbooks: Towards Reconciliation. In *Teaching the Violent Past: History Education and Reconciliation*, ed. E. A. Cole, 81-120). Lanham, MD: Rowman and Littlefield.

Community Access Program Society of Cape Breton County. N.d. *Work Through Time*. http://www.work throughtime.ca/ (retrieved May 10, 2010).

Community Access Program Society of Cape Breton County. N.d. Eel Fishing in Eskasoni. *Work Through Time*. http://www.work throughtime.ca/ Rural/ Eelfishing.php (accessed May 10, 2010).

Community Access Program Society of Cape Breton County. N.d. Mi'kmaq Work Poetry. *Work Through Time*. http://www.work through time.ca/Rural/ Work_Poetry.php (accessed May 10, 2010).

Confederacy of Mainland Mi'kmaq. 2007. *Kekina'muek (Learning): Learning About the Mi'kmaq of Nova Scotia*. Truro, NS: Eastern Woodland Publishing

Crewe, J., R. McLean, W. Butt, R. Kenyon, D. Kessler, D.Minty and E. Schemenauer. 1998. *Atlantic Canada in the Global Community*. St. John's, NL, and Scarborough, ON: Breakwater Books and Prentice Hall Ginn.

Cruxton, J. B. 1993. *Community Canada*. Don Mills, ON: Oxford University Press.

Dalhousie University, Task Force on Access for Black and Native People. 1989. *Breaking Barriers: Report of the Task Force on Access for Black and Native People*. Halifax, NS: Dalhousie University.

Denys, Nicholas . 1979[1672]. *Concerning the Ways of the Indians: Their Customs, Dress, Methods of Hunting and Fishing and Their Amusements*. Halifax, NS: Nova Scotia Museum.

Dion, Susan D. 2009. *Braiding Histories: Learning from Aboriginal Peoples' Experiences and Perspectives*. Vancouver, BC: University of British Columbia Press.

Education Act, Chapter 1 of the Acts of 1995-96. N.d. http://nslegislature.ca/ legc/statutes/education.pdf (accessed June 15, 2010).

Elliott, S. B. 1986. *Nova Scotia in Books: A Quarter Century's Gatherings 1957-1982*. Halifax, NS: Nova Scotia Department of Education, Education Resource Services.

Episkenew, J. A. 2009. *Taking Back Our Spirits: Indigenous Literature, Public Policy, and Healing.* Winnipeg: University of Manitoba Press.

Fairclough, N. 2000. *Language and Power* 2nd ed. New York, NY: Longman.

Fitchett, William Henry. 1897. *Deeds that Won the Empire: Historic Battle Scenes.* London: Smith, Elder & Co.

Fitton, A. (2006). *Canadian Identity.* Toronto, ON: Thomson Nelson.

Flinn, Sean. 2010. Nocturne Spotlight: Ursula Johnson: Elmiet. *The Coast,* October 14. http://www.thecoast.ca/halifax/ursula-johnson-elmiet/ Content?oid=1928051 (accessed December 6, 2010).

Francis, Bernie, Brian Francis and Greg Hancock. 2006. *Meeting of Nations.* [Videorecording]. Moncton, NB: Atlantic Policy Congress of First Nation Chiefs and Indian Northern Affairs Canada.

Francis, D. 1992. *The Imaginary Indian: The Image of the Indian in Canadian Culture.* Vancouver, BC: Arsenal Press

Francis, Michael William and Franziska Von Rosen prod. and dir. 1991. *River of Fire.* [Motion picture]. Big Cove, NB.

Googoo, M. 1992. Quill earrings. In *Voices: Being Native in Canada,* ed. L. Jaine and D. H. Taylor, 49-56. Saskatoon, SK: Extension Division, University of Saskatchewan.

———. 1995. Quill earrings. In *Voices of the First Nations* , ed. F. Ahenakew, B. Gardipy and B. Lafond, 152-59). Toronto, ON: McGraw-Hill Ryerson.

Grove, Miss. 1846. *Little Grace: Or Scenes in Nova Scotia.* Halifax, NS: C. Mackenzie.

Gunn, J. ed. N.d. *Nelson's School Geography: Maritime Edition.* Toronto, ON: Nelson.

Guo, S., and Z. Jamal. 2007. Nurturing Cultural Diversity in Higher Education: A Critical Review of Selected Models. *Canadian Journal of Higher Education* 37 (3): 27-49.

Haig-Brown, C., and D. A. Nock. 2006. *With Good Intentions: Euro-Canadian and Aboriginal Relations in Colonial Canada.* Vancouver: University of British Columbia Press.

Halifax Library Association. 1967. *Nova Scotia in Books: 1752-1967.* Halifax, NS: n.p.

Harris, Michael. 1986. *Justice Denied: The Law Versus Donald Marshall.* Toronto, ON: Macmillan of Canada.

Hayward, P. 1973. *Early Man in Nova Scotia.* Halifax, NS: Nova Scotia Museum.

Henderson, J. S. Y. 1997. *The Mi'kmaw Concordat*. Halifax, NS: Fernwood.

Henry, F. and C. Tator. 2006. *The Colour of Democracy: Racism in Canadian Society*, 3rd ed. Toronto, ON: Nelson.

Henry, F., C. Tator, W. Mattis and T. Rees. 2000. *The Colour of Democracy: Racism in Canadian Society*, 2nd ed. Toronto, ON: Harcourt Brace.

Hulan, R. and R. Eigenbrod, eds. 2008. *Aboriginal Oral Traditions: Theory, Practice, Ethics*. Halifax, NS: Fernwood.

Isaac, T. 2002. *Aboriginal and Treaty Rights in the Maritimes: The Marshall Decision and Beyond*. Saskatoon, SK: Purich.

Jaenen, C. and C. Morgan. 1998. *Material Memory: Documents in Pre-confederation History*. Don Mills, ON: Addison-Wesley.

Johnstone, Roy, Frank Ledwell, John Joe Sark, Brain Pollard, Keith Baglole, Vision TV and Mi'kmaq Pictures Inc. 2003. *The Cross And The Eagle Feather: Spirit World: The Story Of The Mi'kmaq*. Charlottetown, PEI: Mi'kmaq Pictures Inc.

Journal of Education: Being the Semi-Annual Supplement to the Report of the Superintendent of Education for Nova Scotia. 1922. Halifax, NS: Commissioner of Public Works and Mines, King's Printer.

Kanu, Yatta. 2011. *Integrating Aboriginal Perspectives into the School Curriculum: Purposes, Possibilities and Challenges*. Toronto, ON: University of Toronto Press.

King, Thomas. 2012. *The Inconvenient Indian: A Curious Account of Native People in North America*. Toronto: Doubleday Canada.

Kumashiro, Kevin. K. 2000. Toward a Theory of Anti-Oppressive Education. *Review of Educational Research* 70 (1): 25-53. doi: 10.3102/00346543070001025.

LeBel, Susan and Jeff Orr. 2003. *Canada's History: Voices and Visions*. Toronto, ON: Gage Learning.

Leavitt, Robert M. 1985. *Micmac of the East Coast*. Toronto, ON: Fitzhenry and Whiteside.

———. 1995. *Maliseet and Micmac: First Nations of the Maritimes*. Fredericton, NB: New Ireland Press.

Leman, Marc. 1999. *Canadian Multiculturalism*. (93-6E, February 15). Ottawa, ON:

Government of Canada Political and Social Affairs Division, http://publications.gc.ca/Collection-R/LoPBdP/CIR/936-e.htm) (accessed September 17, 2010).

Lischke, U. and D. T. McNab, ed. 2005. *Walking a Tightrope: Aboriginal People and Their Representations.* Waterloo, ON: Wilfrid Laurier University Press.

Lower, A. R. M. and J. W. Chafe. 1958. *Canada – A Nation and How It Came to Be,* 2nd rev. ed. Toronto, ON: Longmans Green.

MacDonald, H. M. 1964. *Memorable Years: A Century of Education in the County of Antigonish.* Antigonish, NS: The Casket.

Machar, Anges M. 1932. The Passing of Gluskap. In The *Atlantic Readers: Fourth Reader,* 123-28. Toronto: Thomas Nelson and Sons.

Mackey, E. 2002. *The House of Difference: Cultural Politics and National Identity in Canada.* Toronto, ON: University of Toronto Press.

MacKinley, M. B. 1929. *Canadian Heroines of Pioneer Days.* Toronto, ON: Longmans, Green.

Macmillan, C. 1974. *Canadian Wonder Tales: Being the Two Collections Canadian Wonder Tales and Canadian Fairy Tales.* Toronto: The Bodley Head and Clarke Irwin. (Original works published 1918 and 1922).

Manual of the Educational Statutes and Regulations of Nova Scotia With Amendments Passed 30th Day of April 1892. 1892. Halifax, NS: Commissioner of Public Works and Mines, Queen's Printer.

Manual of the Public Instruction Acts and Regulations of the Council of Public Instruction of Nova Scotia. 1911. Halifax, NS: Commissioner of Public Works and Mines, King's Printer.

Marshall, L., M. Marshall, P. Harris and C. Bartlett. 2010. *Muin aqq L'uiknek Te'sijik Ntuksuinu'k / Muin and the Seven Bird Hunters.* Sydney, NS: Cape Breton University Press.

Martin, Catherine, dir., Kent Martin and Angela Baker. 2002. *The Spirit of Annie Mae.* [Motion picture]. Ottawa, ON: National Film Board of Canada.

Massey, D. L. 1992. *Our Country, Canada.* Toronto, ON: Ginn.

McGee, H. F. 1974. *The Native Peoples of Atlantic Canada: A History of Ethnic Interaction.* Toronto, ON: McClelland and Stewart.

McGregor, S. L. T. 2003. Critical Discourse Analysis – A Primer. *Kappa Omicron Nu Forum* 15 (1), http://www.kon.org/archives/forum/15-1/mcgregorcda.html.

McKenna, M. O. 1990. *Micmac by Choice: Elsie Sark, an Island Legend.* Halifax, NS: Formac.

McLeod, R. R. 1903. *Markland or Nova Scotia: Its history, Natural Resources and Native Beauties.* Berwick, NS: Markland.

Meuse, T., L. Choyce and J. Swan. 2011. *The Mi'kmaq Anthology* vol. 2. Lawrencetown Beach, NS: Pottersfield Press.

Miller, J. 1991. *Sweet Promises: A History of Indian-white Relations in Canada.* Toronto, ON: University of Toronto Press.

Multicultural Association of Nova Scotia. 1978. *A Survey of Attitudes Toward the Need for a 'Multicultural Kit' as a Teaching Aid; and the Role of the Multicultural Association of Nova Scotia in the Nova Scotia Communities: Final Report.* Halifax, NS: Author.

Nason, K., prod. and C. Martin and K. McTaggart, dir. 1991. *Kwa'nu'te: Micmac and Maliseet Artists* [Videorecording]. Ottawa, ON: National Film Board of Canada.

Newhouse, D. 2005. Telling Our Story. In *Walking a Tightrope: Aboriginal People and Their Representations*, ed. U. Lischke and D. T. McNab, 45-52. Waterloo, ON: Wilfrid Laurier University Press.

Nova Scotia Archives and Records Management, Miscellaneous School Records: 1789-1989. [Textual records]. RG 14, vol. 1-54, 56-61. Halifax, NS: Nova Scotia Archives.

Nova Scotia Department of Education. 1956. *Program of Studies in the Schools of Nova Scotia 1956-57.* Education Office Bulletin No. 10: 1955-56. Halifax, NS: Minister of Education, Government of Nova Scotia.

———. 1962. *Program of Studies in the Schools of Nova Scotia 1962-63.* Education Office Bulletin No. 6: 1961-62. Halifax, NS: Minister of Education, Government of Nova Scotia.

———. 1969. *Program of Studies in the Schools of Nova Scotia 1969-70.* Education Office Bulletin No. 10: 1969-70. Halifax, NS: Minister of Education, Government of Nova Scotia.

———. 1975a. *Program of Studies in the Schools of Nova Scotia 1975-76.* Education Office Bulletin No. 10: 1975-76. Halifax, NS: Minister of Education, Government of Nova Scotia.

———. 1975b. *Social Studies in the Elementary School: A Working Paper.* Halifax, NS: N.p..

———. (1977). *Teaching Suggestions for Local Studies, Primary-grade 12.* Education Office Bulletin No. 22: 1976-77. Halifax, NS: Minister of Education, Government of Nova Scotia.

———. 1979. *Public School Programs 1980/81, 1981/82: Aims and Policies, Program and Course Descriptions, Procedures, Services, Publications.* Halifax, NS: Minister of Education, Government of Nova Scotia.

———. 1981. *Social Studies for Elementary Grade Levels.* Curriculum Development Teaching Guide No. 77. Halifax, NS: N.p.

———. 1984. *Public School Programs 1984-85/1985-86: Procedures, Services, Publications, Program and Course Descriptions.* Halifax, NS: Minister of Education, Government of Nova Scotia.

———. 1992. *Mission, Goals and Action Plans.* Halifax, NS: N.p.

———. 1994. *List B: List of Authorized Instructional Materials, 1995-96: Junior-senior High School Levels 7-12.* Halifax, NS: N.p.

———. 2002a. *Canadian History: Implementation Draft, May 2002.* Halifax, NS: N.p.

———. 2002b. *Racial Equity Policy.* Halifax, NS: N.p.

———. 2003. *Public School Programs 2003-2004: Goals and Policies; Program and Course Descriptions; Services, Procedures, and Publications.* Halifax, NS: Minister of Education, Government of Nova Scotia. http://www.ednet.ns.ca/pdfdocs/psp/psp_03_04_full.pdf.

———. 2005. *Atlantic Canada Social Studies Curriculum: Social Studies, Grade 7; Implementation Draft, September 2005.* Halifax, NS: N.p.

———. (2006). *Atlantic Canada Social Studies Curriculum: Social Studies 8; Implementation Draft, August 2006.* Halifax, NS: N.p.

———. 2011. *Racial Equity/Cultural Proficiency Framework.* Halifax, NS: Province of Nova Scotia, http://www.ednet.ns.ca/pdfdocs/racial_equity/RECPF_WEB.pdf.

Nova Scotia Department of Education and Culture. 1970. *Education Nova Scotia,* 1 (2) September 29.

———. 1972-1973. *Education Nova Scotia,* 3 (12).

———. 1989. *Education Nova Scotia,* 10 (7) February 13.

———. 1981a. *Education Nova Scotia,* 11 (10) June 17.

———. 1981b. *Education Nova Scotia,* 12 (2) September 23.

———. 1988a. *Education Nova Scotia,* 19 (1) September 1.

———. 1988b. *Education Nova Scotia,* 19 (2) December 9.

———. 1993. *Education Nova Scotia,* 23 (4) February 23.

———. 1997. *List A: List of Authorized Instructional Materials, 1997-98: Elementary School Levels P-6.* Halifax, NS: N.p.

———. 1999. *Foundation for Grade Primary Program.* Halifax, NS: Minister of Education, Government of Nova Scotia.

———. 2005. *Achieving Balance.* [Videorecording]. Halifax, NS: Learning Resources and Technology Services.

Nova Scotia Human Rights Commission. 1974. *Textbook Analysis: Nova Scotia.* Halifax, NS: N.p.

Nova Scotia Museum. 1983-84. *Learning Resources Catalogue.* Halifax, NS: N.p.

Ofner, P. 1983. *The Indian in Textbooks: A Content Analysis of History Books Authorized for Use in Ontario Schools.* MA thesis, Lakehead University.

O'Neill, G. P. 1987. The North American Indian in Contemporary History and Social Studies Textbooks. *Journal of American Indian Education* 26 (3): 22-28.

Orr, J. 2004. Teaching Social Studies for Understanding First Nations Issues. In *Trends and Issues in Social Studies*, ed. A. Sears and I. Wright, 164-75). Vancouver, BC: University of British Columbia Press.

Parker, T. 1967. Foreword. In *Nova Scotia: Three hundred years in education*, ed. B. Robinson. Halifax, NS: Nova Scotia Teacher's Union.

Parkin, George R. 1892. *Round the Empire.* Toronto: Copp, Clark, Co.

Paterson, Gilbert. 1933. *The Story of Britain and Canada.* Toronto: Ryerson.

Paul, D. 2006. *We Were not the Savages: Collision between European and Native American Civilizations* 3rd ed. Halifax, NS: Fernwood.

Peabody, G., C. MacGregor, and R. Thorne. 1987. *The Maritimes: Tradition, Challenge and Change.* Halifax, NS: Maritext.

Pellissier-Lush, J. 2009. *My Mi'kmaq Mother.* Charlottetown, PE: Retromedia.

Rand, S. T. 1894. *Legends of the Micmacs.* New York, NY: Longmans, Green.

Reid, J. 1995. *Myth, Symbol and Colonial Encounter: British and Mi'kmaq in Acadia, 1700-1867.* Ottawa, ON: University of Ottawa Press.

Reynolds, Graham and Richard MacKinnon. 2000. *The Peopling of Atlantic Canada* [CD ROM]. Sydney, NS: Folkus Atlantic.

Ricker, D. A. 1997. *L'sitkuk: The Story of the Bear River Mi'kmaw Community.* Lockeport, NS: Roseway.

Robertson, M. 1973. *Rock Drawings of the Micmac Indians.* Halifax, NS: Nova Scotia Museum.

Robinson, B. 1967. *Nova Scotia: Three Hundred Years in Education.* Halifax, NS: Nova Scotia Teachers Union.

Robinson, P. 1979. *Where Our Survival Lies: Students and Textbooks in Atlantic Canada* vol. 22. Halifax, NS: Atlantic Institute of Education: Dalhousie School of Library Service.

Sable, Trudy and Bernie Francis. 2012. *The Language of This Land, Mi'kma'ki.* Sydney, NS: Cape Breton University Press.

Shiu, D. P.-Y. 2008. *"How are we doing?" Exploring Aboriginal Representation in Texts and Aboriginal Programs in Surrey Secondary Schools.* PhD dissertation https://circle.ubc.ca/bitstream/handle/2429/375/ubc_2008_spring_ shiu_daniel_pui-yin.pdf?sequence=4.

Shore, M. ed. 2002. *The Contested Past: Reading Canada's History: Selections from the Canadian Historical Review.* Toronto, ON: University of Toronto Press.

Slapin, B. and D. Seale. 1992. *Through Indian eyes: The Native Experience in Books for Children.* Gabriola Island, B.C.: New Society.

Smith, L. T. 1999. *Decolonizing Methodologies: Research and Indigenous Peoples.* London: Zed Books.

Soosaar, John, prod., and Terry Fulmer dir. 2005. *Wabanaki People of the Dawn* [Videorecording]. Ottawa, ON, and Halifax, NS: Nova Scotia. Office of Aboriginal Affairs Canada and Indian and Northern Affairs Canada.

Sullivan, K. 1989. *Multicultural Assumptions of Selected Schools Boards in Nova Scotia.* Ottawa, ON, and Halifax, NS: Secretary of State, Multiculturalism and Dalhousie University.

Thibeau, P. W. 1922. *Education in Nova Scotia Before* 1811. Master's thesis. Washington, DC: Catholic University of America.

Thomas, C. B. 1972. *Indian Education in Canada.* Master's thesis. http://digitalcommons.mcmaster.ca/opendissertations/5686.

Upton, L. F. S. 1979. *Micmacs and Colonists: Indian-white Relations in the Maritimes 1713-1867.* Vancouver, BC: University of British Columbia Press.

Valverde, M. 1991. *The Age of Light, Soap and Water.* Toronto, ON: McClelland and Stewart.

van Dijk, T. A. 2001. Critical Discourse Analysis. In *Handbook of Discourse Analysis*, ed. D. Tannen, D. Schiffrin and H. Hamilton, 352-71. Oxford, England: Blackwell.

Welsh, J. A. 2005. *Nova Scotia, Nation, and Empire: The Politics of Civic Education and Provincial Textbooks, 1864-1918.* Master's thesis. Halifax, NS: Dalhousie University.

Whitehead, R. H. and H. McGee. 1983. *The Micmac: How Their Ancestors Lived Five Hundred Years Ago.* Halifax, NS: Nimbus.

Whitley, Ray. 1981. Mi'kmaq: A New ETV Native Studies Program for 1981-1982. *Education Nova Scotia* 11 (10): 1-3.

Wicken, W. C. 2002. *Mi'kmaq Treaties on Trial: History, Land and Donald Marshall Junior.* Toronto, ON: Toronto University Press.

Wright, A. 1996. *Multicultural Education Resource Listing.* Halifax, NS: Nova Scotia Department of Education and Culture.

Wyiruim Eva Lis. 1958. Song of a Canadian. In *Canada – a Nation and How It Came To Be* 2nd rev. ed., ed. A. R. M. Lower and J.W. Chafe. Toronto, ON: Longmans Green.

Jennifer Tinkham

That's Not My History! Reflections from Mi'kmaw Students on the Role of Their Teachers in Decolonizing Social Studies Education in Nova Scotia

"They call it Canadian history, but that's not my history." This statement has haunted me since the summer of 2008. Josephine[1] was a Mi'kmaw woman in a Bachelor of Education cohort situated in her home community. I was her instructor, there to teach her a course on inclusion. As the course progressed, Josephine and the other Mi'kmaw students recounted numerous stories of how social studies curriculum was disconnected from their lives and experiences.

When I was a student, I rarely struggled in social studies classes. I often connected with the history I was taught. A white, middle-class female, educated in private schools throughout most of my middle and secondary education, I felt strongly represented in the curriculum. I could see myself in the subject material and given a window into the stories of others. My teachers neither taught nor encouraged me to question the stories in my history classes. This was my history and I was not too concerned with checking the accuracy of the history of others. I assumed that the material was correct. When I taught the inclusion class, my taken-for-granted understanding of history was disrupted by Josephine's and others' stories. I began to understand that many of the Mi'kmaw students I was teaching did not feel represented by the history they had been taught in their public school education. In addition, no one involved in curriculum development seemed to be hearing their voices and no one seemed to be asking to hear them.

I arrived at the University of Alberta to begin my doctoral work in the fall of 2008, a month after the end of that inclusion course. Having completed a Master's degree in curriculum and instruction, I was interested in exploring more in the field of curriculum studies. I kept coming back to Josephine's statement and my area of interest began to take shape. There are many issues contributing to Josephine's story of feeling left out of the prescribed curriculum, such as what she perceived to be systemic or institutional racism or the legacy of residential schooling in this region. Does the curriculum allow counter-narratives to exist alongside the dominant stories of the status quo? Do the teachers? To begin to understand Josephine's experience I thought I should examine the role of curriculum in relation to Mi'kmaw learners as well as the role of counter-narratives and how these alternative perspectives can become more prevalent within formal social studies education. Furthermore, I could examine the complexities of how prepared teachers are to facilitate this infusion of Aboriginal[2] content. This might help me understand the shaping forces of Josephine's public school history experience.

In my master's work on diverse children's identities and individual, community and institutional narratives I found Schwab's (1978) definition of four curriculum commonplaces (teacher, learner, subject matter and milieu) helpful in trying to understand the broader forces involved in curriculum (beyond a particular program of study). I also looked to the work of Dewey (1938) to help me make sense of the connection between the individual and school. Dewey's definition of curriculum encompasses learning styles, society, the individual and the social forces that shape individual experiences. In my master's degree work I connected the theories of Dewey and Schwab with my growing conviction that students' experiences are or should be central to the curriculum of any classroom (Tinkham 2008). Schwab stresses that all four commonplaces are of equal importance and Dewey's theory of the critical role of continuity in successful learning might connect to Josephine's experience. Hearing Josephine's story shortly after finishing my master's work, I began to wonder if she would have felt the disconnect with the curriculum had there been continuity between what she was learning at home and what she was learning in school. How might Josephine's teachers have established connections to prevent Josephine from feeling left out.

My research enabled me to think about the relationship between home and school for children. My participants' experiences in school were influenced by the experiences of home and community that they brought with them. I learned that subject matter and teacher's knowledge and actions were key shaping forces behind this curricular experience. When I returned to Nova Scotia from the University of Alberta in 2009, after my first year of doctoral studies, I was still thinking about Josephine's statement. I asked her if she could tell me a bit more about being confronted with a history that she considered not her own. Josephine talked about her years as a student in a public high school, where she challenged her teachers on the content they were presenting in her classes. Time and time again, her concerns were generally ignored or chalked up to being just another take on Canadian history. When she explained that what she learned at home did not match with what she was learning in school, her high school social studies teacher reminded her of his qualifications as an educator. She was counselled to toe the line, memorize the material and get good grades. The teachers said she could believe whatever she wanted to outside of this classroom context. Josephine referred to this as "curricular assimilation" and said she wished she had fought harder to resist it as a student. She wondered what might have happened if she had stood firm and kept talking until she felt that the teachers were hearing her.

Josephine worried that she had given up too quickly and taken the easy way out. As a self- identified strong Mi'kmaw woman, she felt that it was her responsibility to locate and challenge inconsistencies in provincial curricula for Mi'kmaw students. As a newly certified teacher in a band-controlled school, she was working hard to actively identify, confront and resist curricular assimilation in hopes that her Mi'kmaw students would not have to share her own experience with history education. She worried that this would not be enough and reminded me that "one teacher can only change the lives of so many ... what about the rest?"

Josephine's story left me with more questions than answers. Growing up in Nova Scotia, why was I never presented with examples of early Mi'kmaw conceptions of democracy when we studied democracy in schools? What does being a Canadian mean if you do not identify with so-called Canadian history? Why did I learn about First Nations peoples as if they were living in teepees and dressed in traditional clothing all the time? This would have helped lessen the shock I experienced the first time I visited a Mi'kmaw community and did not see any of these things. Why was I under the impression that Mi'kmaw communities were formed by Mi'kmaw peoples and not the result of centralization (1918), which attempted to move all Mi'kmaw peoples in Nova Scotia to two locations, Eskasoni and Shubenacadie? These are just a few examples of the gaps I have found in my history education. I wondered if these gaps widen in a Mi'kmaw perspective or if, through the colonizing process of schooling, they also miss these pieces in their history education.

Building upon and connecting Josephine's story to my research interests, I intended to establish whether other Mi'kmaw learners share Josephine's Canadian history curricular assimilation experience across individual, commnity and provincial contexts. My sociology and social studies background consistently encourages me to question what I am presented with, whose interests the material is intended to serve, and where the gaps are in the stories being told. With this work, I hoped to get to the root of these wonders by examining which, if any, counter-narratives existed in Canadian history for Mi'kmaw students and how they in turn were able to situate and manage these alongside a larger dominating story.

Josephine's statement "that's not my history" continually led me to wonder what social and/or cultural factors, if any, were contributing to how Mi'kmaw students, like Josephine, interpret their experiences of the integration of Aboriginal perspectives into Canadian history curricula. I wondered how the pedagogical decisions made by teachers in both band-controlled and provincially controlled contexts contributed to how Mi'kmaw students interpret their experiences of the integration of Aboriginal narratives and perspectives. I felt it was important to gain an understanding of what impacts these curricular experiences might have on the cultural identities of the Mi'kmaw students in this research. Based on this interest I wanted to speak with Mi'kmaw students in these same contexts to learn about their experiences of learning Canadian history. I was motivated by Josephine's story, which was profound and real and still affected her many years later. She deeply felt these negative experiences with Canadian history. My work helped me to discover whether this was an experience shared by other Mi'kmaw students.

Using a decolonizing framework[3] and methods of conversations and sharing circles, participants were asked how their social studies courses, particularly in Canadian history, connected (or did not connect) with what they had already learned in their homes and communities. After hearing the participants' candid recollections of connecting their experiences as Mi'kmaw youth to the mostly-Eurocentric curriculum, I analyzed the data using the First Nations Holistic Learning Model (Canadian Council on Learning 2007) and Schwab's four commonplaces (Schwab 1978). I examined how their school social studies experience affected their mental, emotional, spiritual and physical well-being as they made connections between the curriculum and topics such as residential schooling, Mi'kmaw treaty rights and Columbus's "discovery" of North America.

I discovered that, according to the participants, it was the teachers, both Mi'kmaw and non-Mi'kmaw, who made the biggest difference in how the students made connections between their lives outside the classroom and the curriculum. Teachers who showed interest in the students' Mi'kmaw identity and added Mi'kmaw content to the prescribed curriculum promoted holistic well-being for their students. The perception and reality of systemic racism detracted from the students' well-being. Whether or not they were supported by their school environment, students persisted in their efforts to bridge the gap between the curriculum and the lived experiences of Canadian history narrated by members of their community. Listening to the voices of my participants, I now advocate for a reconceptualized curriculum and a culturally responsible pedagogy, which will provide supports for non-Mi'kmaw teachers to create experiences for all students to foster understanding of and respect for Mi'kmaw cultural perspectives.

Successes and Challenges: The Teacher Perspective

Witt (2006) claimed that in order to teach Aboriginal children successfully, teachers, administrators and curriculum developers need to be open and responsive to differing world views. They can then take a critical look at history education, using multiple perspectives and subjective realities. In thinking about ways to reinforce Aboriginal identity, Witt said educators must pay attention to "the identity that was built at home from birth to entering the school, within an education setting that bases in a different culture" (355). Witt explained that some educators have tried to reinforce Aboriginal identity by "teaching some Aboriginal history in university courses and adding so-called Aboriginal contents to the existing school curriculum. However, mere adding of Aboriginal contents, which might also be interpreted as such from a different cultural point of view, will not be enough to reinforce Aboriginal identity" (355). Witt argues that Aboriginal students need educators to transmit knowledge in the same ways it is transmitted at home, through Aboriginal lenses and Aboriginal cultural contexts.

One study, conducted by Orr, Paul and Paul (2002), provides insight into how teachers might connect knowledge learned at home with that learned in school. These authors spoke of reinforcing Aboriginal identity through cultural practical knowledge in an article they co-wrote on decolonizing Aboriginal education. They described the ways in which Mi'kmaw teachers brought their cultural practical knowledge into the classroom using language, activities that integrate a Mi'kmaw world view and conversations where children and teachers shared stories of their culture and communities. These authors saw the Mi'kmaw teachers they interviewed as providing important support for Mi'kmaw students in their schools through the cultural practical knowledge they wove into their teaching.

In speaking with these teachers, Orr et al. found that although Aboriginal knowledge is not part of the official curriculum, the teachers were committed to upholding a collective Mi'kmaw identity through their understandings and privileging of Mi'kmaw values, such as respect and honesty, within the curriculum. Orr et al. found that the teachers in their study brought Mi'kmaw perspectives to the centre of their teaching and that "these teachers strive to overcome inequities by challenging the inaccuracies and inadequacies in school knowledge and making strong linkages between school knowledge and the wider society from which these students come" (344). For me, the work of Orr et al. was hopeful in that it explained some of the key pedagogical decisions made by Mi'kmaw teachers in reaching their Mi'kmaw students. These stories of practice helped me to see how culture is lived in these classrooms. But I was left wondering how non-Mi'kmaw teachers enact this in provincial school contexts. I hoped that this would become clearer as I gathered stories of curricular experience from Mi'kmaw students.

Aboriginal scholars believe that educators must commit themselves to examining the stories told within colonial curricula and Eurocentric structural frameworks (Battiste 2005; Henderson 2000; Witt 2006). In research on First Nations students' perceptions of their learning, Kanu's (2005, 2011) work clearly delineated some of the challenges of integrating Aboriginal perspectives and content into social studies curriculum within a mainstream educational system. The study, conducted with both Aboriginal and non-Aboriginal teachers and students in a large inner-city high school in Manitoba, found that including Aboriginal perspectives was often problematic for non-Aboriginal teachers. The results of this research did suggest that all of the teachers "believed that the integration of Aboriginal knowledge and perspectives into the school curriculum was absolutely crucial" (54) on the grounds that curriculum needs to be culturally relevant for more than just the students of the dominant culture.

Although the teachers in Kanu's (2005) study generally supported integrating Aboriginal cultural knowledge and perspectives in the school curriculum, clear differences emerged among them in terms of how to do so. Kanu found that the non-Aboriginal teachers within the study experienced various challenges in integrating Aboriginal perspectives. Non-Aboriginal teachers tended to add content to the existing Eurocentric curriculum with videos and some Aboriginal literature. Or, they focused on examining significant accomplishments of Aboriginal groups intermittently during the course of their regular social studies teaching. The study found that "on average each teacher had integrated Aboriginal perspectives into the social studies curriculum only six times over the entire academic year" (56). Some teachers in this study relied on videos depicting Aboriginal experiences in Canada. Others taught about Aboriginal issues when they arose in the local and national news media. One teacher used outdated textbooks to examine stereotypes of Aboriginal peoples and the omission of Aboriginal perspectives from the mainstream educational materials.

Overwhelmingly, teachers integrated Aboriginal perspectives in a tokenistic fashion. Although they recognized the importance and the need, many rarely moved beyond an additive approach to incorporating Aboriginal perspectives in their classrooms and curriculum through a limited use of Aboriginal-centred resources. As the teachers in the study outlined the reasons they did not integrate Aboriginal perspectives holistically in their classrooms, it seems evident that many did not know how or where to begin.

The challenges that the teachers in Kanu's (2005, 2011) research identified included a lack of knowledge and familiarity with Aboriginal culture. More significantly, teachers lacked confidence around teaching about Aboriginal cultural knowledge, stating that, as non-Aboriginals, they did not feel that they had the "right" to teach about Aboriginal culture (59). Other problems included school administrators' apathetic attitudes toward integration and racist attitudes toward Aboriginal content. Kanu also argued that the school board provided the teachers with insufficient resources. The persistent lack of resources and funding were found to be barriers for non-Aboriginal teachers. More importantly, they had few or no connections to Aboriginal communities to begin to understand and learn about Aboriginal cultural knowledge. Kanu's work (2011) highlighted the many challenges teachers face in implementing the mandated integration of Aboriginal knowledge into curriculum in Manitoba and outlined numerous areas of concern for them. Agbo (2002) stresses that in order to successfully teach and connect with Aboriginal students, the concerns outlined in Kanu's work must be overcome.

Similar to Kanu's findings, Orlowski's (2008) study with ten veteran non-Aboriginal social studies department heads in British Columbia provided some perspective on the challenges that exist in changing approaches to educating Aboriginal students. According to Orlowski, "Overall, the teachers refused to accept the suggestion that they should alter the curriculum to help make it more relevant for Aboriginal students. Instead they were almost unanimous in their support of the color-blind curriculum" (126). Orlowski's work asked what teachers can do to ensure Aboriginal student success, suggesting that "social studies education is at least part of the problem for the high drop-out rates of Aboriginal students from BC high schools" (ibid.). The teachers in that study believed that the dominant society was not to blame for low Aboriginal student success. Some teachers enacted a "cultural deficit" approach to their explanations as to why Aboriginal students were not succeeding in school. In summary, the responsibility for Aboriginal student success, according to the teachers in this study, rests solely on the shoulders of Aboriginal students and their communities. This belief that Aboriginal education should be relegated to home and community is contradicted by the work of

Orr (2004) who stressed the need for Aboriginal perspectives and content in social studies classrooms. Orr states that it is beneficial for all students to be given the opportunity to discuss and unpack multiple perspectives and multiple values in the classroom.

Successes and Challenges: The Student Perspective

Although band-controlled education has existed in some First Nations communities in Canada since the 1980s, the establishment of the MK school board in Nova Scotia in 1997 was a first-of-its-kind agreement with the federal government that gave the jurisdiction of Mi'kmaw education back to nine Mi'kmaw communities. The agreement now includes eleven communities and was renewed in 2012. It ensured that "education laws of the participating communities with respect to jurisdiction ... shall have paramountcy over Federal and Provincial education laws" (Mi'kmaw Kina'matnewey 2009, Section 6.3: 10). It is important to note that under this agreement, schools within the Mi'kmaw communities falling under the jurisdiction of MK use Nova Scotia provincial curricula. Highlighting one of the key concerns of this curricular agreement, Battiste and Henderson (2000) stated that:

> Some Mi'kmaw communities have their own First Nations schools, which foster the values of the Mi'kmaw people and try to provide a Mi'kmaw curriculum; however, the mandated provincial curriculum continues to mandate a center that is not Mi'kmaq.

While it might be assumed that being educated in a Mi'kmaw system is most culturally beneficial to Mi'kmaw students, it is important to note that not all Mi'kmaw students reside in Mi'kmaw communities and not all attend schools within their communities. Throughout Nova Scotia many Mi'kmaw students live in urban areas and are educated in provincially controlled educational institutions.

I worked with participants from these two contexts. One group of participants were from the Ni'newey First Nation and attended Ni'newey Community School (school, community and student names are pseudonyms). Ni'newey Community School is located in the heart of the community and has approximately 300 students. The school falls under the Mi'kmaw Kina'matnewey agreement, the staff is largely Mi'kmaw, and the school is run by Mi'kmaw administrators.

The study participants from the community were current and former students from the Ni'newey Community School. All the participants were Mi'kmaq and they ranged in ages from sixteen to nineteen. Five participants had recently graduated and three were currently enrolled at the school. The participants had attended the school from grades primary to 12 and had never lived outside the community during their time in school. Some had lived elsewhere as young children but all the participants had started their school years and had finished or intended to finish at Ni'newey Community School. The participants knew each other and each other's families well and had strong bonds with each other prior to this research.

The second group of participants are considered representative of the provincial school context. These participants lived in Welte'temsi (pseudonym), a First Nations community located approximately an hour away from Ni'newey. There is no MK school in Welte'temsi and participants must attend the provincially controlled East Coast High School, located outside of Welte'temsi. East Coast High School is a grade 10 to 12 secondary school with a population of approximately 700 students. East Coast High School serves a large land area and many communities come together under the school's jurisdiction. The staff is largely non-Mi'kmaw (there is only one Mi'kmaw teacher) and the school is run by non-Mi'kmaw administrators.

The participants from the Welte'temsi First Nation were current and former students at East Coast High School. All participants were Mi'kmaq and ranged in age from 16 to 18. One participant had recently graduated and the other four were currently in grade 11.. The participants had attended the high school from grades 10 to the time of the research and only one participant, Kiptu, had lived outside of the community (and province) during his schooling, arriving in Welte'temsi in grade 8. All other participants had attended their school years together at the feeder elementary and junior high schools closest to Welte'temsi and had finished or intended to finish at East Coast High School. All the participants knew each other and each other's families well and had strong bonds with each other prior to this research due to their community connections.

According to the Ni'newey current and former students, their teachers had factored in the participants' well-being into their teaching by being willing to extend the curriculum, rooting their teaching in Mi'kmaw traditions and by being available to help students make sense of their learning in social studies. In thinking about the curriculum that was taught in school, many participants felt that their teachers did a good job but believed that they were adding to the existing curriculum when they taught Mi'kmaw-specific content in the social studies courses. For instance, one of the participants from Ni'newey Community School, Eli, strongly believes that Mi'kmaw content was found in all of his courses because his teachers were Mi'kmaw. He felt that teachers taught what they knew and therefore it was easier for his Mi'kmaw teachers to bring this content into their classrooms. This gave the impression that he—and other participants who made similar statements—believed that Mi'kmaw teachers were better equipped to teach in holistic ways that represent the four themes of development and well-being from the First Nations Holistic Lifelong Learning model.[4] Most felt that their teachers had easily been able to pair Mi'kmaw content with the prescribed curriculum content in ways that strengthened the content and allowed for them to connect to the material.

The participants seemed to feel that their understandings were increased because their teachers at Ni'newey Community School had worked hard to bring out the Mi'kmaw involvement in historical accounts. Examples given throughout our conversations show that the participants clearly believe that the prescribed curriculum was missing significant elements of Mi'kmaw culture and history but their teachers, rooted in Mi'kmaw culture and history, took additional steps to modify this content for them.

Another participant from Ni'newey Community School, Angelina, talked about how her teachers had been there forever; in fact, some of the teachers in Ni'newey Community School had also taught participants' parents. Highlighting this, Eli said that the current principal used to be his grade one teacher and with a big smile announced "she taught me how to tie my shoes." Through our conversations I saw, in my participants' eyes, that the raising of these children was indeed a community responsibility with each member looking out for the other.

The participants expressed that their teachers, being Mi'kmaq, were able to understand things that non-Mi'kmaw teachers would not be able to, such as Mi'kmaw ways of being. While not all teachers at Ni'newey Community School were Mi'kmaq, the participants believe that these non-Mi'kmaw teachers were connected enough to

Mi'kmaw culture and community to be able to do a good job of this. Eli talked about the teachers being able to tie content to people the participants knew in the community. This was especially beneficial in terms of understanding the implications of residential schooling.

The participants believed that teachers did not have to work to bring out elements of being Mi'kmaq because, as Angelina stated, "they live it and we live it, it's in all of our blood" and Eli believes that Mi'kmaw history was easily found in all of his courses because his teachers were Mi'kmaw and, according to him, "teachers teach what they know." All participants praised their former social studies teacher, Mrs. X, for tying everything they learned into Mi'kmaw traditional beliefs, which seemed to allow them to be able to maintain confidence and respect for their individual sense of self as Mi'kmaw people while working with content that wasn't necessarily developed with this in mind.

The participants felt that Mi'kmaw teachers had worked hard to bring out Mi'kmaw involvement in history and consistently attempted to create a bridge for students between being Mi'kmaw and the subject matter, believing that the student-teacher relationship was beneficial because teachers were not afraid to tell them the truth. The level of caring at Ni'newey Community School was similar to a family atmosphere.

There was a sense that the teachers at Ni'newey Community School had done a good job of including Mi'kmaw content and tying it to the curriculum but there was also the belief that these teachers were doing this on their own, without a provincial mandate to do so. Events and activities sanctioned by the school—such as attendance at the Truth and Reconciliation Commission hearings in Halifax—worked to strengthen a connectedness to culture for the participants and in addition helped strengthen the content. The level of teacher involvement and teacher connectedness seemed to foster a sense of pride and confidence in the participants. They expressed hope relating to teaching social studies content with a Mi'kmaw focus and they said they felt that their teachers cared about them. The family atmosphere seemed to create a safe space for the participants to be themselves in their school. They generally showed a high level of respect for their teachers and believe that they had done a good job of connecting with their spiritual selves, helping them to develop a strong Mi'kmaw character and sense of self.

In contrast, the participants from East Coast High School believed that the teachers were sometimes problematic in terms of the development of these participants' mental well-being. The only Mi'kmaw teacher at East Coast High School, Ms. K., was held in high esteem but the participants did not view the non-Mi'kmaw teachers so positively and did not always connect with them. The participants overwhelmingly believed that non-Mi'kmaw teachers saw Mi'kmaw students differently and held them to a lower standard. It was extremely problematic for these participants that teachers did not give the participants' cultural capital (Bourdieu 1986) very much weight. All the participants expressed great love for Ms. K, who also taught them Mi'kmaq Studies 10. The participants felt their love for Ms. K was reciprocated and were comforted by her ability to connect with students on a deep level and her willingness to stand up for Mi'kmaw students. The participants appreciated Ms. K's willingness to arrange learning experiences to promote awareness of Mi'kmaw culture as well as her decision to invite only interested parties to cultural events after negative responses by non-Mi'kmaw students to events like sweat lodges. For the participants this was both good and bad; non-Mi'kmaw students were not exposed to Mi'kmaw history and culture but offensive reactions to history and culture were mitigated through selective invitations to participate.

According to the participants, some, but not all, teachers were well-respected and held high standards for Mi'kmaw students. In talking about the rest of their teachers at East Coast High School, the participants remarked that they liked some of them and did not like some of them. There seemed to be a correlation between how well they liked their teachers and how well the teachers liked them as students. One participant, Kiptu, explained that some teachers viewed Mi'kmaw students as "smart enough" and some did not. Another participant, Helen, felt that some of her teachers believed that she would not do as well in their classes or understand the material because she was Mi'kmaq.

The participants held a positive view of the teachers who took time to engage with the participants, learn Mi'kmaw words or phrases, or take an interest in Mi'kmaw spirituality or traditional practices. Conversely, they had a negative view of the teachers who did not understand general Aboriginal culture or specific Mi'kmaw issues and did not inspire student voices. Ms. K's ability to challenge stereotypical or offensive notions around Mi'kmaw culture or history showed a deep level of care for the participants as individuals. The participants felt that Ms. K loved them and often described her as "like everyone's mom." They said they could trust go to her for whatever they needed in school and they described her as a strong Mi'kmaw advocate and defender of rights. It seems that the participants also viewed her in a protective role, safeguarding the sacredness of their traditions and culture by allowing only those who showed genuine interest in the topics to attend information and awareness events put on at the school.

The Role of the Teachers in Making Meaning

This study did not branch out to include teachers but did provide multiple opportunities for students to voice their experiences. What I found in talking with the participants in both contexts was that the participants at band-controlled Ni'newey Community School saw themselves represented in their learning as a result of action on the part of the teachers and community. The participants at provincially-controlled East Coast High School did not see themselves represented in their learning outside of their classes with Ms. K, which they believe was a result of inaction on the part of their non-Mi'kmaw teachers. The work of Ms. K allowed the participants of East Coast High School to experience a mirrored approach in their learning, where they could see themselves and their community in the content.

For the participants at Ni'newey Community School, the teachers were strong Mi'kmaw role models who worked hard to bring in Mi'kmaw content and celebrate Mi'kmaw culture. These participants discussed their close trusting relationships with their teachers. As mentioned previously, not all teachers at Ni'newey Community School were Mi'kmaw, however, the two non-Mi'kmaw teachers were considered to be adopted members of the community and participants reported that they worked hard to understand and respectfully represent Mi'kmaw culture in their classrooms. For the participants from Welte'temsi, there were some positive responses to teachers who tried hard to understand Mi'kmaw culture and to learn the Mi'kmaw language, but these teachers did not form the majority of the staff at East Coast High School.

Students' understandings/perceptions of the pedagogical decisions made by the teachers in band-controlled Ni'newey Community
School contributed to the participants' understanding of the curriculum and their spiritual connectedness. The open relationships
between the participants and their teachers allowed them to question
the curriculum and ask for more information. The participants in
Ni'newey described their teachers as knowledgeable and helpful. The
teachers at Ni'newey Community School had brought creative elements into their teaching, encouraged an advocacy lens, and provided
support for action. The participants in Ni'newey believe that their
teachers had played a key role in supporting Mi'kmaw ways of being,
tying content to Mi'kmaw culture, supporting attendance at cultural
events and bringing out Mi'kmaw perspectives.

According to Witt (2006), teachers must be familiar with the
cultural backgrounds of their Aboriginal students. The participants
at East Coast High School did not believe that their teachers were
committed to this principle of Aboriginal education. This disconnect
meant the participants had to make their own connections between
the content they were learning and the content they already knew.
There are numerous examples in the data of the Welte'temsi participants trying to make sense of African Canadian, African American
and Jewish history by relating events to local Mi'kmaw narratives. At
times it seemed as if the participants were desperate for some local
content in their social studies courses and most requested that the
content of Mi'kmaq Studies 10 be found in their other social studies
courses. The participants in Ni'newey also showed evidence of making
these connections to other cultural content but this did not seem to
be as much of a requirement for understanding as it was for the East
Coast High School participants. The participants in Ni'newey felt that
the additions and extensions provided by their teachers had allowed
for spiritual development and well-being. They wondered how this
might look in a provincial school with few to no Mi'kmaw teachers
on staff, showing that they understood that the cultural practical
knowledge of the teachers played a large role in their approaches to
curriculum.

Thinking in terms of cultural practical knowledge (Orr et al. 2002),
it is clear to me that—at least according to the students' perceptions
of their learning environment—the teachers at Ni'newey Community
School relied on this to help foster their students' cultural identities.

Using the Mi'kmaw language within the school, doing activities that integrated a Mi'kmaw world view, and making continuous connections to local people and their narratives supported these Mi'kmaw students in all areas of development, as described by the First Nations Holistic Lifelong Learning Model (CCL 2007). Following the logic of Orr et al (2002), the curricular decisions made by these teachers classify them as "political agents" (332) helping to create and foster change in schools and beyond. The teachers at Ni'newey Community School spent considerable time and effort to extend the curriculum for the Ni'newey participants, consistently bringing traditional practices into their teaching, remaining available to students in and outside of the classroom, enacting their cultural practical knowledge and maintaining and fostering close relationships which allowed for open and honest dialogue in the classroom.

When asked about being Mi'kmaw and Mi'kmaw content in social studies, the participants in the band-controlled school in Ni'newey felt that their teachers had been able and willing to approach social studies content from a traditional perspective, using practices rooted in Mi'kmaw culture and representative of Mi'kmaw history, which had helped them further their connections to Mi'kmaw culture. The participants in Ni'newey felt that their teachers had been able to "show the Mi'kmaq in everything," which had in turn helped them to better understand the content.

I believe that the Ni'newey Community School would be beyond able to meet the needs of the Mi'kmaw students it services, even if under a provincial curricular mandate. The school has worked hard to bring traditional culture into their classrooms and celebrate traditionally-rooted practices in their teaching, increasing spiritual connectedness for students. Thechool is grounded in First Nations education and has opened up a space for Mi'kmaw ways of knowing to "be practiced and celebrated" (Brant Castellano et al., 2000: 23). Lipka et al. (1998) felt that "teachers must have the power to structure classroom organization, curricula, and social interaction and the relationships between parents and the school in culturally congruent ways" (87). Based on the participant responses, I believe that the teachers in Ni'newey had been given and were using this power to create an inclusive setting for their students. Similarly, based on participant responses, I do not believe that the teachers at East Coast High School had been given opportunities to determine what the cultural compatibility might be for their pedagogy in relation to their Mi'kmaw students.

The Relationship Between Western and Indigenous Knowledge

Early on in this chapter, I described how Josephine expressed a disconnect between indigenous and Western knowledge, very much believing that they constituted a binary. The participants I worked with in both contexts did not seem to share Josephine's experiences. Thanks to close relationships with their Mi'kmaw teachers, both groups had found a space in which they could speak back to the curriculum when needed. Their main goal seemed to be to add to the existing narratives, not to discard them. When Josephine attended school there were no Mi'kmaw teachers with whom she could have formed close relationships and who could have helped navigate this binary. The school that Josephine attended still employs no Mi'kmaw teachers so I imagine this research would have yielded different results had I conducted it in Josephine's home community.

The participants in Ni'newey were willing to allow Mi'kmaw history and the content found in the prescribed curriculum to co-exist in complementary ways. The participants wanted to see more Mi'kmaw content woven throughout the social studies curriculum alongside, not against, Eurocentric (or Western) content. The participants in Welte'temsi also showed a willingness to lay Mi'kmaw content alongside Eurocentric (and, for them, sometimes contradictory) content. The main difference between the two groups was that the participants from East Coast High School had been left to bridge these gaps on their own. I did not get a sense that the participants wished to replace Eurocentric content with indigenous content. Rather, they wished simply to be included in the curriculum in ways that did not marginalize their culture and history. Both groups of participants recommended including more Mi'kmaw content, especially localized content, in the social studies curriculum.

Learning from this Research

This study has been beneficial to me as a teacher, researcher and learner. I was able to examine some of my own taken-for-granted assumptions and through my interactions with the participants in Ni'newey and Welte'temsi I am beginning to paint a clearer picture of what social studies education might look like for Mi'kmaw learners in provincially controlled and band-controlled school contexts. As the participants from Ni'newey Community School shared their experiences, I heard them say they felt represented in their social studies courses and they thanked their teachers for this. Writing up and analyzing the data generated in Ni'newey was largely a positive experience for me. When I moved to writing the case study for East Coast High School I felt discouraged as I reflected on some of the participants' experiences. As a teacher and teacher educator, it was not easy for me to hear stories about feeling ignored and silenced. The silver lining in these narratives from the participants from East Coast High School was their commitment to a hopeful future for Mi'kmaw representation in social studies. Another positive piece for me within the provincially controlled school case study was seeing the benefits of the relationship between the participants and Ms. K. Through this I was able to inquire further into the importance and impact of individual teachers who enact their cultural practical knowledge in their classrooms.

As I worked with the case studies from Ni'newey and Welte'temsi, I was able to group the participant responses into relevant sub-themes within the analysis. What kept recurring in both cases were instances of othering, exoticness, misinformation, stereotyping and racism. The East Coast High School participants in particular discussed feeling excluded on multiple occasions and the Ni'newey Community School participants discussed their experiences of these issues outside of their school and community. Both groups reflected on their ability to navigate between official and personal narratives in their social studies education. Specific to the band school case study was the position of place and belonging, while specific to the provincial school case study was a greater level of feeling like an outcast within the school. As I reflected on these themes, I kept coming back to thinking about culturally relevant and culturally responsive education practices and I began to wonder how this could help negotiate some of these sub-

themes, especially tensions around race, prejudice and misinformation, for Mi'kmaw students. I reflected on the findings from Kanu's
(2002, 2005, 2011) and Orlowski's (2008) research and realized that
it is not as simple as just asking teachers to be culturally relevant or
responsive in their classrooms. There needs to be a stronger commitment to this type of work at all levels and there needs to be considerable support available for the development of this.

I began to think through what I felt was missing from these approaches and how I could address the needs of my participants in the
midst of the realities of non-Mi'kmaw teachers struggling to meet the
needs of their Mi'kmaw students with limited support and resources.
It was through this reflection and questioning that I decided the term
culturally responsible should replace *culturally relevant*, *culturally
responsive* and *culturally proficient* approaches to education. Rather
than trying to exact cultural proficiency, which is a current focus of
the Nova Scotia Department of Education that is considered to be
problematic for people outside of the culture, I ask educators to adopt
a lens of cultural responsibility. The word proficiency implies mastery,
but can a non-Mi'kmaw person outside of the Mi'kmaw culture ever
be considered culturally proficient? If teachers are responsible to all
students and responsible for engaging students in conversations about
their learning and respecting students' experiences and histories in
teaching, how can they not be responsible for maintaining and fostering cultural identity? I argue that culturally responsible teaching is as
important as, if not more important than the current drive around
achievement-based initiatives in Nova Scotia.

The results of this research contain many implications for teach-
ing and teacher education. There is a call and a demonstrated need for
increased teacher training of Mi'kmaw teachers in Nova Scotia. Based
on the stories of success connected to the work of Ms. K at East Coast
High School, I assert that it is necessary to increase the number of
Mi'kmaw teachers working in provincially controlled schools. More
Mi'kmaw history and cultural content can and should be taught by
Elders. Mi'kmaw students should be supported in learning to speak
Mi'kmaw. Mi'kmaw language learning and tools for retention should
also be a priority in both provincially controlled and band-controlled
schools.

Echoing the words of my participants, I also recommend the
development of a course in teacher preparatory programs that focuses

on aspects of Mi'kmaw learning, building connections in communities, and a relational approach to indigenous and Western knowledge. Such a course would assist teachers in meeting the needs of Mi'kmaw learners across all subject areas. Building upon a recommendation made by Orr (2004), I believe another area for consideration in teacher education is the addition of courses that prepare teachers for teaching Aboriginal students. These courses should focus on readings and resources rooted in Aboriginal perspectives, understandings of Aboriginal ways of learning as described by the First Nations Holistic Lifelong Learning Model (CCL 2007), and opportunities to ask questions about and engage with Aboriginal content and issues. With a course such as this, teachers would be supported in their preparation and increase their understandings of Aboriginal issues. Professional development opportunities for in-service teachers, certificate programs, or a stream in Masters of Education programs across the province would also be helpful. A positive step might be for the provincially-controlled schools in Nova Scotia to negotiate a formal partnership with the Mi'kmaw Kina'matnewey (MK) school board for added support.

In terms of school climate, the participants from the provincially-controlled school demonstrated the need for more celebrations, presentations, information and awareness sessions, and opportunities to attend traditional ceremonies such as powwows and sweat lodges. However, this needs to be handled in ways that highlight respectful attendance and engagement. Having these types of learning experiences mocked by others will do little to foster a positive school climate for either Mi'kmaw or non-Mi'kmaw youth. Creating an inclusive school environment that is welcoming and supportive of Mi'kmaw learners will require engagement with Mi'kmaw educators, students, families, Elders and community members. These close ties to Mi'kmaw contexts will allow students to *be* Mi'kmaq in school and draw upon their connections to home and community.

The participants in Ni'newey felt like the school and community were one big family and they believe that their school was partly responsible for their development of strong Mi'kmaw characters. The school allowed them to be Mi'kmaq. For these participants there was no separation between school and home; both were viewed as safe spaces in which to learn. Educators and administrators can learn from the stories of the participants in Ni'newey and Welte'temsi and from the holistic practices of teachers in the MK school system. Creating an inclusive school for all learners is one of the main goals of education in the 21st century and so it is important to hear the experiences of the various stakeholders in Aboriginal education.

In order for the schools to be respectful of the contexts that shape identities and subjectivities of learners, there must be a commitment to knowing and understanding the life experiences of these students. The participants in Welte'temsi would begin to address this and participate in the reconstruction phase of a decolonizing agenda by incorporating more Mi'kmaw history and culture within the school, allowing more engagement with cultural ceremonies, and fostering more partnerships with local community members who can best share narratives of Mi'kmaw experience in Nova Scotia. Reflective of the premises behind curriculum reconceptualization, notions of place, autobiography, time and context must be taken into consideration because without these, the learner is unable to connect with the curriculum on a meaningful level.

Initially, I believed that the most important avenue that non-Mi'kmaw teachers should consider is simply to listen to the Mi'kmaw students. However, I realize that this isn't always so simple and teachers often feel unprepared, unsupported and undereducated in contexts unfamiliar to their own (Agbo 2002 Orr 2004; Kanu 2002, 2005, 2011; Orlowski 2008; den Heyer 2009; St. Denis 2011). Below, I have a few supports that must be put into place to help teachers navigate this shift.

Teachers should seek out curricular materials with strong Aboriginal content and perspectives, use local connections and people, focus on present-day Aboriginal issues, highlight past achievements and understandings, and encourage all aspects of development and well-being (mental, emotional, spiritual and physical). I do not expect non-Mi'kmaw teachers to enter into social studies classrooms and teach authentically from a Mi'kmaw world view. However, I do expect non-Mi'kmaw teachers to support their Mi'kmaw students by fostering local connections and by encouraging and valuing the voices of Mi'kmaw learners and educators. This is where the term *responsible* over "relevant" or "responsive" comes into play. By making this an imperative, the department of education and provincial school boards would be committed to assisting social studies teachers in meeting the goals specified above. Resources should be provided across the province and a formal partnership between the department of education and Mi'kmaw Kina'matnewey should be established. In addition to this, partnerships between local Mi'kmaw communities and school boards should be developed. Consistent engagement with the Mi'kmaw services division at the department of education would also help schools and teachers evaluate the quality of social studies education delivery for Mi'kmaw students and assist in locating and securing relevant resources reflective of Mi'kmaw history and culture.

Through the words of my participants I have established throughout this research that education about indigenous peoples is not only for indigenous peoples—this is important for all students. Kanu (2011) believes that "refusal to access the knowledge and wisdom of others produces self-fragmentation in us" (15) and she concludes that this self-fragmentation denies the learner the development and understanding needed to understand the world and "impair[s] the capacity for informed action" (ibid.). Social studies education, by its very definition, should produce the capacity for informed action in all students.

I think there is much to be learned from the teachers at Ni'newey Community School with regard to holistic practices for Mi'kmaw education and there is much to be learned from the teachers at East Coast High School in relation to the gaps experienced by the participants from Welte'temsi. A study of teachers could also provide insight into teacher cultural practical knowledge and its applications for non-Aboriginal educators. Further insight into the development and maintenance of positive school climates for Aboriginal students is also needed; however, this should not be attempted without actually talking to Mi'kmaw students to determine what they need in the creation of this environment. My most important recommendation from this research work is that teachers, researchers and curriculum developers seek out the voices of Aboriginal students in order to determine what actually constitute promising practices in Aboriginal education.

Recently, I had a conversation with a colleague wherein we were discussing our thoughts around both Aboriginal and non-Aboriginal teachers being educated within a Eurocentric system and how best to prepare teachers for the diversity of students in the classroom. She told me about a presentation given in her undergraduate education course by two Aboriginal students to a crowd of non-Aboriginal pre-service teachers. The presenters focused on the importance of respecting and valuing Aboriginal identity in the classroom and they discussed their learning to date in their BEd program. Both stressed that they felt supported teaching Eurocentric content to white students and ended their presentation with the following words: "we are prepared to teach your children; are you prepared to teach ours?" This statement stuck with me as it asks both pre-service and in-service teachers to consider their preparedness, comfort level and confidence in teaching Aboriginal students. There will always be non-Mi'kmaw teachers in classrooms with Mi'kmaw students and there are some that do feel prepared, confident and comfortable teaching Mi'kmaw students. It is important to establish that we can also learn from the non-Mi'kmaw teachers in schools that are doing "boundary-crossing" work and successfully creating spaces for the holistic education of Mi'kmaw students in their social studies classrooms by establishing how they too serve the needs of Mi'kmaw students.

This research also contributed to furthering my understanding as an educator and researcher as to how students in general experience curriculum at a personal level. This study highlighted the importance of allowing student voices to help shape curriculum development. While this study was done in a very specific context and the themes that emerged here may not emerge elsewhere, it is important that these questions get asked more broadly across the country and that people in other contexts can learn from this process and repeat it elsewhere, as appropriate to their context. Although this study was unique to the MK context, it exposes a number of issues. Examining social studies curricula elsewhere would lead one to conclude that similar issues exist in other contexts, therefore it is important for others to value these experiences and refrain from seeing these voices as unique to Mi'kma'ki. We can learn from this process and the words of these students and begin to think about what kinds of conversations need to be had with students in other Canadian contexts.

Notes

1. A Pseudonym.

2. Throughout this chapter I have chosen to use the term Aboriginal when referring to a larger context to represent First Nations, Inuit and Metis peoples. I use First Nations and, more specifically, Mi'kmaq, wherever possible to keep this work focused locally and specific to the context in which I worked. In some cases I use the term indigenous to refer to both a local and

global context. When discussing literature I have reviewed I use the terminology that the authors of the literature have specified.

3. Using a decolonizing framework meant I had to understand and interpret my work as I engaged with the community, respecting and understanding the values, traditions and protocols in Mi'kmaw culture. I used methods of conversations and sharing circles and participants were asked how their social studies courses, particularly in Canadian history, connected (or did not connect) with what they had already learned in their homes and communities.

4. According to the Canadian Council on Learning (CCL 2007), the First Nations Holistic Lifelong Learning Model was developed "as a result of ongoing discussions among First Nations learning professionals, community practitioners, researchers and analysts" (1). This model was created as a means to redefine how success in measured in First Nations learning. It is rooted in a First Nations understanding of learning.

References

Agbo, S. 2002. Unstated Features of Cultural Deprivation or Discontinuity: Culture Standards for Administrators and Teachers of Aboriginal Students [Mohawk Education Curriculum Education Project]. *Journal of Educational Administration and Foundations* 16 (2): 10-36.

Battiste, M. 2005. *State of Aboriginal Learning*. Background Paper for the National Dialogue on Aboriginal Learning Conference. Saskatoon, SK: Canadian Council on Learning (CCL).

Battiste, M. and. J. Y. Henderson. 2000. *Protecting Indigenous Knowledge and Heritage: A Global Challenge*. Saskatoon, SK: Purich Press.

Brant Castellano, M., L. Davisand L. Lahache. 2000. *Aboriginal Education: Fulfilling the Promise*. Vancouver, BC: UBC Press.

Bourdieu, P. 1986. The Forms of Capital. In *Handbook of Theory and Research for the Sociology of Education*, ed. J. Richardson, 241-58. New York: Greenwood.

Canadian Council on Learning. 2007. *Redefining How Success is Measured in First Nations, Inuit and Metis Learning*. Ottawa: CCL.

den Heyer, K. 2009. Sticky Points: Teacher Educators Re-examine Their Practice in Light of a New Alberta Social Studies Program and Its Inclusion of Aboriginal Perspectives. *Teaching Education* 20 (4): 343-55.

Dewey, J. 1938. *Experience and Education*. New York, NY: Macmillan.

Henderson, James Sa'ke'j Youngblood. 2000. Postcolonial Ghost Dancing: Diagnosing European Colonialism. In *Reclaiming Indigenous voice and Vision*, ed. M. Battiste, 55-76. Vancouver, BC: UBC Press.

Kanu, Y. 2002. In Their Own Voices: First Nations Students Identify Some Cultural Mediators of Their Learning in the Formal School System. *Alberta Journal of Educational Research* 48 (2): 98-121.

————. 2005. Teachers' Perceptions of the Integration of Aboriginal Perspectives into the High School Curriculum. *Alberta Journal of Educational Research* 51 (1): 50–68.

————. 2011. Integrating Aboriginal Perspectives into the School Curriculum: Purposes, Possibilities, and Challenges. Toronto, ON: University of Toronto Press.

Lipka, J., G. Mohatt and The Ciulistet Group. 1998 *Transforming the Culture ofSschools: Yup'ik Eskimo Examples.* Mahwah, NJ: Lawerence Erlbaum Associates.

Orlowski, P. 2008. "That Would Certainly be Spoiling Them": Liberal Discourses of Social Studies Teachers and Concerns About Aboriginal Students. *Canadian Journal of Native Education* 31 (2): 110-29.

Orr, J. 2004. Teaching Social Studies for Understanding First Nations Issues. In *Challenges and Prospects for Canadian Social Studies*, ed. A. Sears and I. Wright, 164-75. Vancouver, BC: Pacific Educational Press.

Orr, J., J. Paul and S. Paul. 2002. Decolonizing Mi'kmaw Education through Cultural Practical Knowledge. *McGill Journal of Education* 37 (3): 331-54.

Schwab, J. J. 1978. The Practical: Translation into Curriculum. In *Science, Curriculum and Liberal Education: Selected Essays*, ed. I. Westbury and N. J. Wilkof, 365-83. Chicago, IL: The University of Chicago Press.

St. Denis, V. 2011. Silencing Aboriginal Curricular Content and Perspectives through Multiculturalism: "There are Other Children Here." *Review of Education, Pedagogy, and Cultural Studies* 33 (4): 306-17.

Tinkham, J. (008. *Children's Narrative Identity Making: Making Visible Cultural, Family and Institutional Narratives.* Master's thesis. St. Francis Xavier University, Antigonish, NS.

Witt, N. W. 2006. Not Just Adding Aboriginal Contents to a Non-Aboriginal Curriculum: Preparing Saskatchewan Teachers for the Rising Aboriginal School Population. *International Journal of Learning* 12 (10): 347-60.

Lisa Lunney Borden

A Journey to Transforming Mathematics Education for Mi'kmaw students

I have often told my pre-service teachers that the thing I like best about teaching is the on-going learning. I have shared with them how I love learning and how I believe that to become a better teacher we must be always willing to learn with and from our students. This chapter is a story of transforming mathematics, but it is also a story of my own learning journey, working alongside Mi'kmaw[1] people for more than twenty years, as I strive to become a more culturally responsive teacher. This is a story about stories, stories that shaped my understanding of education in a Mi'kmaw context, stories that reminded me to always be a learner first, stories that helped me to learn the value of listening. I share these stories not as a "how-to" but rather as a way to inspire readers to raise questions in their own context, and begin to have important conversations with community partners about what the possibilities might be. The stories I share are, at best, incomplete but they give insight into key moments in my own learning and how that learning has helped me to think differently about teaching mathematics.

Positioning myself and my work

Before I describe my teaching and my research, I believe it is important to share who I am and how I came to this work. Absolon and Willett (2005) have argued that "Identifying, at the outset, the location from which the voice of the researcher emanates is an Aboriginal[2] way of ensuring that those who study, write, and participate in knowledge creation are accountable for their own positionality" (97). My ancestry is rooted in Irish and Acadian heritage. Both of my grandmothers were of French Acadian descent and both of my grandfathers were of Irish descent. In both Acadian family lines I can trace back to Mi'kmaw ancestors at the time of settling in Port Royal, and while I honour this connection, I do not claim any Aboriginal identity. Furthermore, I recognize that my experiences in life have been shaped by the privileges of my white skin.

I grew up in a somewhat diverse neighbourhood and I had friends and members of my extended family who most closely identified with Aboriginal communities (primarily of Mi'kmaw and Wolastoqiyik descent), yet I was surrounded by dominant stories having learned very little about the indigenous peoples in my region. As I reflect back on my own upbringing I realize that I lived my life surrounded by indigenous knowledge and ideas, places of significance to Aboriginal people, yet I never learned the stories. I was completely unaware of what I did not yet know.

A Girl from Indiantown

I grew up in a neighbourhood in the North End of Saint John, New Brunswick—a part of town to this day referred to as Indiantown. I can still recall as a child wondering where that name came from, but no one seemed to know. As an adult, I began searching for information on Indiantown and I learned that it had once been a place of portage as Mi'kmaq, Wolastoqiyik,[3] Passamaquoddy and Penobscot people bypassed the dangerous rapids (a place I know as Reversing Falls) and travelled safely from the Saint John River to the Bay of Fundy. Following the Watertown treaty of 1776, a house for the fur trade was established in this area where each Nation traded with the British and thus, became known as Indiantown (Saint John Heritage n.d.).

In Saint John, I attended St. Peter's Elementary school that was located across the street from Fort Howe National Historic site. As a child my classmates and I would often take walks up the hill on warm fall and spring days with our teachers to work outside and explore the site. I remember being told that this was a fort built to protect the city from possible enemies—a dominant story. I was never told that a Treaty of Peace and Friendship between the Mi'kmaq and Wolastoqiyik Nations and the British was signed in 1779 at Fort

Howe (Aboriginal Affairs and Northern Development Canada 2010). How is it that we were never told this story? How had I not known what an important part my neighbourhood had played in the lives of Aboriginal people in the Atlantic region?

In the summers, I spent my time at a camp that had been built by my paternal grandparents in the late 1940s. Although they had never owned a home in the city, the summer place in Chapel Grove on the Kennebecasis River was a hub for our extended Lunney family. The beach across the road was a place where I spent a good deal of time in the summer, swimming in the river, diving off the raft, enjoying time with my family and friends in the area. Long Island, relatively uninhabited, is across the river from that beach and we would make a trek across in borrowed boats at least once every summer. I remember one time when I was young a neighbour tried to tell me that the Kennebecasis River was named after my uncle Ken. I knew this was not true, but I do not recall anyone ever telling me that this was a name derived from a Mi'kmaw word meaning "little long bay"—perhaps no one in my life actually knew this. After I had been teaching in the Mi'kmaw community of We'koqma'q for a while, someone shared with me a Mi'kmaw creation story. In the story, Long Island was described as the home of beaver—again I was surprised to see how little I knew about that a place that was, and still is, so significant in my life.

I am not surprised that indigenous stories were not part of my upbringing, as Battiste (2013) has stated we have all been marinating in Eurocentrism no matter where we have gone to school, but I feel like there were so many things I did not know and should have known. I am, however, grateful for the opportunities to learn them now and to revisit familiar places with a new lens.

A Spirit of Social Justice

I believe in many ways, although I was not raised with counter-narratives that honoured indigenous knowledge, I was raised to question dominant stories and to understand that we all inherit the world differently. I am one of four children born to Dan and Carol Lunney and the only girl in the family. My brothers and I were raised Irish-Catholic in the Loyalist City and while there was never any overt discussion with us as children of the implications of such an identity, I do recall overhearing the adults in my extended family discuss the challenges such an identity might bring. Violence between the Orange order and Irish-Catholic community in Saint John was common in the mid to late 1800s and the Irish-Catholics were seen as lower class, living in impoverished communities, and inferior to their Protestant counterparts who held great power in the city (Winder 2000). Although the violence had long dissipated in the 100 or so years from those moments to the time of my birth in 1971, a class divide remained in the city and Irish-Catholics would forever be the working class.

The experiences of my Acadian grandmothers were even more complex. There is a story widely known in my family that my maternal grandmother, when she herself was a young mother, would send her children out to play with clear instructions on two things they were not to tell anyone: "You don't tell them I smoke, and you don't tell them I'm French!" My grandmothers both believed they had to hide this piece of their identity opting to appear more English in order to provide a better life for their children. In one generation the language was taken from our family, and while I have learned French in school, it is not the Acadian language of my grandmothers.

These often-overheard conversations of adults in my life helped to shape my identity, and as I grew older and learned more about oppressive agendas used to marginalize peoples, these stories helped me to make connections and perhaps have a greater sense of the injustice of racism and classism.

The impact of socioeconomic status was something I learned at a very early age. The North End of Saint John, New Brunswick was, and continues to be, a working-class community with a considerable amount of poverty. As a child, I believed my family was well off—not as well off as some of the kids I went to school with but very well off relative to some of the families who lived around us. My definition of wealthy growing up was that we got to eat every day and had a warm and welcoming home. My mom worked at Sears. She had a discount and watched for bargains so we always had nice clothes. My dad worked evenings at the railway and was able to pick us up at school during the day. On rainy days, he would load all kinds of neighbourhood kids into the back of the station wagon and make sure everyone got home safely. We lived in a building that was owned by a friend of my late grandfather who rented our flat to us at a reasonable price. My maternal grandmother lived with us and loved to bake so we always had good treats. I knew that there were many children in my school who did not always get enough to eat and many families in my community who did not have the things we had.

Our parents helped us to understand the significant impact that class divides can have on a community and modelled for us a spirit of generosity that helped us to see that a community is made stronger when people work together to lift one another up. My parents raised us to give without letting anyone know you gave, from a true spirit of generosity. They were also involved in a co-op movement in our neighbourhood when I was still in elementary school. They worked with Father Ralph McQuaid, a Redemptorist priest at St. Peter's church, and members of the community to bring a co-op grocery store to the North End so that families could have affordable food options. I can recall many days of my pre-teen years coming home to find my dad and Father Ralph sitting at our kitchen table discussing the damaging effects big business was having on the rain forests of South and Central America, how companies lacked a social conscience and concern for local people in the areas. These were the moments that shaped a spirit of social justice in me. It had been modelled so many times by my parents.

In 1983, things changed for me. The railway was cutting jobs in Saint John and the only way for my father to keep a job was to relocate to Moncton. While we were not keen to move, my parents had been saving funds for a long time to buy a house and this would be their chance to finally have their own home with a yard and grass. I believed they saw it as an opportunity to do a bit better for us. We moved to the town of Riverview, a suburb of Moncton. Riverview was nothing like the North End. It was a town filled with relatively new bungalows and split-level homes that all looked similar, fancy lamp-posts and manicured lawns, corner parks and baseball fields, public pools and playgrounds. There was virtually no cultural diversity and only limited socioeconomic diversity. It was a community of sameness where sameness mattered greatly.

While growing up in the North End, I believed we were relatively privileged in comparison to others in the community; in Riverview I learned we were not quite as well off as I had thought. I found Riverview to a be a community focused on wealth—or at least the appearance there of—and materialism. My new classmates cared about wearing brand name clothes, taking spring break vacations and owning stuff, lots of stuff. My thirteen-year-old soul went through a time of terrible culture shock. These were values I could not share and in spite of what would prove to be an incredible social cost, I chose to resist the pressure to become one of these materialistic teenagers.

My father liked to jokingly ask me if I was a communist, failing to realize the influence he himself had on developing my commitment to social justice. I was a budding champion of equity often debating important social issues with my classmates. The six years I spent in Riverview through junior high and high school were some of the most challenging years of my life. It was a place I felt I never truly belonged and never truly felt welcomed. Yet these experiences helped me to not only understand what I valued with respect to justice and equity, but also to become very clear about what I did not value like materialism and social status.

X – The Unknown Factor

In the fall of 1989 I started my first year of university at St. Francis Xavier University (St. FX) in Antigonish, Nova Scotia. I instantly found it to be a warm and welcoming place and found many people who shared my values and beliefs. In many ways, it felt like coming home although I had never previously been to Antigonish. I joined a student society called X-Project that had grown out of a spirit of community service during the time of the Antigonish Movement in the 1960s. X-Project had begun with a few St. FX students travelling to Lincolnville to help some of the children with their homework in 1964 at the request of the school principal who was a recent St. FX graduate (people.stfx.ca/xproject). Over the years it had grown into a large student society with a commitment to work with children, youth and adults from five African Nova Scotian and Mi'kmaw communities in the surrounding area providing small group educational assistance, recreation and leadership programs. X-Project operated on a philosophy of X as the unknown factor. There was a commitment to work with and learn from communities and to not expect praise or glory for the work, but rather to act as humble servants working behind the scenes to bring about change. This value was reminiscent of the lessons my parents had taught me as a child.

My years in X-Project provided me with numerous opportunities to learn more deeply about diversity and equity. I had the privilege of working with and learning from community leaders, mostly women, for whom the education of their children was both a top priority and a troubling source of cultural oppression. It was as a volunteer with X-Project when I first heard the term "white privilege" and learned how such privilege impacts the lives of people who don't have it. This organization provided me with a space to truly listen to the voices of community members who had experienced racial and cultural oppression and to learn from their stories. I came to see how schools often streamed African Nova Scotian and Mi'kmaw youth into lower levels of math and English courses, and generally held lower expectations for children who were already marginalized within society. I recall a conversation with a leader in her Aboriginal community, as she shared with me her belief that her community needed to have its own school and a different way of educating their children. She told me that she was "not prepared to sacrifice another generation of children" while waiting for public schools to change in ways that would better support Aboriginal learners. These moments helped me to see the systemic racism that was impacting the lives of the children with whom I was working and also helped me to imagine there could be a better way.

Learning as a Beginning Teacher

After graduating with my BEd, I returned to Riverview to live with my parents while trying to find permanent employment. I spent some time as a substitute teacher and then did a small contract as a correspondence teacher for the Province of New Brunswick. One Saturday morning as I was nearing the end of my contract, I was flipping through the paper when I saw it, an ad for a job in a Mi'kmaw school in Cape Breton. They were looking for someone to teach secondary math. Something inside me told me this was my job; this was where I was meant to be. After two interviews, a struggle to find an apartment, and transporting a vanload of found, borrowed and cheaply acquired furniture to Cape Breton, I was ready to begin my new teaching job.

A Tradition of Perseverance.

I felt privileged to become a part of the community over the years. I sang in the church choir, spent time at community events, helped students to do fundraising for school trips at ball games, dances and bingos. Within a short amount of time the community had become home to me as I felt so much more welcomed in We'koqma'q than I did in the neighbouring community where I rented an apartment. Tiny and Karen Cremo became my second family. I learned Mi'kmaw around their kitchen table and was gifted with the privilege of being godmother to their youngest daughter, Tamara.

As a teacher, and adopted community member, I began to hear stories that highlighted a history of perseverance and resilience in the community, including a strong commitment to education, both in formal schooling and in maintaining other traditions. The stories of resistance and survival were told from one generation to the next as part of the oral tradition of the community. At school and community events these stories were (and likely still are) recounted time and again, arising often in seemingly unusual contexts, yet told with purpose.

One story focused on how the community resisted the government's efforts to relocate everyone in We'koqma'q to Eskasoni. Before centralization We'koqma'q was a self-sufficient community; people worked in various jobs, maintained their family farms and always had enough to survive. In the 1940s the Government of Canada initiated a process called "centralization" by which it attempted to remove Aboriginal people from their lands and move them to large, centrally located reserves. In Nova Scotia two designated areas were for Mi'kmaw people; those on Cape Breton Island were to be moved to Eskasoni and those on the mainland were to be moved to Indian Brook. During centralization, the school in the community was burned to insure the families did not return and resistant families were told that they had to move to Eskasoni or their children would be taken to residential school. Families were made promises by the federal government that there would be housing and employment in Eskasoni, but many arrived to unfinished houses and some families were forced to live in shacks or surplus army tents until houses were built. But more often the houses were built without insides completed, and families moved in for the shelter it provided when the tents gave way to winter. There were few jobs and there was no land to farm.

McMillan (2002) has shared the story of a Mi'kmaw elder who recounted the horrible conditions her family, originally from We'koqma'q, faced when they moved during centralization:

> Half of the house was not finished, not even the bottom. My dad said he could not move yet because the house is not finished, I don't have enough lumber. [Indian agent] MacKinnon told him to go to Malagawatch and tear the boards off the school. They

did not give us gyp rock [*sic*] or anything like that. The house is just a shell. [...] We got the water in this swamp area so it was smelly and that. My father said to get it from the brook. We went back and my sister was sick with the measles. We went back to Whycocomagh [We'koqma'q] in the middle of winter. (130)

Many of these families were coerced into moving through threats of harm and were made promises that were never fulfilled. These were the kinds of stories I had the opportunity to hear in the school and around the community during my time as a teacher in We'koqma'q.

I also learned that some families refused to go and an important story in We'koqma'q tells of the six families who stayed, and as a result, helped to save the community. They refused to give up their land or their homes, and they supported other families when they returned to We'koqma'q. Although the school had been burned down, these families were committed to preventing the church from the same fate. The story is told of the men who walked from We'koqma'q to Antigonish (about 100 km) to see the bishop, to tell him that they were still worshipping at the church in the community and did not want it to be destroyed. When the men from We'koqma'q arrived, the nun who served as the bishop's secretary turned them away because they did not have an appointment. Refusing to give up, they found a lawyer and asked if they required an appointment to see the bishop. They returned the next day with a letter from this lawyer and were admitted to see the bishop. The church was saved from demolition.

These same families fought with federal government administrators to have their school rebuilt so that their children could attend school in the community. In 1953, the local school re-opened. In 2003, a celebration was held as part of the secondary school's graduation ceremony to honour fifty years of continuous community-based education and many community members who were students in 1953 attended the celebration.

Although these stories may seem unconnected to teaching mathematics, they are told to remind the students (and staff) of We'koqma'q that they are connected to a long history of perseverance in the face of adversity. These are tales of survival and resistance that remind me, as a teacher, of the strength within this community. In many public schools, such stories would never be heard; Aboriginal students would never have the opportunity to connect with this type of community history. In We'koqma'q School, such connections were foundational.

Learning to Speak Mi'kmaw

In addition to learning about the history of the community, I was also committed to learning the Mi'kmaw language. As the grand-daughter of two Acadian women who married Anglophone men and raised their children speaking English, I knew first hand how quickly language can be lost. This experience made me ever more committed to learning Mi'kmaw and showing my students that I valued their language.

I decided that, since I was the math teacher, it would make sense to learn how to count in Mi'kmaw. I went to some of my Mi'kmaw speaking colleagues and told them that I wanted to learn to count in Mi'kmaw. "Great," they replied, "what are you counting?" "What am I counting? What do you mean what am I counting? I'm just counting: one, two, three...." "Yes, but what are you counting?" I was confused. They laughed and explained to me that in Mi'kmaw *what* one counts determines *how* one counts. Animate objects are counted differently than inanimate objects and the counting words must be conjugated to fit the context. Over the years, I have continued to learn more about counting and have developed a sense for how complex the counting system can be to learn, yet the mathematics curriculum in NS that treats it as the most simple and basic of mathematical concepts. This is clearly a taken-for-granted assumption that needs to be challenged. It is common in mathematics education to claim that context matters but when I think about the complexity of the counting-words, this expression takes on a new layer of meaning.

Over the years I have developed a fairly basic ability to speak Mi'kmaw. Learning to sing hymns for church and other songs helped me to develop an awareness of the sounds. Gradually I began to understand what some of the words meant and, as I became a little more fluent, my friends and colleagues enthusiastically taught me even more words. I also had the privilege of being part of a course in reading and writing for Mi'kmaw speakers that was run for school staff through Cape Breton University. I was the only non-Mi'kmaw person taking the course. This experience strengthened my knowledge of the Smith-Francis orthography and deepened my ability to read and write the language. As this course came to an end, I decided that I would use my new knowledge to write a speech for my graduating class that year. With the help of some colleagues I crafted the words, and during the graduation ceremony for the class of 2000, I delivered my address to my homeroom class entirely in Mi'kmaw!

I was grateful for the opportunity to learn Mi'kmaw and always felt that my willingness and dedication to learning the language was truly appreciated by the community members as well as my Mi'kmaw colleagues. It helped to strengthen a relationship of mutual respect. On occasion, elders used me as an example to parents and teachers, as they declared, "If we can teach Miss Lunney to speak Mi'kmaw we can teach our children!" I developed a deep passion for ensuring all children had the opportunity to speak Mi'kmaw and for me, as a teacher, learning the language was one of the most important professional learning experiences I could ever have had. It taught me more about teaching mathematics in a Mi'kmaw community than anything I had ever learned before or since. I will discuss this idea more fully later in this chapter.

As Good As if Not Better Than.

As a teacher, I committed myself to ensuring that what went on in my classroom was something significantly different than what was happening in most provincially run schools. Inspired by Aboriginal mentors during my university studies, I believed that Mi'kmaw-controlled education would be focused on addressing the needs of Mi'kmaw learners in a direct way through curriculum and pedagogy grounded in Mi'kmaw values, culture and traditions. I was quickly confronted with a reality that did not live up to this vision as I felt immediate and constant pressure to make my classroom the very model of the provincial system.

I was told by the director of education, a Caucasian man from outside of the community, that we needed to be "as good as, if not better than," the provincial schools using the same texts, the same curriculum documents, and the very same mathematics program. The school was not pursuing the vision of Mi'kmaw education I had hoped to find; instead, it was being run by non-Mi'kmaw administrators who believed that the goal should be to imitate the mainstream system. As hard as I tried, I could never understand why we were trying to replicate a system that had consistently failed our students, yet thinking that somehow this time it would work. I made a conscious decision at that time to resist the pressure to conform to provincially imposed regulations and, instead, to work toward culturally responsive teaching believing it would better address the needs of my students and would improve their mathematical achievement overall.

During my master's studies (Lunney 2001), I focused on the conflict between the imposition of mainstream educational values on Aboriginal schools and the expressed desire by Aboriginal communities to substantively embed their own values and culture in their educational system. I was inspired to conduct my own research attempting to determine what a truly Mi'kmaw definition of education would be. Through in-depth conversational interviews with two community members, I developed themes that helped to establish a framework for education that would guide further discussion and investigation. While the focus of this work was not particularly related to mathematics education, several key ideas emerged that strongly influenced my quest to transform my mathematics classroom.

Both participants in the master's study spoke openly about the importance of community culture, language and traditions being incorporated in a meaningful way in the curricular and pedagogical practices of the school, rather than just as add-ons to the Eurocentric system. One participant claimed: "In a Mi'kmaw school, you should have Mi'kmaq in every classroom not just the Mi'kmaw classroom. It shouldn't be a Mi'kmaw course at all. It should be all Mi'kmaq" (Lunney 2001: 116). He felt that this was not simply an issue of improved educational standards for Mi'kmaw students; he instead saw it as essential for cultural survival stating, "To save my culture; that is my concern" (112). His concern became my concern as well, and I strived daily to honour community culture and language in my classroom as a way to begin to address it.

Mi'kmaw Kina'matnewey

As I was finding my way as a new teacher, my school was also undergoing transitions. In 1993, control over education had been transferred from the federal government to the community and with it came many changes. Many of the teachers who had worked there as federal employees chose to leave and go with other federal departments as the new funding arrangements ensured that teacher salaries would be considerably lower than the federal salaries had been. Many of the teachers in the school were young and new to teaching, just like me. I sometimes think this made us more free and creative since we had no old ways to revert back to, but sometimes it also felt scary as we had few mentors who could guide us along. When I arrived in 1995, the community had begun a process of phasing in high school. Our first group of graduates crossed the stage in June of 1997 and the trend of graduates continues to this day with each class getting a little larger.

At this same time, Mi'kmaw communities in Nova Scotia were working collaboratively to negotiate an educational agreement with the federal government. In 1998, nine communities signed on to a unique jurisdictional agreement with the Government of Canada, referred to as the Mi'kmaw Kina'matnewey (MK) agreement, which gives them control over their education system and collective bargaining power. These MK communities have a stated goal of decolonizing education by incorporating indigenous knowledge, culture and values into their curricular and pedagogical practices. At the same time, these communities are also bound by the agreement to offer provincially transferrable curriculum and to demonstrate measures of success based on provincially developed assessments. However, with the arrival of this agreement came a new attitude and enthusiasm about Mi'kmaw education (Orr and Cameron 2004). The collective of nine (now twelve) communities began working more closely together to ensure greater cultural relevance in educational practices. Between 1998 and 2014, through a partnership with St. FX, 120 Mi'kmaw teachers have been trained, most of whom are now teaching in MK schools. Mi'kmaw teachers have been promoted to administrative positions and many of the MK schools have Mi'kmaw principals. Furthermore, in 2013, MK community schools boasted a graduation rate of 88.8 per cent. These schools are experiencing successes both academically and culturally with respect to the development of strong cultural identities of students.

In the early 2000s, I began representing all MK schools on the Nova Scotia Department of Education's provincial math leaders committee. Although I was still a full-time classroom teacher, in this volunteer role I was also sharing information about curriculum and resources with all MK schools. I was also speaking on behalf of MK schools, bringing MK perspectives to the provincial table and striving to encourage consideration of Mi'kmaw perspectives in mathematics education. I often held afterschool PD sessions via video conferencing for teachers in other MK schools and supported the professional learning of all teachers of mathematics within the MK system. The conversations I had with my colleagues across the MK system and the questions we often raised occupied my thoughts regularly. I wanted to make sure that all Mi'kmaw children would learn mathematics in a way that prepared them for higher education while also affirming their identity as Mi'kmaw people.

In July of 2003, while attending a community event at the ball field, I was made the vice-principal and acting principal of the secondary school, with the goal of finding a Mi'kmaw person who would take on the principal's job. This did not happen until the following year when I encouraged one of the elementary teachers who was from the community to become principal. I stayed on to work with him as his VP for one more year. And in 2005, ten years after I had arrived, I took a leave of absence and went back to do my PhD.

The Doctoral Journey

Despite my new identity as researcher, I still saw myself very much as the curious teacher who was (and still is) interested in improving mathematics education for Mi'kmaw students. My questions emerged not only from my own wonderings throughout my career, but also from those ideas and curiosities raised by others in MK schools I interacted with. Initial plans for conducting my doctoral work involved developing culturally responsive mathematics lessons, implementing them in schools and determining their effect. It did not take me long to realize that I needed to do much deeper learning if I were to truly transform mathematics learning for my students.

Becoming a Researcher

The idea of becoming a researcher also brought with it significant tensions for me. As someone who was interested in decolonizing education, who strived daily to work toward transformation of the education system, I had significant concerns about how I would do this work in a way that continued to honour the relationships I had built within the community. For many Aboriginal people, as Smith (1999) states, research has been intimately connected with colonization and imperialism:

> From the vantage point of the colonized ... the term "research"
> is inextricably linked to European imperialism and colonialism.
> The word itself, "research," is probably one of the dirtiest words

in the indigenous world's vocabulary. When mentioned in many indigenous contexts, it stirs up silence, it conjures up bad memories, it raises a smile that is knowing and distrustful. (1)

One friend and colleague, himself a member of the Mi'kmaw nation echoed the feelings cited by Smith. He often asked me during this process how my "research" was going, regularly using his fingers to indicate the quotation marks around the word, speaking in a tone that dripped with cynicism and distrust. He was not distrustful of me; in fact, he was one of my most supportive allies in this work. Rather, he was distrustful of the institution that calls this work "research." He told me that he did not intend to belittle my work but wanted simply to remind me that he does not want to be studied. He was willing to talk *with* me and share ideas, to work together to find solutions to problems but he was very distrustful of the kinds of research that he has seen being done *to* and *on* his community and his people. His words pointed to the damaging effects of research that has been conducted in many indigenous communities.

I knew that there would be institutional pressure to choose an accepted research paradigm that would make my work acceptable within the academy, something Wilson (2003) had argued is a common pressure for many indigenous scholars. Yet, I knew that this was not the kind of work I wanted to do and I knew that pasting indigenous perspectives onto Eurocentric paradigms would not be effective in the decolonization of these paradigms and would not give voice to the indigenous community I was working with (Bishop 2005; Denzin 2005; Smith 1999). Rather, I sought to use a research paradigm that would be rooted in the Mi'kmaw community.

To find a methodology that would work for my doctoral studies, I sought the advice of the elders and Mi'kmaw speakers in my community. I began asking for a word that could be used to describe the process of people coming together to solve a problem or discuss an issue. While many words were suggested, one word that kept coming up over and over again was *mawita'mk* meaning, "coming together to learn together." The word implies that everyone involved in the conversation has something to contribute and everyone has something to learn. What was interesting is that each time I was given this word, the giver would inevitably respond with "but you should ask..." and tell me some names of people who could confirm the word (Lunney

Borden and Wagner 2013). This approach of coming together to learn together shaped my doctoral work, and continues to shape my engagement with communities.

My Role in the Work.

As a non-indigenous person working with an indigenous research methodology (Rigney 1999), I knew there were many ethical considerations that needed to be taken into account. I had grappled with my place in this research as a non-Mi'kmaw person. I had openly questioned my authority to care, my authorization to represent people and ideas, and my responsibility to remain connected to the community after the research. It was understandable to me that there were people within the academy who would question my position in this research because they saw me as an outsider in this context. Yet, within the Mi'kmaw community, my identity was much more complex.

Lipka et al. (1998) refer to "fictive kin" to describe the kin-like relationships that often develop between long-term outsiders and insiders. This term struck a cord with me as it connected deeply to my own experience. I consider many of the people within the community where I worked to be like family; in many ways, this extended beyond that community to the larger Mi'kmaw community. I feel that it is only because of these relationships that I was able to do this work. As Lipka et al. said of their own work with Yup'ik communities in Alaska: "It was the importance of being 'related' that allowed a research agenda to evolve" (209). My research evolved from my experience within the community; yet, many people within the academy might only point out my whiteness.

These concerns about my role in this work bothered me greatly and prompted a conversation with two Mi'kmaw colleagues prior to beginning the doctoral research. Their responses were reassuring. One colleague spoke about the time I had spent in the community, the way I had learned the language and the culture, and assured me that he knew that I had come to work *with* the community. This long-standing relationship is significant. The other colleague jokingly asked me if I wanted to quit now. His teasing was a way of reminding me of our many long conversations about the research I might do some day that would allow us to explore some of these educational issues and questions on a deeper level. They both gave me the sense that not only did I have the privilege to do this work, I had an obligation. They had shared with me the language, the culture, the ways of knowing and being; they gave to me and now I was in a position to give back in a way that honoured the community. This is healthy reciprocity. This gave me the confidence to proceed with the work.

Three and a Thumb

Doctoral studies gave me space to reflect on my own stories of teaching and also gave me the opportunity to re-engage with the many elders who had supported me as a teacher with whom I would revisit old conversations in new ways. My doctoral advisor at the University of New Brunswick was Dr. David Wagner. Dave was new to the region but very interested in looking at the mathematics that people used in their daily lives. As part of a large-scale grant known as CRYSTAL Atlantic, Dave had funds to do ethnomathematical research in communities, and I had communities that I wanted to work with, so this serendipity has always made me think that this work was truly meant to be. Dave and I began having conversations with Elders.

One such conversation took place with Mi'kmaw Elders in the fall of 2005 during my first year of doctoral studies (see Wagner and Lunney Borden 2015 for more detail on this conversation). One participant in this discussion was the late Dianne Toney, a well known quill box maker. Dianne recounted how she used mathematics in making quill boxes although she often referred to her knowledge as common sense and not necessarily math. One story she told was about how to make a ring for the circular top of the quill box, she would take a strip of wood and measure three times across the width of the circle and add a thumb width and it would make a perfect circle every time. As I excitedly declared this to be pi, she reminded me it was knowledge passed down to her by an Elder, knowledge she saw as common sense.

Inspired by this conversation, Dave and I began discussing how enriching this conversation had been, but also how important it would be have Mi'kmaw students have these conversations directly with Elders. We were uncomfortable with how we were learning from Elders to then pass on to teachers and their students and felt it would be much richer for students to have the first hand conversations themselves (see Wagner and Lunney Borden 2012 for more detail). This inspired an idea for an event called Show Me Your Math that would invite Mi'kmaw students to have conversations with elders in their communities about the mathematics they use in their daily lives and share their findings with their teachers and peers (see showmeyour-math.ca).

Initially we suggested that this be a contest hosted by Atlantic Canada First Nation Help Desk (firstnationhelp.com) who had a practice of regular monthly contests for Aboriginal students in the Atlantic region. We arranged to meet with teachers representing each of the MK schools to discuss this idea. While the teachers enthusiastically embraced the intent of the contest, they wanted to do more. It was suggested that we have a math fair to showcase the students' work. Thus was born the regional Show Me Your Math fair (Lunney Borden et al. forthcoming).

Musings about Language

Part of the conversation at that first Show Me Your Math meeting focused on language and, in particular words that can be used to describe mathematical objects and concepts. In what became a somewhat spirited debate, many of the Mi'kmaw-speaking teachers in the room began to discuss what they believed to be the proper word for "circle." There were a few words offered for consideration. A commonly used word for circle in Mi'kmaw immersion classes is *empisqa'wik* or *memqisqa'wik*[4], although another participant at the workshop suggested that he used *empisqa'wik*.

for circle. In consulting other speakers, they have agreed that this latter term could also be used to describe a circle. The discussion of circles on that day led teachers to agree that Mi'kmaw mathematical language would be a wonderful topic for students to explore as part of our Show Me Your Math event.

As I reflected on this and many other discussions about Mi'kmaw words, I was reminded of the importance of examining Mi'kmaw words to understand mathematical reasoning; I was also reminded how complex this might be given the variety that is built into this language. It has been said that speaking an Aboriginal language is like quoting the Elders who walked the land thousands of years ago and who used the language to describe and remember what they saw (Basso 1996). I cannot help but wonder if there are so many different words to describe a circle because there are so many different contexts for talking about a circle in Mi'kmaw. In a later section I will share more detail about the significant role of language in the creation of a framework.

Inspired by the conversations I was having with Elders, the success of Show Me Your Math, and the reflection on my own practice and wonderings and those of my colleagues, I set about to conduct my doctoral research. The primary question in my work was "How can curricula and pedagogy be transformed to support Mi'kmaw students as they negotiate their space between Aboriginal concepts of mathematics and school-based concepts of mathematics?"

Developing a Framework

I spent one full school year working with teachers in two MK elementary schools. At least once each month I would visit each school, volunteering in classrooms during the day and inviting teachers, staff members and elders into conversation after school. Our conversations were focused on supporting students in mathematics education and my questions were often simple asking things like "What do you notice?" or "what are the challenges you see?" Over time, many of the participants would come with their own ideas of things they would like to talk about or their own questions about something they had noticed. After each session I would transcribe our discussion and return with a brief summary of what we had talked about in the previous sessions. By May of that year, themes had emerged and were used to create a model that could serve as a framework for transforming mathematics education for Mi'kmaw students (see figure 10.1).

At the core of this model is the idea that students need to have meaningful personal connections to mathematics. The themes supporting this focus on the need to learn from the Mi'kmaw language, the need to attend to value differences and ways of knowing, and the need to integrate culture into mathematics. In the following sections I will share the details of this model and some of the stories related to each theme.

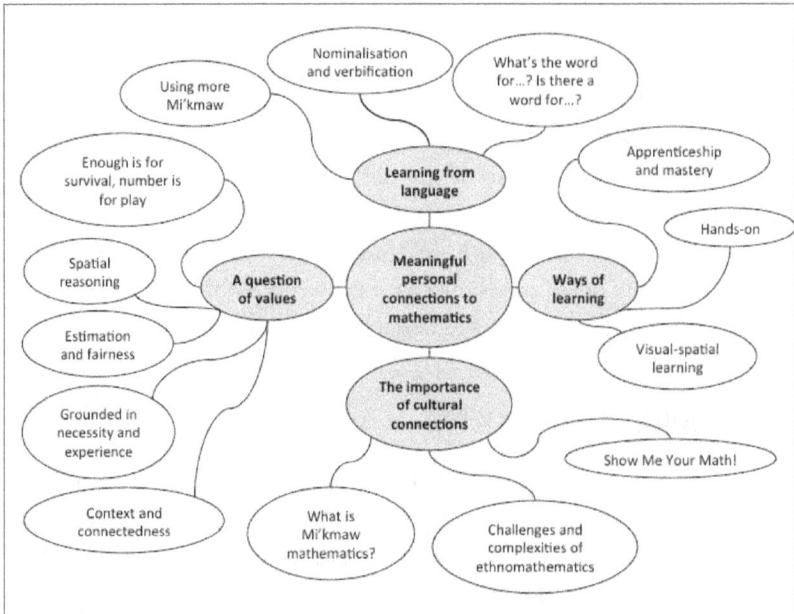

Figure 10.1: Transforming Mathematics for Mi'kmaw Students (Lunney Borden 2010)

Learning from Language

As Emily, a Mi'kmaw school principal, stated during my doctoral work, things can get lost in translation even when both people are speaking English. She talked about the difference between *l'nuita'si* (Mi'kmaw ways of thinking) and *aklasie'witasi* (Anglophone ways of thinking) and suggested that conflicts often arise in the classroom when there is a lack of consistency between these two ways of knowing. Central to her comment is the idea that speaking English is not thinking English. Many children who are speaking English in school are still using their *l'nuita'si*.

When we spoke of language, three significant ideas emerged that could be described as the need to speak more Mi'kmaw, the insights that can be gained by understanding how mathematical words are expressed (or not) in Mi'kmaq, and how we need to consider the implications of a verb-based language on teaching mathematics. Barton has argued that:

A proper understanding of the link between language and mathematics may be the key to finally throwing off the shadow of imperialism and colonialisation that continues to haunt education for indigenous groups in a modern world of international languages and global curricula. (Barton 2008: 9)

In the following sections I will share how our discussions about language pointed out many complexities that could potentially arise for our Mi'kmaw students and gave insight into how these challenges could be mitigated.

Using More Mi'kmaq

Participants in the study argued that it would be helpful to use more Mi'kmaw language when teaching mathematics in Mi'kmaw schools. Many participants shared stories of how they could "say one word in Mi'kmaw" and translate an entire concept for a student. They also talked about the sense of comfort that comes when Mi'kmaw is spoken in schools. Many participants recounted stories of having conversations with children; sometimes the children would simply not open up about what was bothering them when they were being spoken to in English but as soon as an adult would ask "*tala'teken?*" (What's wrong?), the child would instantly open up and begin sharing their story. Emily had shared her own observations that students respond so much more positively when they hear a teacher speaking in Mi'kmaw:

> Emily: Sometimes you tell a child "Ok, lukwaten, apa ke' apa" (work again, please again)—they'll do something for you again but if I say it in English "Okay let's read it again"—un uh [Shakes her head no] but "ke' apa, ke' lukwatamuj" they're more ahhh [letting out a sigh of relief indicating a level of comfort or ease].

The point was also made that even students who are seen as non-speakers likely still know many simple command words in Mi'kmaw and that using Mi'kmaw for managing the class can create a much more welcoming environment. In my own experience as a teacher I found this to be true. I learned words for "come in" (*piskwa'*), "sit" (*pa'si*), "thank you" (*wela'lin*), and "that's enough" (*tepiaq*) that helped me to keep students engaged. These simple communication words helped to build relationships with my students and showed them I had respect for the language.

Learning simple command words is far from being able to teach mathematics in Mi'kmaw however. Immersion programs in MK schools have worked on developing Mi'kmaw mathematics vocabulary, but many MK teachers do not have the language ability to teach math in Mi'kmaw. Yet, that does not mean that they cannot learn from Mi'kmaw language structures.

What's the word for...? Is there a word for...?

As a teacher, I was often asking for translations for mathematical concepts. I found that learning Mi'kmaw words for mathematical concepts also gave me insight into Mi'kmaw ways of thinking about those ideas. Richard, a participant in the study, often argued that students would do better in mathematics if they had a strong language baseand were able to discuss concepts in Mi'kmaw. As part of a discussion about fractions one day, he explained "*pukwe*' is part of something but when you say *aqatayik* that is half of it ... now if a child understood Mi'kmaw very well, it'd be a lot easier for them to understand."

By asking questions about language, I began to develop an appreciation for the contextualized nature of number and shape words within the language. In Mi'kmaw the shape of the object is embedded in the name of the object, for example, *kini'skwikuom* means "a dwelling that comes to a point" such as an A-frame house or a *wikuom* (wigwam). Objects are also described relationally, for example the word for window, *tuo'piti*, describes looking out from the inside. If one was on the outside looking in, the word would change. This contextualization of language is not indicative of a lack of abstract reasoning, but rather demonstrates a difference in world view and what is valued within the culture. "The Mi'kmaw language grammatically encodes details concerning how speakers experience the world and how a speaker and the person spoken to connect with and evidence this experience" (Inglis 2004: 400). Studying ways of speaking about concepts gives insight into ways of thinking about concepts.

Even more powerful than learning about the Mi'kmaw words for mathematical concepts, was realizing sometimes no word exists. If a mathematical concept does not have a direct Mi'kmaw translation, then the English word for that concept may not be part of the everyday language. Barton (2008) has argued:

Different concepts are expressed in different languages, and some concepts are extremely difficult, some say impossible to translate between languages. The implication is that different quantitative, relational, and spatial concepts may also not be easily transformed into each other. (69)

This can mean that a concept that is taken as shared in mainstream mathematics can in fact be quite complex for the child who is unfamiliar with the concept.

The word "flat" is one example of a word that has no Mi'kmaw translation. I have asked on numerous occasions if there is a word for flat in Mi'kmaq and I have attempted to generate scenarios whereby we would need to use the word flat. I asked about a flat tire but I was told by a Mi'kmaw colleague that he would say it was losing air. I asked about the bottom of a basket, suggesting it was flat, but I was told that it just able to sit still. I asked about calm water but was told that this was the negative of rough water, so it had to be able to be rough in order to be calm. I asked about the top of a table but was told that the word for table means you can sit things on it. Having told this story many times to many Mi'kmaw speaking friends and colleagues, the closest word I have been given is one that means "like a plank." We use the word flat often in math class.

An interesting connection to this notion occurred for me during a grade 3 lesson on prisms and pyramids. As we sat on the carpet with students and asked them to say one thing about the prism that was being passed around, one young girl placed the prism on the floor and stated "It can sit still!" Instantly I began to get excited by her answer. It made perfect sense that she would not talk about the flatness of the face but rather its usefulness. This connects directly to the relational way in which Mi'kmaw is used and constructed and reminded me of the conversation about the bottom of the basket. When I later recounted this story during an ad hoc session at the Canadian Mathematics Education Study Group Conference in Sherbrooke, Québec (May 2008), a friend and geometer, Walter Whitely (personal communication) mentioned to me that the word polyhedron actually is derived from the Greek word *hedron* which means "seat," and polyhedron means many seats or many ways to sit.

Many more words were shared that showed how sometimes taken-for-granted words in math class may not be as clear to all children in that class (cf. Lunney Borden 2012). These conversations demonstrated how the contextualized nature of the Mi'kmaw language presents layers of complexity for concepts in the school-based mathematics curriculum. Understanding the structure of the Mi'kmaw language and these ensuing layers of complexity can help teachers to rethink the ways in which they may teach some of these concepts.

Verbification vs. Nominalization

Mi'kmaw is a verb-based language, like all Aboriginal languages in Canada. Alternatively, mathematics as taught in most schools has a tendency toward noun phrases and turns even processes such as multiplication, addition and square root into "things" (Schleppegrell 2007). This process is known as nominalization. The dominance of English in school-based mathematics results in this objectifying tendency. "We talk of mathematical objects because that is what the English language makes available for talking, but it is just a way of talking" (Barton 2008: 127). We could talk differently.

As a teacher, my students would occasionally tell me I was "talking crazy talk" and as I reflected back on those moments, this often meant I was using too many nouns. Math is filled with nouns. When I listened to my students and heard how they were discussing concepts or talking about ideas, they were using more verbs than nouns. They were talking about what concepts were doing. When I shifted my ways of talking about concepts to emphasize actions more than things, processes more than products, more students were able to understand. When I used more verbs, math was easier to learn. I call this process "verbification" to represent the opposite of nominalization. I argue that we need to verbify our mathematics more, ensuring that we emphasize process and action more than definitions and things. (See Lunney Borden 2011 for a more detailed discussion of verification).

Consider the concept of slope commonly taught in Canadian classrooms from seventh or eighth grade on. A common approach is to explain to students that slope is determined by the ratio of the change in the y value (or the rise) to the change in the x value (or the run). This explanation contains a lot of nouns. In my early years I taught students about slope in this way. Some students understood, some struggled. We worked at it. One year I didn't do that. I simply asked students to tell me about the graph and we began to talk about how it was changing. Students talked about how the graph was created by going over and going up, for example they would say things like "you go over 2 and up 3." For the y-intercept students talked about this as being the point where you start. Going over and up or down became how my students spoke about slope. We looked for the numerical values in equation, the table and the graph and students soon became very comfortable with the entire concept. It was only then that I gave them the name: "You know mathematicians name everything. They name that, slope." This proved to be much more effective.

As I share ideas about using more verbs with mathematicians I meet at conferences, I often hear from them that they work in verbs. Exploring change, investigating processes and using lots of verbs are some of the things mathematicians do. As Byers (2007) has argued, mathematics is a creative endeavour that is far more about the *doing* than the objects of mathematics. He referred to mathematics as "a way of knowing" (14). Why then do we teach mathematics as a series of things to learn?

I continue to explore what mathematics teaching might look like if we emphasize verbs more than nouns. In my own teaching I strive to focus on action, process, change, and so on and it seems to have a very positive effect. I believe there is more to be learned about the role of verbification in the teaching of mathematics but I believe allowing students to explore, investigate and discuss the actions they are taking and the changes they are observing is a way to begin to open up space for verbification.

A Question of Values

Mathematics is frequently touted in popular culture as the universal language, a characterization that fails to acknowledge mathematics is, in fact, culturally rooted. To expose this misconception, ethnomathematicians and researchers interested in culturally based mathematics have subjected the field to critical examination that has brought to light some of its embedded cultural biases (cf. Barton 2008; D'Ambrosio 2006) arguing that mathematics could have evolved differently if different cultural ways of knowing had been valued. In exploring strategies to support Mi'kmaw students in mathematics, our research conversations often turned to conflicting values that were apparent between school-based approaches to mathematics and Mi'kmaw ways of reasoning about mathematical questions.

Tepiaq is About Survival

When I first began talking with Elders about mathematics, I would often ask questions to try to understand how number concepts were used within the culture. I would ask questions that involved "How many?" or "How much?" in an attempt to get a numerical answer, but they rarely responded with a number. The answer was almost always "*tepiaq*" (enough) and typically included a spatial gesture to demonstrate the size of enough. I later asked an Elder about this and she told me that a number does not give enough information because there can be so many variables; a spatial description is much more consistent. Space, and not number, becomes foundational for mathematical reasoning because space and shape take into account the variables that connect to the notion of enough.

The meaning of *tepiaq* (enough) points to more than a mere connection to a spatial sense of quantity; it also points to a significant value difference that exists between school-based mathematics and Mi'kmaw community cultural values. The idea of enough continues to define a way of life for many Mi'kmaq, a way of life that has strong ties to their historical roots. As participant Richard explained "The native way of life is you have just enough and to share." Ma'li, an elder, built upon his comment and connected this with a need for survival explaining that enough really means "enough for survival, and that's *l'nu* (our people)." Reflecting on the idea of *tepiaq* generates several questions about the implications for teaching mathematics. We can ask powerful questions such as how might our school-based mathematics be leading students away from valuing enough as a way of living? What is the cost of participation when mathematics comes into conflict with a student's world view? Or more practically, how do we teach mathematics in such a way as to emphasize more spatial reasoning? And how can we incorporate playing with number as a more culturally consistent approach to learning these concepts?

Spatial Reasoning in Mathematics

Mathematics as taught in schools tends to privilege quantitative and numerical reasoning more so than spatial reasoning. The curriculum used in MK schools, and in the majority of schools right across the country, places a high emphasis on number and operation concepts with less value on concepts that are inherently spatial such as geometry. If space is about survival in the Mi'kmaw community, it seems as though number is about survival in school. This can create a challenge for students who tend toward more spatial reasoning approaches to learning mathematics. But number concepts can be learned through spatial approaches such as the use of concrete models and number lines, yet these approaches are not always valued in schools. In the section below on ways of learning, I share some examples of spatial approaches to teaching number concepts.

Counting is for Play

While spatial reasoning seems to be at the heart of Mi'kmaw ways of thinking with respect to concepts that could be seen as mathematical, this does not mean that there is no attention to number concepts. In fact, as I have explained earlier, number is quite complex in Mi'kmaq. Number words need to fit the context of the objects being counted. Counting animate objects is different than counting inanimate objects. Furthermore, number is often embedded as part of a word that describes the entire context. Recently, I was searching the online Mi'kmaw dictionary created by people in Listiguj, QC (mikmaqonline.org/), looking for the correct spelling for three animate objects. I was amazed to see twenty-eight different words to describe the use of three in various contexts. Several words also had shape such as globe-like, cylinder-like and string-like embedded in the word for both animate and inanimate objects. Number in Mi'kmaw is complex but it is not essential for survival. Rather, as Richard and Ma'li explained, it is used for play.

Consider the game of *waltes*, a traditional dice-and-stick game. This game has sophisticated counting techniques and the counting process changes as you go from one round to the next. Although it is not uncommon to see children playing this game, often when the game is being played an Elder or another adult will do the counting. Yet school-based mathematics expects children to learn number early and be proficient with it before moving on to other concepts. In fact, many children who do not develop proficiency with counting in the early years of elementary school are often assessed for learning disabilities and seen as vulnerable with respect to further success in school. What might happen if we shifted how we think about learning number in school and instead allowed children to learn number through play with an adult alongside to help students connect these counting words to their playful learning?

Grounded in Necessity

In addition to problematizing the role of number and space in the curriculum, we also discussed the need for learning to emerge in context and for it to be grounded in necessity. D'Ambrosio (2006) has argued that mathematics emerges "in response to the needs for survival and transcendence in different natural, social, and cultural environments" (42) and Elders I spoke with during my doctoral work, shared this view. Reasoning happens in response to a need for that reasoning. For example, Dianne Toney shared the knowledge she had about circles that she learned by making quill boxes. Thus, by providing rich learning contexts for students so that their knowledge can be grounded in something meaningful might provide a way to make learning more engaging for students.

Ways of Learning

Understanding the grammatical structures of Mi'kmaw and being aware of the value differences that may emerge in exploring mathematics, helped us to think about ways of learning that would support our Mi'kmaw students in a way that would be more consistent with Mi'kmaw ways of knowing. Participants recommended that traditional mastery style approaches and hands-on learning should be important parts of the learning process in schools. But perhaps the most interesting conversation involved a focus on the importance of drawing upon visual-spatial approaches to learning.

Visual-Spatial Approaches

While it is important to remember that "Indigenous teachings provide that every child, whether Aboriginal or not, is unique in his or her learning capacities, learning styles, and knowledge bases" (Battiste 2002: 15), we often found ourselves discussing what the value of spatial reasoning within the Mi'kmaw world view means for teaching. One resource teacher, Donna, shared her concerns with us about the lack of visual-spatial approaches to teaching mathematics in many classrooms:

Spatial and visual learning styles don't fit into the curriculum and that is the problem; that is the whole problem. You can be gifted spatially and visually and it doesn't fit into the way that we present information. Why is that? Why is it not valued as much as the oral or the symbolic? (Lunney Borden 2010: 193)

She truly believed that if students were taught mathematics through a more visual-spatial approach, they would be far more successful in school. Yet, the pedagogy in many mathematics classrooms does not often reflect this approach.

Silverman (2005) has stated that visual-spatial learners tend to think in pictures, relate well to space and understand best through seeing relationships among other things. Students who prefer this approach like to see the big picture thinking whole-to-part rather than part-to-whole. Principal Emily agreed that many of her students need to see the whole picture before they can move on with learning a concept. In mathematics classes, the opposite is often the norm.

Spatial Approaches to Number Concepts

Over the years I have strived to create tasks that draw upon spatial approaches to learning mathematics and I regularly try to emphasize these approaches when working with teachers. I am particularly interested in emphasizing these approaches when working with number concepts. I believe using representations such as area models, ten frames, number lines and so on, can give students a visual-spatial model to support numeracy development. For example, with number lines we can talk about number neighbours and get a sense of the relationship among numbers. Also, when students see seven counters on a ten frame, they learn not only the relationship between seven and ten, i.e. that seven is three less than ten or you need three more to make ten, but they also see that seven is made up of five and two which can help them to understand

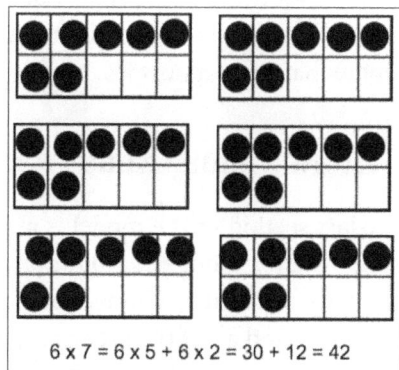

$$6 \times 7 = 6 \times 5 + 6 \times 2 = 30 + 12 = 42$$

Fig. 10.2 – Using a ten-frame to multiply

that when multiplying sets of seven, they can break this into sets of five and sets of two. See figure 10.2 above.

We might also consider how we can make use of area models for teaching operations. We could give students a number of squares and ask the students to arrange these into rectangles and try to find all the rectangles that can be made with these squares leaving no gaps or spaces. This approach can help students make connections between the dimensions of a rectangle and the factors of that number. In effect we are asking students to explore multiplication and division through a concrete and spatial approach. Figure 10.3 below shows that twelve squares can be broken into three rows of four or two rows of six as just two possibilities. Students can use these models to show 3 x 4 = 12 or 12 ÷ 3 = 4 and that 2 x 6 = 12 or 12 ÷ 2 = 6. This enables students to see the relationships between multiplication and division.

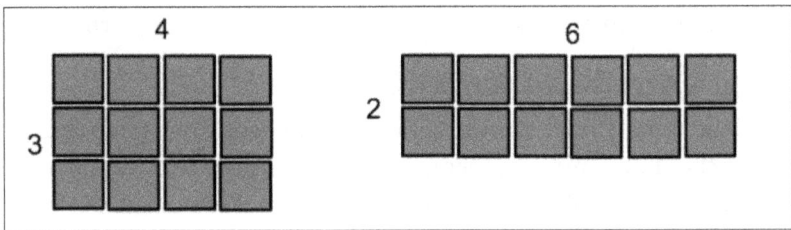

Figure 10.3 – Area Models for Multiplication and Division

Area models can also be used to multiply two-digit numbers, decimals, fractions and algebraic terms. Thus, such an approach not only draws upon a visual-spatial way of learning, it also provides a model that will be applicable in higher grades so that students have a model that can support learning in higher grades.

Cultural Connections

The last section of the model is cultural connections, and this is initially where I thought I would begin, however, I now believe that in order to do cultural connections to mathematics well, it is essential to understand all of the other pieces. Doolittle (2006) has argued that we should examine how school-based mathematics can be pulled into Aboriginal cultures through identifying types of reasoning inherent in the community that can help students to make sense of the school-based mathematics. It also means creating learning experiences that help students see that mathematical reasoning is a part of their everyday lives, and has been for generations. Show Me Your Math has proven to be effective in doing just that, but more so, it has resulted in a new desire in MK schools to do culturally-based inquiry where students begin with a topic to explore and allow the mathematics to emerge because it is needed.

In the past two years, inquiry projects have become increasingly popular for SMYM projects with schools exploring the mathematics needed to make a canoe paddle, to do quill work, to create bead designs, to make maple syrup and even the mathematics involved in birch bark biting, to name just a few. Such projects not only help students to learn mathematics by beginning in a cultural place, but also proves to be affirming of identity by helping students to see the mathematical reasoning inherent in indigenous knowledges.

Concluding Thoughts

Over the past twenty years, I have been deeply embedded in a learning journey with the goal of better supporting Mi'kmaw students in understanding mathematics. There have been many transformative moments along the way and I am grateful to those who have journeyed with me. I feel honoured to have been able to learn together with friends, colleagues, elders and youth. There is still more journeying to be done and more work is needed to transform mathematics education for Mi'kmaw learners. I have shared some stories of my learning journey and some of the important insights I have acquired along the journey. While I do not suggest that the things we have learned together here in Mi'kma'ki can be directly transplanted into other regions, I do believe others could use the model to think about the kinds of conversations that are needed in their own contexts. I am hopeful that such conversations will bring about new insights and create new possibilities.

Notes

1. Throughout this article, Mi'kmaq is used as a noun and can be either singular or plural. Mi'kmaw is used as an adjective and when referingto the languageof Mi'kmaw. While the rules for creating adjectival forms of

words in Mi'kmaq is considerably more complex, it has been agreed to by a working group on Mi'kmaw language learning that, when writing in English, these conventions will be used. For Mi'kmaw words, the Smith-Francis orthography is used.

2. Language and terminology are important. I have attempted to consider the most appropriate words to use, understanding words will mean different things depending on the place and time in which they are used. Several terms are commonly used to represent indigenous peoples. Aboriginal, indigenous and First Nations are all terms that appear in the research. In Canada, Aboriginal is a term used by the federal government to describe First Nations, Metis and Inuit peoples. In this paper I have attempted to use a term that suits the context and intent of the sentence.

3. Wolastoqiyik people are often referred to as Maliseet, however Wolastoqiyik is a more appropriate term meaning "people of the river" referring to the Wolastoq River (Saint John River), meaning beautiful river.

4. Word lists from Eskasoni immersion teachers obtained from Helen Sylliboy.

References

Aboriginal Affairs and Northern Development Canada. 2010. *Treaty of Peace and Friendship 1760*. https://www.aadnc-aandc.gc.ca/eng/1100100028599/1100100028600 .

Absolon, K. E. M. and C. Willett. (2005). Putting Ourselves Forward: Location in Aboriginal Research. In ed., L. Brown and S. Strega, *Research as Resistance: Critical, Indigenous and Anti-oppressive Approaches*, 97-126). Toronto, ON: Canadian Scholars' Press.

Barton, B. 2008. *The Language of Mathematics: Telling Mathematical Tales*. New York, NY: Springer.

Basso, K. 1996. *Wisdom Sits in Places: Landscape and Language Among the Western Apache*. Albuquerque, NM: University of New Mexico Press.

Battiste, M. 2013. *You Can't Be the Doctor if You're the Disease: Eurocentrism and Indigenous Renaissance*. CAUT Distinguished Academic Lecture April 26, 2013. http://www.caut.ca/docs/default-source/default-document-library/you-can%27t-be-the-doctor-if-you%27re-the-disease-eurocentrism-and-indigenous-renaissance.pdf?sfvrsn=0 .

Battiste, M. 2002. Indigenous Knowledge and Pedagogy in First Nations Education: A Literature Review with Recommendations. Prepared for the National Working Group on Education and the Minister of Indian Affairs Indian and Northern Affairs Canada (INAC): Ottawa, Ontario, Canada: National Working Group on Education and the Minister of Indian Affairs

Indian and Northern Affairs Canada (INAC). Retrieved from http://www. usask.ca/education/people/battistem/ikp_e.pdf.

Bishop, R. 2005. *Freeing Ourselves from Neocolonial Domination: A Kua-papa Māori Approach to Creating Knowledge.* In ed. N. Denzin and Y. Lincoln, *The Sage Handbook of Qualitative Research,* 3rd ed., 109-38). Thousand Oaks, CA: Sage.

Byers, W. 2007. *How Mathematicians Think: Using Ambiguity, Contradiction, and Paradox to Create Mathematics.* Princeton, NJ: Princeton University Press.

D'Ambrosio, U. 2006. *Ethnomathematics: Link Between Traditions and Modernity.* Rotterdam, The Netherlands: Sense.

Denzin, N. 2005. Emancipatory Discourses and the Ethics and Politics of Interpretation. In ed., N. Denzin and Y. Lincoln, *The Sage Handbook of Qualitative Research,* 3rd ed., 933-58). Thousand Oaks: Sage.

Doolittle, E. 2006. Mathematics as Medicine. In P. Liljedahl, ed., Proceedings of the 2006 Annual Meeting of the Canadian Mathematics Education Study Group Conference, 17-25. Burnaby, BC: CMESG.

Inglis, Stephanie. 2004. 400 Years of Linguistic Contact Between the Mi'kmaq and the English and the Interchange of Two World Views. *The Canadian Journal of Native Studies* 24 (2): 389-402.

Lipka, J., G. Mohatt and The Ciulistet Group. 1998. *Transforming the Culture of Schools: Yup'ik Eskimo Examples.* Mahwah, NJ: Lawerence Erlbaum Associates.

Lunney, L. 2001. Journeying Toward a Mi'kmaq Definition of Education: Two Voices From One Community. MEd. Thesis. St. Francis Xavier University, Antigonish, NS.

Lunney Borden, L. 2012. What's the Word for...? Is There a Word for...? How Understanding Mi'kmaw language Can Help Support Mi'kmaw Learners in Mathematics. *Mathematics Education Research Journal.* DOI: 10.1007/s13394-012-0042-7.

Lunney Borden, L. 2011. The "Verbification" of Mathematics: Using the Grammatical Structures of Mi'kmaq to Support Student Learning. *For the Learning of Mathematics* 31 (3): 8-13.

Lunney Borden, L. 2010. *Transforming Mathematics Education for Mi'kmaw Students Through Mawikinutimatimk.* PhD dissertation. University of New Brunswick: Fredericton, NB.

Lunney Borden, L. and D. Wagner. 2013. Naming Method: "This is it, maybe, but you should talk to..." In R. Jorgensen, P. Sullivan and P. Grootenboer, eds., *Pedagogies to Enhance Learning for Indigenous Students,* 105-22. New York: Springer.

Lunney Borden, L., D. Wagner and N. Johnson, N. Forthcoming. Show Me Your Math: Mi'kmaw Community Members Explore Mathematics. In C. Nicol, S. Dawson, J. Archibald and F. Glandfield, ed. *Living Culturally Responsive Mathematics Curriculum and Pedagogy: Making a Difference with/in Indigenous Communities*. Rotterdam, NL: Sense Publishers.

McMillan, L. J. 2002. Koqqwaja'ltimk: Mi'kmaq Legal Uonsciousness. PhD dissertation: University of British Columbia. http://www.collectionscanada. gc.ca/obj/s4/f2/dsk4/etd/NQ79241.PDF .

Orr, J., and C. Cameron. 2004. *"We are Mi'kmaw Kina'matnewey": An Assessment of the Impact of the Mi'kmaw Kina'matnewey Self Government Agreement on the Improvement of Education for Participating Mi'kmaw Communities*. Antigonish, NS: n.p.

Rigney, L. 1999. Internationalisation of an Indigenous Anti-colonial Cultural Critique of Research Methodologies: A Guide to Indigenist Research Methodology and Its Principles. WICAZO SA review 14 (2): 109-21.

Saint John Heritage. (n.d). *Old North End Walking Tour of Historical Places*. Saint John NB: n.p.

Schleppegrell, M. J. 2007. The Linguistic Challenges of Mathematics Teaching and Learning: A Research Review. *Reading and Writing Quarterly* 23 (2): 139-59.

Silverman, L. K. 2005. *Upside-down Brilliance: The Visual-spatial Learner*. http://www.qagtc.org.au/conf2005/QAGTC_upside-down.pdf, accessed May 30, 2009.

Smith, L. 1999. *Decolonizing Methodologies*. London: Zed Books.

Wagner, D. and L. Lunney Borden. 2012. Aiming for Equity in Mathematics Education Research in a Marginalized Community: A Perspective From Canada. In J. Choppin, B. Herbel-Eisenmann, D. Pimm and D. Wagner, ed. *Equity in Discourse for Mathematics Education: Theories, Practices and Policies*, 69-87. New York: Springer.

Wagner, D. and Lunney Borden, L. 2015. Common Sense and Necessity in (Ethno)mathematics. In K. Sullenger and S. Turner, ed., *New Ground: The Story of a Research Collaboration Studying Informal Learning in Science, Mathematics, and Technology*, 113-28. Rotterdam, NL: Sense Publishers.

Wilson, S. 2003. Progressing Toward an Indigenous Research Paradigm in Canada and Australia. *Canadian Journal of Native Education* 27 (2): 161-78.

Winder, G. M. 2000. Trouble in the North End: The Geography of Social Violence in Saint John, 1840-1860. *Acadiensis* 29 (2): 27-57.

Jaime Battiste

Mi'kmaw Humanity:
On Belonging and Identity and Citizenship

If identity can be proven by any number of ways, with varying demands and standards set sby agencies that regulate identity, then what does that say about the very "provability" of indigenous identity? Who is an Indian? Clearly it depends on who is asking, and why they are asking. It also depends on who is answering, and why they are answering. (Forte 2013: 33)

In 2012, I wrote an editorial for the *Mi'kmaq Maliseet News* attempting to generate discussion about what makes a person a Mi'kmaq. It was titled "What's in our blood?" and explored some of the misconceptions around identity being somehow tied to a concept of "minimum blood quantum" level. In this essay I would like to expand on that idea and discuss what I have come to accept as a more complex topic of subject identity and one's citizenship in a renewed Mi'kmaw nation relationship with Canada. In this essay I discuss race characteristics dispelled as belonging to peoples, the historical use of race-based policies and the courts' contesting of those criteria, governmental decisions and tribal government's use of citizenship criteria, and teachings from our Elders to arrive at my own thoughts on how identity is or might be forged.

Scientists have long recognized that, despite physical differences, all human populations are genetically similar—in fact, 99 per cent of the human genome is shared by all human beings (Rosenberg et al. 2002). This affirms what scientists and world experts have previously stated—there is no biological difference among human beings, and nothing within an individual's blood can actually separate them or identify them as belonging to any specific category of "race," other than blood type which belongs to all humans.

The scientific finding of being 99.9 per cent alike was not shocking to the general global consensus of the United Nations who have long noted that race is not a scientific or biological phenomenon but rather a cognitive or culturally constructed phenomenon. In December 1960, the United Nations General Assembly adopted a strong resolution condemning "all manifestations and practices of racial, religious and national hatred" as violations of the United Nations Charter and Universal Declaration of Human Rights. The UN called on the governments of all states to "take all necessary measures to prevent all manifestations of racial, religious and national hatred" (UN 1960: n.p.).

In the preamble to the United Nations Convention on the Elimination of All Forms of Racial Discrimination (UN 1965), the nations asserted they were "convinced that any doctrine of superiority based on racial differentiation is scientifically false, morally condemnable, socially unjust and dangerous, and that there is no justification for racial discrimination, in theory or in practice, anywhere (cite)." They further "reaffirm[ed] that discrimination between human beings on the grounds of race, colour or ethnic origin is an obstacle to friendly and peaceful relations among nations and is capable of disturbing peace and security among peoples and the harmony of persons living side by side even within one and the same State." They were further "convinced that the existence of racial barriers is repugnant to the ideals of any human society." The Convention entered into force on January 4, 1969.

In Article 2 of United Nations Educational, Scientific, and Cultural Organization (UNESCO) Declaration of Race and Racial Prejudice (1978) further reaffirmed this idea that:

> Any theory which involves the claim that racial or ethnic groups are inherently superior or inferior, thus implying that some would be entitled to dominate or eliminate others, presumed to be inferior, or which bases value judgments on racial differentiation, has no scientific foundation and is contrary to the moral and ethical principles of humanity. (UNESCO 1978: n.p.)

The United Nations Declaration of the Rights of Indigenous Peoples (2007) affirmed these principles, and of the forty-six articles in the preamble of the UNDRIP, nowhere does it attempt to define who is "indigenous." Rather, the article 33 reflects that indigenous people have the right to determine their own identity or membership in accordance with their customs and traditions. The idea of race as a systematic classification of human population has been an artificially constructed discourse of peoples often constructed in binary opposites of white groups, taught and socialized by European societies to assert the superiority of their society over others. The fatal invention of race is the foundation of, and embedded in, the social construction of colonialism, racism and eugenics. Pulitzer prize winning author Jared Diamond, in his book *Guns, Germs, and Steel: The Fates of Human Society* wrote: "History followed different courses for different peoples because of differences among peoples' environment, not because of biological differences among peoples themselves" (1997: 25).

The global consensus has solidly affirmed that all stereotypes or traits that are referenced to certain groups of people are not a result of a "race" characteristic. Yet, despite the science of genetics and the discrediting of race, the idea of race lives in the modern consciousness and has not been eliminated. It is a concept that is still used to artificially and arbitrary segment people into groups with many negative impacts on peoples over generations. In many societies throughout history, social groups of peoples have subsequently devised artificial racialized categories, fought wars, legalized discrimination and divisiveness based on these categories. The social proliferation of racism thus continues to create many injustices and has distorted many views about humanity and livelihood.

The Mi'kmaq are just one indigenous group that has had to live in Canadian societies where schools have perpetuated false knowledge and stereotypes about themselves or have read biased depictions and stereotypes recorded about them in print (see Nancy Peters, pp. 165-227, in this collection). They have had to submit to generations of peoples of various origins coming to Canada to project various racialized colonial constructions on Mi'kmaq or indigenous peoples in general across the globe. Such depictions, coming from the earliest explorers and missionaries, like Chrestien Le Clercq's journal (Ganong 1910[1697]), were complete with European claims of their superiority. There is, however, no scientific proof or validity to the claims that they are or were physically any better or any worse than any other humans or that their culture, language and values were superior as well.

If no scientific evidence exists that any human group is smarter, more athletic or more prone to succeed than any other, social scientists and educators have tried to understand what are the factors that have led some to succeed and others not. Dr. Pam Palmater pointed out in her book *Beyond Blood: Rethinking Indigenous Identity* that:

> Eugenics was a social philosophy based on the idea that human traits could be improved through various kinds of intervention in order to produce a healthier, more intelligent society. Eugenics led to forced sterilization and selective breeding, and served as one of the justifications for the holocaust. (2011: 183)

While some early writing came complete with eugenics causations for depicting some with more or less brain capacity, what we have since learned is what has been pointed out as among the scientists of UNESCO (1978) who has emphasized in Article 1 (5): "The differences between the achievements of the different peoples are entirely attributable to geographical, historical, political, economic, social and cultural factors. Such differences can in no case serve as a pretext for any rank-ordered classification of nations or peoples (n.p.)."

The awareness of race and culture are important, then, for the current discussion about identity, citizenship and membership for indigenous nations. If there is nothing in our blood that can be identifiable as being Aboriginal, Indigenous or First Nations, Metis or Inuit, what might be the determining factors to include in a citizenship code for nations of people? As former Citizenship Coordinator for Kwilumuk Maw Klusuaqn Negotiating Office in Nova Scotia, I have had many fascinating conversations with many different situations and communities throughout Nova Scotia over what makes us Mi'kmaq. How do we decide who is and is not a member of our nation? During these conversations at community gatherings or just at dinner tables or socializing with people, I have had to pause to reconsider what the conversations were about, what assumptions they held and what false concepts they continued to hold onto, such as those around race and blood and about Mi'kmaw identity and citizenship. I have heard people say, "We can't water down our blood" or "we have to keep our bloodlines strong." I've often pondered during these moments, What is it within our blood that we are trying to maintain; Is there anything within our blood that really makes us Mi'kmaq? Based on my research and conversation on biology, blood genetics and law and citizenship, I find that nothing in science or law affirms the racialized concept that blood makes us more or less Mi'kmaq.

Mi'kmaw scholar Dr. Pam Palmater (2011) and Lakota scholar Dr. Kimberly TallBear (2013, 2014) have rejected the use of blood quantum as a part of determining one's membership or inclusion within a nation. Palmater noted that the existing literature rejects blood quantum as a standard for "Indianness." She asserts that historically the blood quantum rules have been and are based on the idea of race, and its purposes have served to terminate people from governmental obligations and responsibilities. For example, in the United States, the 1930s law of the Bureau of Indian Affairs (BIA) ignored the terms of the treaties and terminated its responsibilities to several tribes—including the Menominee Osage and others—based on eugenics or faulty premises about their ability to survive on their own individual sociocultural resources. Eugenics was a flawed racist science and a basis for the use of blood quantum laws. Eugenics was a failed scientific attempt to create policy based on the disputed notion that certain races were inferior to others and which led to destructive racist regimes such as Nazi Germany and Apartheid South Africa (Palmater 2011: 183). Like racism itself, the federal blood quantum law has generated injustice, unfairness and resistance. Membership within the Native American tribes has always been a complex combination of factors but primarily was decided by the people themselves.

Both Professors Tallbear and Palmater point out that under the current regulations in Canada for First Nations as "status Indians," it is expected that within decades some Indian reserves may not have any children born who are considered as having federal status Indians. In Canada, the federal *Indian Act* has two distinctions: a child with two parents who are registered status Indian s.6(1) are characterized as full blood, those children with only one parent who is a registered status Indian are considered as half blood or s.6(2). This has led to many "6(2)" registered Indians being unable to pass on their status to their children unless they have a child with another registered Indian. Palmater wrote:

> If a single mother wishes to register her child she must list the fathers's name on the birth certification to prove that he is an

Indian, otherwise the child is automatically registered under section 6(2). Many mothers do not wish the father's name on the birth certificate so it often results in a number of cases known as unstated paternity. (2011: 106)

The discriminatory federal laws of deciding which child is or is not a registered Indian perpetuates the giving or taking away relative status as Indians. As pointed out by anthropologist David Maybury-Lewis, the co-founder of Cultural Survival, an international organization that works toward a future that respects and honours indigenous peoples. "It is one of the many ironies of the American experience that the invaders created the category of Indians, imposed it on the inhabitants of the New World, and have been trying to abolish it ever since" (Forte 2013: 3).

In both the United States and First Nations in Canada, many indigenous tribes continue to use the governmental blood standard as part of their determination of who belongs to a tribe or First Nation. Whether it was because the government urged this upon them to hold up the status quo or if they could not decide what was a better option, it is not known. While the United States Bureau of Indian Affairs (BIA) has often used the "1/4 blood quantum law" to determine an individual's eligibility to receive federal benefits and tribal membership, certain tribes such as the Cherokee have used more relaxed thresholds with ancestry of 1/4096 of Cherokee ancestry for allowing membership. As daunting as the math is within that statement, the Cherokees' focus has been more on one's heritage and ability to demonstrate "the historical political citizenship of one's immediate ancestors" (Forte 2013: 38).

Some tribes have tried to use the widely used identification of DNA (deoxyribonucleic acid) to apply a test to replace the blood quantum law, but they have also realized that these tests cannot give an accurate portrayal of genetic ancestry. Professor Kimberly TallBear, a citizen of the Sisseton-Wahpeton Oyate of the Dakota Nation, stated in both her book *Native American DNA* (2013) and her article "There is no DNA test to prove you're Native American" (2014) that science cannot prove an individual's identity as a member of a cultural entity such as a tribe. It can only reveal one individual's genetic inheritance or partial inheritance. The two concepts of identity and inheritance are not synonymous. No scientific system exists for determining federal benefits or tribal membership; they are all imperfect systems (Cussins 2012).

Furthermore, the Indigenous Peoples Council on Biocolonialism (n.d.) concluded that any DNA ancestry test that is used to dictate who is and who is not a member of a Native American tribe undercuts tribal sovereignty. It declared that Indian tribes do not differ from one another in ways that geneticists can detect. Moreover, the Council states that even if DNA ancestry tests are only considered for the additional scientific "facts," the frequency of false positives and false negatives in the test means they are not a reliable way to determine complex ancestral histories.

To try and summarize the problems with DNA, briefly: the current DNA markers being used by some to identify Native Americans in USA, or Aboriginals in Canada, are not exclusively found in those groups. Rather, these DNA markers can be found in other populations around the word; and they just occur more frequently in Native Americans/Aboriginal. What is further troubling about trying to use DNA is when looking at one's biological inheritance that both women and men inherit the specific mitochondrial DNA from their mothers only. That means that if you look at your great-grandparents, you are getting your inheritance for this test only from your great-grandmother, on your grandmother and mother's side. Therefore, one's DNA will not have these markers if any of the other seven great-grandparents were Aboriginal. Understandably, genetic inheritance can be very confusing and unreliable; it's like trying to cut soup. There are no distinct places to cut it, and any cut will always end up mixed again anyway.

The existing Canadian federal *Indian Act* policy uses sections 6(1) and 6(2) as described earlier in this essay. A full blood member in the United States having a child with a full status member in Canada becomes a half blood in the United States and a 6(2) designated status in Canada because the child does not have one parent with full status. In the United States, most federally recognized tribes retain a requirement that a certain level of blood quantum (ranging from full Indian blood to 1/32 Indian blood, or as in rare occasions 1/4096 as stated earlier) is calculated by child parentage from their grandparent and great grand parentage.

The racial distinctions existing in the federal *Indian Act* of Canada that determine eligibility for Indian status has been rejected as unconstitutional in the aptly titled *Loving v. Virginia 388 US 1* (1967). The United States Supreme Court invalidated Virginia's *Racial Integrity Act* of 1924 prohibiting interracial marriage between a "black" woman (who was also of Rappahannock Native American ancestry) and "white" man as unconstitutional under the due process clause and equal protection clause of the Fourteenth Amendment. Chief Justice Earl Warren stated:

> Over the years, the court has consistently repudiated "distinctions between citizens solely because of their ancestry as being odious to a free people who institutions are founded upon the doctrine of equality. [...] There is patently no legitimate overriding purpose independent of invidious racial discrimination which justifies this classification. The fact that Virginia prohibits only interracial marriages involving white persons demonstrates that the racial classifications must stand on their own justification, as measures designed to maintain White Supremacy. [...] Under our constitution, the freedom to marry, or not marry, a person of another race resides with the individual and cannot be infringed by the state. (11-12)

In *McIvor v. Canada* (2009) 2009 BCCA 153, the Court of Appeal for British Columbia ruled that the *Indian Act* discriminates on the basis of gender with respect to registration of men and woman as status Indians and violates the Canadian Charter of Rights and Freedoms [*Canada Act* 1982]. In that ruling, the Court gave the Government of Canada one year, until April 6, 2010, to amend certain registration provisions of the *Indian Act* that were found to be unconstitutional.

Unfortunately, recent Canadian case law has done little to help with the question of identity and how to determine identity. Perhaps the biggest case involving determination of identity is the Metis case of *Powley* (2003). In *Powley*, the Supreme Court of Canada attempted to determine how one can identify as belonging to the Metis people. The question was answered partially with a test developed by the court that focused on three important factors: 1) ancestral connection, 2) self identification and 3) acceptance by a Metis group or community.

Prior to 1985, Indian Status was the federal method used to determine whether one was or wasn't an Indian; however, over the years the *Indian Act* has been found to be discriminatory against women. Initially, in *Lovelace* the UN Human Rights Committee found that the

Indian Act discriminated against women and the right to enjoy their culture (1981), and *McIvor* (2009) stated that the *Indian Act* still discriminated against women in their ability to gain status. In response, Canada created temporary "band aid" solutions, but has yet to replace the rules within the *Indian Act* that still causes many to lose their status as Indian because of inter-parenting (inter-marriage) between Indians and Non-Status Indians.

The way in which the *Indian Act* determines whether one gets Indian status is an issue to many Mi'kmaq, but in the case of Lavigne (2007) in the Court of Queen Bench in New Brunswick addressed the question of whether a Mi'kmaq person required a federal status card to assert a hunting rights under existing constitutional rights. In the absence of any document created by Mi'kmaq for Mi'kmaq the court found that the trial judge use of the constitutional test of *Powley* for Metis "equally applicable to the question of who is an Indian." In the Lavigne case, Justice Macintyre stated:

> There is evidence, that the respondent has Indian Ancestry, he self-identified as a Mi'kmaq from an early age and even lived on a Mi'kmaq reservation for a while ... with respect to community acceptance there was sufficient evidence before the trial judge to allow him to conclude that the Mi'kmaq community of Pabineau First Nations has accepted the respondent as one of their own. (par. 42)

Of particular interest in this case was the evidence of the presented by Mr. Lavigne and accepted by Justice Macintyre in determining Indian ancestry. Justice Macintyre distinguished a previously decided case of *Acker* (2004) where Mr. Acker was able to demonstrate Indian Ancestry but wasn't able to satisfy whether he had self-identified or that he was accepted by a Mi'kmaw community. In the *Aker* case, trial court noted that Mr. Acker had only at the age of forty discovered his Mi'kmaw ancestry, he only attended a few meetings with the New Brunswick Aboriginal Peoples Council, he had no communication with a Mi'kmaw reserve despite being only twenty miles away, and had generally had no contact with other Mi'kmaq and, further, his lifestyle did not change after discovering his Mi'kmaw heritage. In comparison with the *Lavigne* case, the evidence called by Mr. Lavigne was accepted showed (1) an ancestral connection five generations removed from a recognized Indian; (2) evidence of self-identifying as Mi'kmaq and living on reserve at an early age; and (3) community acceptance that was supported by testimony of New Brunswick Aboriginal Peoples Council, a district representative of the Mi'kmaw Grand Council, and the support of an anthropologist. Weighing the evidence presented, and without hearing testimony from any member of the Pabineau First Nations community, the judged ruled that Lavigne was accepted by that community. It is important to note that Mr. Lavigne's fiancé/common-law wife at the time was also a full status Mi'kmaq of the Pabineau reserve.

When reading the case of Lavigne, I noticed that the evidence being offered to prove one's affiliation with Mi'kmaw people was that Mr. Lavigne participates in Aboriginal Day, dances at pow-wows, has an Indian name of "Lintuk" and also has built and has sufficient knowledge of the sweat lodge. While I can make no judgment whether the decision was correct, I do note that the evidence accepted seemed to weigh heavily on the romanticized version of what it means to be Indian, with the feathers, regalia, dancing and ceremonies as the focus. This reminded me of a Mi'kmaw Elder from Pictou Landing who stated "being Mi'kmaq isn't about beads and feathers," yet this seems to be at least some of the evidence a court looked to in determining who is a Mi'kmaq.

Looking at these judicial decisions, it is clear that the constitutional test of *Powley* is being used to determine identity, as opposed to any determination based on blood quantum. Sections 6(1) and 6(2) of the *Indian Act* continue to remove federal status from many people based on Ancestry and blood lines: but we are now seeing the courts begin to back away from the statutory rules of *Indian Act* with a preference for the ancestral connection, self-identification and community acceptance factors.

The Supreme Court of Canada in *Daniels v. Canada* (2016) ruled comprehensively that Canada has misinterpreted the meaning of "Indians" in the Constitution since confederation in 1867; it held that constitutional term "Indians" applies to non-status Indians and Metis. It held that Canada had denied Indian status to more than 600,000 people. These people have a right to negotiate with Canada for federal benefits consistent with those applied to status Indian on reserves. Unfortunately, the Supreme Court did not help clear up any of questions surrounding how to determine constitutional identity, rather,

Justice Abella preferred a case-by-case analysis stating that "cultural and ethnic labels do not lend themselves to neat boundaries" (par. 17).

In July of 2016 Minister of Justice of Canada, Jody Wilson Raybould, indicated that the new federal approach would be "a nation to nation relationship" rather than imposed standards of the *Indian Act* (Canada 2016b). The Court and federal government signals that indigenous nations themselves can and should determine identity and citizenship. Together with the judicial corrections of the past standards of Indian status in *Indian Acts* epitomise the invalidity of federal standards and authority over constitutional rights of Aboriginal peoples. They denote that that under the constitution of Canada, Aboriginal people have the right to determine their standards of belonging and the responsibilities of citizenship in their nations (Henderson 2002). These standards should be developed from their theory and traditions of Mi'kmaw humanity (Battiste 2008).

The UN Declaration of the Rights of Indigenous People (2007) affirms the inherent rights of indigenous peoples to determine their own identity or membership, in accordance with their customs and traditions (article 33). It affirms that "Indigenous peoples and individuals have the inherent right to belong to an indigenous community or nation, in accordance with the traditions and customs of the community or nation concerned. No discrimination of any kind may arise from the exercise of such a right" (art. 9). "Indigenous peoples have the inherent rights to maintain and strengthen their distinct political, legal, economic, social and cultural institutions, while retaining their right to participate fully, if they so choose, in the political, economic, social and cultural life of the State" (art. 5). On May 10, 2016, Canada became a full supporter of the Declaration without qualification and declared it intended nothing less than to adopt and implement the declaration in accordance with the aboriginal and treaty rights of Aboriginal peoples in the Canadian Constitution as part of its commitment to a renewed, nation-to-nation relationship (Canada 2016).

The normative standards that have informed Mi'kmaw humanity and inherent aboriginal law have been derived from the concept of empathetic love. In terms of the Mi'kmaw creation story, Kiju' revealed to Kluskap the forces of love (*ksalsuti*) in nature as well among the standing animals to be introduced in the Living Lodge. This teaching would become one of the most sacred gifts to the Mi'kmaq from the Life Giver. It became the overarching framework of Mi'kmaw thought and society (*kesaltimkewey*). As part of the spiritual covenants, and integral to the structure of the knowledge keepers, the people were taught to respect the force of love in their community, nation and living lodges of the ecologies. While comprehending the need for harmony in a diverse and changing ecology, the Mi'kmaq teaching of *kesaltimkewey* seeks adherence to the intimate ordering of loving, empathy, kindness, caring, compassion and respect as the proper bonds of peaceful relationships with all the flows of life energies. The concept of love regenerated the families over the generations in the natural environment, the knowledge systems, laws and their alliances with other families to form the allied families into the kinship system of the Mi'kmaw nation. This is reflected in the concept of Mi'kmaq, which has either been translated in English as "our kin" or "allied people," or "people of the red earth," depending on dialect and how it was pronounced.

Steven Augustine (1992; 1996) has persuasively suggested that Mi'kmaq is from the concept of *nokamaq* (these are my relatives) or *niskamij* (my brother, my friend) a word of the Lnu'k civilization that was also used as a term of endearment by a husband for his wife. These concepts reflect that being a Mi'kmaq is to be a relative of the allied families based on mutual respect and responsibilities. The allied families or Mi'kmaq were organized through extended family structures. Each extended family became identified with and belonged to a certain tribal territory (*saqmawti*). Certain places and communities (*wikamou*) came to be recognized as the responsibility of certain families. Within the structure of Mi'kmaw values, our Elders, such as Joe B. Marshall, have stated on many occasions "that being Mi'kmaw comes with rights and responsibilities." They are interconnected and you cannot practice rights without understanding the reciprocal responsibilities.

These Mi'kmaw stories and teachings confirm one of my favorite witty remarks from Guy Harrison's book *Race and Reality: What Everyone Should Know about Our Biological Diversity* (2010) who notes there is no end to people mating with great enthusiasm with anyone they want and across many cultural borders regardless of the efforts used to stop them. This freedom to love and marry has been the prevailing constitutional rights of each Mi'kmaq. In many of the Mi'kmaw families and communities, despite whatever boundaries or teaching our young are given, many of our community members fall in love, marry and have children without any concern for their being status or non status, Indian or non-Indian, or Canadian or non-Canadian.

In 2005, social worker Dr. Michael Yellow Bird, a citizen of the Three Affiliated Tribes, captured the complexity of this issue:

> It seems to me that if tribes are determined to maintain the blood quantum system, we must do either of the two following things to avoid ending up with the majority of our tribal population having less than the "required" level of Native blood: (1) Institute an arranged marriage system that ensures our children and grandchildren, who want to have children, marry within the race and tribe so they can produce more "little Indians" with the "proper" blood quantum required by our tribes: or (2) adopt citizenship criteria that do not care whether our children or grandchildren are quarter, half, or full blood but, instead, that they are productive, happy, committed, contributing members of our nations, who will keep our languages alive, protect our homelands and resources, and maintain a tribal way of life based upon the teaching of our ancestors. I personally vote for number two. (2005: 181)

Along with the complexities of policies that seem to be assimilating Mi'kmaw out of existence, there are other factors such as custom adoptions that must be noted as well. There have been customary adoptions, especially in the early colonial period when many non-Mi'kmaw settlers left their children born out of wedlock to the care of Mi'kmaw families. These adopted children have always been treated as belonging to the Mi'kmaw families who cared for and nurtured them. They became members of the families of the Mi'kmaw nation and entered into the multifaceted relationship and responsibilities of relatives in Mi'kmaw law—of protection and duty, obligations and rights. Their long-lived legacy among Mi'kmaq assured them to become often fluent speakers, even cultural icons and leaders.

Dismantling or decolonizing racism and blood lines in Mi'kmaw thought is more than simply exposing the concepts of Eurocentric illusions of self-induced power and superiority or as a discourse of cognitive imperialism, it requires comprehending Mi'kmaw humanity in our knowledge system. What this boils down to is when Mi'kmaq speak of blood, what they actually mean is not talking about what fluid actually flows in our blood or our genetic markers in its composition, but rather our heritage from our ancestry, knowledge system, our stories and teachings. It was through the language and stories that the Mi'kmaq constructed their nation, which we wish to preserve. I have often heard that it is important to remember our teachings and to understand our heritage as part of what is important to being Mi'kmaq. In many of the articles in this book, I understand how crucial Mi'kmaw humanities and its teachings and stories are to rebuilding the Mi'kmaw nation. Mi'kmaq have decided on who we are by our relations, by families' oral traditions, and by teachings of how we learn, keep our faith, our hearts and our love of our land and our people by duty and responsibility. We all have a responsibility to each other and to the nation and to the land that secures our communities. These have been the foundations of reciprocal relations and ultimately about belonging and citizenship.

Colonial societies and their unjust practices of residential schools, scooping children from families and sending them to live with non-indigenous people, and the losses of our languages and relations present us today with new challenges and new imperatives to find a fair and just way to know ourselves and all those who have been left out of our nations and communities. It is a difficult process and our communities are both concerned for and about the consequences of accepting everyone who declares themselves Mi'kmaq. We are stronger when we stand together, rather than fighting with one another over scraps given by the federal government. Yet, nations are nations because among other criteria, they select who will become members or citizens of the nation. This is a time for Mi'kmaq to mobilize their nationhood to ensure that they have the right to choose and it is not the federal government to choose for us. We are treaty nations and we have and will continue to decide our own membership and citizenship. Our humanity and the survival of our peoples and our knowledges depend on it.

References

Augustine, Stephen. 1992. Presentation to the Royal Commission on Aboriginal Peoples. Big Cove, NB, October 20. N.p.

———. 1996. English translation of the Creation story. In Report of the Royal Commission on Aboriginal Peoples, *Looking Forward Looking Back* 46-50. Ottawa: Minister of Supply and Services Canada.

Battiste, Jaime. 2008. Understanding the Progression of Mi'kmaq Law. *Dalhousie Law Journal* 31:311.

Canada Act 1982 (UK). 1982. c 11 Canadian Charter of Rights and Freedoms, Schedule A.

———. *The Constitution Act 1982*, Schedule B.

Canada. 2016. Indigenous and Northern Affairs Canada United Nations Declaration of Rights of Indigenous Peoples, https://www.aadnc-aandc. gc.ca/eng/1309374407406/1309374458958. accessed August 10, 2016.

Canada. 2016b. Statement of Minister of Justice and Attorney General of Canada, Jody Wilson-Raybould to General of Assembly of First Nations Annual General Assembly, Niagara Falls Ont. July 12, 2016.

Cussins, Jessica. 2016. DNA Ancestry Testing: What Can It Say About Native American Identity." *BioPolitical Times* December 20, http://www.biopoliticaltimes.org/article.php?id=6588, accessed August 10, 2016.

Diamond, Jarred. 1997. *Guns, Germs, and Steel: The Fates of Human Society*. New York: W. W. Norton.

Forte, Maximillian C. 2013. *Who is an Indian? Race, Place and the Politics of Indigeneity in the Americas*. Toronto: University of Toronto Press.

Harrison, Guy P. 2010. *Race and Reality: What Everyone Should Know About Our Biological Diversity*. Amherst, NY: Prometheus.

Henderson, James (Sa'ke'j) Youngblood. 2002. *Sui Generis* and Treaty Citizenship, *Citizenship Studies*, 6(4): 415-40.

Indian Act Canada (R.S.C., 1985, c. I-5).

Johnson, Eleanor. 1990. "Mi'kmaq Tribal Consciousness in the Twentieth Century" in *Paqtatek*, eds. Stephanie Inglis and Joy Manette. Halifax, NS: Garamound Press.

Indigenous Peoples Council on Biocolonialism (n.d.). http://www.ipcb.org/ publications/briefing_papers/files/identity.html, accessed August 10, 2016.

Le Clercq, Chrestien. 1910[1697]. *New Relations of Gaspesia: With the Customs and Religion of the Gaspesian Indians*. Trans. William F. Ganong. Toronto: Champlain Society.

Palmater, Pamula. 2011. *Beyond Blood: Rethinking Indigenous Identity*. Saskatoon, SK: Purich Publishing.

Rosenberg, Noah A., Jonathan K. Pritchard, James L. Weber, Howard M. Cann, Kenneth K. Kidd, Lev A. Zhivotovsky and Marcus W. Feldman. 2002. Genetic Structure of Human Populations, *Science* 298: 2281-85.

TallBear, Kimberly. 2013. *Native American DNS: Tribal Belonging and the False Promise of Genetic Science* Minneapolis, MN: University of Minnesota Press.

———. 2014. There is no DNA test to prove you're Native American. *New Scientist*. Issue 2955, February 8, https://www.newscientist.com/article/mg22129554-400-there-is-no-dna-test-to-prove-youre-native-american/, accessed September 14, 2016.

United Nations. 1960. General Assembly Resolution 1510 (XV) December 12.

———. 1965. General Assembly Resolution 2106 (XX). International Convention on the Elimination of All Forms of RacialDiscrimination, http://www.ohchr.org/EN/ProfessionalInterest/Pages/CERD.aspx.

———. 2007. General Assembly Resolution 61/295. United NationsDeclaration on the Rights of Indgenous Peoples, http://www.un-documents.net/a61r295.

United Nations Educational, Scientific, and Cultural Organization (UNESCO). 1978. Declaration on Race and Racial Prejudice, November 12, http://portal.unesco.org/en/ev.php-URL_ID=13161&URL_DO=DO_TOPIC&URL_SECTION=201.html, accessed August 10, 2016.

Yellow Bird, Michael. 2005. Decolonizing Tribal Enrollment. In *For Indigenous Eyes Only: A Decolonization Handbook*, ed. Angela Wilson Waziyatawin and Michael Yellow Bird, 179-88. Santa Fe, NM: School of American Research Press.

Judicial Cases Cited

Daniels v. Canada (2016) SCC 12.

Loving v. Virginia, 388 US 1 (1967).

McIvor v. Canada, (2009) 2009 BCCA 153.

R. v. Acker, [2004] N.B.J. No. 525 (P.C.N.B.).

R. v. Lavigne, 2007 NBQB 171.

Ashley Julian

Thinking Seven Generations Ahead: Mi'kmaq Language Resurgence in the Face of Colonialism

Mi'kmaw language learners, speakers and linguists are engaged with the survival of our language with the seven generations in mind: for me, that would be my great-great-great grandchildren. Currently First Nations students across Canada and Turtle Island (North America) live in "shame" for not knowing their culture and indigenous identity. A resurgence of Mi'kmaw in Mi'kma'ki territory and within our communities is urgent—for learners and educators in mainstream education, immersion schools, language nests and even more so with the access to language online, using technology.

Much work has been done in Canada and beyond with respect to language revitalization. Relatively speaking, however, little is known about our own Mi'kmaw context and the issues arising from colonialism and the influences of modern communication forms. Education systems in the western world today continue to show resistance when confronted with indigenous cultures, often failing to include language training, much less third language training, resulting in the imposition of dominant perdagogies—a form of linguicide. Positive efforts can be found—for instance in Mi'kmaw-medium schools in indigenous communities in Nova Scotia—but by-and-large, Eurocentric pedagogies fail indigenous people. Language revitalization cannot succeed in isolation. Revitalizing and sustain indigenous culture must observe indigenous knowledges through a pedagogy of the land.

This chapter represents my findings and conclusions drawn from my Master's of Education journey at the University of New Brunswick. My interest in understanding Mi'kmaw language changes and, more importantly, its growth led me to conduct an indigenous auto-ethnographic narrative. Two primary questions guided my research: What are the existing actions indigenous communities are contributing toward Mi'kmaw language resurgence? What additional resources are required to support Mi'kmaw language resurgence in developing sustainable tools for the present and future generations?

As a Mi'kmaw woman living in Mi'kma'ki (Mi'kmaq territory), I do my best to teach and do research by following indigenous[1] beliefs and ways of doing. Our territory includes both the Wolastoqey and Mi'kmaw people, and we are known as Wabanaki, which means, *people of the dawn*. Wabanaki territories include the Maritimes, Newfoundland, Quebec, Maine, Vermont and Massachusetts (Sable and Francis 2012). It is my hope that this work honours and builds on the work of indigenous scholars who have gone before me, and like Wilson (2003), I hope that future indigenous researchers will be able to continue indigenizing the academy and continue to connect us with our traditional ways of knowing.

According to Wilson (2003) and Rigney (1997), it is important to highlight and reshape the terminology now used to define us as Mi'kmaq on the eastern Canadian seaboard. Terms such as Indian, Metis, Inuit, First Nations or Native (used in Canada) or Aborigine (used in Australia) or Aboriginal no longer seem inclusive enough to situate the growing resurgence of knowledge that encompasses Mi'kma'ki. The term indigenous knowledge is now more often used to describe the knowledge system that is inclusive to all traditions. Indigenous people are in the process of reshaping, redefining and re-explaining their positions through redefining the research, outlining the ethical protocols and explaining the culturally congruent methodologies (Wilson 2003: 170). Rigney states, "Indigenous peoples think and interpret the world and its realities in differing ways to non-Indigenous peoples because of their experiences, histories, cultures, and values" (1997: 8).

What the literature tells us

Language Genocide/Linguicide

European imperialism includes a chronology of harsh events directed at indigenous peoples related to discovery, conquest, exploitation, distribution and appropriation (Smith 2012). The assaults and attacks on indigenous language loss include intrastate violence, mass atrocity and historical injustice (Simpson and Coulthard 2014;), which can now be framed as language genocide.

For centuries, these assaults have been a part of a forced assimilation (Battiste 2013). Language genocide/linguicide are enshrined in our current patriarchal system and contemporary education. Battiste describes this assimilation plan:

> Imagine the consequence of a powerful ideology that positions one group as superior and gives away First Nations peoples' lands and resources and invites churches and other administrative agents to inhabit their homeland, while negating their very existence and finally removing them from the Canadian landscape to lands no one wants. Imagine how uncertain a person is whose success is only achieved by a complete makeover of themselves, by their need to learn English and the polished rules and habits that go with that identity. They are thrust into a society that does not want them to show too much success or too much Indian identity, losing their connections to the land, [language], family, and community. (23)

As a result of forced assimilation, language genocide and Eurocentric education policies, indigenous peoples across Canada have witnessed a global loss of their languages, ways of knowing and world views.

Cultural revitalization and preservation informs and animates knowledge systems (Battiste 2013) and embeds culturally sustaining pedagogy (Paris and Alim 2014) within inclusive curriculum outcomes. Education systems in the Western world often fail to teach second and third languages and, in turn, impose dominant pedagogies (Battiste 2013; Kincheloe 2008).

Anders-Baer et al. (2008) discuss linguistic genocide as a result of dominant language pressures in educational institutions. Dominant language pressures assert that linguistic, pedagogical and psychological barriers prevent the right to mother-tongue-medium (MTM) education for most indigenous peoples and minorities. Indigenous peoples in Canada learn the dominant language at the cost of their mother tongue which becomes displaced. Perley (2011: 78) uses the term "linguicide" to describe language endangerment and indigenous language loss. Linguicide implicates colonialist programs such as assimilation, boarding schools and neocolonialist agendas as the primary causes of indigenous language death. These colonialist programs act as ideological state apparatus (ISA) (Brookfield 2005) with hidden dominant ideologies that are hegemonic, manipulative and oppressive for indigenous paradigms, Mi'kmaw pedagogies and language resurgence.

To conquer these tools of colonization embedded in the Western ideological state apparatuses, we, as indigenous academics, need to listen to our Elders, our own people, and recognize the relationships and connections within our communities. Elders are often the only fluent Mi'kmaw speakers in our communities today, and only a small number of the seventh generation are fluent. The Elders have inspired many actions being taken toward defying Wolastoqey and Mi'kmaq language death (Perley 2011) and confronting linguist genocide (Corntassel 2012; Perley 2011; Bear Nicholas 2008) and their actions have influenced our optimism in the fight against linguicide.

Language Resurgence:
Maintaining, Recovering and Reclaiming

In the face of continued colonialism, language resurgence becomes our responsibility as the seventh generation (Simpson 2011). Resurgence includes the embedding of instruction within the indigenous knowledges that drive indigenous people to maintain, recover and reclaim culture and language. The continued use of the tools of colonization and Western discourses are sparking the empowerment of indigenous peoples to shift back to their traditional knowledge systems (Battiste 2013; Grande 2004; Wilson 2008). This shift back to traditional knowledge systems must be driven by a desire-based research approach versus the current damage-centered perspective. Damage-centered research fuels tools of colonization and oppression through the documented history of indigenous peoples' pain, loss and brokenness (Tuck 2009).

Damage-centered research has been academically documented through a lens of colonial and cognitive imperialism. These imperial lenses continue to be the blueprint for vehicles that drive political, cultural and language genocide in ISA policies, practices and theories (Tuck 2009; Battiste 2013; Simpson 2011). As a result, the drive for language resurgence is vital in the survival of indigenous culture and language. Perley (2011: 39) shares staggering statistics that frame language death in Canada suggesting: That of the fifty-three distinct Native languages in Canada, only three have a chance of surviving the next ten years, eight are facing extinction, twenty-nine are deteriorating very rapidly, and thirteen are moderately endangered. This is essentially why indigenous academics are using cultural and language resurgence as the engine to drive desire-based research (Tuck 2009). This desire-based approach to research is recommending academics to construct a fuller representation of indigeous peoples' past toward an epistemological shift of cultural and language resurgence and renewal (Tuck 2009: 418-19).

I believe it is through my spiritual connection to the land that I am able to respect and understand the survival of our languages. Indigenous people are traditionally taught how to nurture our spirits and how to interact with the two legged, four legged, water spirits, land spirits and sky spirits that exist together on mother earth. These indigenous knowledges are coded into the pedagogical and ontological scriptures of the land and this is why language recovery is vital for the protection of mother earth.

Pedagogy as Land and the Land as Pedagogy

The value of nurturing mother earth, is to ensure the survival of our language and culture. The survival of our Mi'kmaw language is scripted in the movement and flow of mother earth. The movement and flow of mother earth captures what it means to be indigenous. The land teaches, the land provides and the land demands respect. The colonial mentality has alienated and disconnected indigenous from the land, creating confusion and despair in the 21st century. Land-based education is considered an appropriate practice for resurging and sustaining indigenous life and knowledge (Wildcat et al. 2014). Corntassel (2012: 87-88) assures the importance of land-based education by asking: What happens when the medicines, waters and traditional food that indigenous peoples have relied on for millennia to sustain their communities become contaminated with toxins? What resources do we have against those destructive forces and entities that have disconnected us from our longstanding relationships to our homelands, cultures and communities?

Indigenous lands of Turtle Island are currently occupied by the Canadian state. Indigenous peoples, as the protectors of mother earth, have been in the longest running resistance movement in Canadian history for the repatriation of indigenous lands. Prior to colonization, indigenous peoples lived in independent, sovereign nations and held strong spiritual foundations rooted in the land (Simpson 2008).

Having a relationship with the land, to the spirits and with each other, defines being indigenous (Wilson 2008; Corntassel 2012). The relationships to the land have been challenged by legacies of settler-colonialism, including the appropriation of land and forced resettlement, making us question what makes us indigenous today. Thus, the rehabilitation and acts of renewal and remembrance, through relationship-building with the land, are the foundations to language resurgence (Corntassel 2012; Alfred and Corntassel 2005). Indigenous academics are now advocating for the reclamation and repatriation of land as pedagogy (Wilson 2008; Corntassel 2012). The land holds indigenous intelligence, life skills, embedded knowledges and values to rebuild, revitalize and restore our lands.

In promoting land-based education, indigenous people are using indigenous theory beginning with mother earth or Turtle Island as the holder of indigenous philosophies, pedagogies, epistemologies, ontologies and ideologies. The traditional practices encoded in land pedagogy including intergenerational sharing and teaching between family and community. Elders who choose to live in the bush hold an abundance of knowledge of the land. They are our intellectuals, philosophers, theorists, medicine people and historians. Building relationships between youth and Elders helps foster a generation of people who are attached to the land. This essentially is a form of land-based education, utilizing a generation who are committed to indigenous culturally inherent ways of knowing. Simpson and Coulthard (2014), Alfred and Corntassel (2005) make it clear that we risk losing what it means to be indigenous (Mi'kmaq) within our own thought systems and within the use of our lands, if we cannot bring about resurgence to our nations.

This Study

Indigenous Methodology

Indigenous methodologies are congruent with in-digenous paradigms, including linguistic elements such as storytelling and oral traditions in exchange for documented history. Throughout this chapter, I have tried to embed indigenous paradigms, epistemologies and praxis. This study used an indigenous auto-ethnographical approach (Whitinui 2014). Indigenous auto-ethnography seeks to resist the more dominant ideologies by deconstructing and reconstructing various historical accounts (George 2015; Whitinui 2014). It is about finding a voice, or way of voicing concerns, fears, desires, aspirations, needs and questions as indigenous issues relate to research (Smith 1999: 93). Through indigenous auto-ethnography, this chapter examines the narrative stories in three papers. The first paper included my grandmother from Sipeknekatik, the second paper included conversations with three Mi'kmaw immersion educators: the Principal, the Grade 2 teacher and the curriculum development educator. The final paper included two Mi'kmaw Elders from Listuguj and Metepenagiag, and two youth adovates from Gesgapegiag and Eskasoni.

Indigenous research has become a way of universal inquiry for indigenous and non-indigenous scholars around the world. Indigenizing methodologies and decolonizing methodologies provide settler allies with inclusive indigenous paradigms to learn from. Indigenous methodologies and research are not to be appropriated by Western researchers or reframed as another colonialist tool for imperialistic aims to favour Canadian policy, but rather seen as a pathway for greater understanding. According to Smith, "...decolonization must offer a language of possibility, a way out of colonialism" (2012: 204).

Collected Data and Findings

In "Speaking With My Elder About Technology: Mi'kmaq Language and Culture" (Julian 2015), I interviewed my grandmother and in this paper I refer to my grandmother as Grandmother. Grandmother is an Elder from Indian Brook (Sipekne'katik Band), and she is a grandmother/mother, a Indian Residential School survivor, basket maker, arts and crafts artisan, and a language and cultural teacher at Ln'u Sipuk Kina'muokom School (LSK). Elders are still the fluent Mi'kmaq speakers in many of our Mi'kmaw communities and my grandmother reminds me that technology is an important tool for language preservation and resurgence. Technology is most commonly used by youth of today, and if Mi'kmaw would like to see the next seven generations using the Mi'kmaw language, it is important to use technology today. Grandmother's stories helped narrate and instruct ways of integrating the Mi'kmaw language and culture within the classroom. Grandmother mentioned the importance of land pedagogy and language of the land, for example, how language preservation and resurgence exists in our hands during the process of basket weaving.

Language fluency has changed in our communities. Throughout Grandmother's acts of remembrance, I asked her how many speakers are fluent in our community today, and she said "not that many, mostly the Elders, the ones who are in their seventies, some in their sixties, very few who are in their fifties. And the younger ones don't speak it," she added, "well the ones who are learning Mi'kmaw in school now" are speaking. Grandmother believes language revitalization is important and the difference between the amount of Mi'kmaw used historically and today exists because of the Western forms of education being used in most schools. Our youth are being educated through English language and Eurocentric discourses about themselves and others that continue to strip them of their language while learning in the dominant English language. Grandmother has witnessed the diminishing use of our Mi'kmaw language. Regarding our community, Grandmother says "it is seldom that you'll find someone who speaks Mi'kmaq to their children. Maybe enough to count on my fingers, if that. But in Cape Breton, [Nova Scotia], them places, there is a lot [of youth speaking Mi'kmaw]." Grandmother says youth today "understand and speak English much better than when we were kids."

Grandmother sees youth learning Mi'kmaw if they are taught pride and she wants to see more culture in the classrooms, a classroom that teaches culture in the Mi'kmaw language. I asked grandmother to describe our Mi'kmaw cultural practices. She shared:

> ...how to cook deer meat, moose meat, how to skin a rabbit, take the children on culture camps, moose hunts, out fishing, ice

fishing. But our children are so spoiled, or whatever you want to call it. They are not prepared when you take them to these places, they don't wear the right clothing. We took a group out to Cape Breton, we [the Elders] went with them, and what I noticed is that our kids from our community here in Indian Brook, they wore sneakers, jeans ... this is in the middle of winter, they were suppose to go ice fishing and sleep in a wigwams over night. They couldn't do that because they weren't dressed properly, and they weren't prepared because no one told them. Or they could be taught how to prepare wood. Up here, old people like your grandfather are too old to go out there and get the wood, and now his one of the only ones to know how to do this.... How to get wood ready for splints, there's a lot of work to it, and now these young guys don't know anything about it, but they all know technology and about the video games. How those two thumbs work.

Grandmother continues to describe cultural practices,

Basket making, fishing for eels, learning how to clean them, learning how to cook them. People would look at them and say, "Eee, I ain't eating that" they don't even know what it taste like, that they are good. Eel skins [used for medicine], it was used for splints [when injured]. I remember when I sprained my ankle when I was young, we didn't have no doctors, didn't have no car, we were out in the woods, so my father skinned one, and took one, opened it up and wrapped it around my leg. And it stayed on there until it dried and I wore it for about a week, and my leg didn't hurt no more. Then they took it off by putting it in water again, that softened it up. The doctors use couple of sticks, and tape.

Grandmother commented that our language is connected in the culture, saying:

If we don't use our culture, we lose half of our language. All the [Mi'kmaw] words used for making baskets for instance, wood splints for making baskets – *lipkite'knapi'l*, shaving splints by using a hand tool – *naltaqmin*, making splints with my teeth – *elipketmin*, I'm wrapping the splints and the putting the rim on – *elokwistoq*, I'm weaving the basket bottom – *elaqpa'toql*,

I'm weaving the sides of the basket – *elisqapeka'tu'nl*, all the process of making baskets, you loose all that [language], and it's the same with hunting. If you don't go hunting, you don't track the animal, you don't know how to walk in the woods. Your grandfather use to tell me, jeez you make a lot of noise, so after a while I didn't go in the woods with him ... Grandmother laughs.

A story like this makes me wish I spent more time in my community learning from my grandmother and grandfather, rather than spending eleven years away from home, trying to get a Western education.

The second portion of my study highlights success stories from the Eskasoni Immersion school titled "*Kina'muanej Knjanjiji'naq mut ntakotmnew tli'lnu'ltik*" (in the foreign language, "Let us Teach our Children not to be Ashamed of Being Mi'kmaq") (Julian and Denny 2016). From 1997 until September 2015 a Mi'kmaw immersion pilot project was conducted in Eskasoni. Students were taught through a Mi'kmaw immersion program within the context of the English language school. In 2015, the Mi'kmaw immersion program was moved to its own separate building, with 128 kindergarten to grade 4 students. The students stay for lunch and are immersed in Mi'kmaw all day. Three immersion educators shared their successes with me: the Principal, the grade 2 teacher and the Ta'n L'nuey Etl-mawluk-watmumk / Mi'kmaq Curriculum Development Centre educator (TLE). Through their stories and practices, they affirm their belief that Mi'kmaw immersion schools are required to support Mi'kmaw language resurgence in the 21st century.

The educators interviewed suggested that for many of the younger generation of Mi'kmaq, relationships with the land have been almost nonexistent. Teachers in the English language school were not allowed to take children out of school, and had few opportunities for field trips. Now that they are in their own school, the immersion teachers take the students outside onto the land as much as possible. The principal says:

> If I went to go pick berries, I knew every plant and berry, the name of every part of the tree, I grew up with that. Lots has changed; at the other school, there is a little bush there with blackberries and I'd tell the kids to pick them ... times have changed ... apple

trees are full of apples because no one is picking them anymore, all these little traditions are no longer practiced.

This example describes how simple steps like outdoor classrooms can educate children through the pedagogy of the land and advance the survival of Mi'kmaw and indigenous languages

The Eskasoni immersion school teachers believe this is the first time there has been so much content being delivered in Mi'kmaw. The school's immersion teachers believe that land-based pedagogies instill respect in the students. They learn implicitly to be respectful to mother earth. The teachers teaching the "Mi'kmaw way of life" within their classrooms through the language notice that they have not seen any major discipline problems.

The benefit of having a Mi'kmaw immersion school is in providing a safe place for Mi'kmaw speakers, where students are exposed to their mother tongue continuously: in the hallways, in the classrooms and outside all day. Students converse in Mi'kmaw from the time they come into the school doors until they leave. The TLE educator, who has been teaching for thirty years, said,

> Thirty years ago, you never heard English in the hallways; you never heard it anywhere, just in the classroom, now it's switched. You can hear the students speaking English even though they are in the immersion school, but as soon as the students are told "*l'nu'isi*" [speak Mi'kmaw], the students begin speaking in Mi'kmaw. As Mi'kmaw educators, it is necessary at times to remind the immersion students how important it is to speak in Mi'kmaw. Having this new immersion school is an enriching activity and enriching experiences for the students.

Educators help translate literature and textbooks. The language itself is sophisticated and complex. Mi'kmaw is a verb-oriented language; the words themselves might include a verb, a pronoun and the object all embedded into one word, such as "*nemiatl*" (he or she sees him or her); the word is all in one. The immersion school teachers do a great deal to promote the language in all its complexities, and really have to work on the spoken language in particular in order to ensure it continues into the next generations. As the grade 2 teacher said:

> We need to keep in mind that in the generations before us, language educators were referred to as pioneer teachers, the

hard knock teachers, and these teachers were really enthused about using the language and getting the children to speak the language.

Many of the challenges for immersion teachers are a lack of materials, curriculum documents, subjects, activities and lesson plans in Mi'kmaw. And some subjects pose particular challenges. Math, for example, is a tricky subject; educators find it to be a huge undertaking to translate and transcribe a math book for several reasons. Currently in the math program, students learn a great deal of vocabulary but need to keep the English vocabulary for words that don't exist in Mi'kmaw; for example, the English words for equal, odd, even, estimate and balance are used.

Strong culture and language in education embeds pride in students and builds confidence in their speaking and motor skills. Teaching the language within immersion schools makes both students and teachers more culturally aware. As the TLE educator stated:

> The students are learning the language, learning the culture, values, customs and traditions that students are not getting in a regular English curriculum. Mi'kmaw students studying in a Nova Scotia social studies course only receive minimal information on their history and culture, whereas in an immersion school, students are not only getting a language but also learning their way of life, their history; they are getting a well-rounded Mi'kmaw education and students are learning about themselves.

The Eskasoni principal further said:

> Since the school opened its doors, the immersion school has done what we could not do at our previous school. We can focus on community people and bring in speakers. Elders want to come see the school and speak to the students.

I believe Eurocentric discourses in education are continuing to assimilate indigenous peoples across Canada. In order for these stories to exist for seven generations to come, it becomes our responsibility to ensure that Mi'kmaw epistemologies, ontologies and philosophies are embedded into curriculum. An indigenous approach like the Eskasoni immersion school will teach our young children to have pride in their cultural identity, and with the use of language of the land, the land itself becomes the pedagogy, a place for reclaiming and recovering our language.

In the third portion of the study, "Thinking Seven Generations Ahead: Mi'kmaq Language Resurgence in the Face of Settler Colonialism" (Julian 2016), the first community Elder I spoke with was a linguistic Elder from Listuguj, Québec, called Wilmot. Listuguj has a population of around 3,000 with approximately 200-300 people who can speak and understand Mi'kmaw. In the late 1950s, Mi'kmaw was spoken regularly in homes, the community and at community gatherings. The elders in the 1950s would have only known ten to twenty words in English, and Mi'kmaw language was rich. For our linguistic Elder, Wilmot, the Mi'kmaq language began to change in the early 1970s. For many communities, Mi'kmaw is quickly becoming "Mi'k-lish" (Mi'kmaw and English spoken together).

The second conversation I had was with a spiritual *ji'nm*/leader from Metepenagiag, New Brunwick, named John. Metepenagiag has a population of approximately 700 and roughly twenty-five are Mi'kmaw speakers. According to the spiritual *ji'nm*, our Mi'kmaw is a beautiful language taught and learned verbally. When he was in his twenties, our language was not seen as being so beautiful and both our language and culture were changing because of assimilation, colonialism and materialism.

The third conversation held was with a young inspiring linguist, named Al, from Eskasoni, Nova Scotia. The population of Eskasoni is about 4,500 and approximately half are fluent in Mi'kmaw, at least fluent enough to carry on a conversation longer then five minutes. Al is of the younger generation, he is fluent, immersed in the Mi'kmaw language from birth, raised in a Mi'kmaw-speaking home and is teaching Mi'kmaw. Mi'kmaw fluency levels in Eskasoni are recognized as very high because Elders there can still carry on a conversation in Mi'kmaw for longer then three hours without little to no Mi'k-lish.

My fourth conversation was with a young cultural leader from Gesgapegiag, her name is Larocque. Gesgapegiag is surrounded by French speakers and is near Listuguj, Quebec. In Gesgapegiag there are numerous speakers of Mi'kmaw and many are trilingual, adding French and English. Larocque continues her Mi'kmaw fluency in the home by passing the language down to her daughters. For her it is important that Elders, her parents and other speakers continue to speak "pasik l'nuisi" (only Mi'kmaw) to her and her daughters.

What Conversations with Youth and Elders Reveal

Language Genocide – Linguicide

In the face of Mi'kmaw language resurgence, it is important for language revitalization and survival to create a healthier thriving Mi'kmaw nation as well as understand the impacts of colonization. We have been culturally stripped of soul, mind and spirit (Moore 1999). Our younger generations continue to learn that the language we are trying so hard to revive and continue to communicate is somehow not seen as acceptable, likeable or usable in today's society. It was forbidden in Indian Residential Schools, and day schools; and today, in the 21st century, our language is heading toward extinction at a tremendous rate. During the Residential School era, many Mi'kmaq finished school speaking little to no Mi'kmaw. In Wilmot's case, his mother was able to relearn the language through her husband. He taught her, corrected her and only spoke in Mi'kmaw to her until she became fluent and began helping others with Mi'kmaw translation. As Wilmot got older he said, "I would never stop speaking Mi'kmaw consciously, and if there were other Mi'kmaq speakers around to speak to, I would speak to them in Mi'kmaw." Wilmot was fifty years old when he learned to read and write, and today he is using old and new Mi'kmaw dictionaries, social media websites, digital resources and fellow Mi'kmaw speakers to keep an online living dictionary up to date (http://www.mikmaqonline.org).

In all four interviews, my participants suggested that when our young people and Elders perceive difficulty communicating in Mi'kmaw, they switch to English if they can. For Elders who have a hard time speaking English today, Al iterates how it is easier for them to speak in Mi'kmaw. The described relationships between Elders and youth indicated the stigma around languages today and Al asserts, "that it has to do with that colonialist kind of thinking." The stigma around languages and keeping up with colonialism has divided Elders and youth. The spiritual *ji'nm* from Metepenagiag says, "In the past, everything was shared verbally, nothing was on paper," and he continues saying, " very little is being done today, there's no more sharing verbally, everybody got lost with the negative impacts of [settler] colonialism."

Larocque feels that with the language comes respect and identity. She says, "Our younger generations feel ashamed for being Mi'kmaq." As our spiritual *ji'nm* noticed:

> If our younger generations are not 100 per cent Mi'kmaq, they grow up torn; it plays an awful role on them psychologically and their hearts and minds all suffer. Today our young people are walking around blemished, trying to refer to other Mi'kmaw people to educate them about their Mi'kmaw history, culture, language and identity.

When Larocque was in school, she noted, "Even though the school was in the community of Gesgapegiag, Mi'kmaq language was only spoken in language class." When Larocque attended school off reserve, they also weren't allowed to speak Mi'kmaq in class, in the hallways, or on the playground. "When I was caught by my teacher or monitor, I was continuously told to speak the English or French language that [the teachers] understood," Larocque believed this was because of their own insecurities, "They thought we were talking about them when they heard us speaking our Mi'kmaq language."

The participants believe language shaming is stopping young people from speaking Mi'kmaw today. Al asserts that "Language shaming is hurtful, not just in Mi'kmaq but in English too." Al remembers, "When I started learning English, I was terrible at it, and the ones that knew English would make fun of me. Our young generations need to learn how to cope with language shaming when learning Mi'kmaq or learning English." Al stopped speaking Mi'kmaw when he was a teenager, in high school, because it became easier to communicate with his peers and teachers in English. Al also recalls when he came out of Mi'kmaw immersion class; he struggled to learn English from his non-native English-speaking teachers. Although he went all through grade school with his immersion graduates, as soon as they were ready to graduate or pursued post-secondary, only a handful of immersion students were speaking Mi'kmaw. According to Al, "I don't know what is causing the decline in language, but I believe it is more than just one issue." Larocque believes it is because Mi'kmaw is not being the first language taught to young people in education. She believes that if you speak your mother language first, then you'll be academically successful.

Information and Communication Technology Works as a Resurgence Tool

Information and Communication Technology (ICT) supports learning, education and training. Members of our Mi'kmaw communities are active users of social media and many other online tools for language learning opportunities. ICT can be a tool delivered online for professional development and can be planned, accessible and cost-efficient for all Mi'kmaw learners (Beaton and Carpenter 2014). Both Al and Wilmot reported being active users of Facebook and both are accessing the Mi'kmaw living dictionary to practice and share the language. Al says, "A lot of people learn new things online, like myself, I learn something new every day, every time someone shares a word, this is how to say this word, this is how to use this word, this is how this sounds, it amazes me." Even for current fluent speakers like Al's uncle, ever since the Facebook group was created, they are discovering new words that are not found in the current number of existing Mi'kmaw dictionaries and, to Al, that's how technology can act a positive resource for language learners.

Social networking sites are populated by community members for the purpose of networking with each other. This provides Mi'kmaw language learning to those communicating both within and outside of the geographical communities (Molyneaux et al. 2014). This allows for the seven Mi'kmaw districts within Mi'kma'ki to communicate quicker and establishes networking. Wilmot asserts that:

> Technology is always ready to go, its always right there, push of a button and it's on. Everything is stored on electronics, its endless and you'll never run out, but you can run out of [fluent speakers] like myself.... *Teluwisit* (what's it called) computers, they are babysitters today, kids aren't learning from us anymore, before, the Elders use to be our teachers, it was our tradition, this is how you learned from the people that were around you, you learned your language and everything you're suppose to do, we don't do that anymore.

Given the relative ease of accessing technology (i.e., computers, iPhones, iPads, mobile phones and other forms of technological communication) in today's world, meeting indigenous people face-to-face is a culturally preferred and legitimate means of communication, engaging and interacting with indigenous peoples on their terms (Whitinui 2014).

According to Wilmot, today "we are trying to come up with Mi'kmaw words for computers, iPhones, laptops, printers, cell phones, and telephones ... words that do not exist in our language." He believes there is a lot of time wasted on electronics/technology, however; personally he uses technology/computers daily for using the Mi'kmaw language and tracking/adding words on the online dictionary. Wilmot has strong feelings about gathering all our information on computers due to cultural artifacts collected in communities for museums. Wilmot says:

> When people came around to gather all our tools, for the usage of the land, how we made things, and put it on display in Ottawa, it disappeared from our communities, even though they didn't take it all, they just took samples. Since that time it disappeared, the only place you can see it is if you go to a museum. Now my point is, our Mi'kmaw language, by putting it into computer, its like writing books that end up on dusty shelves, this however [Wilmot holding his dictionary made in 1988] is my bible.

Wilmot fears that if we store our language all online, we will wait two and three generations after the language is gone before we try to revitalize it; however if that happens, there will be access to recording, digital stories, videos and young language learners will make use of it all.

In Larocque's household, her daughters love the online Mi'kmaq storybooks and applications. Although the words are not spelled the same because of the different dialects and spelling, her daughters can still hear the books, the books can be read to them, and if they are looking for a word, they can access it through the books and applications. Larocque says that "Maybe technology applications could be developed regionally making it accurate in preserving the dialects in language ... technology could be a tool for our community."

For Larocque, her first language was Mi'kmaw, and her father tells her she learned English from television. He told her its that easy to learn English but harder to revitalize our language. Larocque says revitalizing our languages starts with using it. She continues:

Its our responsibility as parents to speak to our children, being a mother that knows the importance is passing the Mi'kmaq language down to my child, whether it be through games, through storytelling, through songs, using imagination, its bringing back pride, and letting people know and understanding our culture and what makes Mi'kmaw people is we are distinguished by language, our language is one of the key elements to culture. If people start understanding that and feeling that sense of pride and knowing that for 500 years we've been resilient and our language had survived this long, then our language will survive 500 more.

Resilience is about the ability of the individual or community to cope, manage and bounce back in times of crisis, dislocation, grief, loss, hardship or trauma. This can also relate to a loss of identity (loss of language), self and culture within a world focused on material wealth and societal regulation (Whitinui 2014). Both Larocque and Al have hope for the future generations and believe our generation will keep our languages alive because we understand how important it is to be fluent and be proud of our Mi'kmaw language.

Immersion Schools Work as a Resurgence Tool.

Wilmot believes that segregating our schools from current provincial English curricula would mean our children would be more comfortable around our Mi'kmaw speakers. The schools should be immersion schools and go from Kindergarten to Grade 5. These immersion schools would provide learning in Mi'kmaw and the language learners would gain fluency in the language before moving on to learning English. According to Wilmot, "The immersion school would have a seasonal curriculum and the classrooms would be more of a home setting instead of a classroom, with everything in the language." Wilmot supports the steps taken in Eskasoni to open a total immersion school in Mi'kmaw.

The spiritual *ji'nm* says:

Today in our Mi'kmaq communities, you do not hear the beautiful Mi'kmaw language spoken, changes are taken place that cannot be stopped; there is too much colonialism and too much materialism, too much non-native influences ... nobody has respect for our language, it's alarming about the Mi'kmaq.

Revitalizing the languages takes working together, the spiritual *ji'nm* says.

The Mi'kmaq people have to come back together, despite the hardships and the hatred, we have to go back and learn the old ways. It's very hard the old ways, but no matter how and what we do, we will never be white [non-native].

Spiritual *ji'nm* says I insulted him during our conversation:

Talking is not winning, you come here today, you put all this paper in front of me, you almost like disrespecting me, you're insulting me, which I don't like. Don't get me wrong, and I have no disrespect for anyone or you, I have a lot of respect for Mi'kmaq, and how much we lost, and how had our [languages] are today.... I feel the pain, there is a lot of things that need to be answered about the past, they can't sweep our past under the rug and make them go away... what have we [the Mi'kmaq] done so wrong in life to deserve all this [colonialism, Eurocentric way of life].

As a researcher and Mi'kmaw woman, after ten years of post-secondary education and feeling as though I have accomplished my educational endeavours, I am still reminded that all those years could have been spent gaining my own language fluency, cultural teachings, living off the land and practising our traditional ways of knowing. Wilmot reminded me that he wants help from the younger generation with language resurgence. Wilmot says:

Most young Mi'kmaw people today are busy doing exactly what you're doing, research, getting an education. How many decades ago, is a high school graduation enough, how many years ago was that? Getting a degree now is not enough; you have to have Masters. Even a Masters is not enough; you go for a doctorate, that's where everybody is heading. So by the time you finish, lets say you go for your doctorate, that's another six to seven years depending on you, you have to make a living somewhere [off-reserve], maybe ten years later you are now into your forties, you decide you're ready to settle down, by that time you are forty, [you are ready to learn your language], I may be gone by then, guys like me and women that are speakers, will be a memory. (Wilmot)

As indigenous people we are reminded that we cannot stop people like myself, who spent a decade in post-secondary from moving forward. Our whole lives we hear the mantra "get an education, get an English education, it will get your further in life." However, as a nation, perhaps we are loosing time with our fluent speakers in our communities, and in the end we are going to have to work twice as hard to get our Mi'kmaw back to fluency.

Pedagogy as Land and the Land as Pedagogy

Through resistance and resurgence, indigenous students are responding to hegemonic forces by contesting colonizing pedagogy and demanding indigenous education. Truly indigenous education is inseparable from landscape and can be taught through land-based education, also referred to as indigenous cultural practices with the land. Indigenous academics attest that indigenous land-based education is a powerful and strategic pedagogical practice and acts as a site of resurgence for indigenous sovereignty and epistemologies (Ottmann 2013; Scully 2012).

According to our spiritual *ji'nm*, "We have to accept a lot of things, but we still need to go back to the old ways and clean ourselves, our land, everything." If we do this, it truly is indigenizing the academy and acknowledging indigenous histories, philosophies, traditions and practices (Ottmann 2013). During the discussions with the spiritual *ji'nm*, experiences about learning Mi'kmaw, he says,

> We learned by word of mouth, passing it down from mothers, family, siblings and repetition of Elders words and some of your extended family will pass a word down or share something. Today I am grateful I have 70 to 80 per cent, I don't know all because there is so much to know that's not heard today.

This experience is about learning with and on the land as pedagogy of land, he describes our nations as once a complete circle, but today we are but fifty million broken trees that disconnect our circle, the Mi'kmaw nation. His reference to trees, using mother earth descriptions contends to language resurgence, as language genocide's connotation is the destruction of mother earth. Spiritual *ji'nm* said, "I had to jump into the spiritual teachings, side of life, to give myself more power to learn more about myself, the culture, and the language."

Spiritual *ji'nm* describes his relationship with the land through our sweat lodge practices:

> As a person of spirituality, I would say the connection between language and land is about respect, it makes you feel like you are a part of something, and makes you feel good about who you are and all the love and respect you have for the land, when we go to get wood and rocks for the sweat lodge, alder, we put our tobacco down and show our respect that way. I don't really understand or what happened years ago to show our [younger generations] how the respect is shown.

This relationship with the land through ceremonies is key to revitalize our language, and is a way to ensure the survival of Mi'kmaw for the next seven generations to come. Spiritual *ji'nm* agrees by asserting,

> We have to do it together, to clean up our land, take out all the garbage, tires, washers, cars, everything, because if we do that, we will get rewarded. It will take everybody ... cultural practices are more beautiful and powerful than anything else and it comes from honouring our ways of life, honouring our culture, everything on the land."

He goes on to say,

> We pray for a clean body, mind, and spirit, the cleansing medicine of mother earth. The ancient sweat lodge ceremonies will always be there, on the land, everything you learn in the sweat lodge is pure, its about who you are, its about showing respect for mother earth, everything that is being used comes from mother earth and we have to show our respect by tobacco, prayer, singing, pipe carriers, we feel the spirit world, and we love the spirit world, and we ask for good medicine and healing for not just Mi'kmaq but for the 7.2 billion people on Turtle Island.

The sweat lodge ceremony is a cultural practice that can be a place to begin language resurgence and land-based education. Spirital *ji'nm* added some final comments about language resurgence,

> We have to pull together, despite all the colonialism, materialism, hatred and let go of our differences because of the destruction that was created and is still being created. How many trees has

it taken you to do research, write this thesis, how many libraries and schools in the world, how many trees does it take to fill
these libraries and schools, how many trees does it take to get an
education?

From one generation to the next, land pedagogy, land-based
education, must involve forms of education that reconnect indigenous
peoples to land and languages that arise from the land.

By acknowledging and listening to our peoples' stories of connections to land and place, it facilitates the bonding between storytellers
and listeners. Stories are important because they help community
members, particularly the youth, to understand their lived experiences, help with language learning, and builds a stronger relationship
within the community (Moyneaux et al. 2014). Al asserts that, "we
need language nests in Eskasoni. We have a lot of speakers here, but
we need language nests to keep the language here ... it doesn't matter
what age you are, you can pick up Mi'kmaw language fluently any-
time." One of the connections Al draws between language and the
land is that,

> We have names, not just for Nova Scotia but all of Mi'kmaw
> territory, covering Nova Scotia, New Brunswick, Prince Edward
> Island, Newfoundland, Québec, Maine, and the Mi'kmaw place
> names, when you read them, the translations describe how the
> land looked. Our Mi'kmaw ancestors knew everything in the
> language, if you point to a tree, they can describe it to you, the
> grass, the different kinds of grass, the blades of the grass, every
> type of descriptions, they knew, they knew everything in the
> language because there was barely any English back then, the
> difference today between language and the land is fluency.

The beginning of language resurgence is being on the land, being
around language nests and participating in storytelling. Al says:

> Cultural practices, smudging, sweat lodge ceremonies, and even
> storytelling are our ways of language resurgence, when you lis-
> ten to our people, our speakers, our elders, tell stories, they use
> a lot of words, and its almost like you have to paint the picture
> when your speaking in Mi'kmaw, a lot of storytellers especially
> the fluent Mi'kmaw speakers, when you listen to them telling

stories, they are using words that make you go, "wow," they are describing everything and that plays a huge role.

These are safe environments for language learners and open up pathways for speakers to teach through storytelling.

Larocque remembers the times she would try to translate a Mi'kmaw story to English, "You lose translation from Mi'kmaw to English; the descriptions are not as funny." She says

> When I was growing up we had plays in Mi'kmaw on bullying, drinking, parenting, etc. They were Mi'kmaw plays the youth used to do in the community, and there is humour in the language, and when you hear it in Mi'kmaw it is super funny but once you translate it, you loose the humour.

These storytelling traditions have not continued over the years. Larocque understands the connection between culture and land:

> Culture, land, and language tie together because culture is our language and our language is connected to land, they all fit together because who we are as Mi'kmaq is the essential element of our culture, and how we describe things in our language are the elements from mother earth. It's the land, and the true Mi'kmaw words come from the land.

Today our language teachers are bringing visual pictures of the outdoors into the classroom as teaching tools instead of taking the students and the language learning outdoors and Larocque assert's "that's how they are teaching the language in the schools today."

Discussion and Conclusion

My conversations with Mi'kmaw speakers remind me of the importance of my own quest for language fluency and how fluency will root me in my culture. This strengthens my belief that, "within a Mi'kmaq epistemology, ways of knowing, spiritual knowledge is a tremendous, ubiquitous source of wisdom that is the core of every system in the physical world" (Simpson 2014: 12). We must continue to find ways of reinserting people into relationships with and on the land as a mode of education. Especially in the conversations with the elders, we are reminded that:

histories of dispossession have hindered young people from acquiring bush skills and denied them access to the land ... a recommendation would be, increasing capacity to offer land-based education is going to require a discussion of how various First Nation governments and organizations might cooperate with each other in order to foster these sites of learning. (Wildcat et al. 2014: XII)

The Wildcat et al. recommendations echo those of the Mi'kmaw speakers in this study. Throughout my conversations, I was reminded by Simpson's (2011) quote that in the face of continued settler colonialism, language resurgence becomes our responsibility on behalf of the seventh generation. Resurgence needs to be the force behind the regeneration and revitalization of indigenous ways of knowing in order to combat the oppression placed on indigenous peoples through Western discourses.

Notes

1. I use the term indigenous to refer to the original peoples of Turtle Island, North America. It is a globally inclusive word for original peoples than many of the current Canadian labels (e.g., Indian, First Nation, Aboriginal, Metis, tribal, Inuit) that have been imposed on us.

References

Alfred, T. 1999. *Peace, Power, Righteousness: An Indigenous Manifesto.* Oxford, U.K.: Oxford University Press.

———. 2005. *Wasase: Indigenous Pathways of Action and Freedom.* Toronto: University of Toronto Press.

Alfred, T. and J. CorntasselJ. 2005. Being Indigenous: Resurgence Against Contemporary Colonialism. *Politics Of Identity: Government And Opposition* 40:597-614.

Anders-Baer, L. R. Dunbar and T. Skutnabb-Kangas. 2008. Forms of Education of Indigenous children as crimes against humanity? In *Education Policy for First Nations in New Brunswick: Continuing Linguistic Genocide and Educational Failure or Positive Linguistic Rights and Educational Success?*, ed. Andrea Bear Nicholas, Chair of Native Studies, St. Thomas University, Fredericton, NB.

Battiste, Marie. 2008. Research Ethics for Protecting Indigenous Knowledge and Heritage: Institutional and Researcher Responsibilities. *Handbook of Critical and Indigenous Methodologies*, ed. N. K. Denzin, Y. S. Lincoln, and L. T. Smith, 497-509. Los Angeles, CA: Sage.

———. 2013. *Decolonizing Education: Nourishing the Learning Spirit.* Saskatoon, SK: Purich.

Bear Nicholas, A. 2008. *Education Policy for First Nations in New Brunswick: Continuing Linguistic Genocide and Educational Failure or Positive Linguistic Rights and Educational Success?* http://www.educatorsforimmersion.org/LI_pdf/Genocide_in_Educational_Policy.pdf.

Beaton, B. and P. Carpenter. 2014. A Critical Understanding of Adult Learning, Education, and Training using Information and Communication Technologies (ICT) in Remote First Nations. *Canadian Association of Indigenous Education.* Brock University: St. Catherines, Ontario.

Brookfield, S. D. 2005. *The Power of Critical Theory: Liberating Adult Learning and Teaching.* San Francisco: Jossey-Bass.

Corntassel, J. 2012. Re-envisioning Resurgence: Indigenous Pathways to Decolonization and Sustainable Self-determination. *Decolonization: Indigeneity, Education and Society* 1 (1): 86-101.

Grande, S. 2004. *Red Pedagogy: Native American Social and Political Thought.* Lanham, MD: Rowman and Littlefield.

George, C. 2015. *Nikma'jtut Apoqnmatultinej: Reclaiming Indigeneity via Ancestral Wisdom and New Ways of Thinking.* Paper presented at the Canadian Sociological Association, University of Ottawa, ON.

Julian, Ashley. 2015. Speaking with My Elder about Technology: Language and Culture. Paper presented at the Canadian Sociological Association, University of Ottawa, ON.

———. 2016. Thinking Seven Generations Ahead: Language Resurgence in the Face of Settler Colonialism. Paper presented at the Canadian Sociological Association, University of Calgary, AB.

Julian, Ashley and Ida Denny. 2016. Kina'muanej Knjanjiji'naq mut ntakotmnew tli'lnu'ltik (In the Foreign Language, Let us Teach our Children not to be Ashamed of Being Mi'kmaq). *Special Issue: Indigenous Education in Education, Exploring our Connective Educational Landscape* 1 (22): 148-60.

Kincheloe, J. L. 2008. *Critical Pedagogy.* New York: Peter Lang.

Molyneaux, H., S. O'Donnell, C. Kakekaspan, B. Walmart, P. Budka and K. Gibson. Forthcoming. Social Media in Remote First Nation Communities. *Canadian Journal of Communication.*

Moore, D. 1999. The Value of Mother Tongue Education. *Revue Quebecoise de droit international* 12(1): 163-73. http://www.sqdi.org/fr/the-value-of-mother-tongue-education/.

Ottmann, J. 2009. Canada's First Nations People: Ethnicity and Leadership. *Education and Ethnicity* 6 (2): 100-16.

———. 2013. Indigenizing the Academy: Confronting "Contentious Ground." *The Morning Watch.*Ed. Kirk Anderson and Maura Hanrahan, 40(3-4): 8-24. http://www.mun.ca/educ/faculty/mwatch/vol40/winter2013/indigenizingAcademy.pdf.

Paris, D. and H. S. Alim. 2014. What are We Seeking to Sustain Through Culturally Sustaining Pedagogy? A Loving Critique. *Harvard Educational Review* 84 (1): 85-100.

Perley, B. C. 2011. *Defying Maliseet Language Death: Emergent Vitalities of Language, Culture, and Identity in Eastern Canada.* Lincoln, NB: University of Nebraska Press.

Rigney, L. 1997. *Internationalisation of an Indigenous Anti-colonial Cultural Critique of Research Methodologies: A Guide to Indigenist Research Methodology and its Principles.* Paper presentation at the HERDSA Annual International Conference, Adelaide, AU.

Sable, Trudy and Bernie Francis. 2012. *The Language of this Land, Mi'kma'ki.* Syndey Nova Scotia: Cape Breton University Press.

Scully, A. 2012. Decolonization, Reinhabitation and Reconciliation: Aboriginal and Place-based Education. *Canadian Journal of Environmental Education* 17:148-58.

Simpson, L. 2008. *Lighting the Eighth Fire: The Liberation, Resurgence, and Protection of Indigenous Nations.* Winnipeg, MB: Arbeiter Ring.

———. 2011. *Dancing on Our Turtle's Back*: Stories of Nishnaabeg Re-creation, Resurgence and a New Emergence. Winnipeg, MB: Arbeiter Ring.

———. 2014. Land as Pedagogy: Nishnaabeg Intelligence and Rebellious Transformation. *Decolonization: Indigeneity, Education and Society* 3 (3): 1-25.

Simpson L. and Coulthard G. 2014. Leanne Simpson and Glen Coulthard on Dechinta Bush University, Indigenous land based education and embodied resurgence. *Decolonization: Indigeneity, Education and Society blog*, https://decolonization.wordpress.com/2014/11/26/leanne-simpson-and-glen-coulthard-on-dechinta-bush-university-indigenous-land-based-education-and-embodied-resurgence/

Smith, L. T. 1999. *Decolonizing Methodologies: Research and Indigenous Peoples.* New York: St. Martin's.

———. 2012. *Decolonizing Methodologies: Research and Indigenous Peoples,* 2nd ed. London: Zed Books.

Tuck, E. 2009. Suspending Damage: A Letter to Communities. *Harvard Education Review* 79(3): 409-27, http://pages.ucsd.edu/~rfrank/class_web/ ES-114A/Week%204/TuckHEdR79-3.pdf.

Whitinui, P. 2014. Indigenous Autoethnography: Exploring, Engaging, and Experiencing "Self" as a Native Method of Inquiry. *Journal of Contemporary Ethnography* 43 (4): 456-87.

Wildcat, M., M. McDonald, S. Irlbacher-Fox and G. Coulthard. 2014. Learning from the Land: Indigenous Land Based Pedagogy and Decolonization. *Decolonization: Indigeneity, Education and Society* 3 (3): I-XV.

Wilson, S. 2003. Progressing Toward an Indigenous Research Paradigm in Canada and Australia. *Canadian Journal of Native Education* 27 (2): 161-78.

———. 2008. *Research is Ceremony, Indigenous Research Methods.* Winnipeg, MB: Fernwood.

Marie Battiste, Lynne Bell, Isobel Findlay,
Len Findlay, Sa'ke'j Henderson

Afterword – Mobilizing the Indigenous Renaissance and Humanities

Now that this project has been completed, we reflect on our research and offer some insights and lessons learned on the significance of the work. The contributing authors in this book have revealed and reaffirmed the Mi'kmaw humanities have been, and continue to be, ignored or denied by the various educational systems in Atlantic Canada. We came from a number of disciplines and colleges, from law, arts and science, education and commerce, and have been strategically and deliberately hybrid, collaborative, interdisciplinary and trans-systemic between our respective knowledge systems. Our collaborations were part of our original research design, aimed as it is to locate the knowledge in and with Mi'kmaw Elders, leaders, educators and students in the various districts of the Mi'kmaw nation, from Cape Breton, Nova Scotia, to Fredericton, New Brunswick, to Listiguj, Québec. We hope we succeeded in our objectives in a respectful re-encounter of indigenous and colonial knowledge systems while also pointing the way ahead.

Made possible by a Social Science and Humanities Research Council of Canada grant, the collaborations among Mi'kmaw Elders, scholars, students, leaders and teachers within focused dialogues on the situations that have created and confronted Mi'kmaw awareness of themselves in three Atlantic reserve sites and the nature of their Mi'kmaw humanity. The major issues confronting us arose around Mi'kmaw humanity not being understood, or taken seriously and the historical events of Canadian policy and discourses and ideologies of superiority and assimilation that Mi'kmaq and our allies have resisted and ultimately rejected. The need to understand colonial and neocolonial conceptions of settler thought led us to further our study of Nova Scotia curricula over the last 100 years to understand the ideological formulations that created "Indians" of different eras and how those constructions created the hostility, superiority and amnesia of their situation.

Understanding and translating how Mi'kmaq define themselves was in part to understand the situation from their origin and its transformability in the modern context. The deep problems associated with the government's forced assimilation and destructiveness of Indian residential schools on Mi'kmaw humanity have required us to confront the classic Eurocentric view of individual "character," dispositionalism and fate that have corrupted our version of human nature to favour compulsions of habit and character, and a vicious cycle of individual confusion, distrust and conflict. Mi'kmaw humanity emerged as story, as dialogue, as spiritual connection to land and place, to the Creator, and as relations not severed by time and place and history. Mi'kmaw humanity has deepened understanding of ecology and animal and plant connections from continuous experience within a particular place. The research has generated conversation, affirmations, realizations and spiritual unity as well as long lasting friendships and relations, periodic conference presentations, workshops, two books, the Mi'kmaw Archives website resource, community events, poetry, essays and continuing generation of new projects and ideas for indigenizing the academy and universities in the Atlantic region and beyond.

Our research design activated stories that both centred Mi'kmaw perspectives and the knowledge of themselves—and their histories and their change agents—and reflects our comprehension of the current situation affecting our origins, heritage, transformability and the standards by which they ought to be assessed. Change is the aspiration for this book for educators within educational institutions. The ameliorative purpose of this transformation in education is to change their depiction of Mi'kmaq and Mi'kmaw knowledge. The generative purpose is to initiate a pedagogy and practice of an inclusive humanity within which Mi'kmaq and indigenous youth might more fully see themselves. An inclusive humanity in education should be designed for all students to learn to embrace and implement a different world view than one consumed with power over the land and the people—a world view where there is shared awareness of and faith in how we can learn from each other through our diverse knowledge of human nature and humanity.

Our own inspirations came from many sources, but ultimately hit home within the dialogues we had with the Elders, knowledge keepers and community members in many Mi'kmaw communities. At the beginning of our study, we met with the Elders on Cape Breton Island (Unama'ki), who shared with us their aspirations and their teachings, like Elder Albert Marshall who shared a common concern:

> Children are confused today. They don't see a good way with one another. The[ir] world models war, consumerism, and competition. The[ir] world needs to know another humanity, another way to be in the world.... Knowledge is not static but alive and we use knowledge for the benefit of all. Our challenge is to make knowledge practical not just philosophical, to build peace and harmony. Current structures of education need to analyse and apply our own [Mi'kmaw] teaching. Who will move this forward? Who will do this and make the changes needed? Due diligence requires that we do this for love, compassion, and in humility.

These early discussions confirmed our resolve to understand and transform the growing nihilism of Mi'kmaw youth. Our dialogical approach with the Mi'kmaw communities reaffirms the colonial, racial and lateral violence that reverberates among them and the consequential replacement of cognitive solidarity by contradictions that have resulted in living with confusion, violence and the predicament of a troubled and alienating particularity. We found their hope for a better future resided in their own knowledge systems and language, anchored in knowing who they were. They want to live as people and communities that are not disconnected from their unique heritage, knowledge system and identity but lived with other heritages, knowledge systems and identities. Albert Marshall's wisdom encapsulated what many said to us:

> The language is central to our being Mi'kmaq. Education needs to be the place where we learn from Mi'kmaq to be Mi'kmaq. [...] Today's education does not support that and we need to tell

those in charge to make education connected to our past for our future. Our kids may ask us in the future, why didn't you teach us?

In this final searching question lies the seed of a renewed cognitive solidarity across generations, cultures, their languages and values—an anticolonial mobilization.

As we struggled to develop our thoughts about the true heritage and identity of Mi'kmaw humanities, Elder Jane Meader reminded us that others who tried to interpret Mi'kmaw humanities from what they took from the outside could not do it. Mi'kmaw humanities, she said, "has to come from perspectives of *KINU* (us) away from the individual and on the collective WE (*ninen*): we inclusive." Based on the belief that the capabilities and the demands of a Mi'kmaw knowledge system can resolve the challenges of the compulsory education of the current situation, our research has aimed to bring various perspectives from many sources that impact on Mi'kmaw consciousness, experiences and behaviour, all the while insisting that these parts and particulars reflect the whole. Through our dialogues Elders often lamented that they needed to have more of their own knowledge system and language in the schools. In that regard, Dianne Denny pointed out, "We need teachers who are Mi'kmaq and who bring that perspective. We need those who are understanding Mi'kmaq who can translate on our behalf." In other words, at last being understood in Mi'kmaw terms: "Nothing about us without us," as the maxim goes.

Storying and Healing

Despite the weight of colonization with which we have lived and which has made its living at our expense, the Mi'kmaw maxims came with some characteristically Mi'kmaw lightheartedness. In the many dialogues, sometimes we cried, and in all instances we laughed. Reflecting on the burden of colonization, however, Elder Murdena Marshall reminded us that "we have magic in the use of humour as an important ingredient to our development. It is used in all our relations, our mistakes and our discipline. Humour is an important part of our lives and a way to poke fun at ourselves and as places to show how we learn and heal the heart." Murdena shared how telling stories provides healing moments as well, just as in tenses of the Mi'kmaw language there is one that is said to be a healing tense. As a Mi'kmaw story unfolds, the storyteller reveals their self-acknowledgement of their own personal change, a marker of their growth, and a moment to be reflective of and on their now past mistake and the resultant change in their being. Mi'kmaw stories work in relations to places, objects and humans. Stories are not only performed; they perform, and they act in the world. Stories inform people's sense of justice and law, of what is good or bad, of how to act and how not to act. Stories are about the principle of responsibility. They depict the profound, the difficult and often the risk of choosing how to live. The values of these stories are to offer sufficient clarity without betraying the complexity of life-in-flux. Thus, storying helps to unfold the personal lessons as well as the collective ones.

Mi'kmaw storying, in their own language, generates a new story to Euro-Canadian humanities. Thomas Berry, author of *The Dream of the Earth,* asserts:

> It's all a question of story. We are in trouble just now because we do not have a good story. We are in between stories. The old story, the account of how we fit into it, is no longer effective. Yet we have not learned the new story. (qtd. in Suzuki 1997: 4)

Indeed, the collective crafting of this new story has been an ongoing project, as Paul Hawkin (2007) relays in his provocatively titled book *Blessed Unrest: How the Largest Movement in the World Came into Being and Why No One Saw it Coming.* The implicative movement relies on increased awareness, and more resolute and creative activism and actions of many people and organizations worldwide that focus on three interrelated foci—indigenous peoples, social justice and the environment—that is creating the largest movement in the world while strengthening the audacity of hope, not the mendacity of fear.

The emergence of a Mi'kmaw humanities is a new story. It is a story that involves a conscientization about the limits of the colonial Eurocentric education, its foundations and ignorant or insensitive or convenient presumptions, and the recognition of the integral role indigenous peoples and their humanities, sciences, perspectives and contributions can have in an interdependent world for the futures of all peoples.

Elder Albert Marshall noted the life-in-flux in the Mi'kmaw knowledge system, and the challenges and opportunities that enfolding dynamism brings in using "knowledge for the benefit of all." His challenges were picked up in the words and thoughts of others who talked about love and spirituality in many stories, animating the experiences and relationships of Elders, of themselves and their environment. Mary Ellen Googoo concluded, "We need our spirit of love to guide us." A spiritual ceremony led by Jane Meader offered an introduction to how spirituality connects and guides us and helps with vision and purpose, bringing light where there was darkness: "within each of us burns the light of Creator and we have the power to walk out of the dark. Fire of Creator can leave love of spirit of Creator in that dark hole. We carry that gift."

The necessary new story arose as social justice, equity and cultural pursuits that became sites of regeneration, when the first generation of indigenous scholars and professionals sought to obtain their university and professional degrees. We were educated within Euro-Canadian knowledge systems that sought to avoid, swallow without trace or constrain other knowledge systems, which traumatically resisted these violent and profoundly damaging incursions. Their cognitive journey was one of awareness of the imbalance and limitations of what Eurocentric universities and scholarship had to offer them as they struggled to find the appropriate theories and methodologies to describe their cognitive struggles and help them to find ways out of the dark corners of colonial educational system and institutions.

Perhaps one of the greatest contributions to that discourse from indigenous peoples around the globe was their thirty-year struggle to enact the United Nations Declaration of the Rights of Indigenous Peoples (2007). Those long years in dialogue and collaboration, as frustrating and defeating as they felt at the time, helped to build momentum across the generations and borders to shape the necessary new story asserting indigenous rights and responsibilities which now ground and energize the current generation of scholars, teachers and communities (Henderson 2008). The global voice and consciousness of indigenous peoples generated a significant source of the indigenous renaissance, as many peoples over those years spent much time and effort to convince the nations of the world of the consequences of their colonial plight, to assert rights that others had already won at the international level, and to prove the value of indigenous knowledges and languages to peacefully resolve contemporary challenges. Indigenous lawyers, professionals, educators, scholars and politicians used the formation of international fora to help expose the prejudices and policies of Eurocentrism against indigenous peoples that the settler states refuse to acknowledge.

In 2007 the government of Canada signed onto the United Nations Declaration of the Rights of Indigenous Peoples. In 2008, the Grand Council of the Mi'kmaq adopted the Declaration as part of its constitutional law of the Mi'kmaw nation. The success of acquiring the global consensus on the importance of inherent indigenous rights in the Declaration energized an educational, political and cultural indigenous renaissance, the renewal of indigenous peoples' teachings and the commitment to preserve our knowledge systems and languages as expressed in the voices of our Elders and wisdom holders who enrich, inspire and guide our youth (Battiste and Henderson 2000). These "extended and revitalised humanities are dedicated to public re-education, to rebuilding institutions and disciplines, and to displacing Eurocentric singularities and nominal universals that deny and distort the realities of difference and commonality that define us all" (Findlay 2003: n.p.). The professions of law, education and social work have been the first professions that indigenous peoples have sought out to help deal with the problems they felt empowered to solve, and they have become the source of first-line workers intent on developing indigenous, antiracist and culturally inspiring approaches to education that are already building a culturally inclusive discourse and culturally responsive programming within school systems.

In 2016, Canada adopted the Declaration without qualification as the foundation for moving forward in all relations with indigenous peoples (Canada 2016). Canada's policy of renewing the nation-to-nation relationship based on Aboriginal and treaty rights affirmed in the constitution of Canada has been encouraging. The transition of a renewed nation-to-nation relationship reflects the changing story and aspirations of indigenous peoples. This constitutional relationship requires a structural change and transition from existing governmental and administrative monopolies in the systems of health, education and governance over indigenous peoples to renewed self-determining nations.

The indigenous renaissance and their allies has generated this visionary new story in Canada. Most of the provinces and public institutions in Canada have begun to take steps toward addressing the inequities and the structurally unfair access to education for indigenous peoples. Notable in this regard have been the Canadian Council of Ministers of Education in their prioritization of Aboriginal education in the provincial school systems since 2010, and the many provinces that have registered awareness of the need to include indigenous peoples in their institutions' curricula and primary goals, including the mandate to teach treaty education throughout the grades as has been done in Saskatchewan and Manitoba and, more recently, Nova Scotia. While much has been done, a re-visioning of Mi'kmaw humanity is needed in the curricula of Atlantic Canada. Curriculum revisions cannot be restricted to adding content about indigenous peoples, but must rather include what they choose to share from their perspectives, from their holistic envisioning of success based on learning that is holistic, lifelong, experiential, communally activated, spiritually consistent, linguistically and culturally relevant, and embraced in indigenous and Western content (Bouvier et al. 2016).

The essays in this book swirl around Mi'kmaw humanity and the needed revisions. These essays unfold Mi'kmaw humanity to empower a better education system for all students. They come from the continuing struggle to try and comprehend the complexities of human nature and consciousness. Evolution, revision or correction of current understandings of humanity is important in generating an inclusive and engaged citizenship. After generations of cognitive struggle with various socially constructed ideologies—"isms"—that have nearly buried alternative notions of humanity in many knowledge systems, such versions are now making themselves known to contemporary educators, if only as flashes of knowledge, grace and peace, and possibility. Some of the thoughts we offer require revisions and rethinking but, as bell hooks noted, "that twirling, changing, is part of the empowerment" (hooks 1999: 128).

These essays seek to protect Mi'kmaq from the persistent echoes of the Eurocentric stereotypes and stories that have been released to the world in the guise of reality, inevitability and progress. The essays insist instead on the new storying of Mi'kmaq as an essential and active part of a more just and sustainable future. They employ a decolonizing approach that has followed the well placed advice of Linda Tuhiwai Smith in *Decolonizing Methodologies: Indigenous Peoples and Research* (2012[1999]) to indigenous peoples to *re*-write their own histories as a way of *re*-righting how they were positioned in the past, how they are positioned in the present, and how they might be *re*positioned in the future.

As a closing thought, we are drawn to the inspiration of Cherokee writer Thomas King in the *Truth about Stories* (2003). In a refrain about what to do with his stories, he asks his audience to consider what they have heard and do what they will with this knowledge. We too offer our stories on the Mi'kmaw humanities and suggest if you got this far in the read, to learn from them and dream on them. Work them into your life, your scholarship or not, as King's storytelling ethic goes: "don't say in the years to come that you would have lived your life differently if only you had heard this story. You've heard it now (2003: 29)." Every story or essay has the power to shape and transform the lenses through which we see and live in the world. What is important to us is that these essays have been written about Mi'kmaw humanities so as to comprehend another version of humanity, maybe even yours. You have choices and a responsibility, as the Truth and Reconciliation Commission instructed us to act now so each of us can add to what the future and our legacy can bring. These essays and stories are thus gifted to you.

The late Rita Joe was a poet laureate from the Mi'kmaw nation. Her experience in Indian Residential Schools is a constant guide for reconciliation:

> *I lost my talk*
> *The talk you took away.*
> *When I was a little girl at Shubenacadie school.*
> *You snatched it away:*
> *I speak like you*
> *I think like you*
> *I create like you*
> *The scrambled ballad, about my word.*
> *Two ways I talk*
> *Both ways I say,*
> *Your way is more powerful.*
> *So gently I offer my hand and ask,*
> *Let me find my talk*
> *So I can teach you about me.*

References

Battiste, Marie and James (Sa'ke'j) Youngblood Henderson. 2000. *Protecting Indigenous Knowledge and Heritage: A Global Challenge*. Saskatoon, SK: Purich Publishing.

Berry, Thomas. 1988. *The Dream of the Earth*. San Francisco: Sierra Club.

Bouvier, R., M. Battiste and J. McLaughlin. 2016. Centring Indigenous Intellectual Traditions on Holistic Lifelong Learning. In *Indigenous Perspectives on Education for Well-Being in Canada*, ed. T. Falkenberg and F. Deer, 21-40. Winnipeg, MB: Education for Sustainable Well-being Press, University of Manitoba. http://www.eswb-press.org/publications.html.

Canada. 2016. Statement of the Minister of Justice and Attorney General of Canada, Jody Wilson-Raybould to General Assembly of First Nations Annual General Assembly, Niagara Falls, ON, July 12,2016.

Findlay, Isobel. 2003. Working for Postcolonial Legal Studies: Working with the Indigenous Humanities. *Law, Social Justice and Global Development Journal*. http://www2.warwick.ac.uk/fac/soc/law/elj/lgd/2003_1/findlay/.

Hawken, Paul. 2007. *Blessed Unrest: How the Largest Movement in the World Came into Being, and Why No One Saw it Coming*. New York: Viking.

Henderson, James (Sa'ke'j) Youngblood. 2008. *Indigenous Diplomacy and the Rights of Peoples: Achieving UN Recognition*. Saskatoon: Purich Publishing.

hooks, bell. 1999. *Remembered Rapture: The Writer at Work*. New York: Holt Paperback.

Joe, Rita. 1988. "I Lost my Talk." In *Song of Eskasoni: More Poems of Rita Joe*, ed. Lee Maracle. Charlottetown, PEI: Ragweed.

King, Thomas. 2003. *The Truth about Stories: A Native Narrative*. Toronto: Anansi Press.

Smith, Linda Tuihiwai. 2012[1999]. *Decolonizing Methodologies: Research and Indigenous Peoples*. London: Zed Books.

Suzuki, David. 1997. *The Sacred Balance: Rediscovering Our Place in Nature*. Vancouver: Grey- stone.

United Nations. 2007. Declaration on the Rights of Indigenous Peoples. http://www.un.org/esa/socdev/unpfii/documents/DRIPS_en.pdf.

About the Authors

Stephen Augustine is hereditary chief and *keptin* from Elsipuktuk, representing Sikniktok "district" on the Mi'kmaw Grand Council. Holding a master's degree from Carleton University, he is the Dean of Unama'ki College and Aboriginal Learning at Cape Breton University.

Jaime Battiste, a Mi'kmaq from Potlotek First Nations, residing in Eskasoni in Unama'ki, is a graduate of Mi'kmaq Studies at Cape Breton University and law school of Dalhousie University. He is former assistant professor of Mi'kmaq Studies at CBU. Currently he is working on a treaty education project in collaboration with the Mi'kmaw chiefs of Nova Scotia, Mi'kmaw Kina'matnewey and the province of Nova Scotia. He is a published writer and researcher on Mi'kmaw history, culture and law.

Marie Battiste is a Mi'kmaw educator from Potlotek First Nations, Nova Scotia, and full professor in the Department of Educational Foundations at the University of Saskatchewan. With degrees from Harvard and Stanford Universities, she is widely published in initiating institutional change in the decolonization of education and activating social justice and postcolonial educational approaches that recognize and affirm the political and cultural diversity of Canada.

Lynne Bell is Professor of Visual Culture in the Department of Art & Art History at the University of Saskatchewan. She has published widely on decolonizing visual culture in Canada. Her publications include: "Unsettling Acts: Photography as Decolonizing Testimony in Centennial Memory" in *The Cultural Work of Photography in Canada*, 2011; and "Singing the Colonial Blues in the Settler Archive" in *Adrian Stimson – The Life and Times of Buffalo Boy*, 2014. She is co-editor of

Decolonizing Testimony: On the Limits and Possibilities of Witnessing, a special issue of *Humanities Research,* 2009.

Lisa Lunney Borden is an Associate Professor and Chair of the Department of Teacher Education at St. Francis Xavier University, where she teaches mostly mathematics education courses at both the undergraduate and graduate level. She began her career teaching grades 7-12 mathematics at We'koqma'q First Nation Secondary School, a Mi'kmaw community-run school where she credits her students and the Mi'kmaw community for inspiring her to think differently about mathematics education. She is most interested in examining strategies to transform mathematics education for Aboriginal students with a focus on equity, diversity and the inclusion of multiple world views.

Isobel M. Findlay is Associate Professor, Edwards School of Business; University Co-director, Community-University Institute for Social Research; and Scholar, Centre for the Study of Co-operatives, University of Saskatchewan. She publishes and presents widely on communications, cultures and communities; partnerships, participation and democratic governance; corporate social responsibility, performance indicators and reporting standards; transcultural law and justice; and Aboriginal co-operatives and community economic development, cultural revitalization and ecological sustainability for healthy communities

Len Findlay is Professor of English and co-director of the Humanities Research Unit at the University of Saskatchewan, and President of Academy One of the Royal Society of Canada. Widely published in 19th-century comparative studies, literary theory, academic freedom and the nature and role of universities and the humanities in Canada, his more recent work includes the several-times reprinted "Always Indigenize! The Radical Humanities in the Postcolonial Canadian University." He is currently editing a special issue of *English Studies in Canada* on "Rethinking the Humanities."

Marjorie Gould is a retired teacher and former originator and founding director of Mi'kmaw Kina'matnewey, the first legislated educational authority for the thirteen First Nations communities in Nova Scotia. She is an Elder in the community of We'koqma'q and the daughter of the late Roddie and Caroline Gould. Marjorie received an honorary doctorate at St. Francis Xavier University, where she received her education degree, in tribute to her years of work and service to Mi'kmaw education. She has worked as an education director and former superintendent of education with the Department of Indian Affairs.

J. Youngblood (Sa'ke'j) Henderson is a member of Chickasaw Nation. He is the former research advisor to Union of Nova Scotia Indians, advisor to the Mi'kmaw Grand Council and professor and lecturer at Cape Breton University. Currently, he is the Research Director for the Native Law Centre of Canada, College of Law, University of Saskatchewan.

Ashley Julian is a Mi'kmaw woman from the Indian Brook First Nation, Sipekne'katik Band, Nova Scotia. Ashley currently lives in Metepenagiag (Red Bank First Nation), New Brunswick. A success leader in all her endeavours, she has a Master of Education, she is a traditionalist, activist and Head Coach for Team Atlantic girls' hockey team at the National Aboriginal Hockey Championships (NAHC). Ashley works as the First Nation Cultural Transition Coordinator at Miramichi Valley High School (MVHS) under First Nation Education Initiative Inc. (FNEII).

Nancy Peters received her PhD at the University of Saskatchewan in the College of Education. Her interests are in learning how to stand as a settler ally with Aboriginal peoples and helping other people of privilege do so as well. Nancy was one of the early graduate student researchers of the SSHRC grant Animating the Mi'kmaw Humanities in Atlantic Canada focusing on the Nova Scotia schools and curricula approach to teaching about Mi'kmaq in Nova Scotia.

Margaret Robinson is a bisexual and two-spirit scholar from Eski'kewaq, Nova Scotia, and a member of the Lennox Island First Nation. She holds a PhD in theology from the University of Toronto and is an Assistant Professor of indigenous studies at Dalhousie University in Halifax, Nova Scotia. Her research examines food justice and the impact of intersecting oppressions on health. She has been a community-based researcher since 2009, incorporating participatory, action-based, feminist and indigenous research methods. She has been a vegan since 2008 and lives in Halifax with her partner of 22 years and four cats.

Jennifer Tinkham is an Assistant Professor and Bachelor of Education Practicum Coordinator at the School of Education at Acadia University. She has a PhD from the University of Alberta. Her thesis is entitled "That's Not My history! Examining the Role of Personal Counter-Narratives in Decolonizing Canadian History for Mi'kmaw Students."

Index

Page numbers refer to print version

www.ingramcontent.com/pod-product-compliance
Lightning Source LLC
Chambersburg PA
CBHW020654270326
41928CB00005B/122